The Communist Party of Indonesia

DONALD HINDLEY

The Communist Party of Indonesia 1951-1963

UNIVERSITY OF CALIFORNIA PRESS

Berkeley and Los Angeles

1966

UNIVERSITY OF CALIFORNIA PRESS
BERKELEY AND LOS ANGELES
CALIFORNIA
CAMBRIDGE UNIVERSITY PRESS
LONDON, ENGLAND

© 1964 BY THE REGENTS OF THE UNIVERSITY OF CALIFORNIA

SECOND PRINTING, 1966

LIBRARY OF CONGRESS CATALOG NO.: 64-24889

PRINTED IN THE UNITED STATES OF AMERICA

PARA LOS DE ABAJO

Preface

On May 23, 1920, the first Asian communist party was founded: PKI (Partai Komunis Indonesia), the Communist Party of Indonesia. Since then PKI has had a varied history. Its ill-planned anticolonial rebellion at the end of 1926 was ruthlessly repressed by the Dutch. From 1926 until the end of the Japanese occupation in August 1945, Indonesia's Communists were forced to operate in exile and in a diminutive underground fashion within Indonesia. The Party failed to exploit fully the possibilities of the Indonesian revolution for independence, waged from August 1945 to November 1949. In fact, while the military phase of the revolution was still in process, a part of PKI staged a fresh rebellion in September 1948. The results were disastrous, and yet, in the long term, perhaps beneficial. Most of the prominent Communists were either shot after capture or killed in the fighting. Until the end of 1950 the Party continued to exist, but barely so, with some 3,000 or 5,000 disorganized members. Then, in the first week of January 1951, a Central Committee meeting placed the leadership of the Party in the youthful hands of the Aidit leadership. The most eminent members of this leadership were and are D. N. Aidit, M. H. Lukman, and Njoto.

Since the Aidit leadership won control of PKI, the Party has become the largest nongoverning communist party in the world. By 1963 there were over 2 million members of the Party itself, and over 12.5 million members of Communist mass organizations. This study is concerned with the years since January 1951. It seeks to define and to trace the development of the Aidit leadership's over-all national united front strategy. It endeavors to portray and explain the implementation of that strategy in its three main aspects: the creation of a mass communist party, the winning of mass support extending far beyond the boundaries of the Party itself, and PKI's interaction with the other major political forces in Indonesia. At all times I have attempted to ascertain the political value of the mass support so painstakingly and so successfully garnered by the Aidit leadership. The book necessarily ends with 1963. As it does, the ultimate success of the national united front strategy, that is, the victory of the Indonesian Communists, is still in the balance.

This study makes no pretense to place the Aidit leadership's PKI in its international Communist setting. To do that would require an entirely different study. I have attempted to show how a particular strategy has been formulated and implemented in a particular underdeveloped country. The whole emphasis, then, is on Indonesia. More than this, the emphasis is on Java and the ethnic Javanese because they have provided the Aidit leadership with the overwhelming bulk of its support. For this reason I have included in the Introduction a description of Javanese society. Such a description should help explain not only why the particular form of the national united front strategy was chosen, and why mass support could be readily won, but also why the Aidit leadership, despite its mass support, is still unable to achieve power. The Introduction also sketches the history of PKI up to January 1951. It is only a sketch because many available secondary sources are concerned with the earlier phases of the Party's history.

My thanks are readily extended to the many persons who rendered assistance in the collection of materials and in the actual writing of this study. Most of the work was done while I was a doctoral candidate at the Australian National University. While at that institution, I received considerable encouragement and advice from the late Professor Leicester Webb, from Dr. Bruce Graham, and from Dr. Herbert Feith. My greatest debt is to the large number of Indonesians who afforded hospitality and assistance during my stay in their country in 1959 and 1960. The great majority of them must remain anonymous. Officials of the Ministries of Labor and Agriculture were especially helpful, as were national and local leaders of non-Communist and anti-Communist political parties and mass organizations. I received invaluable information from many tens of cadres of PKI and its mass organizations in Djakarta, Surabaja, Surakarta, and Jogjakarta. With few exceptions, they were young and friendly people, dedicated to the welfare of the impoverished Indonesian masses. I also wish to give special thanks to Ken Thomas, John Gare, and Lance Castles for their kindness and assistance. And I am grateful to Brandeis University for defraying the expense entailed in preparing the index to this book.

Finally, a note about the translations. The translations from Indonesian to English are my own. At times Indonesian English-language materials are quoted. Where the original Indonesian was available, I have at times corrected the English because I felt that it did not accurately represent the meaning of the original.

DONALD HINDLEY

Brandeis University
Waltham, Massachusetts
July 1963

Contents

Part five

THE NATIONAL UNITED FRONT AND THE OTHER POLITICAL FORCES

Abbreviations and Glossary

NAMES OF POLITICAL PARTIES

The following are the abbreviated names of parties most frequently used in this study:

NU=Partai Nahdatul Ulama, Party of the Association of Islamic Scholars. NU was founded in 1926 as an association of Moslem scholars adhering to the orthodox schools of Islamic law. It became a member of Masjumi, the all-embracing Moslem party founded on November 7, 1945, but withdrew in August 1952 to constitute itself as a separate political party. In the September 1955 parliamentary elections, NU emerged as one of the four large parties, alongside PNI, Masjumi, and PKI.

Perti=Partai Islam Pergerakan Tarbijah Islamijah, Islamic Party of the Islamic Educational Movement. Perti was founded originally as an educational association in Central Sumatra in 1928. In November 1945 Perti reconstituted itself as a political party.

PIR=Partai Persatuan Indonesia Raya, Party of the Union of Great Indonesia, founded on December 10, 1948.

PKI=Partai Komunis Indonesia, Indonesian Communist Party, founded on May 23, 1920.

PNI=Partai Nasional Indonesia, Indonesian Nationalist Party, founded in its present form on February 1, 1946, but tracing its history back to a PNI founded in 1927. PNI is the only major secular nationalist party.

PSI=Partai Sosialis Indonesia, Indonesian Socialist Party. A Socialist Party was founded shortly after the proclamation of Indonesian independence on August 17, 1945. PSI was formed as a separate party in January 1948 after the Socialist Party had fallen under Communist control.

PSII=Partai Sjarikat Islam Indonesia, Indonesian Islamic Association Party, was founded in 1947, though a party of the same name and with some of the same leaders had been active before World War II.

NAMES OF MASS ORGANIZATIONS

The following are the abbreviated names of Communist mass organizations frequently cited in this study:

BTI=Barisan Tani Indonesia, Indonesian Peasants' Organization, founded on November 25, 1945.

CGMI=Consentrasi Gerakan Mahasiswa Indonesia, Concentration of Indonesian Student Movements, founded in November 1956.

Gerwani=Gerakan Wanita Indonesia, Indonesian Women's Movement. Gerwani is the new name given to Gerwis in March 1954.

Gerwis=Gerakan Wanita Indonesia Sedar, Movement of Enlightened Indonesian Women, founded on June 4, 1950.

IPPI=Ikatan Pemuda Peladjar Indonesia, League of Indonesian High School Youth, was formed, with a slightly different name, in September 1945.

LEKRA=Lembaga Kebudajaan Rakjat, Institute of People's Culture, formed on August 17, 1950.

Pemuda Rakjat=People's Youth. Shortly after the declaration of Indonesian independence on August 17, 1945, a socialist youth organization was established, Pemuda Sosialis Indonesia (Indonesian Socialist Youth, or Pesindo). The name of Pesindo was changed to Pemuda Rakjat in November 1950.

Perbepsi=Persatuan Bekas Pedjuang Seluruh Indonesia, All-Indonesian Union of Veterans, established on December 30, 1951.

SAKTI=Sarekat Tani Indonesia, Indonesian Peasants' Association, established on December 17, 1949.

Sarbupri=Sarekat Buruh Perkebunan Indonesia, Indonesian Estate Workers' Trade-Union, founded in February 1947 and constituting the largest union in SOBSI.

SOBSI=Sentral Organisasi Buruh Seluruh Indonesia, All-Indonesia Organization of Trade-Unions, established on November 29, 1946.

NAMES OF NEWSPAPERS AND PERIODICALS

BB=Bendera Buruh, Workers' Flag, the periodical of SOBSI.

BM=Bintang Merah, Red Star, PKI's monthly ideological journal.

FALP=For a Lasting Peace, for a People's Democracy!, the journal of the Cominform.

HR=Harian Rakjat, People's Daily, the PKI newspaper, published in Djakarta.

ITUN=Indonesian Trade Union News, an English-language periodical issued by SOBSI.

KP=Kehidupan Partai, Party Life. This was the successor to *PKI-Buletin* and became primarily a forum for the exchange of practical experiences in the different fields of Party work.

PKI-B=PKI-Buletin, a multipurpose Party journal issued from February 1952 to early in 1955 when its name was changed to *Kehidupan Partai.*

RI=Review of Indonesia, a PKI English-language monthly published from January 1957 to October 1960. Its mimeographed predecessor, *Monthly Review,* had been issued from 1954.

ST=Suara Tani, Voice of the Peasants, the official journal of BTI.

TI=Times of Indonesia, an English-language, politically independent newspaper published in Djakarta from 1952 until October 31, 1960, when its license was revoked.

GOVERNMENT ADMINISTRATIVE AREAS

The following two terms are used in this study:

Kabupaten=Indonesia is divided into provinces, the provinces into residencies, and the residencies into *kabupatens.* In 1960 there were 209 *kabupatens* in Indonesia, including 80 in Java.

Ketjamatan=Each *kabupaten* is divided into several *kewedanaans,* and these in turn into *ketjamatans.* In 1960 there were 2,936 *ketjamatans* in Indonesia, including 1,455 in Java. The average *ketjamatan* in Java contained 15 villages or groups of hamlets.

Part one

INTRODUCTION

1

THE SOCIOECONOMIC
SITUATION IN JAVA

The Indonesian census of 1961 registered a population of 95,889,000 on 735,268 squares miles.[1] Java, including Madura,[2] contained 62,733,000 persons on only 51,032 square miles; the next most populous island, Sumatra, trailed far behind with 15,439,000 inhabitants. For PKI, however, Java has been and remains more important than these figures suggest because the people of Java have provided the overwhelming majority of the millions of members recruited to PKI and its mass organizations after 1951. The nature of social and economic conditions in Java has been the decisive factor in the determination of the precise form of the national united front policy formulated by the Aidit leadership. It is the decisive factor in understanding why the Aidit leadership has been able to build mass support. And it is a major factor in explaining why Communist mass support is still an inadequate weapon for the seizure of power.

1. A GENERAL VIEW OF RURAL JAVA

The Indonesian population in 1930 was 60.4 millions. At the end of 1961 it had reached over 96 millions and was growing at a rate of over 2 millions per year. The urban population is growing faster than rural population, but urban growth is far too slow to absorb even a significant part of the rural increase.[3] The population of Java increased from 41.7 millions in 1930 to 63 millions in 1961. This increase occurred on an already crowded island. In 1961 the population density for West Java (including Djakarta) was 441 persons per square kilometer, for Central Java (including Jogjakarta) 550, and for East Java (including Madura) 455. The high density is not, in general, the result of urbanization but of a dense rural population. The greatest concentrations of rural population occur along the north coast from Tjirebon to Pekalongan; along the south coast from Banjumas to Jogjakarta, and then inland to around Surakarta; and along the lower Brantas from Kediri to Surabaja.[4] The highest densities are in the *kabupaten* of Klaten (an estimated 1,038 persons per square kilometer in 1955), and the *kabupaten* of Tjirebon (an estimated 773 persons per square kilometer).[5]

Within Java approximately 60 per cent of the total land surface is used by peasants for food production and some cash crops, 7.6 per cent is used by estates for export crops, and 8.8 per cent is occupied by towns, roads, and rivers.[6] Only 23.4 per cent is forest-covered, although forestry experts estimate that 30 per cent of forest is the minimum required to safeguard the water supply. The forest is in scattered pockets, and much of it is planted teak stands. There is virtually no land available in Java for a further expansion of agriculture,[7] and migration from Java to the thinly populated outer islands has been on a small scale.[8] In other words, the increase in rural population has to be absorbed on the present agricultural area.

The basic crop in Java is irrigated rice, with maize, cassava, peanuts, and soybeans grown in the dry season and on unirrigated land. Cultivation is everywhere labor-intensive, and agricultural implements are primitive. Little fertilizer is used, and yields are low: 22.7 quintals of dry stalk paddy per hectare in Indonesia, compared with 37.8 in China and 74.8 in Italy.[9] Livestock (buffaloes, goats, and sheep) and fishing (sea and inland) form an important additional source of food. Although the geographical limits of agriculture have been reached in Java, indications are that yields could be much improved by relatively simple measures, such as increased supply of fertilizers. Similarly, it is generally agreed that fish production could be greatly expanded.

The population pressure in Java has led to the fragmentation of holdings. Statistics provided by the Ministry of Agrarian Affairs for 1957 [10] give the area of *sawah* (irrigated rice land) in Java as 3,227,694 hectares, owned by 5,788,247 persons, that is, an average of 0.56 hectares per owner. The statistics for unirrigated land were: 4,369,099 hectares, 9,845,936 owners, and an average of under 0.5 hectares per owner.[11] Landholdings were distributed as shown in table 1. Although the

TABLE 1
LANDHOLDINGS IN JAVA, 1957
Sawah

Area*	Under 0.5 ha.	0.6–1	1.1–2.0	2.1–5	5.1–10	10.1–20	Over 20
A	1,395,307	359,424	156,216	56,283	8,153	1,449	363
B	1,388,352	405,067	115,304	25,787	3,265	905	111
C	933,615	464,532	167,565	40,954	4,369	577	93
Total	3,717,274	1,229,023	439,085	123,024	15,787	2,931	567

Unirrigated Land

	Under 0.5 ha.	0.6–1	1.1–2.0	2.1–5	5.1–10	10.1–20	Over 20
A	1,908,821	304,079	198,663	92,785	11,993	2,268	756
B	2,956,974	376,873	187,844	70,227	6,373	754	137
C	2,278,143	393,332	237,814	111,394	13,968	1,748	421
Total	7,143,938	1,074,284	624,321	274,406	32,334	4,770	1,314

* A=West Java; B=Central Java; C=East Java.

figures do not categorize landowners according to total landholdings, that is, *sawah* plus unirrigated land, and do not show how much land was owned by the few landowners with more than twenty hectares, details published by the Ministry of Agrarian Affairs do at least indicate the absence of large landowners over much of Java. There were no *sawah* owners with more than twenty hectares in 3 of the 19 *kabupatens* in West Java, none in 14 of the 28 *kabupatens* of Central Java, and none in 10 of the 29 *kabupatens* of East Java. Over half of the "large" landowners in West Java were in the residency of Djakarta which covered less than one-fifth of the province, and 71 of the 111 "large" *sawah* owners in Central Java were concentrated in the residency of Pekalongan. In Central Java there were nine *kabupatens* with no owner of more than 10 hectares of *sawah,* and four, all around Surakarta, with no owner of more than 2 hectares. In East Java two *kabupatens* had no owner of more than 10 hectares of *sawah.*[12]

The peasant organization BTI claimed in 1950, and PKI claimed in 1951, that 70 per cent of landowners in Java had less than 1 hectare of land (*sawah* plus unirrigated land), 20 per cent had 1 to 2 hectares, 8 per cent 2 to 4 hectares, and 2 per cent more than 4 hectares.[13] Despite the land fragmentation indicated in these figures and those of the Ministry of Agrarian Affairs, the intense population pressure on the limited agricultural land has caused the growth of a landless peasantry generally estimated at about 50 per cent of the rural population. With the collapse of Dutch authority in 1942, many land-hungry peasants moved onto estate and forestry lands. Official government sources in 1954 estimated that 28,000 peasant families were occupying 80,000 hectares of estate lands in Java, and that in Java and Sumatra combined about

400,000 hectares of forestry land were occupied.[14] Such squatters had no legal right to the land they were occupying, and after the transfer of sovereignty in December 1949 they came into conflict, often violent, with estate and government authorities endeavoring to evict them.

Alongside the fundamentally subsistence agriculture of the great majority of the Javanese peasantry has been juxtaposed modern estate agriculture. In 1958, estates occupied 629,900 hectares in Java, of which 342,600 were in West Java (mostly in the residencies of Bogor and Priangan), 209,100 in East Java, and 78,200 in Central Java.[15] At the end of 1955, estates in Java with over ten permanent workers were employing 327,000 permanent workers and 102,000 temporary workers.[16] Sugar mills rented 52,000 hectares of land for sugar cane in 1957,[17] at rents fixed by the government. Forestry also provides rural work outside the sphere of subsistence agriculture, and in 1958, 245,349 laborers were employed in forestry work in Java.[18]

2. THE JAVANESE VILLAGE [19]

OCCUPATIONS, LANDHOLDING, AND SOCIAL STATUS

The percentage of villagers engaged directly in agricultural production varies considerably with such factors as the size of the village, and its proximity to towns, communications, the sea, estates, sugar mills and forests, and workable raw materials such as clay. In some villages 100 per cent of the population engages directly in agriculture, but such villages must now be only a small minority. Nonagricultural villagers include petty traders and owners of small shops (often of Chinese descent), craftsmen in a diversity of work from basketry, weaving bamboo walls, and food preparation to masonry, tile-making, and bicycle repair. There is often a learned group, consisting of one or more of the following: *gurus,* teachers of traditional Javanese lore, *dalangs,* conductors of puppet theaters or producers and instructors of Javanese dance drama, *kiajis,* Moslem scholars, *imams,* mosque officials, and elementary schoolteachers.[20] Where they are present, the learned people receive great respect from the other villagers. On occasion even the learned engage in agriculture, while most of the indigenous petty traders and craftsmen are only part-time specialists, pursuing their trades when agricultural work is slack. Each village also has its own village officials, at least a *lurah* (village head), and a secretary, and often an irrigation official, a religious official, a messenger, and *kamituas,* heads of hamlets. These village officials, too, usually engage in agriculture besides performing their official functions.

An American sociologist has explained concisely the relation between land and social status in the Javanese village: "There is an extremely complex organization of rights in land, labor and the use thereof, and a clearly graded hierarchy of villagers based on clustering of these rights." [21] Any description of the pattern of landholding in Java is complicated by the continued village, that is, communal, right of disposal over about one-quarter of all landholdings.[22] The "kernel" villagers, those who are envisaged as being the descendants of the original settlers in the village, and who may comprise up to 50 per cent of the village households,[23] receive lifelong right of usufruct over equal areas, usually less than two acres, and this right is inheritable, while the land involved cannot be subdivided or sold. Should a kernel villager die without heir, commit a serious crime, or leave the village, a meeting of all kernel villagers decides to whom to transfer the land, usually to a villager who owns a house but no land and who has been waiting the longest. No person may own two shares. The village officials receive extra land in proportion to their position.[24] Along with the right to village land are many obligations, such as maintaining village roads and irrigation channels and taking part in the night watch. The individually owned land may be disposed of at will, but there is strong social pressure against alienation of this land to people outside the village.[25]

The landless peasants and those with only diminutive holdings must seek land to sharecrop or supplementary work outside the village or of a nonagricultural nature, such as petty trading, trades, handicrafts, and transportation (much of transport is done by human back). Conditions for sharecropping are often heavy, the sharecropper usually receiving only one-third to one-half the crop from *sawah,* and in some areas there is added "key money" and the obligation to work without recompense for the landlord.[26]

However, exploitation of landownership has not developed to the extent that it has in some other countries. Jay, investigating villages in East Java, found that "a poor family without land rights, in this area at any rate, may reasonably expect to be able to claim a sharecropping right from a well-to-do neighbor without much fear of rejection." [27] Willner writes that the wealthier in the village "feel some measure of responsibility in providing work [for the landless laborer] even when rationally of dubious economic gain to himself." [28] Geertz has suggested two main factors as retarding the growth of a large "genuinely alienated and politically disinherited agricultural proletariat": the capacity of the village to absorb an increase in population through an intensification of agriculture, and the capacity of the social structure to adapt to a more complex pattern of social differentiation.[29] Thus, Geertz points out, one piece of land of one acre may have an owner, a renter, a major tenant, a subtenant, and a wage laborer, all drawing shares from its output, shares that are unequal but not radically so.

Many Javanese peasants are forced, by their general poverty, the seasonal nature of their income and the high expense of occasional ritual feasts, to borrow goods or money from moneylenders or to sell their crops at low prices long before they are harvested. Interest rates in the capital-scarce village are high.[30] Where the moneylenders are ethnic Indonesians, rather than Chinese, their operations have led to a certain degree of concentration of landholdings, apparently more so in West Java.[31] However, "risk capital is . . . chronically short, and thus becomes the sought rather than the seeking." [32] This fact may partly explain the apparent lack or weakness of peasant resentment at the moneylenders who are helping to meet the great demand for capital that is as yet unmet by government or coöperative enterprise.[33]

Are the poor villagers conscious and resentful of their unfavorable social and economic position? Geertz believes that village society "has, in fact, proved remarkably capable of absorbing a very dense population without developing a sharp class segregation of haves and have-nots." [34] Jay found a clear distinction between the "patrons" and those who must sharecrop, but also a refusal by the villagers to conceptualize the community as divided into two socially unequal categories.[35] Jay further found that there was much movement across this division, and that about half the families on the wealthier side had started in their youth on the poorer side.[36] Kattenburg, studying a village near Salatiga, reached the conclusion that "to my mind at least, class distinctions play no effective role in the village . . . in final account, rights, obligations, privileges and, indeed, status, are pretty well the same for all the villagers." [37]

While it would be rash to generalize from the experience of a few research workers, their general conclusions as to the minimal nature of social antagonisms are supported by my own conversations with many Javanese and by the great difficulty experienced by PKI and its mass organizations in their efforts to create or increase such antagonisms. The impact of the 1945 revolution, with the concomitant penetration of political parties and mass organizations into rural areas, election campaigns,[38] and increased primary education,[39] has undoubtedly led to increased material and social expectations among the poorer villagers and perhaps to the beginnings of social conflict. But the poorer villagers are still far from the point of expressing violent verbal or more active dissatisfaction with the inequalities that exist.

VILLAGE GOVERNMENT

In each *ketjamatan* there are about fifteen *kelurahans,* which in turn consist of two to seven hamlets. The lowest administrative unit is the *kelurahan,* which may have a population of up to several thousand persons. Since 1945 the *lurah* has been elected by all village males aged 18 and over. The *lurah* is generally elected for life, or until he resigns or is dismissed by a member of the central government rural administrative service. He usually nominates the other village officials, but his choice must be endorsed by the administrative service. Formerly the position of *lurah* was generally hereditary,[40] and the *lurah* acted as a paternal despot. Since the revolution the *lurah* has become less of a "little king," although he still retains a monarchist character in the more remote villages. He still retains the respect of his villagers, but has been no effective barrier to the entry of an array of political parties and mass organizations into the village. Politically he is becoming increasingly the nominee and dependent of a political party, or he attempts to maintain political neutrality so as not to antagonize any major group in his village.

The members of the rural administrative service used to exercise considerable power and authority over the villagers, but such power and authority have been "radically curtailed by the upsurge of nationalist and democratic feeling and by the development of political parties and mass organization at the local level." [41] The influence of the rural administrative service is still felt politically, especially in the more remote areas, and PNI is still dependent upon it for mobilizing much of its votes in elections, but like that of the *lurahs* it is on the wane and has been unable to prevent the growth of political parties and mass organizations in the villages.

Village meetings, of everyone over 18 and all married men, are called when necessary. After independence the central government at first required that such meetings be held regularly, but when they led to breaches of Javanese etiquette and to the intensification of factionalism, local officials were given permission to discontinue regular meetings. When they are held, important decisions are reached not by voting but by talking and modifying, and if a considerable body of objection remains to a particular proposal, then the proposal is dropped or postponed. This method of procedure satisfies a deeply held desire for *mufakat,* consensus, and for the prevention of external display of disagreement.

While the authoritarian control of *lurah* and the administrative service is everywhere on the decline, the individual villagers have been slow to take spontaneous initiative in village or wider politics. Fagg found that

Perhaps the fundamental element of the Javanese world-view and value-system . . . is the division between the leader and the masses. . . . The great mass of the people consider themselves unworthy of positions of leadership; such posts are reserved for those adjudged superior in critical respects.[42]

This division has tended to bolster the authority of persons holding "position," but it has presented no obstacle to the expansion of political parties and mass organizations, as their present large membership shows. It is significant, however, that as yet virtually no first, second or even third echelon leaders or cadres of the parties and mass organizations have arisen from the ranks of the rural and urban poor. It would appear that the Javanese poor are willing to join organizations led by educated urban people, so long as the organizations are for their own immediate benefit, but that their membership is largely passive. The Javanese poor are still loath to take action against the traditional authorities around them or against wealthier neighbors to whom they continue to pay at least overt respect.

THE VILLAGE AND SOCIAL SERVICES

Geertz, after working in villages in east-central Java, wrote:

Javanese villages are very large . . . , and their sense of internal solidarity is rather weak. These are broad generalizations and they will not, perhaps, hold equally well everywhere in Central Java, but in a comparative sense I think they are not misleading: the organic, communal, confidently tranquil sort of society we associate, perhaps romantically, with peasant life is not, in general, characteristic of the Javanese village today. More characteristic is an inability to cooperate or to organize anything very effectively; a reluctance, born of an uncertainty of how precisely to proceed, to undertake complex and extended projects; and a certain aimlessness, a dissatisfied, bewildered, restlessness.[43]

Jay has likened Javanese village life to American suburbia, with the same rows of self-contained nuclear family households, the same complete ignorance of and indifference toward those living more than a short distance away.[44] Geertz adds another similarity: boredom.[45]

Mutual assistance, *gotong rojong*, was once common, especially for tasks that an individual was unable to accomplish alone, such as housebuilding, certain work on the land, and major ritual feasts for deaths, births, and circumcisions. While mutual assistance is still highly regarded, the effects of a monetary economy have been felt, and "Nowadays, . . . the rendering of these various services without recompense is confined to very near neighbours." [46]

After national independence the village was unable to cope with the new demands produced by parliamentary democracy, greatly increased education and generally increased awareness of the outside world, and the stimulated desire for economic improvement and social advancement. The "under-organized" village has therefore accepted with little opposition an array of political parties, mass organizations, religious associations and the like. These parties and organizations, under literate urban leadership, have provided means of social and economic advance or the promise of them, they have provided the leadership necessary to revive mutual assistance and to undertake any major action for village improvement, and they have provided "entertainment" and action, a breath of modernity, to relieve the boredom of Javanese "rural suburbia."

RELIGIOUS SCHISM IN JAVA

As a result of uneven Islamization, Javanese society is divided into two culturoreligious groups.[47] On the one hand are the *santris,* the more devout Moslems who have rejected much of earlier Javanese culture and syncretic religion. On the other are the *abangans* and *prijajis,* the latter a more sophisticated, urbanized, aristocratic version of the former. The *abangans* and *prijajis,* for the most part nominal Moslems, range from the villagers and urban poor with a more indigenous, animistic set of beliefs and practices incorporating vestiges of Hinduism, to the aristocratic *prijajis* with often a highly developed theosophical world view based on Hindu-Javanese cosmology, and occasionally fully secularized and antireligious. The *santri-abangan* division (and here I include the *prijajis* as a part of the *abangans*) split the pre-independence nationalist movement into two main streams, and the post-independence political parties into *santri* and non-*santri,* avowedly Moslem and secular.

In many areas syncretic *santri-abangan* practices still persist without friction between the more orthodox Moslems and the more *abangan*-inclined, but antagonism between the two groups would now appear to be general and to be increasing as a result of the political competition that spread through all levels of society after the proclamation of independence. Geertz has observed that "for all intents and purposes, no *kampong* or village *santris* follow urban *abangan* leadership, and vice versa";[48] while Jay wrote of the village he studied that "overt political factionalism between *santri* and *abangan*" had dominated local politics since the revolution.[49]

The *santri-abangan* division has had considerable influence on political developments since 1949. Firstly, approximately 40 per cent of the population of Java (including the Sundanese in West Java and the Madurese of Madura and adjacent areas of Java proper) are sufficiently *santri* to vote for Moslem political parties, and from the results of the September 1955 parliamentary elections and the 1957 local elections it would appear that their political loyalty to Islam is not easily shaken.[50] From the election results, it is evident that the *santri* population is not evenly distributed, but is concentrated in the Sundanese areas of West Java, along the north coast from Indramaju to Djepara, and in East Java in Madura and along the north coast.[51] Significantly, the few relatively extensive areas of mountains and forests, suitable for guerrilla warfare, are strongly *santri*. Elsewhere the *santris* are generally small islands in a basically *abangan* population, and are almost absent in a belt of country from Pati south to Gunung Kidul.

A second major political repercussion of the *santri-abangan* division is that the choice of political affiliation for the large *abangan* population cannot include the Moslem, *santri* parties. The choice is between the secular parties, of which only PKI and, to a far less extent, PNI have made widespread organizational efforts. Having been carefully insulated from political activity during the period of Dutch and Japanese rule, the *abangan* poor after independence had no traditional loyalty to a particular party and could judge the parties only on their present appearance. Because PNI has largely relied for winning popular support on the elite of government officials, village officials, and schoolteachers, and, despite much talk to the contrary, is clearly a party of "haves," PKI and its mass organizations have had a virtual monopoly in channeling whatever social protest or aspirations there have been among the poorer *abangan* population. PKI has gone further and, in many *abangan* areas, deliberately exploited the *abangan* fear and dislike of the *santris* in order to win support.

3. THE URBAN SETTING

In 1961 there were eleven towns in Java with a population exceeding 100,000. Their combined population was 6,904,000. Djakarta was by far the largest, with 2,922,000 inhabitants, followed by Surabaja with 990,000, Bandung with 966,000, and Semarang with 487,000. In general, the largest towns grow the fastest,[52] while the smaller towns seem to do little more than keep pace with the rural areas around them. The population of the six largest cities increased by approximately 400 per cent between 1930 and 1961, while the population of Java as a whole increased by only about 53 per cent. This means that a large proportion

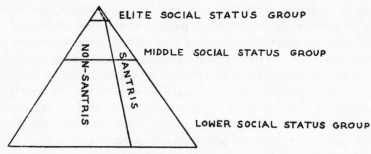

ELITE SOCIAL STATUS GROUP

MIDDLE SOCIAL STATUS GROUP

NON-SANTRIS

SANTRIS

LOWER SOCIAL STATUS GROUP

Urban Social Status Groups, Java

of the present urban population does itself come from villages or is only one generation removed from the village. In other words, a large proportion of the present urban population still retains peasant modes of behavior, and, of great political significance. the "tradition of open obedience" [53] that is most marked among the peasantry.

Little recent research has been made into the social and economic situation in the Indonesian towns. The urban population may be divided arbitrarily into three broad categories according to social status: elite, middle, and lower (see diagram above).

The main determinants of status are occupation (and rank within that occupation), wealth, birth, and formal education.[54] As the diagram illustrates, the *santri* and non-*santri* may be thought of as two subcommunities, but they are not completely exclusive because, by and large, each subcommunity recognizes the prestigeful persons in the other subcommunity. Further, there appears to be a tendency, especially at the elite level, for the two communities to merge as one national status system embracing persons of different ethnic and religious background.

THE ELITE STATUS GROUP

The social elite, of a few thousand persons, is a national conglomeration that includes members of the old Javanese aristocracy but also many more who have risen to prominence by a number of channels: political parties and mass organizations, the bureaucracy, business, the armed forces, education, and so on. The *santris* are not as well represented in the elite as in the middle and lower social categories. The *santris* have, by and large, scorned employment in the bureaucracy, which is one of the main avenues to membership in the social elite, because they are, in general, the indigenous commercial and industrial group with economic and religious outlets for initiative which the non-*santris* do not have (the remainder of private commerce and industry

being in the hands of the Chinese). Or, if *santris* do enter the bureaucracy, the armed forces, political parties, and so on, and enter the
social elite by those channels, they tend to lose their *santri*-ness and
become absorbed by and indistinguishable from the non-*santris*. Furthermore, although *santris* comprise a high percentage of the small
indigenous commercial and industrial group, they were largely excluded from a new element of the social elite created by the PNI-led
first Ali Sastroamidjojo cabinet (which itself excluded the largest
santri party, Masjumi): the government-sponsored and protected "national businessmen."

It should be noted that a position of prominence in such as the political or economic sphere does not necessarily bring entry into the social
elite. For example, almost no persons prominent in PKI or the Communist mass organizations are in the social elite; nor are more than
a handful of the wealthy ethnic Chinese of Indonesian citizenship. It
is also true that while most of the social elite are readily recognizable
by obvious status indicators—a large house in the right location, a large
new car (preferably a Mercedes Benz), fine quality textiles purchased
abroad, large receptions and even cocktail parties—not all members
of the social elite need to possess such material attributes, nor does
possession of them automatically ensure a position in the elite. The
only sure way to recognize a member of the social elite is to know if he
is invited to the homes of other members of the elite, and if he or his
children marry other members of the elite.

THE MIDDLE STATUS GROUP

In Indonesia the middle status group comprises that large number of
white-collar citizens between the elite and those who have a blue collar
or no collar at all. This middle group could almost be called the
pegawai (government employee) class because the great majority of its
members are associated with the government: officials, clerks, technical
staff, teachers, officers in the armed forces. The tremendous growth of
the bureaucracy since the establishment of the Indonesian republic has
been largely caused by three factors: the government's belief that anyone with qualifications, educational or revolutionary, is entitled to a
position in the bureaucracy; the political and family padding of
ministries by individual ministers and their subordinates; and the
increase in work performed by the government, compared with
colonial times. Employees of the central government apparatus increased from about 150,000 in 1940 to 570,000 in 1953.[55] One effect of
this expansion of the bureaucracy has been to prevent the growth of a

literate unemployed, a source of radical politicians in many countries. A significant indigenous commercial or industrial class has not yet emerged. After the transfer of sovereignty in December 1949, the major commercial and industrial enterprises were in the hands of Europeans or Chinese, and the Chinese, of whom about one million live in Java, dominated most other forms of economic activity requiring more than a minimum of capital and business skill. There were exceptions, indigenous Indonesians in some medium- and small-scale industry, commerce, and repair shops, and they were mostly *santris*. In 1957, the Indonesian government confiscated all Dutch enterprises, which opened up a new range of positions for Indonesians, but as the larger concerns were retained under government control the new managers were, in fact, government employees, members of the bureaucracy. Indigenous Indonesians also constitute a part of the free professions, doctors and lawyers, and their more eminent members are in the social elite.

THE LOWER STATUS GROUP

The gulf between the middle group and the lower group is a marked one in Java. In general the urban lower status group lives in the *kampongs,* though it must be noted that the housing shortage and the low government wages have forced many lower government employees also to live in *kampongs*; they are in the *kampongs,* but not of them.

Although I frequently asked Indonesian politicians and government officials how all the *kampong* dwellers earned a living, none was able to give a satisfactory answer. Under Dutch rule, at least until the 1930's, industrial development was discouraged, and in 1940 only an estimated 200,000 workers in Java were in industry using modern machinery; 2.5 millions, of whom many would be in the small towns and villages, were estimated to be employed in small-scale industry.[56] A survey of industry in 1955 indicated a little over 400,000 workers in Java employed in undertakings with over 50 workers.[57] Only 140,248 workers were employed in undertakings with over 249 workers. Furthermore, about 35 per cent of those employed were women.[58] Medium- and large-scale manufacturing accounts, therefore, for only a small part of the urban labor force. The rest is employed in a bewildering array of occupations, in small-scale manufacture and processing, transportation (by lorry, jeep, *oplet, betjak,* bicycles, carts, and human back), repairs of all kinds, small-scale trade, domestic service, and laboring jobs on such as construction, road-sweeping, and grass-cutting.

In the smaller enterprises, which employ the great majority of the

16 Introduction

urban labor force, it would be broadly correct to say that the employer, whether Chinese, *santri*, or *abangan*, still exhibits a certain fatherly concern for his workers, a certain responsibility for them in time of family illness, death, or other difficulties.

The *kampongs*, especially in Djakarta and Surabaja, are densely crowded collections of bamboo houses that have arisen behind the shops and better houses on the paved roads. Conditions in the *kampongs* vary greatly from *kampong* to *kampong* and from city to city, but in general the homes are without their own water and electricity, and sewerage arrangements are primitive. The poor living conditions of the *kampong* dwellers is reflected in their health and nutrition. The death rate among all Indonesians in Djakarta in the 1930's was 30 per thousand, and about 30 per cent for children under one year; and, as Wertheim comments, conditions have, if anything, deteriorated since then.[59]

In 1957 the Ministries of Labor and Health made surveys in Djakarta of a random sample of the families of workers in manufacturing enterprises.[60] From a subsample of 166 families, the Ministry of Labor found that an average 95.83 per cent of expenditure was on consumption "in order to live," and 4.17 per cent on such as taxes, interest on loans, and entertainment. Of the expenditure on consumption, 60.0 per cent was on food, of which 49.12 per cent was on rice alone. The ministry's report, written in 1959, added that "It can be estimated that the present situation is already very different and is becoming worse." The Ministry of Health survey covered 180 families. It found that only 30 per cent ate three times a day; that the average worker's calorie intake was only 70.4 per cent of the calculated minimum requirements, and for the members of his family, only 80.1 per cent. Vitamin deficiency was widespread.

Wage statistics are useless unless put against cost of living indexes—which are not available in Indonesia. Continual inflation, especially rapid iń the period 1957 to 1963, has meant that any wage increases have quickly lost their purchasing power.[61] Careful studies suggest that real wages are lower than prewar. To quote Higgins:

Available data indicate that national income per capita is below the 1939 level, probably below the 1929 level, and may even be below the level of 1919. There is no clear evidence that per capita real income is currently rising.[62]

The Communist trade-union federation has estimated that real wages of government workers fell from an index of 100 in 1954 to 58 in 1959.[63]

In the absence of industrial expansion that equals the rate of urban growth,[64] there is less work per head of urban population. This situation has not led to a massive army of unemployed, rather it has led to a pattern similar to that in the villages: greatly increased underemployment, more persons doing the same amount of work, but not the creation of a socially disinherited, unemployed proletariat.[65]

II

THE INDONESIAN COMMUNIST PARTY, 1920-1951

1. 1920—1948

The first socialist-oriented organization in Indonesia was the ISDV (the Indies' Social Democratic Association), founded in 1914 by four Dutchmen resident in Indonesia. By 1920 the more extreme leftists in the ISDV had established close contact with Indonesian leftists in the nationalist Sarekat Islam (Moslem Association). On May 23, 1920 the Indonesian Communist Party was established, with its headquarters at the Semarang branch of Sarekat Islam.[1] During the next six and a half years, the Communists attempted first to capture control of Sarekat Islam, and, when they failed, to establish a parallel organization. A change in policy turned the Party's major effort to trade-union activity. The Dutch colonial government was quick to exile the more prominent Communists, leaving the Party in the hands of extremists who led the Party into an ill-organized series of revolts in West Java in November 1926 and on the west coast of Sumatra in January 1927. At the time of the revolts, there were about 3,000 Party members.

The government easily quelled the revolts, arrested 13,000 suspects, imprisoned 4,500, and interned 1,308 in a concentration camp in West Irian. PKI was declared illegal. Although the Party did not reëmerge as a significant political force until 1946,[2] its anti-Dutch action in the early 1920's placed it in a position of nationalist honor as the first modern nationalist martyr at the hands of Dutch colonialism.

PKI was reëstablished on October 21, 1945, but the exiled veteran leaders did not return until 1946, when they took control and ensured that the Party pursued a policy of coöperation with other socialist and nationalist political forces.[3] It is to be noted, however, that many of the returning Communists, and many of those who had been members of the Communist underground, did not enter PKI. Many went into the Socialist Party, the Indonesian Labor Party, and Pesindo (Indonesian Socialist Youth). Kahin does not consider this development to have been part of a long-term plan.

For two years during the revolution, the open and covert Communists followed a policy of support for the Republican government, especially in its negotiations with the Dutch. In return they received large representation in the appointed parliament and, at times, significant representation in the cabinet. At the same time the open and covert Communists were active in the mass organizations (of which the labor federation SOBSI, the peasant organization BTI, and Pesindo were the most important), and were later to use their positions to capture control of them.

The first Republican cabinet, installed on August 31, 1945, included Amir Sjarifuddin. He was then known as a left-wing socialist leader of the wartime underground but was to declare in 1948 that he had been a Communist for thirteen years. The first working committee of the appointed parliament included Sjarifuddin as vice-chairman, and also Tan Ling Djie, then known as a leader of the Socialist Party but who was already a member of the "illegal PKI" which was coördinating the work of the Communists in the various parties. Sjarifuddin was included in the first Sjahrir cabinet as minister of defense, a position he retained in the second Sjahrir cabinet that also included a Communist, Wikana, as minister without portfolio.

Sjahrir's third cabinet, appointed on October 2, 1946, included among its 31 members one open Communist and three covert Communists. Sjarifuddin retained the post of minister of defense. In March 1947, PKI was rewarded for its support of the government by an increase in its parliamentary representation from 2 to 35 when the size of parliament was enlarged from 212 to 514 members. After the enlargement of parliament, two young Communists, who were to win control of the Party in January 1951, became prominent in parliamentary work: Njoto as chairman of the PKI group in the working committee of parliament, and D. N. Aidit as chairman of the PKI group in the full meeting. In the new working committee of parliament, the Communist-Socialist alliance, Sajap Kiri (Left Wing), received 17 of the 47 seats.

The cabinet which succeeded Sjahrir's third, and which was in office from July 5, 1947, to January 23, 1948, went far toward giving the Communists a position from which they might have been able to win full control of the Republican government. Of the 34 ministers, Sjarifuddin was both prime minister and minister of defense, two open Communists were ministers of state, a covert Communist was deputy prime minister, and another was a third minister of state. It was widely believed that Sjarifuddin was using his position to advance his allies within the army and to establish secret arms and ammunition caches in the mountains. The Communists were unable, however, to consolidate their position for two main reasons. First, the Dutch began their first major attack on the Republic at the end of July 1947, and the cabinet was therefore preoccupied with the struggle for survival and then with precarious negotiations with the Dutch. Second, the government felt forced to sign the highly unfavorable Renville agreement with the Dutch. This caused the opposition, already concerned at Communist strength, to combine and bring down the government after less than seven months of existence. The post-1950 Party leadership was to criticize "the transfer of state power to the bourgeois class in February 1948" as "the peak of basic errors committed by PKI during the revolution." [4] "In this way the most important instrument in the class struggle, that is, state power, was entirely removed from the hands of the people, and from that moment became the instrument for oppressing the people."

The Sajap Kiri refused to accept a junior position in the next cabinet, that of Vice-President Hatta, but in January 1948 a large part of the intellectuals and other democratic socialists in the Socialist Party split away to form PSI which supported the new cabinet. On February 26, 1948, the Sajap Kiri was reorganized as the Front Demokrasi Rakjat (People's Democratic Front). The Front soon launched strong attacks, including strikes, against the cabinet, and rejected further offers from Hatta of cabinet posts.

On August 11, 1948, Musso, a Communist veteran of the 1920's, returned to Indonesia after over twenty years of exile in the Soviet Union and was immediately acknowledged as the leader of PKI. Musso drew up a lengthy resolution which called for the reorganization of the Communist forces into one openly Communist party, and presented a new formulation of the national united front policy.[5] The plenary meeting of the Central Committee of the PKI adopted the resolution on August 27, whereupon the leaders of the Socialist and Indonesian Labor parties publicly declared that they had been Communists for many years and announced the dissolution of their parties.

On September 1, 1948, the new 16-member Politbureau of the enlarged PKI was announced, and incorporated the prominent leaders of the three former Communist-led parties. Party leaders toured the country to explain the new organizational and political policies to cadres and members of PKI and the now-dissolved parties, and a start was made in sifting and registering those members of the dissolved parties who were considered suitable for membership in the enlarged PKI. But before the new policies could be fully implemented, the Madiun rebellion began on September 18, 1948.[6]

It appears that the Madiun rebellion began when Communist and pro-Communist civilians and army officers in the Madiun area panicked at the government's plan to demobilize many of the Communist-led armed units. Although it is probable that PKI was preparing for an eventual armed struggle, the rebellion in Madiun was premature and posed the PKI leaders the difficult question of what to do: to do nothing, and see their positions in the armed forces eliminated; or to join the rebels, and try to turn the premature uprising into a successful revolution. Some of the Politbureau members, including Alimin, merely went into hiding; others were arrested before they could take any action; but the majority of the top echelon leaders went to Madiun and took over the direction of the rebellion.

The government acted swiftly, recapturing Madiun within two weeks, and totally crushing the rebellion within two months. Musso was killed in a skirmish at the end of October, but most of the other Communist leaders were captured. In all, some 36,000 PKI members, sympathizers, and suspected sympathizers were imprisoned.[7] Many second-echelon leaders were killed in the fighting or shot after capture, but PKI suffered the most severe blow in December 1948 when the army executed the eleven most prominent Communist prisoners rather than free them in face of advancing Dutch troops. Among those shot were five Politbureau members, including Amir Sjarifuddin, and the two top leaders of SOBSI, the trade-union federation. The chairman of the Indonesian Labor Party was also killed during the rebellion.

Most of the Communists captured or arrested at the time of the rebellion were freed when the Dutch attacked and before charges could be brought against them. Many took to the hills and joined the Republican guerrilla bands. When the Dutch finally withdrew at the end of 1949, the government took no further action against them.

2. DECEMBER 1948—JANUARY 1951

In the period between December 1948 and the final Dutch withdrawal in December 1949, a provisional PKI Central Committee worked spasmodically in an effort to maintain a rudimentary Party organization. The great majority of the surviving leaders and members were afraid, however, to associate openly with the Party until they were certain it was not going to be persecuted further for its rebellion at Madiun. When the Dutch withdrew, Ngadiman Hardjosubroto, who was acting secretary-general, was chosen by the Party to sit in the working committee of the Republican parliament, and took his place there in December 1949. Ngadiman was then appointed a member of the Indonesian parliament and moved from Jogjakarta, in which city the PKI headquarters were still located, to Djakarta in January 1950. Djaetun took over the post of acting secretary-general.[8] He was a veteran Communist who had been active in PKI in the 1920's and had suffered exile in West Irian and Australia from 1926 to 1946. But Djaetun was only a front figure.

Throughout most of 1950, PKI operated on three levels. First, there was the legal PKI, with an office in Jogjakarta, and with Djaetun as secretary-general. Second, the Socialist and Indonesian Labor parties were revived. The leader of the Socialist Party was Tan Ling Djie, an Indonesian citizen of Chinese descent. The Indonesian Labor Party was led by Asmu and Sakirman. Third, there was an "illegal PKI" which directed the work of the open parties, and also maintained a clandestine Party organization. In other words, Musso's plan for the organization of the Communist parties into a single, public Marxist-Leninist party was quietly ignored.

During 1949 and 1950 no one person exercised leadership of the "illegal PKI," and therefore of the legal PKI and the Socialist and Labor parties. The foremost leader was Tan Ling Djie,[9] with Ngadiman Hardjosubroto perhaps the second figure. These two were the survivors of the four-man General Secretariat of the Politbureau that had been announced on September 1, 1948, and their rise to the top two places in the Party was a natural process after the death of the other two members of the General Secretariat. Alimin, a veteran Party member, retained considerable prestige, and in March 1950 he was reported to be the head of PKI's Agitation and Propaganda Secretariat, of which he had been a member in 1948. But Alimin could not be a serious contender for control of the Party because of his age (he was born in 1889), and of marked ill health which began in late 1949.[10] Also within the leadership, but of a lesser stature, was Wikana, who had been a minister of state in the Amir Sjarifuddin cabinet from July 1947 to January 1948, and who had been elected head of the youth section of the Politbureau announced on September 1, 1948.

In July 1950, two young Communists returned to Indonesia after eighteen months abroad: Dipa Nusantara Aidit, and M. H. Lukman. They had left Indonesia at the time of the Madiun rebellion and had gone to Viet Nam where they reportedly fought with the Viet Minh guerrillas,[11] and to China, where they attended the Asian-Australasian trade-union conference in Peking in December 1949, ostensibly as representatives of the trade-union federation SOBSI.[12] Aidit[13] was 26 years old on his return, but already had been active for several years in the left-wing movement in Indonesia. He claims to have joined PKI as early as 1943, and to have taken part in the semilegal youth organizations which prepared the August 17, 1945, proclamation of Indonesian independence. In the middle of 1946 he went to work for the PKI Central Committee and at the Fourth PKI Congress in January 1947 was elected to membership of that committee. In 1947 he became a member of the Republican parliament and chairman of the PKI parliamentary group. In the same year he was also a member of the executive board of the Indonesian Socialist Youth, and of the executive council of the People's Democratic Front which united most of the socialist and Communist organizations. At the beginning of 1948 Aidit became a candidate member of the PKI Politbureau and in August became a full member and a member of its Labor Secretariat. His companion, Lukman,[14] was 30 years old and had been raised in the Dutch concentration camp in West Irian to which his father had been sent for his part in the 1926 Communist rebellion. Lukman, too, had taken part in the youth movement during the Japanese occupation and in the early days of the revolution, and had also worked for the PKI headquarters from mid-1946. He was elected to the Central Committee in 1948, and in August 1948 to the Politbureau, in which he was a member of the agitation and propaganda section.

Upon their return Aidit and Lukman worked for the Politbureau's Agitation and Propaganda Secretariat which on August 15, 1950, and despite obstruction from Tan Ling Djie, began to republish, twice a month, the Party's periodical *Bintang Merah* (Red Star). Also on the editorial staff were Peris Pardede, then only 32, and Njoto.[15] Njoto, Aidit, and Lukman were to constitute a triumvirate which still controls PKI. In August 1950 Njoto was 25 years old, and like his companions already had an active record in the Communist movement. He had taken part in the underground movement during the Japanese occupation, and in November 1945 had helped establish the PKI organization in Bekasi, of which he soon became secretary-general. Later he represented PKI in the working committee of the Republican parliament, and became chairman of the PKI group in the committee. In mid-1948 he became a member of both the Central Committee and Politbureau of the Party.

The *Bintang Merah* editors claimed in the issue of January 1-15, 1951, that the periodical had reappeared "at a time when Party members were seeking a way out of the darkness caused by the confusion of the Party leadership, at a time when Party members . . . did not receive clear leadership in the organizational and political spheres." [16] The editors further claimed that the reorganization of the Party in the regions, which gathered force after August 1950, was in large part due to the stimulus and leadership given by *Bintang Merah*. They also claimed that the periodical gave the basis and leadership for developing the criticism and self-criticism among Party leaders and ordinary members which led to the ouster of those leaders who clearly "did not fulfill conditions." And if the claim is correct that *Bintang Merah* circulation was increased from 3,000 in August 1950 to 10,000 at the end of the year,[17] then presumably the periodical would have had an influence also extending far outside the Party, which at that time had perhaps 3,000 or 5,000 members.

The influence of the newly-returned leaders was soon felt. On October 19, 1950, the Indonesian Labor Party officially dissolved itself in accordance, as it declared, with Musso's plan, and its leaders expressed the pious hope that Tan Ling Djie's Socialist Party would soon follow suit.[18] However, not all the "old" Communist leaders were willing to accept meekly and without question the new leaders and their policies. As prominent Communists from the previous period, at least Wikana, Ngadiman Hardjosubroto, Tan Ling Djie, and Alimin openly disagreed with the Aidit leadership on matters of policy. But the older leaders did not present a compact resistance and were quickly eliminated one after the other.

The first of the older leaders to be publicly disciplined was Wikana. In the third conference of the Indonesian Socialist Youth, which was held from November 4-12, 1950, he was not reëlected to that organization's executive committee. Further, an article of his in *Bintang Merah*, entitled "Mass Youth Organization," was severely criticized by the editorial board for "erroneous and confused thought." [19] The board called him in for long discussions and obliged him to recant. On December 29 he was made to resign from a study group organized by the nationalist-Communist Murba party, and which the new leaders denounced as a "Trotskyite effort" harmful to PKI.[20]

Ngadiman Hardjosubroto was also disciplined in December 1950. On December 2, a statement was issued in the name of the PKI Secretariat which called for a confederation between a "Democratic Republic of Irian, free from the Round Table Conference agreement, and the Unitary State of the Republic of Indonesia not yet freed from the agreement." [21] The PKI Central Committee immediately denounced the statement as the work of "the Trotskyite and adventurist group," and disclaimed authorship.[22] When it was found that Ngadiman, apparently with Tan Ling Djie's knowledge, had issued the statement, the Central Committee removed him as a PKI member of parliament,[23] and he was excluded from the leadership of the Party.

The other prominent "old" Communist to resist openly the policies of the young leaders at this time was Tan Ling Djie himself. By the end of December the new leaders were sufficiently entrenched within the Central Committee to take Tan to task in a plenary session of the committee held in the first week of January 1951. There he "deviously defended his reformist and legalistic policy concerning West Irian, and also deviously defended the importance of continuing the Socialist Party in order, he said, to gather people who were pro-Communist but 'dare not enter PKI.' " [24] The Central Committee went against him, cancelled his statement on West Irian, and decided to dissolve the Socialist Party. His defeat "resulted in his being deserted by the centrist group in the Central Committee." [25]

The new, five-member Politbureau elected by the Central Committee was announced on January 7, 1951.[26] It consisted of Aidit, Lukman, Njoto, Sudisman, and the aged and ailing Alimin. Aidit, now occupying the post of first secretary, and Sudisman were elected as the leadership of the Central Committee Secretariat. Sudisman,[27] aged 30, had a similar political background to that of the new triumvirate leadership: he had joined PKI during the Japanese occupation, was secretary-general of the Indonesian Socialist Youth from its formation in November 1945, worked in the leadership of the People's Democratic Front, and in August 1948 became a full member of the PKI Politbureau, in which he headed the organization section. From June 1950 to January 1951 he was joint secretary-general of the legal PKI, and lent his support to the Aidit-Lukman-Njoto triumvirate. Aidit, Lukman, Njoto, and Pardede were chosen as the editorial board of *Bintang Merah*. Sakirman was chosen to head the PKI parliamentary group, a position held previously by Ngadiman Hardjosubroto. The Central Committee itself consisted of fourteen persons,[28] still including Tan Ling Djie and Wikana, but not Ngadiman.

The new leadership had met little opposition from the older leaders, for several reasons. First, the more prominent and capable of the "old" leaders had been killed, and the surviving leaders did not have a sufficiently large or loyal following within the Party to stand against the new leadership. Tan Ling Djie had the added disadvantage of being of Chinese descent, and was thereby unable to occupy publicly the top position of PKI in a country where anti-Chinese feeling was strong. Second, the "old" leaders were divided among themselves on matters of personality and policy, and did not present a united front against the new leadership. Third, and partly because of the divisions in the "old" leadership, the Party during 1950 was in a chaotic condition. Little progress was being made in the task of reshaping the Party organization that had been shattered by the Madiun rebellion and the second Dutch attack, and there was a lack of leadership on both organizational and political policy. Into this situation came the new, young, dynamic leaders. They claimed to have clear ideas on organizational and political policy, and they claimed, in defense of their legitimacy, to be the true implementers of Musso's August 1948 resolution. Perhaps they also claimed to have the approval of the Chinese Communist leaders, from whose country they had just returned. Of great, and perhaps crucial, importance was their dynamism. They launched into the publication of *Bintang Merah*, feverishly began to rebuild the Party organization, and worked hard to subdue their opponents. The result was that by January 7, 1951, PKI had a new leadership.

Part two

THE AIDIT LEADERSHIP'S
STRATEGY IN THE INDONESIAN
REVOLUTION

PROLOGUE

When they won control of PKI in January 1951, D. N. Aidit and his colleagues were faced with an unpropitious situation. The Party itself was broken and disorganized. Nearly all Communists and open sympathizers had been purged from the armed forces and the government bureaucracy. The military phase was ended in the revolution against the Dutch. Governmental power was in the hands of rightists who were either openly anti-Communist or at best wary of Communist activities. And "the people," the workers, peasants, and petty bourgeoisie, were far from a revolutionary frame of mind. On the other hand, the Party was not declared illegal, nor were the Communist-infiltrated trade-unions, and peasant and youth organizations. Also, the political elite was fragmented. Instead of a single victorious nationalist party as the Indian Congress Party or the Anti-Fascist People's League of Burma, Indonesia had many and competing parties. The secular nationalists were divided among the PNI and many lesser parties; Protestant and Catholic parties existed; the left wing was split into Socialist, Communist, and national-Communist groups; and even the devout Moslems were divided, with the main party, Masjumi, as an uneasy coalition that was to fall apart in 1952.[1]

Aidit and his fellow leaders were faced with a post-independence situation in an underdeveloped country. As Marxist-Leninists they analyzed the Indonesian revolution in terms of the broad theories of

Marxism-Leninism and of the experience of the Chinese Communists, at that time the only Communists who had won power unaided in an underdeveloped country. But, like Mao Tse-tung, the Aidit leadership was impressed with the need to formulate its own policies and tactics with direct reference to the objective facts (as it saw them) of the Indonesian situation. As Aidit said in March 1957:

We Indonesian communists are not dogmatic in the application of Marxist-Leninist teachings; we are creative. Marxist-Leninist theory is only a guide, the decisive thing in our policy being the concrete situation in Indonesia.[2]

The Aidit leadership has frequently acknowledged its indebtedness to the revolutionary and parliamentary experiences of foreign Communist parties. It insists, however, that the Indonesian revolution possesses certain characteristics that are unique. While there is, for example, a close parallel between the PKI analysis of Indonesian society and the Indonesian revolution, and Mao Tse-tung's analysis of Chinese society and the Chinese revolution, the PKI leaders have been at great pains to show that there are important differences between the circumstances of the Indonesian and the Chinese revolutions. One major difference was that the Chinese Communist Party could win power by armed struggle: it had the politically beneficial environment of the anti-Japanese war which weakened the Kuomintang and allowed the Party to gather about it Chinese nationalist feeling; it had a large territory in which to retreat and maneuver when strongly attacked; and behind its liberation base it had a friendly frontier which prevented encirclement and across which supplies could come.[3] In short, foreign experience must be studied:

But the most important thing for the Indonesian communists is the problem of welding the general truths of Marxism-Leninism with the concrete practice of the Indonesian revolution itself.[4]

The evidence strongly suggests that the repeated assertions of the need to formulate a policy based on the Indonesian situation were not a verbal smoke screen masking effective control and direction of PKI by either Moscow or Peking. Clearly the PKI leaders analyzed Indonesian society along lines closely parallel to those used by Mao Tse-tung in China. It is true, also, that a broad national united front strategy of alliance between the workers, peasants, petty bourgeoisie, and national bourgeoisie against imperialism and feudalism, was indicated by both Chinese experience and the analysis of the Indonesian situation presented by Musso in August 1948 after he had returned from over twenty years residence in the Soviet Union. But the form the united front was to take was developed independently by the Aidit leadership from their own experience with and analysis of the actual Indonesian situation.

That the definition of the national united front strategy was effected independently by the Aidit leadership is strongly suggested by two factors: first, the apparent lack of interest in PKI shown by Moscow for some years after the Madiun rebellion; and second, the quite evident groping by the Aidit leadership toward a definition of the national united front in the context of Indonesian politics and society. It is probable that after the fiasco of Madiun, Moscow wrote off the Indonesian Communists as a lost cause. That is, Moscow considered the distant PKI no longer worthy of attention. Only after 1954, when the success of the Aidit leadership's form of the national united front had become amply apparent, did the interest of Moscow focus anew on PKI. At this stage, the Cold War was entering a more complex stage, with the Russians and Chinese attempting to extend their spheres of influence by winning favor among the neutralists in the underdeveloped and newly independent countries of Asia, Africa, and Latin America. This renewed interest did not take the form of interference. Rather, the foreign parties studied PKI in order to see if its policies could have wider application. Hence, many PKI delegations were invited abroad, and PKI received considerable attention in PKI-written articles in the Cominform journal.[5] The Aidit leadership's search for an Indonesian form of the national united front will be discussed below.

There are certain parallels between the circumstances in which Aidit and Mao Tse-tung formulated their own definitions of the national united front. Both Aidit and Mao won control of parties that were freed from Soviet guidance in policy. Earlier Soviet intervention in both Indonesia and China had helped cause the near extinction of the local Communist parties, with the result that Moscow considered the small, decimated parties to have little if any chance of winning power, and therefore to be no longer worthy of intervention. In the formulation of their own over-all policy, both Aidit and Mao used Marxist-Leninist analytical tools and studied the experience of foreign parties. But each of the leaders was deeply imbued with the atmosphere of his own country, and used his own assessment of the local situation as the principal basis for defining a strategy designed to bring his party to power. In each case, a broad, national united front policy was chosen. Mao has led the Chinese Communist Party to power in the highly favorable circumstances of the Japanese War. The success of Aidit's form of the national united front in post-independence Indonesia is still in the balance.

IV

A SEMICOLONIAL,
SEMIFEUDAL COUNTRY

The Aidit leadership's theory of the Indonesian revolution is based on the assumption that Indonesia is a semicolonial, semifeudal country.[1] At first the Party leaders merely asserted this to be self-evident.[2] The semicolonial position of Indonesia was widely recognized by Indonesians outside PKI, and was emphasized by the heavy terms of the Round Table Conference agreement which had ended the war with the Netherlands,[3] by the control of Indonesia's export and import trade by large foreign companies, by the extent of foreign estate agriculture, and by the exploitation of Indonesia's oil wealth by foreign companies. On the other hand, PKI at first did not elaborate on what was termed the semifeudal nature of Indonesia, perhaps because it was not until 1953 that the Party was concerned with expanding into the rural areas.

An early account of Indonesia's semicolonial position was given by Aidit in May 1953.[4] He repeated the PKI assertion that by the Round Table Conference agreement the Dutch imperialists had retained their control over Indonesia. Among the terms of the agreement that he particularly attacked were the position of the Netherlands monarch as head of the Indonesian-Dutch Union, the alleged control by the Dutch government of Indonesia's financial and foreign policies, the enormous debt to the Netherlands, the restoration to the colonialists of their former rights in industry, commerce, finance, and agriculture, and the alleged control by Dutch civil and military officials of the Indonesian state apparatus and armed forces.

That means Indonesia has what is called "the right of self-government," but in fact real power, in the political, economic and military spheres, is retained in the hands of the Dutch imperialists, and the Indonesian door is opened wide by the RTC agreement to political, economic and military penetration by the American imperialists and other imperialist countries.[5]

Although the first agrarian program drawn up under the Aidit leadership and issued on November 10, 1951, had referred to the "landownership of a feudal and imperialist nature," [6] a clear definition of what was meant by semifeudalism was not given until July 1953. In that month Aidit wrote a major article, "The Future of the Indonesian Peasant Movement," which marked the beginning of intensive Party work in the rural areas.[7] He stated that after capitalism had operated in Indonesia complete feudalism no longer existed, but that "important and heavy remnants" remained. The most significant remnants he listed were:

1. the continued monopoly rights of the large landowners, with the result that the majority of peasants could not own land and were forced to rent land on the landowners' terms;

2. the payment of most of the crops as land rent in kind, so that the majority of peasants were kept in poverty;

3. the payment of land rent in the form of work on the landlords' land, "which places the majority of peasants in the position of serfs"; and

4. the heavy debts of the majority of peasants, which placed them "in the position of slaves vis-à-vis the landowners."

In short, Aidit argued, "there is still feudal exploitation of the peasants."

Such semifeudal conditions, Aidit claimed, made impossible the economic development of Indonesia. Agricultural techniques were primitive, the internal market was shrinking as agricultural production declined and the relative prices of manufactured goods increased, and industrialization was impossible so long as 70 per cent of the population remained too poor to afford industrial goods.

The PKI program endorsed by the Fifth National Congress in March 1954 devoted its first section to a description of Indonesia as being semicolonial and semifeudal.[8] Once more the Round Table Conference agreement was attacked because it "enslaves Indonesia and maintains her position as a semicolony." As a result of the colonialists' control of the Indonesian economy, "our country is in the grip of a continuous economic crisis and is already close to collapse," so that talk about development plans, industrialization and the like came to nothing.

Although our land is fertile there is not enough food in our country to meet the people's minimum needs. . . . As a result of the unlimited power of monopoly and of the embargo against trade with China enforced by the American capitalists, the price of export goods . . . declines gravely, and it is increasingly difficult to find markets for these goods. Indonesian money declines and the price of goods rises. As a result of competition from the Netherlands, America and Japan, the very small number of national industries and trading enterprises is crushed and bankrupt. Except for a small number of feudal landlords, compradores and high officials, the greater part of the Indonesian people lives miserably.[9]

The program also pointed out that 20 per cent of all cultivated land, that is, the best and most fertile land, was still in the hands of colonialist estates. On the matter of feudal remnants in Indonesia, the program added nothing to Aidit's article of July 1953.

When Indonesia unilaterally abrogated the Round Table Conference agreement in April 1956 and then canceled her debts to the Netherlands, PKI was forced to show new grounds for continuing to describe Indonesia as semicolonial. This Aidit did in a booklet *Indonesian Society and the Indonesian Revolution* written in July 1957.[10] He examined the degree of political and economic sovereignty enjoyed by Indonesia. Dealing with the political question, he pointed out that West Irian, comprising 20 per cent of Indonesian territory, was still occupied by the Dutch, and that as for the rest of the country:

The political independence which the Indonesian people now possess is not full and stable political independence but only half and is under the constant threat of the reactionaries. The internal reactionaries working in collaboration with the Dutch, American and other imperialists are doing all they can to restrict and destroy the political independence of the people. And besides this, the national bourgeoisie is trying to limit the political independence of the working class and other progressive people.[11]

According to Aidit, an analysis of the economic sphere also gave "extremely clear evidence that Indonesian society is still semicolonial." The big foreign capitalists, "by utilizing their dominant position in the sphere of the economy and by means of their mercenaries . . . also participate in determining political developments in Indonesia." They controlled the oil reserves, estates, sea transport, some land transport, the import, export, and internal trade, and the banks. As if to emphasize that the abrogation of the agreements with the Netherlands had not altered the situation, Aidit claimed:

The policy of the imperialists in the field of economic affairs is not in principle different from what it was at the time when Indonesia was fully colonized. They have continued to run their old enterprises and have opened up some new ones. This means that they can directly make use of Indonesia's raw materials, extract

Indonesia's mineral wealth, and utilize cheap Indonesian labor power. They are economically squeezing national industry, that owned by the state and that owned by the national bourgeoisie. The result is that the big foreign capitalists stand in the way of developing the productive forces in our country. The banks and finances as well as the goods for sale in the hands of the imperialists play the decisive role in the economic life of our country at the present time.[12]

In order to safeguard their capital and facilitate their exploitation of the people, Aidit continued, the imperialists used compradores and usurers "to throw out wide nets of exploitation extending from the busy commercial harbors on the coast and from the towns right out to the most remote villages." Furthermore, they had placed their compradores in the bourgeois parties and so converted those parties into faithful servants of their interests.

In December 1957 the Indonesian government took over all Dutch businesses.[13] Once again PKI had to justify its continued description of Indonesia as semicolonial, and in December 1958 the Central Committee submitted a new compilation of evidence to support its case.[14] A blow had been struck against the Dutch, the Central Committee admitted, but the Dutch still occupied West Irian; the position of the confiscated Dutch enterprises was still uncertain; Indonesia still made much use of Dutch capitalist channels in its foreign trade; Dutch capital in the oil industry, that is, in the Anglo-Dutch Shell Company, was still untouched; Dutch puppets still occupied important positions in the government, the state apparatus, and the economic field; armed gangs were still actively operating in the interests of the Dutch colonialists; the sky, sea, and coastline of Indonesia were still constantly threatened by Dutch aircraft and submarines; and the Dutch colonialists still had influence in the fields of education and culture. The Central Committee declared that as a result of this situation, "Dutch imperialism is still the first enemy of the Indonesian people."

The Central Committee must have been aware that the diminished economic position of the Dutch had made it difficult for PKI to persist in attributing a semicolonial status to Indonesia, and Party leaders began talking of American imperialism as "increasingly occupying important positions in Indonesia in the economic, political, and cultural spheres." According to the Central Committee, the American imperialists maintained military bases in West Irian, controlled right-wing parties and individuals to promote their interests, carried out cultural infiltration via films and education, and were engaged in a program of assistance to the rebels in Sumatra and Sulawesi. All this was cited as "proof that U. S. imperialism already constitutes a constant danger threatening Indonesia's sovereignty and independence."

In the Central Committee report presented to the Sixth National Congress in September 1959, Aidit once more stated:

For the imperialists, Indonesia continues to be a place for the investment of their capital and a storehouse for cheap labor. They strive not only to defend what capital they already have invested in Indonesia, but also to increase it.[15]

He also added an extra paragraph in denunciation of American imperialism.

Lukman, in his speech to the Sixth Congress, justified at some length the Party's continued description of Indonesia as semicolonial, semifeudal.[16] He said that except for Dutch-occupied West Irian, Indonesia had political independence. On the other hand, the Indonesian economy was in large part still controlled by the imperialists and dependent upon the economy of the imperialist states.[17] In order to emphasize the political importance of economic considerations, he declared:

Supposing the whole of Indonesian territory was already under the control of the Indonesian Republic, but the Indonesian economy was still controlled by or very dependent on the imperialist countries, in such a situation Indonesia could not yet be said to be completely independent because political power cannot possibly be separated from economic power, and economic power is even precisely the basis of political power. Therefore it is impossible for a country to have complete power in the political sphere if its economy is still controlled by or greatly dependent on other, imperialist, countries. Thus it is clear that if a country is not yet independent in the economic sphere, neither is it yet completely free in the political sphere.[18]

Lukman added nothing to Aidit's July 1953 description of the semifeudal condition of Indonesia, a description which remains the basic Party exposition of the matter largely because there have been no subsequent fundamental changes in agrarian relations.

In short, PKI chooses to envisage Indonesia as being still semicolonial, semifeudal. The continued presence of colonial and feudal elements ensures that the great majority of the Indonesian people remain in a state of poverty, and obstructs general economic and industrial development. It is only "a small number of feudal landlords, compradores and high officials," to requote the March 1954 PKI program, who do not suffer from the country's semicolonial, semifeudal condition.

V

THE BASIC TARGETS OF
THE INDONESIAN REVOLUTION

The PKI general program issued by the Central Committee in April 1951 declared that the Indonesian revolution "is aimed against imperialism, feudalism and the compradore bourgeoisie." [1] This bald statement was expanded in the program of March 1954:

As long as the [semicolonial, semifeudal] situation in Indonesia is unchanged, that is, as long as the power of imperialism has not been overthrown nor the remnants of feudalism eradicated, the Indonesian people cannot possibly free themselves from poverty, backwardness, lameness and powerlessness in facing up to imperialism. The power of imperialism and the remnants of feudalism in Indonesia will never be abolished in Indonesia while state power in our country is still held by the landlords and compradores who are firmly connected with foreign capital because they want to preserve imperialist exploitation and feudal remnants in our country, because they are most afraid of the Indonesian people.[2]

Thus the main targets of the revolution are imperialism, with its Indonesian compradore agents, and feudalism.

The Aidit leadership has, however, made a clear tactical distinction between the two main enemies. This distinction was most lucidly explained by Aidit in his speech to the PKI First National Peasants' Conference in mid-April 1959.[3] He declared that the two tasks of overthrowing the power of the foreign enemy, imperialism, and the internal enemy, feudal landlord domination, were "from the strategic angle

. . . very closely interconnected and inseparable." Strategically inseparable because the imperialists were using the feudalists in order to
govern and exploit the people, and because for the revolution to succeed it had to mobilize the peasants, which could only be done by
providing them with land, which in turn meant taking the land from
the feudal landlords. Aidit then went on to say:

If viewed from the tactical angle these two tasks, namely the tasks of overthrowing
the power of imperialism and the power of feudalism, cannot be executed at one
and the same time. If viewed from the tactical angle of the particular conditions of
the present moment, the head of the revolutionary spear should in the first place
be pointed at the foreign enemy (imperialism) and those feudalists and bourgeois
who have become the agents of this foreign enemy. The oppression of foreign imperialism is widely felt by our people. Imperialism is the most criminal enemy with
the most intensive exploitation.

Thus, at a certain moment and under certain conditions as at present, we must concentrate all our efforts for a blow against imperialism in order thus to be able to
settle the first contradiction, the contradiction between the Indonesian nation and
imperialism.

In other words, the enemies of the revolution are considered too
strong to be tackled both at the same time. They must be smashed in
turn, first imperialism and then feudalism.

VI

THE DRIVING FORCES
OF THE REVOLUTION

As Communists, the PKI leaders believed that the proletariat constituted the basic driving force of the Indonesian revolution, the basic
support of the Party. An analysis of the strength of the proletariat
showed, however, that the proletariat was far too weak to destroy the
power of imperialism and feudalism. Because the proletariat was so
weak, the Aidit leadership undertook a sociopolitical analysis of the
other major social forces in Indonesia in order to determine which
might be won as disciplined allies, which might be won as allies under
certain circumstances, and which were implacable enemies.

1. THE PROLETARIAT

According to Aidit, the Indonesian proletariat consists of about 500,000
workers in modern industry (transport workers, factory workers,
miners, workers in repair shops, and so on), more than 2 million workers
in small industry and handicrafts in the towns, and a large number of
workers on estates, in forestry work, and in miscellaneous occupations.[1]
Their total number is about 6 millions or, with their families, about
20 millions. They therefore comprise about 25 per cent of the total
population.[2]

The exploitation and poor living conditions suffered by the Indonesian proletariat are obvious to all Indonesians. Aidit could state, without fear of contradiction, that "the Indonesian proletariat is exploited by three forms of brutal exploitation, that is, imperialism, capitalism and feudalism." [3] In December 1958 the Central Committee reported that "the living conditions of the Indonesian workers are getting worse and worse" [4]—which was a deterioration in an already deplorable situation. The decline was stated to be the result of the rapid and continuous rise in the price of basic daily essentials, and the increasing contraction of work opportunities because of the failure to develop state and private industry.

According to PKI's analysis, the Indonesian proletariat, "as is also the case of the proletariat in other countries," has "very fine qualities." [5] First, because it works in the most advanced economic units, the proletariat has a strong understanding of organization and discipline. Second, because it owns no means of production, the proletariat is not individualistic in nature and cannot fear the loss of its property in the revolutionary struggle. Third, because it suffers the three forms of brutal exploitation, the proletariat is more resolute and thoroughgoing in the revolutionary struggle than the other classes. Fourth, because Indonesia unlike Europe is not fertile soil for social reformism, "the proletariat in its entirety is very revolutionary indeed, of course with the exception of the small number who have become the scum." And, fifth, because the Indonesian proletariat has been led by PKI since it first appeared in the revolutionary struggle, it is politically the most conscious class in Indonesian society. Therefore the proletariat is

the basic force pushing the Indonesian revolution forward. The Indonesian revolution will not succeed unless it is under the leadership of the Indonesian proletariat. . . . Without the proletariat taking an active part, nothing will ever run properly in Indonesian society.[6]

On the other hand, the PKI leaders recognize that the Indonesian proletariat has "certain unavoidable weaknesses." [7] It is numerically weak compared with the peasants, it is young compared with the proletariat in capitalist countries, and it has a low cultural level compared with the bourgeoisie. By itself it is not strong enough to win victory. It must build "revolutionary unity in all situations with all other revolutionary classes and groups."

2. THE PEASANTRY

What PKI means when it refers to the peasants "is mainly the poor and middle peasants that make up the majority of the inhabitants of the villages." [8] As a group, the peasantry is viewed as suffering not only the remnants of feudalism, but also the depredations of bandit gangs that allegedly have received assistance from the landlords and foreign estate owners as well as arms from the imperialists.[9] Because of their suffering, the peasants as a whole "can be, for the working class, not only the most numerous ally but also the most loyal and most trusted ally." [10] In recognition of the size and revolutionary nature of the peasantry, the PKI agrarian program issued in November 1951 stated that the worker-peasant alliance was all-important for the success of the revolution.[11] The Aidit leadership's increased awareness of the role of the peasantry in the revolution was shown in Aidit's declaration in July 1953 that "The agrarian revolution is the essence of the people's democratic revolution in Indonesia." [12]

Once the Aidit leadership accepted the peasantry as a revolutionary force, it proceeded to grade separate groups within the peasantry according to their revolutionary potential. The November 1951 agrarian program included a guide for classifying the peasantry into rich peasants, medium peasants, poor peasants, and agricultural laborers.[13] But it was not until mid-1957 that Aidit gave a public explanation of the revolutionary value of the respective peasant groups.[14]

Aidit wrote that although some rich peasants lend money, exploit peasant laborers, and are by nature semifeudal, they generally participate in labor themselves and so form part of the peasantry. If a correct approach is made to them, they can take a neutral stand in the struggle against the landlords and can join the struggle against imperialism. The medium peasants are economically independent, generally neither exploit others nor earn interest on loans, and suffer from the exploitation of the imperialists, the landlords, and the bourgeoisie. Some do not own enough land for their own use and must rent land from the landlords. Therefore, they

can not only become part of the anti-imperialist revolution and the agrarian revolution, but they can also accept socialism. This is why they are one of the important forces pushing the revolution forward and are a reliable ally of the proletariat.

Aidit even stated that

their attitude to the revolution is a decisive factor for victory or defeat because the medium peasants will comprise the majority in the countryside after the agrarian revolution.

Prior to the agrarian revolution, Aidit continued, the poor peasants and the agricultural laborers would continue to form the majority in the villages. They do not own land or do not have sufficient land for their own use, and must rent land or work as laborers for the land-owners. In short

they are the village semi-proletariat, they are the largest force pushing the revolution forward and it is natural for them to be the most reliable of the allies of the proletariat and a basic part of the forces of the Indonesian revolution.

However, they can attain their emancipation, Aidit claimed, only under the leadership of the proletariat.

3. THE PETTY BOURGEOISIE

Aidit, writing in 1957, defined the petty bourgeoisie, "other than the peasantry," as "the urban poor, the intellectuals, the small traders, the handicraft workers, the fishermen, the independent workers and so on." He declared that these groups

have a status which is almost the same as that of the middle peasants. They also suffer the oppression of imperialism, feudalism and the big bourgeoisie and are every day pushed further and further towards bankruptcy and ruin. This is why they are one of the forces pushing the revolution forward and are a reliable ally of the proletariat. They can attain their freedom only under the leadership of the proletariat.[15]

Aidit also pointed out that as some sections of the petty bourgeoisie fell easily under the influence of the bourgeoisie, the Party had to devote special attention to revolutionary propaganda and organiza-tional work among them.

Aidit's description of the composition and political character of the Indonesian petty bourgeoisie is an almost direct translation of sections of the analysis of the Chinese petty bourgeoisie contained in Mao Tse-tung's *The Chinese Revolution and the Chinese Communist Party*[16]—though Aidit added fishermen and the urban poor to the definition. Earlier in the period of the Aidit leadership, for example in the April 1951 PKI general program, the petty bourgeoisie was not specifically included among the driving forces of the revolution.[17] In fact, the only group to be listed in 1951 as a revolutionary force and later included in the definition of the petty bourgeoisie was the intelligentsia. Only when the national united front policy was being implemented success-fully and when the Party leaders were tidying up their theoretical analysis of the Indonesian revolution, did the Aidit leadership define their concept of the petty bourgeoisie and list the petty bourgeoisie as the third of the three basic driving forces of the revolution.

The groups that comprise the petty bourgeoisie as defined by Aidit vary greatly in social status and in political behavior. To put the Indonesian urban poor and fishermen in the same category as the high-status and wealthy doctors and lawyers is almost ludicrous. Politically, the urban poor, the fishermen, small traders, and handicraft workers, unless they were *santri,* have provided a ready source of support for PKI and its mass organizations. On the other hand, the intellectuals and independent workers have been, in general, leaders, members, or supporters of what the Communist leaders call the national bourgeois and reactionary parties.

Why, then, has the Aidit leadership defined the petty bourgeoisie as it has, and why has the petty bourgeoisie been described as a revolutionary force? Perhaps the PKI leaders do believe that given the correct policy and tactics the Party could rally as revolutionary forces all the groups within the petty bourgeoisie as defined. Such a belief could arise from a study of the success of the Chinese Communist Party. It is also possible that the Aidit leadership used the category of petty bourgeoisie as a potpourri of groups that did not fit into the other more readily identifiable sociopolitical categories—and if this is the case, it would account for the heterogeneous nature of the petty bourgeoisie as defined.[18] The Party leaders have been aware, too, that they needed members of the petty bourgeoisie, who are generally more self-assured, better educated, and financially better off than the workers and peasants, as cadre and financial sources for the Party and its mass organizations.[19]

4. THE BOURGEOISIE

According to the usage of the Aidit leadership, the bourgeoisie is as much a political as a social category. The bourgeoisie comprises those persons of social status higher than the petty bourgeoisie (not including the doctors and lawyers), and who lead, join, or support political parties other than those of the extreme left. The bourgeoisie is subdivided into the compradore bourgeoisie and the national bourgeoisie.

The Aidit leadership labeled as compradore bourgeois those sections of the bourgeoisie which were pro-Western, or not so outspokenly anti-Western, and which were avowedly anti-Communist.[20] Although the label compradore bourgeois has been applied irrespective of whether the victims had business relations with foreign capitalist companies, Aidit has attempted to remain within the bounds of Marxist-Leninist orthodoxy by explaining that some of the compradores had capital alliances with the large foreign capitalists, while others were paid "out of special funds or other forms of bribes provided by the imperialists." [21] But despite their obvious hatred for the compradore bourgeoisie, the PKI leaders have been aware of the possibilities of exploiting the "contradictions" between the compradores serving different imperialist masters:

When . . . the Party's policy at a given time is directed against only one particular imperialism, then a part of the compradore bourgeoisie can be an additional force in the fight against that particular imperialism. But, even so, the compradore bourgeoisie remains very reactionary and still aims at crushing the Communist Party, the proletarian movement and other democratic movements.[22]

The national bourgeoisie, according to the usage of the Aidit leadership, is that section of the bourgeoisie which is outspokenly opposed to Western imperialism, and which is not implacably anti-Communist. The Aidit leadership envisages the national bourgeoisie as having a dual character: on the one hand its development is stifled by imperialism and feudalism; but on the other, because it is economically and politically weak and has class ties with imperialism and feudalism, the national bourgeoisie does not have the courage to attack in a fundamental manner the two basic targets of the revolution.[23] The vacillating character of the national bourgeoisie was explained by Aidit in his speech to the Fifth National Congress of the Party in March 1954:

The Indonesian national bourgeoisie, because it is also oppressed by foreign imperialism, can, in certain situations and within certain limits, participate in the fight against imperialism. In such certain situations, the Indonesian proletariat must build unity with the national bourgeoisie and defend that unity to the utmost. . . .

Because the Indonesian national bourgeoisie is weak in the economic and political fields, under certain historical conditions the national bourgeoisie, which is by nature vacillating, can become unreliable and betray. Therefore the proletariat and PKI must always be prepared for the possibility that in a certain situation the national bourgeoisie will not participate in the united front but, in yet another situation, it may possibly rejoin the front.[24]

The PKI leaders have shown widely varying degrees of confidence in their own ability to win the national bourgeoisie to the side of the revolution. In mid-1957 Aidit wrote that because of the weak character of the national bourgeoisie, "it is not very difficult to pull this class to the left and make it stand firmly on the side of the revolution" provided that the progressive forces were strong and the PKI tactics were correct.[25] Much of this confident tone was removed by national and international events in 1959 and 1960. In February 1960, Aidit wrote directly of the Indonesian situation that "some groups of the national bourgeoisie, jointly with the compradore bourgeoisie, want to take the road of military or personal dictatorship." [26] In 1963 the PKI leaders were still confident, at least in public, of being able to maintain an alliance with the bulk of the national bourgeoisie. However, by 1961

Aidit had already admitted that "now a part of 'our' bourgeoisie has turned to the right, sabotaging the national economic policy . . . ." [27] Since then, these "bureaucratic capitalists," the officials of state enterprises who use their positions for self-enrichment, have been placed alongside the compradore bourgeois as implacable enemies.

5. THE LANDLORD CLASS

The Aidit leadership sees the landlords as oppressing the peasant masses, as opposing their emancipation, and as possessing the land that is required for distribution to the peasant masses in order to mobilize those masses on the side of the revolution. Therefore the landlords are "a target of the revolution." [28] They are not necessarily, however, an immediate target. The PKI leaders have concluded that when, for tactical reasons, the primary target of the revolution is foreign imperialism, then it is desirable and possible to obtain the neutrality and even alliance of sections of the landlord class in the struggle against imperialism. Furthermore, even in the antifeudal struggle, Aidit has been conscious of the relative political weakness of the peasants and the need to antagonize as few groups as possible. In July 1961, for example, he stressed that "concerning the landlords, who are the target of the peasants' actions, it is necessary to take different attitudes, meaning that they must not all be considered the same." [29] That is, "patriotic landlords" who implement progressive agrarian laws are approached differently from the "deceitful landlords" or "bandit landlords" who resist such laws and consequently are "the enemies of the peasants, of the people, of the nation and of the state."

When the Aidit leadership won control of PKI in 1951, and during succeeding years, PKI possessed only insignificant support in the armed forces, the bureaucracy and the other major political parties. A coup-type seizure of power was impossible, and adventurism despite the objective situation was ruled out by the recent memory of the bloody Madiun failure that had been executed while PKI still controlled important sections of the Republican armed forces. The Aidit leadership was therefore forced to carry out a fresh and deep appraisal of Indonesian society in order to find a successful road to power. As Communists, Aidit and his colleagues assessed the political potential of the proletariat. Finding it too weak to complete the revolution alone (that is, bring the Party to power), the Communist leaders looked at the other major groups in society. A Marxist-Leninist analysis of society and the experience of foreign parties indicated that the peasantry and petty bourgeoisie could be reliable allies. But even this combination was insufficient to guarantee victory in view of the low level of organization and political consciousness of the Indonesian masses. It was thus necessary to seek and possible to forge an alliance with the national bourgeoisie which was also dissatisfied with Indonesia's semi-colonial, semifeudal status. As Aidit declared in 1957:

Based on the above analysis of the classes in Indonesian society, it is clear which classes and groups are the pillars of imperialism and feudalism, that is, the landlords and the compradores. They are obstacles standing in the way of the revolution and that is why they are the enemies of the people. The above analysis also makes clear which classes and groups are the basic driving force of the revolution, that is, the working class, the peasants and the petty bourgeoisie. It also makes clear which class can take part in the revolution, that is, the national bourgeoisie. This is why the workers, the peasants, the petty bourgeoisie and the national bourgeoisie are the people and make up the forces of the revolution, the forces of the national united front.[30]

But, to be doubly certain of victory and to avoid any repetition of the 1948 defeat, the Aidit leadership deemed it necessary and possible to extend the limits of the national united front even further to the right. Sections of the compradore bourgeoisie and landlord class should and could be won over or at least neutralized in the step-by-step struggle against imperialism and feudalism.

VII

THE NATIONAL UNITED FRONT

From the first the Aidit leadership accepted as its over-all strategy the national united front. This strategy was a legacy of Musso's 1948 analysis of the Indonesian situation as well as of foreign Communist, especially Chinese, experience. It was also confirmed by the new leaders' own analysis of Indonesian society. Thus Aidit and his colleagues believed that in order for the revolution to succeed:

The working class, the peasants, the petty bourgeoisie and the national bourgeoisie must unite in one national front.

The alliance of the working class and the peasants must be the foundation of this national united front.

The working class must lead the national united front.

Only a national united front that is formed on the basis of the worker-peasant alliance, led by the working class and formed as the result of the broadest people's movement and the revolutionary struggle of the masses, will make possible the establishment by the Indonesian people of a people's democratic government that implements the program of people's democracy and leads the people to victory.[1]

In possession of such a general formulation, the Aidit leadership was faced with the task of giving the national united front a precise form within the Indonesian context. At the end of 1961, Aidit was to speak of "Indonesianizing Marxism-Leninism." [2] By this he meant that "we must hold fast to the principles of Marxism-Leninism and creatively determine the policy, tactics, form of struggle and form of organization of our Party on the basis of the concrete situation in our country." The major creative period of the Aidit leadership was in the later part of 1951 and early 1952. The political experience of the Party in 1950 and 1951 plus the knowledge of Indonesian society were used to determine the major tactics, form of struggle, and form of organization that have guided PKI down to the present. In short, the Indonesian situation as analyzed by the young Communists molded the precise form the national united front was to take.

1. THE EXPERIENCE OF 1950

In the year between the transfer of sovereignty to Indonesia on December 20, 1949, and the assumption of complete control over PKI by the Aidit leadership in the first week of January 1951, three major political developments of importance took place: a split appeared between the two largest parties, the secular nationalist PNI and the Moslem Masjumi; some political parties showed a willingness to coöperate with PKI; and other political forces demonstrated their strong antagonism to the Communist Party.

When the federal state was dissolved and a unitary state inaugurated on August 17, 1950, discussions were held between PNI and Masjumi for the formation of a new cabinet. A dispute arose not over the cabinet's program but its composition. When Natsir, of Masjumi, finally formed a cabinet which included members from Masjumi and four minor parties, PNI was excluded from cabinet office for the first time since 1946.[3] This was the beginning of the division between PNI and Masjumi that was to increase during the succeeding years. PNI, bitter at its exclusion from office, declared that Western capitalists had exerted some influence in the formation of the cabinet,[4] and began to work with the other opposition parties, including PKI, toward the downfall of the government.

In the period of the federal republic, from December 27, 1949, to August 17, 1950, PKI had coöperated, both inside and outside parliament, with PNI and many of the lesser parties on a variety of matters. After the formation of the Natsir cabinet, PNI was much more willing to coöperate with the Communists. The first opportunity PKI had after the creation of the unitary state to demonstrate its usefulness to the non-Communist parties came on August 19 and 21, 1950, when the new parliament met to elect its speakers. Due to PKI votes, Sartono of PNI was able to defeat the Masjumi candidate for the post of first speaker, and Arudji Kartawinata of PSII was elected second deputy speaker.

The new Natsir government won a vote of confidence on October 25 by 118 votes to 73, but, by coincidence or not, the general alignment of parties in the vote has continued down to the present: Masjumi, the Sjahrir socialist party PSI, and the Protestant and Roman Catholic parties on the one hand, and PNI, PKI, and the minor Moslem parties PSII and Perti on the other. Coöperation between PNI and PKI in the formulation of motions to embarrass and harass the government continued until January 1951 when the Aidit leadership gained full control of PKI.

The third major political development of importance to PKI that had occurred by the beginning of 1951 was the display of antagonism toward PKI by Vice-President Hatta, Masjumi, and many army officers. Hatta (unlike President Sukarno)[5] and Masjumi (unlike PNI) had no inhibitions against attacking PKI and its associated organizations, and indeed led an outright attack on them. Hatta, for example, on October 25, 1950, declared PKI to be a Russian tool.[6] Natsir's cabinet demonstrated its strong hostility to PKI in a series of actions. In November 1950, for example, a ban was placed on a proposed SOBSI demonstration to mark the reburial of a Communist leader shot during the Madiun rebellion; then PKI was forbidden to hold mass meetings to celebrate the anniversary of the 1926 Communist rebellion; and on November 19, the Djakarta military command twice raided the PKI and SOBSI headquarters. Toward the end of the year, after a SOBSI-directed wave of strikes, many regional army commanders prohibited strikes in "vital" enterprises and offices—a ban which the central military authority made nationwide on February 13, 1951.

2. THE EXPERIENCE OF 1951

The Aidit leadership took over a small, disorganized party confined largely to certain towns in Java. Communists had a loose control of the higher echelons in the largest trade-union federation, SOBSI, but little organization among the peasantry or youth or women. As a result of the Madiun rebellion they had been largely purged from those positions they had gained in the armed forces and the bureaucracy. The new leaders, therefore, could hardly pursue a forceful policy—unless they were to risk what they most feared, a renewal of the "White Terror" that followed Madiun. During their first months in full control of PKI, they did little more than watch political developments in order to sense more clearly the demarcation between foe and friend or potential friend, to ascertain just what possibilities existed for increasing PKI's strength. As yet they had no new approach, continuing the *ad hoc* coöperation, whenever possible with other political forces, of their predecessors in 1950.

Toward the end of 1950 and the beginning of 1951 a division became visible between PNI and Masjumi on matters of policy. The division stemmed, basically, from their attitudes to the revolution and, from this, to the Western powers. For Masjumi and such as Hatta, the transfer of sovereignty marked the end of the revolution and the beginning of what should have been a period of construction; for PNI and other nationalists, including Sukarno, the transfer of sovereignty was merely a stage in the revolution because the revolution would be completed only when all forms of "imperialist" political, economic and cultural power in Indonesia had been eradicated.[7] For Masjumi, once sovereignty had been transferred the Dutch and the West in general were looked upon as friends or potential friends, while for PNI and Sukarno they remained imperialist opponents. From this major difference in concepts of the revolution arose major differences on questions of policy—economic policy, foreign policy, and the means of liberating West Irian. The transfer of sovereignty meant that the Indonesian government and parliament had to formulate a wider range of internal and international policies than they had during the revolutionary war. It was inevitable that the different attitudes of PNI and Masjumi to the revolution and to the Western powers would result in disagreement over many concrete issues which emerged and that, as a result, the gap between the two parties would be widened further.

PKI naturally lent its support to PNI in its dispute with Masjumi because PNI was evidently more anti-Dutch, anti-imperialist, and, unlike Masjumi, was willing to coöperate with PKI when convenient and was circumspect in references to the Madiun rebellion.

In January 1951 PKI was presented with the opportunity to lend its support to PNI on two important parliamentary motions. The first, jointly sponsored by PNI and PSII, called for the immediate entry of West Irian into Indonesia with the same status as the other regions, the immediate abolition of the Indonesian-Dutch Union, and the cancellation of the Round Table Conference agreement within three months. This motion was narrowly defeated in January 10, 1951, by 66 votes to 33. PNI initially had accepted the Round Table Conference agreement, but soon changed its mind. Even as early as January 1951 coöperation between PNI and PKI for the cancellation of the agreement was not confined to parliament, for in that month, a 40,000-person demonstration was organized by 49 parties and organizations in Surabaja to demand cancellation.[8]

On January 19, 1951, discussions began in parliament on a joint motion of PNI, PKI, PSII, and three lesser parties which led eventually to the downfall of the government. The motion called for the cancellation of a government regulation which had become law on August 14, 1950, and which permitted the government to appoint local representative councils. The motion was passed on January 22, 1951, by 76 votes to 48. PNI, PKI, PSII, the nationalist-Communist Murba, the Labor Party and a number of nonparty members boycotted the session of March 20 which was called to discuss the government's statement on the motion. A quorum could not be found. On the same day the minor nationalist party PIR withdrew its support from the government, and the cabinet thereupon resigned.

The PKI parliamentary group immediately announced that the Party would support the next cabinet if the cabinet would cancel the Round Table Conference agreement and would pursue an independent, anti-imperialist foreign policy.[9] On March 21, the PKI Central Committee proposed a "provisional national government of a coalition nature" consisting of "democratic parties, groups and peoples," that would first cancel the agreement as a major step toward creating a "truly free national, political, economic, cultural and defense system." [10] The Central Committee proposed, too, that the cabinet's program be jointly formulated by the democratic parties and groups. *Sin Po*, the pro-Communist newspaper, reported that "we have the impression that PKI is prepared to sit in the cabinet provided that the program it proposes is accepted as the cabinet's program." [11] PKI thus offered its support for a cabinet with a basic program acceptable to PNI.

On March 24, 1951, the leaders of the minor Moslem party PSII called a meeting of leaders of several political parties to seek a basis for overcoming the problems facing the nation, in particular the current cabinet crisis. PNI, after some hesitation, withdrew from the negotiations, but on March 30 a Political Parties' Consultative Council (BPP) was formed. The council included, besides PKI, the Moslem parties PSII and Perti, the Murba party, the Labor Party, and the small nationalist parties Parindra, PRN, and PRI. These eight parties signed a charter of coöperation, a joint program, and a constitution for the new council.[12]

Despite certain qualifications, the PKI leaders were jubilant at the formation of the BPP. They warned Party members that the BPP "is not yet in accordance with the concept of the national united front as we desire it," and that the other parties in the BPP were not yet prepared to accept the PKI proposal that individuals as well as organizations be admitted as members of the new organization.[13] But they also said that "we can do much, very much!" with the BPP. Lukman wrote that "the Consultative Council with its joint program is one form of the national united front at a certain stage." [14] He was certain, he wrote, that the joint actions based on the joint program would force the BPP to adapt its organization along lines desired by PKI. On May 11, 1951, Aidit declared that the creation of the intended national united front had already begun with the creation of the BPP.[15]

The optimism of the PKI leaders was soon proved to be groundless. Most members of the BPP viewed it as a short-term means of applying pressure in the current cabinet crisis. When the BPP was ignored by the cabinet formateurs,[16] the majority of its members lost interest in it. Although PKI and its mass organizations worked hard to build the BPP into a nationwide system of committees, the other members showed no further interest and within a year it had disappeared completely.

Sartono of PNI was the first formateur, but he failed to reach agreement with Masjumi not only on the composition of the cabinet but also on policy matters, primarily the question of Indonesian-Dutch relations and the implementation of the motion halting the appointment of representative councils. *Sin Po* also reported that PNI objected to Masjumi's insistence on giving the pro-Western PSI control of foreign policy.[17] On April 18, 1951, PNI and Masjumi joint formateurs were appointed, and on April 26 the new Sukiman cabinet was announced. Of the twenty cabinet members, five were PNI, five Masjumi, and the rest were either nonparty or from minor parties.

PKI at first abused the new cabinet which disappointed its hopes. On May 31 and during the first two weeks of June, Communist members of parliament roundly rejected the cabinet's composition and program.[18] They expressed disgust at PNI's participation and hinted that PNI was interested only in obtaining posts, attacked Sukarno for "undemocratic" practices in choosing the cabinet formateurs, and strongly intimated that the United States and Britain had exerted great pressure, particularly on Sukarno, to have this cabinet formed. But even during the period of greatest disappointment, the PKI leaders declared that they were not being negatively oppositionist. Aidit, for example, stated on May 23 that PKI was always ready to cease its opposition the moment the government stopped implementing the Round Table Conference agreement.[19]

By the formation of the Sukiman cabinet the Aidit leadership was posed the question: did the new cabinet mean that the national bourgeoisie, represented by PNI and Sukarno, had once more allied itself with the anti-Communists, and would it again be party to an anti-Communist drive as in 1948? The young leaders could not yet see the fundamental division within the other political forces, and overestimated the anti-Communist forces. For example, Sukarno was believed to be among the Party's enemies. Throughout 1951, and particularly in the first three quarters of that year, he was attacked for his part in choosing the cabinet formateurs, for being a false and demagogic Marxist,[20] for playing a primary role in the Madiun affair,[21] and for selling out his country in the Round Table Conference agreement. He was always identified in Party speeches and documents with first the Natsir and then the Sukiman cabinet.

Fears of a second "Madiun provocation" became intense at the beginning of July 1951. On July 3 the Politbureau protested the searches made of the homes of many prominent progressives, and also some arrests that had taken place.[22] It called to all democrats "to coöperate as closely as possible in order to defend democratic rights, to prevent Indonesia's becoming a military or police state." Then, on August 6, an armed attack was reported to have been made on a police station in Tandjung Priok, the port of Djakarta, by persons using the hammer-and-sickle as a symbol.

The PKI Central Committee Secretariat at once denied PKI participation in the attack and warned Party members to be on the alert against possible provocation.[23] On August 11 many leading PKI cadres in Medan were arrested, on the 15th arrests and searches began in Djakarta, and the arrests then spread throughout Indonesia until, according to PKI information, about 2,000 "Communists and other progressives" were imprisoned.[24] It is significant that although the government justified the arrests on the grounds that a coup was being prepared, none of the arrested was brought to trial and no evidence in support of the allegation was ever presented.

Aidit, Lukman, and Njoto evaded arrest and went into hiding. Their reaction to the arrests was very different from that taken by Musso in September 1948. In the words of a Central Committee statement of August 24, 1951, PKI had "already begun to be adult and knows how to face the imperialists' criminal provocations," and therefore could not be dragged into a second Madiun affair.[25] The leaders in hiding declared that PKI would not attempt a coup, and ordered the Party to continue above-ground activity.[26]

The blame for the "fascist coup d'etat" attempt was not fixed on the government as a whole, but only on "a small group in the government that wishes to castrate democracy." [27] The group was named as "the Sukiman-Wibisono-Suprapto clique" [28]—Sukiman and Wibisono being members of Masjumi, Suprapto of the Labor Party. No PNI cabinet ministers were implicated.

In their search for allies to demand justice for the arrested, the PKI leaders met a mixed response which provided political lessons that were a stimulus to the formulation of a new concept of the national united front. Prominent members of PNI, PSI, PSII, Perti, and the Protestant Party "with sincerity and courage stood on the side of democracy in face of the danger of fascism." [29] PNI as a party refused to vote against the government on a parliamentary motion of November 1, 1951, though it expressed dissatisfaction with the government's explanation of the arrests.[30] On the other hand, PSI, although an "agent of imperialism," was the staunchest non-Communist opponent of the arrests.

3. THE NATIONAL UNITED FRONT DEFINED

At the time of the August 1951 arrest of Communist leaders, Aidit, Lukman, and Njoto went into hiding, from which they did not emerge for several months. This period was spent in analyzing Indonesian politics and society. Many lessons and conclusions were drawn. When the leaders emerged, a national united front concept had been formulated that was to guide the Party for over a decade.

The primary lesson drawn was that present tactics were bringing PKI no nearer to governmental power. It was apparent that none of the other major political forces would allow PKI easily to reëstablish its pre-Madiun role. That is, the other political parties, Sukarno, and Hatta were not prepared to permit PKI to resume its place in the process of cabinet formation and in the cabinet itself. Some might coöperate with Communist parliamentarians in order to strengthen their own bargaining position, but when actual cabinet formation was in process, PKI was firmly ignored. It was apparent, also, that the other political forces effectively blocked PKI's efforts to create a national united front in the form proposed by Musso in the August 1948 "New Road" resolution.[31]

The "New Road" resolution had called for the creation of a national front in which PKI would play the leading role. A widely acceptable national program was first to be drawn up in order to attract "all progressive and anti-imperialist people" into the front. The front was to be formed from below, with members of all parties as well as nonparty persons eligible for membership as long as they agreed to the program. Front committees were to be established at the center and in the regions, their members to be elected democratically. Here, then, was a plan for the creation of a national front organization, linked with but separate from the political parties, and with which the PKI leaders hoped to win disguised control over the members of other parties and over nonparty persons. But the Madiun rebellion made all parties wary of too close a coöperation with PKI.

However, as Lukman was to write later, "For some time after the 'New Road' resolution, there . . . existed rather widely among we communists stiff and formal thinking about the organization of the national united front." [32] During 1950 and 1951, PKI made frequent calls for the formation of "one complete national united formation" or "a national united front," but gave no further details of what the front would involve.[33]

With the formation of the Political Parties' Consultative Council at the end of March 1951, the PKI leaders believed, briefly, that they had been presented with the possibility for creating a national united front along "New Road" lines. Their disenchantment came quickly. The failure of the council drove home forcibly to them the certainty of what they must already have felt probable: that no political party was likely to transfer part of its control over its members to another political organization which, covertly but still obviously, was controlled or strongly influenced by PKI. That is, no other political party would give PKI access to its own supporters and sympathizers.

In short, *ad hoc* coöperation with PNI and minor parties failed to produce Communist participation in the government. The "New Road" concept of a national front was impracticable. Further, the arrest of a few leading cadres could gravely disrupt the Communist organization. The question then arose, what strategy would be most likely to increase Communist strength?

The Aidit leadership concluded, first, that any strategy must be long-term. The ruling elite was impervious to Communist infiltration or trickery. Victory was a distant prospect. Certainly the enemies of the revolution, namely the imperialists, compradores, and feudal landlords, "are in a stage of disintegration and decay." [34] On the other hand, "it would be a mistake for us to underestimate the strength of these enemies." Because the enemies were and are still strong, the struggle to defeat them "is . . . bitter, difficult and protracted." "It is a mistake to believe that this struggle can be completed within a short space of time and hastily."

A second conclusion was that in order for PKI to have increased weight in Indonesian political developments, it must greatly expand its own independent basis of support—the other political parties being alert to Communist attempts to subvert their own support. A Marxist-Leninist analysis of Indonesian society indicated that there were several major sectors and groups which were actual or potential allies of the working class (that is, of the Communist Party). Fortunately, these masses were not only economically deprived, but also largely ignored by the organizations of other political parties. But because their political consciousness was so low, they could not be approached immediately by the Party. Thus Aidit declared in August 1951 that the national united front should consist of

the workers' front, the peasants' front, the cultural front, the youth front, the students' front, the women's front, the poor urban people's front, the ex-armed fighters' front, the peace front, the Irian struggle front, the parties' united front, and the national industrialists' front.[35]

On April 26, 1952, the Agitation and Propaganda Secretariat of the PKI Central Committee declared that the Communist mass organizations would organize the fronts uniting the various sectors of society.[36] In short, the PKI leaders set the Party the task of uniting the masses through the Party's own mass organizations. This was a long-term task, but the leaders had acknowledged the protracted nature of the revolution. The period of futile appeals for national coalition governments was ended. PKI would build its own mass support with which to force or bargain an entry into the national government.

In order to win the support of and leadership over the other revolutionary classes and groups, it was recognized that the proletariat

must aid the peasants' struggle for land, the intellectuals' struggle for their basic rights, the national bourgeoisie's struggle against foreign competition, and the entire Indonesian people's struggle for national independence and democratic liberties.[37]

A third conclusion was that PKI must undertake a drastic revision of its attitude toward the other political forces. The Aidit leadership recognized that it was essential to gain the toleration and coöperation of as many as possible of those political forces that were not anti-Communist. Given the relative weakness of the Party, toleration and coöperation were necessary for the successful pursuit of several goals: government toleration of the growth of the Party and its mass organizations, the destruction of the strength of imperialism and feudalism in Indonesia, the isolation and destruction of the anti-Communist Indonesian political forces, and Communist participation in a "national united government" as a step toward Communist control of a People's Democratic Republic of Indonesia. The events of 1950 and 1951 had demonstrated that broad possibilities existed for the successful implementation of this new approach to the other political forces. The "bourgeois" forces were divided, even deeply divided. On the one side, such as Masjumi, PSI, and Hatta were at considerable odds with such as PNI and Sukarno. It appeared, from a Communist viewpoint, that even the "enemy" was divided: the pro-American Masjumi versus the pro-British PSI. Further, some of the other political parties were willing, for a variety of reasons, to tolerate or coöperate with PKI. PNI sought allies in its struggle against Masjumi, which it conceived to be its chief enemy; the minor Moslem parties PSII and Perti sought allies against their Moslem rival, Masjumi; and most parties, with the notable exceptions of Masjumi and PSI, sought Communist support in their opportunist scramble for office. Some higher cadres [38] of PKI were reluctant to view parts of the bourgeoisie as allies or potential allies, regarding the entire class as an enemy of the people,[39] but the Aidit leadership persuaded the hesitant that the bourgeois political forces were rent by divisions that could be exploited by the Party.

A detailed exposition of what the national united front policy meant in terms of PKI's relations with the non-Communist political forces was given by Aidit on July 31, 1956.[40] He divided the Indonesian social-political forces into three broad categories: the diehard force, consisting of "feudalists and compradores who plot with foreign imperialism"; the progressive force, consisting of workers, peasants, urban petty bourgeoisie, and revolutionary intellectuals, and by which he clearly meant those people who could be brought into or influenced by PKI or its mass organizations; and the middle force, consisting of "the national bourgeoisie and all other patriotic and anticolonial forces including the left (rather progressive) landlord group." Aidit said that PKI's political line must be "with all its might and tirelessly to build up the progressive force, to unite with the middle force and to isolate the diehard force."

Aidit went on to say:

It is a fact that in the parties that represent the diehard force and the middle force there exist several groups which can basically be divided into left, center and right groups. In order to be able to unite the greatest strength, the Communists must analyze these groups so that we can always establish a correct attitude in order to be able to unite all that can be united, and in order to isolate the truly diehard.

Even within the diehard parties, he continued, some leaders and members were anti-Communist but not pro-imperialist, not yet aware that to be anti-Communist assisted the imperialists, while others were anti-imperialist and not averse to coöperation with the Communists. "The communists must unite with such people." This readiness to seek coöperation with as many as possible of the political forces, even the most reactionary, in the pursuit of certain common goals, is a major characteristic of the Aidit leadership's concept of the national united front as applied to the non-Communist political forces. It stems from the leadership's analysis of the relative weakness of the progressive force in face of the other internal and external forces, and the resultant need to build the broadest possible unity in order to advance step by step against the enemies of the revolution.

Aidit has been aware that in order to win the vital tolerance and coöperation of other political forces the Communists had to create and maintain a new public image of themselves. One of the more important characteristics that have been cultivated is apparent self-abnegation: [41]

The basic principles we must adhere to in the conduct of the national struggle is to subordinate the class struggle to the national struggle. . . . Only by subordinating the class and Party interest to the national interest, which is the interest of the whole revolutionary people, and by defending the class and Party interest in a limit-conscious manner, can our coöperation with the other classes and groups be profitable and can coöperation be achieved.[42]

In other words,

class political and economic demands must be based on the condition that they will not harm the coöperation between the classes which, according to their common interest, must coöperate; and . . . all demands in the class struggle must be based on the needs of the national struggle.[43]

The last major conclusion drawn by the PKI leaders during their period in hiding after August 1951 concerned the nature and role of the Party. PKI must be made a mass party and a disciplined, indoctrinated party. Such a party was necessary in order to organize, control, and indoctrinate mass organizations; in order to afford its leaders sufficient strength to warrant other forces seeking alliance with them; in order to deter or counter a rightist attack against the leaders; in order to prevent the establishment of a bourgeois dictatorship once imperialism and feudalism had been shattered. In other words, the Aidit leadership concluded that only by the creation of a mass party would they be able to shape political developments in Indonesia. The first step on the road to a mass party was taken in March 1952. In that month a campaign was launched to increase Party membership within six months from 7,910 to 100,000.[44]

Thus, in the later months of 1951 and the early part of 1952, the Aidit leadership defined its own concept of the national united front in conformity with foreign Communist experience, past PKI experience, and its own analysis of the social and political forces present in the Indonesian revolution. Aidit made this concept clear in a speech on July 31, 1956.[45] He said that the revolution would be successful "only if there is a united front, if the proletariat has many friends," and went on to add that "there are two kinds of front and two kinds of friend."

There is the united front between the proletariat, the peasants, and the petty bourgeoisie; and the unity or friendship between the proletariat and the people who exploit it, that is, between the proletariat and the employers and government people who represent the interests of the national bourgeoisie. In other words, the Aidit leadership came to conceive of the national united front as entailing unity in two separate spheres and of two distinct qualities: the unity of the masses directly led and controlled by the Party and its mass organizations, a disciplined unity embracing the truly revolutionary classes; and the unity, in the form of friendship and coöperation, between PKI and the non-Communist political forces, a unity that PKI must work painstakingly to create and maintain.

The national united front policy envisaged and even now envisages no rapid victory, but many years of hard and patient work to alter the balance of forces in Indonesia. In the implementation of this policy, PKI has faced three main and inseparable tasks: (1) to build PKI into a disciplined, mass party; (2) to attract, mobilize, organize, and lead the three most revolutionary classes—and to do the same for any other elements in society which might prove susceptible; and (3) to gain the tolerance and coöperation of as many as possible of those political forces that are not anti-Communist.

Part three

BUILDING THE PARTY

VIII

THE PARTY LEADERSHIP

On January 7, 1951, the new leadership of PKI was announced. The Politbureau consisted of Aidit, Lukman, Njoto, Sudisman, and Alimin, with Aidit as first secretary. Among the fourteen members of the Central Committee were three who were discontented with the new leaders, the new policies and the relatively lowly status to which they had been relegated: Tan Ling Djie, Alimin, and Wikana. As soon as the Aidit leadership had established firm control over the lower organizations of the Party and was assured of the loyalty of most members of the Central Committee, it moved to expel the three recalcitrants from the Central Committee.

The first move was made against Tan Ling Djie. In August 1952 the Central Committee established a control commission to investigate those of his activities which were held to conflict with Party policy.[1] Although he dutifully performed self-criticism and admitted many errors, the Central Committee termed his self-criticism as not completely sincere. The Central Committee plenum which met from October 6-8, 1953, drew up a resolution which accused him of maintaining his "errors of subjectivism, legalism and liquidationism" and of insincerity in performing the tasks set by the control commission.[2] A campaign against "Tan Ling Djie-ism" was launched as a means of purifying the Party ideologically, and Tan himself was removed from the Central Committee. He was not expelled from the Party, but was given the opportunity "to purge himself of non-Communist ideology, to correct his errors, to proletarianize his ideology, and to develop himself as broadly as possible in order to become a good Party member" by performing tasks to be set by the Politbureau and by greater study of the theories of Marxism-Leninism in relation to the practice of the Indonesian revolution.

In June 1953, at a time when discussions were being held concerning the formation of a new cabinet, there were reports of disagreement between Alimin and the Aidit leadership over what course of action PKI should take. On June 25 Alimin was made to issue a statement that no such disagreement existed, and that he agreed fully with Aidit's views.[3] Despite this, the October 1953 Central Committee plenum removed him from the Politbureau "in view of his activities and health,"[4] though for the time being he retained his position on the committee. He was replaced by Sakirman, who was already chairman of the PKI parliamentary group and a loyal supporter of the Aidit leadership. Sakirman[5] was a useful addition to the PKI leadership as one who was able to cement personal contacts vital to the creation of a national united front between the Party and the non-Communist political leaders. He had a higher level of education than the other PKI leaders, having graduated before the war from the Bandung technical high school. And he had a long record of coöperation with the non-Communist nationalists. In 1941 he had joined Gerindo (Movement of the Indonesian People), which included a few Communists and many nationalists, and within which he became a member of the West Java commissariat, thereby gaining the acquaintance of many nationalist leaders. During the revolution he had become first the chairman of the People's Army stationed in Magelang, and later a major-general in the Indonesian national army, serving in the headquarters. In January 1950 he became a member of parliament. Furthermore, he was the brother-in-law of Sartono, a prominent PNI leader and speaker of parliament from 1950 to 1959.

At the Central Committee plenum of October 1953 Aidit was elected secretary-general of the Central Committee Secretariat, with Lukman and Njoto as his deputies. Sudisman, who had shared the leadership of the Secretariat since June 1950, lost this position but remained on the five-member Politbureau.

By the time of the PKI Fifth National Congress, which ended on March 21, 1954, the number of full members of the Party, that is members with voting rights, had reached 49,042 [6]—a tenfold increase since January 1951. This large increase in itself consolidated the Aidit leadership's control over the Party because the new members had been attracted into PKI by Aidit's policies and programs, they were receiving political education from cadres loyal to the Aidit leadership, and they had no ties of loyalty to the "old" leaders. The Aidit leadership was already assured of the support of the central and local Party cadres, and from this position of strength made the Fifth Congress the occasion for removing the last of the disgruntled "old" leaders from the central leadership. Although Alimin sat on the five-man congress presidium,[7] he failed to receive enough votes to be reëlected onto the Central Committee.[8] It was not announced whether Wikana stood for reëlection, but he too lost his place on the Central Committee. Alimin and Wikana were replaced by Nursuhud and Karel Supit,[9] who had proved themselves able and disciplined Party workers under the Aidit leadership. The membership of the Central Committee remained at 13.

As the claimed membership of the Party increased from about 4,000 or 5,000 in January 1951 to 165,206 in March 1954, and one million by the end of 1955, the work to be done by the Party's central leadership increased considerably, and it became necessary to widen its membership. It appears that the Aidit leadership was at first reluctant to incorporate new members in the central leadership, perhaps through fear of unwittingly importing potential opposition into what had proved to be a reliable Central Committee. But as time passed, the Aidit leadership was able to judge which of the lower Party workers were most able and most loyal. In the March 1954 congress, three young Communists were elected as candidate members of the Central Committee: A. Anwar, Anwar Kadir, and Siswojo, born in 1926, 1916, and 1925 respectively. The Central Committee plenum which met on August 7, 1955, endorsed the election of three more candidate members: Tjugito, S. Utarjo, and Ruslan Kamaludin,[10] born in 1921, 1923, and 1919 respectively. The Central Committee plenum which met from July 31 to August 3, 1956, elected Siswojo to full membership of the committee,[11] to replace Bachtarudin who had died in June. At the same time the Central Committee Secretariat was enlarged to include Sudisman, Jusuf Adjitorop, and Siswojo.

These slight increases in the membership of the central leadership were soon found inadequate to meet the increased work entailed by a further increase in Party membership to one and a half millions at the beginning of 1959, and by the greatly increased Party work in parliament, the Constituent Assembly, and the local councils.[12] The expansion and reorganization of the central leadership organs were undertaken by the Central Committee plenum which ended on April 3, 1958.[13]

The Politbureau was enlarged by the promotion of Adjitorop to candidate membership, and a Politbureau daily council, consisting of Aidit, Lukman, Njoto, and Sudisman, was established to provide leadership to the Party between Politbureau meetings. All five candidate members of the Central Committee were elevated to full membership, thus increasing the size of the committee from 13 to 18 members. Ten of the members had continued to sit in the committee since January 1951. The Central Committee Secretariat was reorganized, and given the task of performing the committee's routine daily work. Its seven members consisted of Sudisman and Adjitorop from the Politbureau, plus five other Central Committee members of whom only one had sat in the committee since January 1951. The inclusion of so many post-1951 Central Committee members in the Secretariat demonstrated the Aidit leadership's confidence in the loyalty of the new members.

The PKI Sixth National Congress, held from September 7-14, 1959, resulted not only in the confirmation of the control of the Aidit leadership, but also in the further enlargement of the Party central organs, and the readmission of the previously ousted "old" leaders, presumably purified, to positions within the central leadership.[14] Aidit was chairman of the commission which drew up the lists of candidates for all central leadership organs, and the lists were adopted unanimously and unchanged by the congress. It is certain, therefore, that the enlargement of the central organs and the return of "old" leaders were in no way a threat to Aidit's leadership.

Aidit was elected to the new post of Central Committee chairman, with Lukman and Njoto as his deputies. The Politbureau was unchanged except for the addition of Njono, the chairman of SOBSI, as a candidate member. The Central Committee was enlarged to 35 full members and 11 candidate members. The Central Committee Secretariat, with Sudisman at its head, was further enlarged to a total of eight members by the addition of Karel Supit.

The rehabilitation of the "old" Party leaders had begun some time before the Sixth Congress. Alimin, Wikana, and Tan Ling Djie had been elected as PKI representatives to the Constituent Assembly in the December 1955 general elections, and in December 1956 Tan Ling Djie and Wikana were elected as second deputy chairman and secretary respectively of the Party group in the assembly.[15] Ngadiman Hardjosubroto was reported, in 1959, to be chairman of the PKI Central Election Committee entrusted with the task of preparing the Party's campaign in the forthcoming general elections. In the Sixth Congress, Wikana returned to the Central Committee as a full member, Tan Ling Djie and Ngadiman were elected to membership of the Central Verification Commission, and Alimin was honored by a place on the congress presidium. Aidit was sufficiently sure of his own control of the Party to reëmploy the undoubted talents of Wikana, Tan Ling Djie, and Ngadiman in useful, but, in terms of power, unimportant, positions.

The latest enlargement of the central leadership took place in February 1963.[16] It may have been necessitated by a number of factors: the large amount of time spent by the highest Party cadres in the efflorescing advisory councils instituted after July 1959 by President Sukarno within the framework of Guided Democracy; a desire to grant promotion to loyal lower cadres; and the constantly increasing work of controlling and supervising the ever-expanding Party, its mass organizations, and their new educational institutions. The membership of both the Politbureau and the Central Committee Secretariat was increased. Adjitorop and Njono became full members of the Politbureau, while Rewang and Anwar Sanusi became candidate members. The total was now seven full members and two candidates. Two more members were added to the Central Committee Secretariat, making ten in all. The Central Committee, which may be enlarged only by a party congress, remained at 35 full members and 11 candidate members.

A notable feature of the central leadership of the PKI since January 1951 has been the continuity of the membership of the inner core. Of the 14 Central Committee members in January 1951, 11 are still members. Only Bachtarudin, who has died, Alimin, who is too senile for such a position, and Tan Ling Djie are no longer in the committee. And of the five full members of the Politbureau elected in September 1959, four were members in January 1951. The control over the Party of these four—Aidit, Lukman, Njoto, and Sudisman—is complete. Not only do they control the Politbureau and its daily council, and the Central Committee and its Secretariat, but they also have exercised personal supervision over Party work in parliament, the Constituent Assembly, and other legislative, advisory, and organizational bodies created by President Sukarno since July 1959, such as the Provisional People's Consultative Council, the National Advisory Council, and the National Front. Furthermore, they have maintained a close personal supervision over Party publications. When PKI began to publish its own newspaper, *Harian Rakjat* (People's Daily), in July 1951, Njoto was given the task of supervising its contents, a task he still performs.

With the publication of the newspaper, the importance of the periodical *Bintang Merah* was reduced, and its editorship was transferred in August 1951 to the veteran, Djaetun, and later to Supeno, a member of the *Harian Rakjat* editorial staff. In January 1957, however, the editorship was returned to Sudisman and Pardede who continued in that function until the periodical was suspended by the government in October 1960.

IX

THE EXPANSION AND EDUCATION
OF PARTY MEMBERSHIP

1. 1951

The Aidit leadership took over a party that was small and ill-organized, and most of whose members were lacking even the rudiments of Marxist-Leninist knowledge. The two primary tasks of the new leaders were to put the Party organization into order, and to begin the work of political education.

In January 1951 the Party organization was still chaotic as a result of the Madiun rebellion, the second Dutch attack on the Republic, and the failure of the post-Madiun leaders to give clear and energetic direction. Total Party membership was about 4,000 or 5,000.[1] The task of reëstablishing the Party organization was begun in earnest after the return of Aidit and Lukman to the Party leadership in July 1950. In September 1950, the newspaper *Sin Po* reported that PKI branches were already active throughout Sumatra (where the Party had stayed aloof from the Madiun rebellion and so continued its public activities unimpaired) and in Java in Djakarta, Banten, Sukabumi, Jogjakarta, Surakarta, north Kedu, Blitar, and Banjumas.[2] It was expected that branches would soon be revived in Semarang, Bandung, Besuki, Pekalongan, and Tjirebon in Java as well as in Menado, Makasar, Banjarmasin, and Timor in the outer islands. During October 1950, the Party was revived in Surabaja, Bodjonegoro, Madiun, and Malang.[3]

The revival of former PKI branches and the establishment of new ones continued after the Aidit leadership won full control of the Party in the first week of January 1951. In each locality where reorganization was effected elections were held and leaders chosen who were in agreement with the new central leadership. The Party in Sumatra, however, required special treatment, probably because the pre-Madiun leaders had remained unchanged. On February 1, 1951, the Central Committee sent Pardede and Hutapea to reorganize the Party there. By March it was already reported that undesirable elements had been excluded from the Sumatran leadership, and Central Committee commissariats, led by trusted pro-Aidit members of the Central Committee, were established in North, Central, and South Sumatra.[4]

By May 1951, Aidit declared that the Party organization was being built not only in Java and Sumatra as in the past, but also in Kalimantan, Sulawesi, and Nusatenggara.[5] He also claimed that the number of Party members and candidate members was already far more than in 1948, and that the basic Party organizations in places of work and residence, as well as Party fractions within mass organizations, had already begun to function. The work of expanding the Party organization suffered a temporary reversal when, in August 1951, the government arrested some 2,000 Communists and "other progressives" on an unsubstantiated charge of plotting a *coup d'état*.[6] Many of the leaders who evaded arrest, including Aidit, went into hiding from which they did not emerge until the formation of a new government in April 1952.

Thus, a year after the Aidit leadership had won control of the Party and despite the August 1951 arrests, the Party organization was functioning not only throughout the major centers of Java and Sumatra but also in the other islands. Furthermore, the leadership of the Party had become more homogeneous than ever before. The Aidit leadership had exercised its power under the January 1947 and April 1951 Party constitutions to nominate the commissars who headed the organizations at the regional level, and had insured that the leaders in the newly organized or revived branches were persons amenable to the central leadership. At the beginning of 1952 there were 7,910 full and candidate members of PKI.

At the same time as reviving and expanding the Party organization, the Aidit leadership began the ideological and organizational education of the cadres and members. This task was of continuingly vital importance given the Indonesian situation. Mass following might be relatively easy to achieve if the Party and its mass organizations espoused the demands and desires of large sectors of the population. But how could this following be molded into a disciplined force that correctly implemented the directives of the leadership? The only answer available was education: education to instill in the members of the Party and its mass organizations a united concept of the Indonesian revolution and of the strategy and tactics that must be used to bring "the people" to victory; a united concept of the nature and role of the Communist Party. From the moment of winning control of PKI, the Aidit leadership perseveringly undertook the education of their supporters. Their success is at least part of the explanation of over twelve years free from overt factionalism, purges, or defections in a Communist Party that was to become in this period the largest outside the Sino-Soviet bloc.

Aidit, in an article written at the beginning of March 1951, warned that the Party suffered from ideological deficiencies and that during the struggle for victory, PKI could be affected by the dangers of "left" and right opportunism, that is adventurism and capitulationism.[7] At the same time he warned against sectarianism, which entailed ignoring the importance of attracting the broad mass of the workers and the importance of the national united front. The Party's general program, included in the April 1951 constitution, introduced the Party members to other dangerous deviations that could isolate PKI from the people and had to be fought and avoided, "tailism, commandism, closed door policy, isolation policy, paternalism, individualism, liberalism, bureaucracy, intrigue, nepotism and militarism."[8] An article by Aidit in May 1951 pinpointed two other diseases present in the Party which led sometimes to "left" and sometimes to right deviation.[9] They were dogmatism, which did not accept that "Marxism is not a dogma but a guide for action"; and empiricism, whose adherents held firmly to their own restricted experiences, and who did not understand or wish to understand the importance of theory for revolutionary practice. In order to remedy or avoid such ideological deviations, the new central leadership emphasized the need to study not only the concrete situation in Indonesia, but also the more important and relevant Marxist-Leninist literature. At the beginning of 1951 this literature was virtually unobtainable in Indonesia.

In order to provide study materials, the Central Committee announced on March 1, 1951, that it had formed a commission to translate Communist works into Indonesian.[10] The first books listed for translation were: Stalin's *The Foundations of Leninism,* Leontiev's *Political Economy, The History of the CPSU(B),* and Liu Shao-chi's *On the Party.* They were to be followed by Lenin's *Imperialism, the Highest Stage of Capitalism, State and Revolution,* and *Left-wing Commu-*

nism, an Infantile Disorder, Mao Tse-tung's *On New Democracy,* Stalin's *Marxism and the National and Colonial Questions,* Engels' *Utopian and Scientific Socialism,* and Rutger's *Indonesia.* And so began the systematic translation into Indonesian of selected Communist classics, basic tools with which the PKI leaders hoped to create a Party united behind themselves.

Brochures and pamphlets were not the only means used to make known international Communist writings. For example, the periodical *Bintang Merah* contained Mao Tse-tung's *Strategic Problems of China's Revolutionary War* in serialized form during the later part of 1950 and the first part of 1951, and during 1951 the translated works included Stalin's *Theory* and *The Foundation of Leninism,* Mao Tse-tung's *On Eradicating Liberalism in the Party,* and Hong Ha's *The Victory of the Vietnamese People and its Army.* From July 1, 1951, the PKI published its own daily newspaper, *Harian Rakjat,* which began with only 2,000 copies, but which played and plays an important role in disseminating Party instructions and in providing materials for the organizational and political education of its readers. As soon as *Harian Rakjat* was published, *Bintang Merah* became a monthly instead of a semimonthly, and was then temporarily forced by financial problems to cease publication from the end of 1951 to August 1952.[11] When *Bintang Merah* temporarily closed down, the Agitation and Propaganda Secretariat of the Central Committee began to publish a mimeographed periodical *PKI-Buletin* which appeared on average about once every three weeks. The new periodical contained Party statements and news, articles by Party leaders on a wide range of ideological, political, and organizational matters, and an increasing number of translations from the Cominform journal *For a Lasting Peace, For a People's Democracy!* In Surabaja, from about the end of 1950, a large "weekly of people's democracy," *Zaman Baru* (New Age) was published under PKI control. By the end of 1952, when its editor, Naibaho, was appointed chief editor of *Harian Rakjat, Zaman Baru* appeared irregularly. Miscellaneous Party publications during 1951 included the April 1951 Party constitution, and a short history of PKI.[12] One of the PKI-led peasant organizations published a translation of Stalin's *The Peasant Question.*[13]

According to Aidit, the government's mass arrest of Communists in August 1951 resulted in a fresh burst of study of those of Lenin's works which in a popular way expounded Marxist strategy and tactics.[14] The Party leaders in hiding turned to Lenin's works in order to seek a way out of the difficult situation PKI was in. As a result, extra effort was made to translate Lenin's works, adding to those begun in March 1951 such as *What is to be Done, From Where to Begin, To the Village Poor, Thesis,* and *Marxism and Revisionism.*

Little information has been published as to the work of formal cadre training in 1951. On April 16, 1951, the Djakarta Raja section of the Party opened a course for Party functionaries at which Aidit, Lukman, Njoto, and Sudisman gave instruction on the fundamentals of Leninism, the history of the Communist Party of the Soviet Union, utopian and scientific socialism, and Party organization.[15] A leading Party cadre told me in 1960 that he had attended a Central Committee cadre school in Djakarta in 1951, but this might have been the one officially organized by the Djakarta section. A report in *Harian Rakjat* mentioned in April 1952 that courses had been organized in Subang and Krawang, on the initiative of the Communist-led mass organizations, in order to give cadres the minimum knowledge required in building the national united front.[16] But although this report added that it was hoped to extend these courses into other areas, it did not say how long the original courses had been in operation. Within the Party itself, from the time of the August 1951 arrests, periodic discussions concerning theory and concerning practical work were begun in the Party committees, fractions in mass organizations and representative councils, and in lower levels of the organization.[17]

2. THE FIRST MEMBERSHIP DRIVE

During 1951 the Aidit leadership had reorganized the Party, purged the national and regional leadership of elements considered hostile to itself, and had begun the work of ideological and cadre training. The Party was strong enough to bring in new members on a large scale, and to begin the primary task of the national united front policy, that is, to build the Party into a mass, nationwide machine. Only a great increase in PKI membership would enable PKI to find large numbers of capable cadres, to successfully build and control mass organizations among the different sections of society, to mobilize millions of voters in the coming elections, to seek entry into the civil service and armed forces which contained only insignificant numbers of Party members, and so to mobilize and control a broad national united front which, it was hoped, would eventually control political life in Indonesia. It is possible, too, that the August 1951 arrests spurred the Aidit leadership to expand the Party, for the arrests showed that the removal of only a relative handful of leaders could virtually paralyze the small Party, and they also showed that PKI control over its mass organizations was still extremely tenuous.[18]

A PKI national conference, which met early in March 1952, made two important decisions.[19] First, it decided to promote the study of theory within the Party, as a means of combating sectarianism, capitulationism, and adventurism which had appeared among the Party ranks at the time of the August arrests. Second, it endorsed the plan to expand membership to 100,000 within six months. On March 7 the Central Committee published a resolution calling for a membership drive which would result in the Party becoming a mass party,[20] an objective that had not been envisaged since 1926 at least.

It would have been surprising had there not been some opposition within the Party to the new policy, and the resolution in fact incorporated a series of arguments designed to counter objections to the creation of a mass party. To those members who said that the Party needed quality, not quantity, the Central Committee explained that "quantity is necessary in order to achieve quality. From a large quantity it is far more possible to achieve higher quality. Therefore we need quantity as well as quality." To emphasize this point the Central Committee stressed that "Party cadres cannot appear all of a sudden. People cannot enter the Party as good cadres" but must enter as ordinary members, the best among them being selected and trained as new cadres. The resolution also explained that only by increasing the number of members could the Party broaden and strengthen its relations with the masses, and that only with the organized strength of the broad masses could the Party achieve its goals. In order to remove the fear that the membership drive might lead to the recruitment of undesirable elements or to the lowering of the quality of members, the resolution explained that organizational methods would prevent this. That is, the implementation of the stringent provisions embodied in the April 1951 constitution governing the entry of new members and the elevation of candidate members to full membership, and the practice of criticism and self-criticism would prevent such an occurrence. Finally, the resolution stated that in order to maintain the political and theoretical level of the Party, the membership drive had to be accompanied by the implementation of the other Central Committee resolution concerning the education of Party members and cadres.

The success of the membership drive was immediate. Toward the end of May 1952 PKI already claimed 100,000 members.[21] This was followed by a period of consolidation in which the membership rose more slowly to 126,671 at the end of 1952 and 165,206 in March 1954.[22] In May 1953, the Central Committee gave its comments on the drive.[23] By the end of 1952 the Party had 8,467 committees, fractions,[24] and groups. But not all was satisfactory. Only 1.5 per cent of members and candidate members were women, and the Party leaders in Banten, Tapanuli (North Sumatra), and Kalimantan still did not consider that women were "mature" enough to enter the Party. Some Party committees even had shown indifference to the whole membership campaign. For example, after the delegates from Kedu returned home from the March 1952 national conference, "the instructions and plan were discussed a little in the daily committee, and then . . . deposited in the refrigerator" and forgotten for a year.

In terms of social targets, the campaign appears to have been aimed primarily at the towns in general and SOBSI activists in particular. PKI, since 1926, had had very little experience of work in the rural areas, and it was natural that the drive was aimed at the towns, with which the cadres were familiar and where the possibilities of rapid success were greatest.[25] Reportedly one of the main objectives of the drive was to consolidate control over SOBSI by bringing a greater number of lower-level activists under Party direction.[26] That is, to ensure that if the government tried to curb SOBSI's activities, as it had in August 1951, it would have to arrest not merely a few national leaders, but would have to ferret out and arrest thousands of Communists. As for the geographical spread of the Party, Aidit claimed that the first membership drive had extended PKI to Madura, Sulawesi, Kalimantan, Maluku (Moluccas), and Nusatenggara,[27] although the great majority of members remained in Java and, secondarily, Sumatra. The geographical spread of the Party was illustrated by the establishment in October 1953 of a Party subsection in Lombok, Nusatenggara.[28]

As the March 7 Central Committee resolution on the expansion of membership had emphasized, the campaign was to be accompanied by the implementation of a Central Committee resolution on the education of Party cadres and members. The latter resolution was not published, but Lukman, in September 1952, did write his comments on the work done to implement it.[29] He stated that the Party had only recently begun to effect the education of Party cadres and members in a wide and more organized manner; but, as according to the resolution, all Party organizations in the regions were obliged to organize courses for all Party members, arrange periodic discussions of theory, organize self-study, arrange lectures, organize public meetings and other efforts to propagandize Party policy, and arrange for regional publications by either the Party or other progressive groups. By such efforts it was hoped gradually to raise the theoretical and political level of all members, as well as gradually to increase the public's understanding of Party policy. Such efforts, which Lukman recognized would be at first accompanied by all kinds of deficiencies, were expected in the long run to give birth to "a number of course leaders, discussion leaders, lecturers, speakers in public meetings, writers for regional publications, etc., from the most progressive Party members. This means the creation of a Party propagandist and agitator group."

In order to improve the work of cadres, Lukman also recommended regular meetings of the propagandists and agitators to discuss experiences gained in carrying on their work, and pointed to the need for especially the cadres to master both Indonesian and the local language of the area in which they worked. Indonesian was necessary for writing letters and reports, giving news to the press, and writing articles and translations; mastery of the local language would enable the cadres to work far more efficiently among the masses, whose knowledge of Indonesian was often slight.

Little evidence remains as to the materials studied within the Party during 1952, although Aidit did mention that they included Mao Tse-tung's *On the Practice and Extermination of Liberalism in the Party* and Liu Shao-chi's *On the Mass Line*.[30] In March 1953, Sudisman reported that education courses had begun in an organized manner at all levels of the Party organization and that the section and subsection committees were giving lectures at least once a month on the history and policy of PKI, the task of building the workers' united front, the PKI agrarian program, the policy of peace, people's democracy, the cultural struggle, the national united front, and the question of the national industrialists.[31] He also stated that within a period of six months all Party members had to study and understand seventeen specified Communist works, including six written by Indonesians, five by Chinese, three by Russians, two by unidentified authors, and the Communist Manifesto.[32]

That not all went well with the plan for education within the Party was shown by a Central Committee statement in May 1953.[33] The Central Committee pointed out, for example, that the plan for Djakarta Raja was only 15 per cent achieved because of absenteeism among both members and cadres, and that higher cadres had made only "fragmentary" study of theory, while the staff of the Central Committee commissariats and the members of the section committee daily councils "often 'forget' to study theory and to hold discussions concerning theory." Lukman, in his article of September 1952, had predicted that many shortcomings would appear when the Party launched its first large-scale education campaign, but he had also stated that despite inevitable shortcomings a body of teachers and cadres would be formed which could, with the practice of criticism and self-criticism, teach others, expand their own knowledge, and thus gradually raise the quality of Party education.

In the sphere of publications, great though uneven strides were made between the opening of the membership drive and the Fifth National Congress in March 1954.

Harian Rakjat slowly increased its circulation from 2,000 in July 1951 to 12,500 in October 1953 and to 15,000 in February 1954.[34] *Bintang Merah* did not fare so well. It was republished in August 1952 and continued as a monthly until October 1960.[35] From a peak of over 10,000 copies in the first half of 1951, when it was the only official Party periodical, it had declined to only 7,500 or 8,000 copies in May 1953.[36] During 1952 and 1953 *Bintang Merah* contained Central Committee comments on national and international affairs, articles on theory and practical work, and translations of works by foreign Communists. In order to increase its circulation, and thereby its educational importance, the Central Committee Agitation and Propaganda Secretariat early in 1953 ordered all Party functionaries to read *Bintang Merah* from cover to cover and to send in their criticisms every month.[37]

PKI-Buletin was published regularly, but in October 1952 its form was changed. For the first time it was printed, instead of mimeographed, and so became available in sufficient numbers for all lower Party committees to receive it. The translated editorial of *For a Lasting Peace, For a People's Democracy!* became a regular feature added to its usual contents of official Party statements, occasional articles by Party leaders, and comments on methods of work within the Party. When the form was changed, the editors stated that the lower Party committees would still have to translate *PKI-Buletin* into the regional languages.[38]

During 1952 few translations were yet available of works by foreign Communists, but in 1953 translation and publication was greatly increased. By the end of 1953 at least forty, mostly booklet-size, works were available. Lenin, Stalin, Dimitrov, Kalinin, Mao Tse-tung, and Liu Shao-chi were among those whose works were translated, and from the available evidence [39] it would appear that Mao Tse-tung and Lenin, in that order, were most frequently translated at that time. A report by an American observer suggests, however, that the large number of translated Chinese works was due not to the efforts of PKI but to the Chinese government which was shipping in large quantities of pamphlets and booklets translated into Indonesian.[40]

A Central Committee note of January 18, 1953, expressed continued dissatisfaction with the circulation of Party publications and with the collection of funds for them.[41] The note complained that many Party committees were not doing a good job of circulating Party and other progressive publications, and as a remedy ordered all committees to appoint a Party member to be an agent for the publications. These agents were to supplement, not replace, the work of existing non-Party agents. The note also listed 30 Party committees which owed money to *Bintang Merah* and 36 with debts to *PKI-Buletin*, and called upon them to pay their debts.

The preparations for the Fifth National Congress were converted into a massive campaign not only for the propaganda of Party policies and programs among the general public, but also for educating Party members and candidate members. The congress materials, including the new constitution and program, were drafted in the Central Committee plenum of early October 1953, and were then widely circulated and publicized. 150,000 copies of the draft program were published, in Sundanese, Batak, and Madurese as well as in Indonesian.[42] About 1,500 public meetings, attended by over 2 millions, were held to explain the draft program to people outside the Party. Within the Party, in the four months prior to the congress, meetings were organized at all levels and conferences held between equal levels of the Party organization to discuss the draft constitution, program, and the Central Committee general report.[43]

3. THE SECOND MEMBERSHIP DRIVE

The PKI Fifth National Congress which met in March 1954, made two decisions of importance to the education and expansion of Party membership: it endorsed the campaign against "Tan Ling Djie-ism," and it endorsed the plan for a second membership drive.

Although Tan Ling Djie was removed from his position on the Central Committee in October 1953, the campaign against the error of Tan Ling Djie-ism was developed on a large scale only in the period around the Fifth National Congress. The congress endorsed both the Central Committee resolution of October 1953 which condemned Tan Ling Djie's activities,[44] and the more important "Report on Tan Ling Djie-ism." [45] The campaign against Tan Ling Djie-ism was not used to expel Tan Ling Djie, for he was allowed to remain within the Party because he accepted the Central Committee's decisions and promised to correct all his errors.[46] Nor was it used to purge his followers because, in the words of the "Report," he had received only the passive help of several centrists who later abandoned him when he was defeated in January 1951. No announcements were ever made of anyone else being accused of Tan Ling Djie-ism. It is probable that the campaign, which was carried out intensively throughout the Party, had an educational purpose, that is, to increase the cadres' and members' knowledge and understanding of the basic organizational, ideological, and political content of the Aidit leadership's national united front policy. In other words the campaign was a useful framework within which to undertake the political education of old and new members.

The "Report on Tan Ling Djie-ism" analyzed the error in detail. In the field of organization, Tan Ling Djie-ism was condemned as basically liquidationist. It advocated the creation of a working-class party other than PKI. This was "tailism" because the working class already had sufficient political consciousness to support an openly Communist party. In the sphere of policy, Tan Ling Djie-ism was described as "legalistic," as "nothing other than bourgeois liberalism," because it wished to tone down the Party program, to divert the members too much from the class struggle, to place excessive emphasis on the parliamentary struggle. This error in policy, declared the "Report," had its roots in a grave underestimation of the strength of the masses and a gross exaggeration of the strength of the reactionaries. But it was in the realm of ideology that Tan Ling Djie-ism received most bitter condemnation.

"Tan Ling Djie-ism in the ideological field has its source in subjectivism," which resulted in dogmatism and empiricism. It was dogmatist because it attempted to imitate uncritically overseas experience without taking into consideration the conditions in Indonesia. It was empiricist because it considered unimportant the work of raising the theoretical knowledge of Party members.

As the result of the two subjectivist ideologies, dogmatism and empiricism, our Party was tossed about between two diseases. Subjectivism caused our Party to be unable to take a correct attitude, that is, an objective, truly scientific attitude. In one situation our Party committed errors by pursuing a rightist policy, reformist policy, following behind the masses who were already more progressive. But in another situation our Party committed "left" errors, pursuing adventurism, going far ahead of the masses who were still trailing behind. Therefore the history of our Party after Tan Ling Djie-ism gained control was the history of right and "left" errors at the same time, the history of capitulationism and adventurism together.

Besides endorsing the campaign against Tan Ling Djie-ism, the Fifth National Congress also endorsed a one-year plan for the second membership drive.[47] At the time of the congress, membership was 165,206, of whom 49,042 were full members and 116,164 candidate members.[48] The goal of the second membership drive was not published. Aidit, however, wrote on May 23, 1954, that in view of the Party program, the current tactical and organizational lines and cadre activity, "it will not be simply luck if PKI at the end of this year is a Party with a million members and candidate members," not just registered but organized and receiving political education.[49]

The second membership campaign did not achieve as rapid a growth as Aidit had hoped. Probably the figure of one million by the end of 1954 was unrealistic given the number of cadres and members and the still-limited geographical spread of the Party organization in March 1954. It seems that the Party leaders had allowed themselves to become overoptimistic as a result of the ease with which the first membership campaign had been completed. At the end of October 1954 Aidit claimed a total of half a million members and candidate members, and in February 1956 one million.[50] Membership figures were not published between these two dates, but available evidence suggests that the greatest growth occurred before August 1955. Feith, in his monograph on the 1955 elections, mentioned the rapid extension of Party membership prior to the September elections,[51] while Aidit, in his report to the Central Committee plenum on August 7, 1955, referred to the success already achieved in the campaign to extend the Party's organization and membership.[52]

The second membership drive was spurred by both the approach of general elections for parliament, and the start of intensive PKI activity to attract and organize the peasantry. To ensure PKI a greater role in national politics, more members, more widely spread, were needed in order to mobilize voters as politics still largely revolved around parliament. And in July 1953, a major article written by Aidit turned the main focus of Party attention to the as yet untapped potential of the peasants.[53] Prior to this, the still-limited Party resources had been concentrated on the more accessible and more politically aware urban population.

The success of the drive was indicated by the results of the parliamentary elections held in September 1955. Not only did PKI emerge as the fourth largest party, with over 6 million votes, or 16.4 per cent of the total; but the great majority of PKI's votes came from rural areas. PKI also received votes in all of the fifteen electoral districts. And if 88.7 per cent of Communist votes still came from Java, PKI also won more than five per cent of the total votes cast in the three districts of Sumatra and in East Kalimantan and West Nusatenggara.[54] Thus, in the second membership campaign, PKI grew numerically, extended geographically, and at the same time widened the social basis of its membership. PKI was now a mass party.

The rapid rise in Party membership again posed the problem of how to maintain the ideological, political, and organizational unity of the Party. As Aidit told the Central Committee in November 1954:

It is wrong if we think that bourgeois ideology and bourgeois influence is only outside the Party, especially as many new people have entered our Party bringing with them bourgeois and feudal ideological vestiges and habits. . . . Besides, the enemies of the Party certainly try to enter our Party in order to break the Party's organization from within and to weaken the ideology of the Party members.[55]

Because of this situation, Aidit declared, it was necessary to intensify the vigilance of members and cadres, and ideological work within the Party. Every new member had to be given an understanding of the structure of the Party organization, of the limitless strength of the people, of the Party's leadership role, and of the importance of the national united front. Every political view expressed by the Central Committee or the province committees or the Party congress had to become material with which to educate the members politically.

In the same speech, Aidit also devoted special attention to the need for the proper education of cadres some of whom, he declared, still did not understand either the essential character of the worker-peasant alliance or the agrarian relations in the villages. As a remedy for the cadre shortcomings, cadre courses had to be extended to Party committees at all levels, and at the same time made more systematic and practical. Furthermore, the cadres from the level of section committee upward were expected to accustom themselves to reading and discussing the classical writings of Marxism-Leninism. Aidit said that in July and August 1954 a beneficial campaign had been organized for the study by cadres of Lenin's *Left-wing Communism, an Infantile Disorder*, although several provinces still had not seriously implemented the campaign.

Despite the insistence by the central Party leadership in the second half of 1955 that the cadres and members should be given a systematic political education,[56] several factors prevented the implementation of this task. In the first place, the Party was obliged to concentrate all its resources on the campaign for the September 1955 parliamentary and the December 1955 Constituent Assembly general elections.[57] In the second place, the cadres' low level of general education proved a serious obstacle to their understanding of Marxist-Leninist texts, and the Party was obliged to institute general knowledge courses, ranging from the eradication of illiteracy to geography, history, and languages, before it could proceed with courses in Marxism-Leninism.[58]

Njoto, speaking to the Central Committee plenum on August 1, 1956, summarized the educational work actually performed by PKI since it had become a mass party with over a half million members.[59] He said that the Party had as yet been unable to establish a centralized system of political education, but that on several occasions the central leadership had issued instructions to the lower Party organizations that:

a. all members and candidate members should be given a thorough understanding of the Party constitution and program, and that they also should follow and understand all Central Committee and Politbureau statements;

b. Party cadres should study classical works of Marxism-Leninism such as Lenin's *Left-wing Communism, an Infantile Disorder* and the *History of the CPSU(B)*. Furthermore, Party committees from the provincial level downward had already begun to organize various kinds of courses which used Central Committee instructions and guides, and had made their own experiments in methods of teaching. But in the period of the second membership drive, education was concerned primarily with cadres. Njoto explained that this was necessary "because they are the backbone in carrying out the Party's tasks," and because without prior cadre education it would not be possible to educate the rest of the Party or have unity of ideology, policy, and organization in the Party. In short, the rapid expansion of Party membership had created a grave shortage of cadres. As the Party was not yet in a position to provide thorough political education for all members, its educational work was concentrated primarily on the creation of an informed and ideologically attuned cadre force.

Party publishing also made considerable strides between March 1954 and August 1956. *Harian Rakjat* increased in circulation from 15,000 in February 1954 to 23,000 in January 1955 and to 55,000 in January 1956.[60] At the last date its circulation compared with 48,000 for the socialist newspaper *Pedoman*, 40,000 for PNI's *Suluh Indonesia*, 38,000 for the independent but pro-PNI *Merdeka*, and 34,000 for Masjumi's *Abadi*.[61] A three-month campaign to extend sales was launched in January 1956, but succeeded in increasing circulation by only 3,000.[62] *Bintang Merah*, from a low of 7,500–8,000 copies at the end of 1952, increased its circulation to 20,000 in the second half of 1954 and to 25,000 at the end of 1955.[63] At the end of 1953 *PKI-Buletin* became a monthly, whereas previously it had appeared every two or three weeks. On January 1, 1955, its name was changed to *Kehidupan Partai (Party Life)*, with the intention that henceforth it would provide a place for short articles by regional and local cadres on their experiences, as well as for important Party statements and some articles translated from foreign Communist sources.

A surprising new Party monthly appeared in the middle of 1954— an English-language *Monthly Review* providing news of PKI and also of the major political developments in Indonesia. At first *Monthly Review* was mimeographed, but from January 1957 was printed, illustrated, and well produced under the title *Review of Indonesia*. The purpose of the review is uncertain. Its editor told me simply that it was intended for comrades and friends abroad. One can only surmise that its appearance reflected the growing prestige of the PKI in the international Communist world, and that it was intended firstly to keep the foreign Communist parties informed, in a language they understood, of national and Party events in Indonesia, and secondly, perhaps, to serve as comparative material especially for such as the Indian Communist Party.

By the beginning of November 1954 PKI had issued, besides translations from foreign Communist literature, 150,000 copies of the Party program, 100,000 copies of its constitution, and 250,000 copies of its election manifesto.[64] 150,000 copies of the election program were printed in Javanese, Sundanese, Batak, and Indonesian in Arabic script. At the end of 1955, the PKI publishing company, Jajasan Pembaruan, reported that during the year it had published 30 different books and pamphlets in a total of 1,136,000 copies.[65] Of this number, the translations from foreign sources appear to have been predominantly from Chinese authors, with some also from Lenin and Stalin.

The educational importance is clear of the increasing circulation of *Harian Rakjat* and the Party periodicals, and of Marxist-Leninist classics translated into Indonesian. At the same time, the 1955 election campaigns also provided valuable education: for ordinary members and candidate members through the availability and study of the Party constitution, program, and election manifesto; for all, but especially cadres, through the practical work of winning and mobilizing millions of electors.

As the Party membership swelled rapidly during the second membership drive, a new organizational form had to be found that could permit the control, education, and activation of the ordinary members and candidate members. The old branches were swamped by large numbers of new members and could no longer perform this function. It was therefore decided to organize all members into groups of at the most seven persons.

The group was incorporated into the March 1954 constitution,[66] but intensive work to bring all members into groups was started only at the beginning of 1955 when Aidit wrote an important article on the subject.[67] The purpose of the groups was fourfold:

1. to eradicate illiteracy among members by organizing anti-illiteracy courses or obliging members to attend government courses;

2. to organize their members to report on the conditions, thoughts, and activities of the people with whom they lived and worked, and send these reports to the branch committees, which in turn sent them to the higher committees;

3. once a group had been established some months and was already holding periodic meetings, it was to begin the basic political education of its members by discussions on Party organization, the responsibilities of members, the Party program, the unlimited strength of the people, and the importance of the national united front; and

4. to collect membership fees.

At the beginning of 1955 the PKI began to establish special groups for women.[68] This was deemed necessary in face of the traditional bashfulness and self-effacement of Indonesian women.

4. THE FIRST 3-YEAR PLAN OF ORGANIZATION AND EDUCATION, 1956-1959

The Central Committee plenum which met from July 31 to August 3, 1956, drew up a three-year plan for organization and education which went into operation on August 17, 1956. The actual plan was not made public, but its outline as well as its results may be gathered from a number of PKI sources.[69]

From the available sources, the organizational objectives of the plan were:

1. to extend membership by 50 per cent from one million to one and a half millions;

2. to spread membership and organization more evenly throughout Indonesia;

3. to open new Party offices and improve the organization of all offices, to activate the various committees' bureaus, and increase the number and improve the distribution of full-time cadres;

4. to organize every member into a group, with women in special groups, and to make the groups active;

5. to promote all candidate members to full membership after they had completed their supervised period of candidacy; and

6. to increase the payment of membership fees and donations, and to ensure that they be forwarded in stipulated percentages to the higher committees.

The education objectives were:

1. to eradicate illiteracy within the Party;

2. to organize Party schools and courses;

3. to organize seminars at the Central Committee and provincial com-

mittee levels on such matters as economic problems, and also to organize conferences in theory;

4. to extend Party publishing and to increase distribution of the publications, with an emphasis on increasing the circulation of *Harian Rakjat*;

5. to establish libraries in committee offices; and

6. to establish educational institutions for non-Party progressives, especially to create a people's university.

Quotas were set for each Party committee, and special bureaus were created in the Central Committee and the provincial committees to supervise the implementation of the plan.

Although not all the plan's objectives were realized, important gains were made: Party membership was increased, organizational work advanced, and educational activity systematized.

Claimed membership had reached the goal of one and a half millions by the beginning of 1959,[70] at which figure it remained until the Sixth National Congress held from September 7-14, 1959. Peasants had still constituted less than half the total membership in March 1954, but by December 1958 they had become the majority group.[71] The proportion of peasants in the membership was still growing at the time of the Sixth Congress, while that of workers remained the same, despite the fact that their number was increasing.[72] The promotion of candidate members to full membership was accelerated until by September 1959 about 50 per cent, or 750,000, of the total members were full members, compared with only 30 per cent, or 49,042, at the time of the Fifth Congress in March 1954.[73] Thus between the two congresses the number of full members had increased fifteenfold. Aidit, however, still complained that the percentage of candidate members was still too high due to the tardiness of some committees to promote them, and to the insecurity in the rebel areas which prevented the smooth operation of the Party there.[74]

A significant result of the plan was the large increase in the number and percentage of women members. The Party instruction of January 1955 to increase the number of women members and to organize them into special groups was at first implemented slowly owing to the shyness of Indonesian women, but also because many male committee members refused to see any value in women as Party members.[75] In February 1957 guidance was published on how to attract women from the different social strata; during 1957 several provincial committees held conferences on how to attract and activate women members; and not only special groups but also special political schools and courses were organized so as to permit the more rapid political development of women members.[76] In September 1957 the number of women members had been 100,000, with the percentage of women members ranging from 6 to 17 per cent in Java and lower in the outer islands.[77] As late as May 1958 the number of women members was still given as 100,000, but a PKI national conference to discuss Party work among women and held at the end of that month[78] heralded a rapid increase. By December 1958 there were 150,000 women members, and 258,000 at the time of the Sixth Congress.[79] At the time of the national conference of May 1958 there were already five women sitting in parliament, six in the Constituent Assembly, and 180 in regional and local councils, who had been elected on the PKI ticket.

As for the geographical spread of the Party during the period of the plan, the chairman of the Central Planning Bureau, Amir Anwar Sanusi, told the Sixth Congress that "the activities of the Party are now evenly spread over all parts of the country." [80] He backed the statement by claims of membership increases of 38 per cent in West Sumatra and 40 per cent in North Sulawesi, despite atrocities committed on Party members by rebels in these areas, and of 63.5 per cent in Kalimantan. In Java, the increase had been 36 per cent, with the lowest, 31 per cent, in East Java. As for the growth of the Party organization, Anwar Sanusi reported that in Kalimantan the number of subsections had increased by 45 per cent, while in Java the number of branches had risen 250 per cent, and of subsections 42 per cent. At the end of the plan, within Java only 1.3 per cent of the 1,449 *ketjamatans* (the level at which the subsection is established) and 15.8 per cent of the 21,047 villages (the level at which the branch is established) were without a Party organization.

In order to cope with the increase in membership and organization, the number of full-time functionaries in the provincial and island committees was almost doubled. The number of full-timers in the sections (established for each *kabupaten*, for medium-sized towns, and for areas of large cities) increased 400 per cent and in the subsections 300 per cent. The number of committee members at all levels was increased sevenfold. From these statistics it appears that during the plan PKI increased its cadre force even more rapidly than membership. At the same time, the equipment of the Party offices was increased. For example, the number of typewriters in the provincial committee and section committee offices was increased by 600 per cent.

Although a rapid increase in membership was effected, great care was still taken to prevent the entry of undesirable elements into the Party. This is illustrated by an article published in *Kehidupan Partai* in May 1958, which detailed the method used in bringing a new person into the Party.[81] Four stages were listed: preparation, watching over the recruit, caution, and investigation. The basic targets were those who had voted Communist in the last elections. First, for "rather a long time," the cadres would note the potential recruit's name, age, residence, social origins, education, work, and so on, questioning his friends and acquaintances to obtain the information. Then began the second stage, that of educating him to live selflessly and to be progressive in his political outlook and method of thinking. To encourage him in such ways, Party workers would pay periodic visits to his house in order to explain Party policy and convince him of the correctness of the Party's political position; they would provide him with progressive reading materials (at least *Harian Rakjat* every day); invite him to art evenings, receptions, or lectures organized by the Party and other progressive organizations; invite him to public meetings and demonstrations; encourage him to take part in delegations to press both social-economic and political demands; and, if necessary, give him the responsibility of leading small actions. The aim of the second phase was to develop the recruit's political and organizational awareness so that he voluntarily requested to join the Party.

But, at that stage, caution was required. A close check would be made of his friends and associates to see whether they were reactionary or progressive. If they were reactionary, the cadres had to convince him of the criminal nature of the reactionaries' actions. Finally, if the recruit passed through the first three stages successfully, there was the period of investigation. A thorough check would be made of the records of the preceding stages, especially of his assistance in implementing Party policy, his diligence in reading Party literature, and his loyalty to the people's everyday demands. If he passed this check he was accepted into the Party. At the end of the article the author warned committee members not to use the guide in order to keep the entry of new members to a minimum, not to practice "closed-doorism"; that is, the cadres were exhorted to use great care with potential members, but not to the extent of impeding the growth of the Party. Although it was not mentioned in the article, the careful supervision of those who entered PKI was continued during the period of candidate membership when any undesirable elements that had evaded earlier detection could be weeded out.[82]

Little information has been published on the success achieved in pursuing the last objective of the organizational section of the first three-year plan, to increase the entry of membership fees and donations and to ensure that they were forwarded in stipulated percentages to the higher committees. From the little evidence available, it appears that by the end of the plan PKI was still unable either to solve the problem of collecting a large percentage of membership fees or to ensure that the lower committees forwarded the stipulated percentages of income to the higher committees.[83]

PKI educational work also expanded considerably during the plan. In fact, the Sixth National Congress. claimed that "in general, the quotas achieved in the field of education are much better than that in the field of organization." [84]

The work to eradicate illiteracy within the Party has not been discussed publicly. In mid-1957, at a time when the number of illiterates in the Party was "not small," [85] the agitation and propaganda section of the Central Committee issued two booklets for use in the eradication of illiteracy both within and outside the Party.[86] The organization of members into groups must have facilitated anti-illiteracy work, but in 1960 committee members complained to me of the continued existence of illiteracy among not only ordinary members but functionaries as high as the section and subsection levels.

Under the three-year plan a system of political schools and courses was established through all levels of the Party organization from the Central Committee to the branches. The Central Committee ordered that all schools and courses teach four subjects whenever the educational level of the participant would permit.[87] The four subjects were: the history of society, which was designed to acquaint students with the Marxist-Leninist view of society and the laws of social development; the basic problems of the Indonesian revolution, which was directed toward creating unanimity of thought on the strategy and tactics of the Indonesian revolution; the problems of the national united front, aimed to secure unanimity in the PKI's implementation of this policy in the Indonesian situation; and the building of the Party, which showed the importance of the Leninist-type party and of the active participation of all Communists in its development. Texts were published for each subject adapted to the different levels of education and political awareness of the students.

Each "shift" of the central school, organized by the Central Committee, lasted full time for one month. It included two extra subjects: dialectical and historical materialism, which was also taught by some provincial-level schools, and the international working-class movement. The duration of each "shift" in the provincial, section, and subsection schools has not been published, but information is available about a provincial-level school for women cadres held in Makasar.[88] In order to avoid the women students' staying in a hostel, which was the normal practice for male students, the school was held for three hours, three days a week for five weeks—or for 45 hours in all. The time was spent in lectures, discussion groups, and discussion classes; self-study at home was required; and the course ended with an examination. From Surabaja there is information about the duration of branch schools.[89] As the Party leaders had determined that a branch political school should be completed within seven days, the students met for two hours on each of the seven days, making a total of fourteen hours of classwork.

At the lowest level the Party faced great difficulties in giving political education because the students in the branch schools were people "whose general knowledge is still low, a large part of them are illiterate, while those who are not illiterate still have a very limited desire to read." [90] Not all branch schools covered the four subjects stipulated by the Central Committee. One in Surabaja, for example, met for two and a quarter hours on six successive nights but taught only the history of the development of society; the people who attended were heads of Party groups.[91]

Absenteeism was also a problem in the schools and courses. Where the students stayed in a hostel for the period of the school, which occurred on at least the central and provincial levels, absenteeism was not significant. But in the lower levels absenteeism occurred for a number of causes: students had to work overtime, or were too tired or too lazy or lost interest. An added cause was the wet season. Leaders of all Communist-led mass organizations complained to me of the fall in attendance when the roads were quagmires and the students had no rainclothes and could not afford to come by transport. The Madiun section committee reported that during rain, attendance at the political school fell by 30 per cent.[92]

Less than a year after the plan went into effect, Aidit told the Central Committee plenum of July 4, 1957, that "In general there is already rather enough attention to education for high and middle Party cadres."[93] After this speech, the emphasis of Party education was shifted to the lower cadres and activists, the committee members in the subsections and branches, and the leaders of groups. By the time of the Sixth Congress over 270,000 cadres and activists had graduated from the Party schools or had completed a Party course.[94] They "form the Party's backbone, which can never be broken." According to Aidit, the 270,000 comprised "the majority of cadres from the centre to the basic committees."[95]

Concerning the implementation of the plan for seminars and conferences, Aidit told the Central Committee plenum which met from March 31 to April 3, 1958, that conferences in theory were not yet being held as desired, but that the Central Committee and some provincial committees were already arranging seminars on specific topics. The seminars and special conferences arranged by the Central Committee during the period of the plan included a seminar on Party work among students, held at about the beginning of 1958, a national conference on Party work among women, held in May 1958,[96] a national seminar on economics, held in February 1959,[97] and a national conference on Party work among peasants and fishermen, held in April 1959.[98] The provincial committees also arranged conferences and seminars which were probably devoted to the same topics as, and held in preparation for, the national meetings.

One of the principal goals of the seminars and conferences was to exchange experiences in the work of building the Party among the different sections of society. But for the high and middle cadres who took part, there was the danger that their work within the Party organization might result in their losing contact with the actual condition of the masses. To avoid this danger, the Central Committee organized a six-month "go down" and "three-togethers" campaign in preparation for the national conference on Party work among peasants and fishermen.[99] All Party committees from the Central Committee down instructed certain cadres to "go down" to the villages to study at first hand agrarian relations and the living conditions of the peasants. While in the village, in order to understand the peasants better and win their support, the cadres had to practice the "three-togethers": "living together, eating together, and working together with the peasants, especially with . . . the poor peasants and agricultural laborers."[100] The Communist-led mass organizations followed the Party and organized "go down" movements among their own cadres and activists. "Going down" has continued since the national conference on work among the peasants, and cadres have been sent into urban *kampongs* and fishing villages as well as into rural areas. The movement has a greater value than just educating cadres in the realities of the life of the masses, for it has also provided the Party leadership with a store of social and economic data which permits the Party to formulate popular demands and slogans attuned to local, provincial, and national situations.

During the period of the first three-year plan, the Party cadres and activists were expected to do more for their political education than attend schools and courses, participate in seminars and conferences, and join in the "go down" movement. They were also expected to study on their own, and guides to self-study were published in *Kehidupan Partai*.[101] Anwar Sanusi reported in September 1959 that cadres at the provincial and section committee levels were studying on their own such classical Marxist-Leninist works as the *Communist Manifesto,*

Lenin's *Left-wing Communism, an Infantile Disorder,* and his *Two Tactics of Social Democracy in the Democratic Revolution.*[102] The cadres were also encouraged to read Communist novels which had been translated into Indonesian. Cadres were also expected to read *Harian Rakjat,* the various Party periodicals, pamphlets, and booklets, and all Party documents that were circulated to their respective committees.

The schools, courses, seminars, conferences, "go down" movement, and self-study movement of the first three-year plan were concerned with the Party cadres and activists. The Party did not yet have the resources for an intensive education campaign among the ordinary members. For the 1.2 million or so members and candidate members who had not achieved the position of cadre or activist, basic political education continued to be received through the group. Instruction on the Party constitution and program was continued, but apparently a special effort was made to organize study movements that would familiarize the ordinary members with the line of the moment taken by the central Party leadership.[103] Cadres from the subsection or even section, that is, those who had benefited most from the education campaign, went into the groups to explain decisions taken by the Central Committee plenums, and any important Party document which laid down the Party line at a given time. The meetings of ordinary members would then discuss how to implement the Party line in their own locality.

The fourth objective of the educational section of the plan was the extension of Party publishing and the distribution of Party literature, especially raising the circulation of *Harian Rakjat.* Work toward this objective had mixed success.

The greatest failure, perhaps, in the whole plan was met in the attempt to increase the circulation of *Harian Rakjat.* In March 1956, five months before the plan went into effect, the circulation of *Harian Rakjat* was 58,000. By February 1957 it had reached 60,000, compared with a total circulation of the 75 daily newspapers in Indonesian of 747,250.[104] Despite campaigns to increase circulation, in which even Aidit and other Central Committee members took part, and despite the great increase in the number of Party members, committee members, and organizations, the circulation was still 60,000 four years later.[105]

All the periodicals from the period before the plan continued publication. *Bintang Merah* appeared regularly. *Kehidupan Partai* reappeared in October 1956. From May to December 1957 it appeared only twice because of technical printing difficulties and the lack of articles being sent in from the regions. During 1958 and 1959 it was published regularly. The English-language monthly *Review of Indonesia,* initially mimeographed, was printed from January 1957 and appeared regularly.

Apart from the periodicals continued from the previous period, several new ones appeared during the three-year plan. The first was *PKI dan DPR (PKI and Parliament)* which began publication in June 1956. Its title was changed to *PKI dan Perwakilan (PKI and the Representative Councils)* after the 1957 local elections. This quarterly was intended to give news of PKI activities in parliament, the Constituent Assembly, and the local representative councils. In January 1957 appeared the first number of *Mimbar Komunis (Communist Forum)* which had the subtitle *Problems of Peace and Socialism.* *Mimbar Komunis* contained translated articles and speeches by foreign Communists, and sought to familiarize the PKI cadres with the experience of foreign Communist parties. It was at first published every two months, but then became a monthly. Early in November 1957 PKI began to publish an English-language quarterly entitled *Marxist Science* which was aimed at the intelligentsia and scientists and contained news of the scientific advances in the Soviet bloc. It was soon changed to *Ilmu Marxis (Marxist Science)* in Indonesian. The latest periodical was the quarterly *Ekonomi dan Masjarakat (Economics and Society).* This appeared in March 1959 and contained articles by both Indonesians and foreigners on economic, financial, and social matters. All the new periodicals were published regularly.

During 1956, PKI published 700,000 copies of books, booklets, and pamphlets[106]—a decrease compared with 1955, but the 1955 figure had been bloated with the large printing of the new PKI constitution and program, and the election manifesto used in the 1955 election campaigns. A target of one million copies was set for 1957, but there was no report of whether it was achieved. In 1958, the Communist publishing house issued 52 different books and pamphlets as well as over 50 issues of different periodicals.[107] By the end of that year there were available in Indonesian in booklet, pamphlet, or article form many works of Lenin, Stalin, and Mao Tse-tung, as well as some by Liu Shao-chi, Ho Chi Minh, Marx and Engels, Dimitrov, Sharkey, and lesser foreign Communist figures. Communist fiction available in Indonesian included works by Gorki, Julius Fucik, Sholokov, and Ilya Ehrenburg. This wealth of translated material enabled the Party cadres to study many of the classical writings of Marxism-Leninism as well as much that has been written of the practical experiences of foreign Communist parties, especially those of the USSR, China, and Vietnam.

Although translations from foreign Communist sources constituted a majority of the titles published by the PKI, the great majority of total copies were of PKI materials: speeches and articles by the Party leaders, documents of Central Committee plenums, new printings of the Party constitution and program, the materials for discussion in the Sixth Congress, course guides for Party schools and courses, and occasional important Central Committee statements, such as New Year messages. The largest publishing undertaking was the two volumes of Aidit's selected works, covering the period from August 1951 to the Sixth National Congress in September 1959. The first volume, of 537 pages, appeared in mid-1959, but the second volume was delayed until May 1960.[108] These two volumes made readily available for study the most important articles and speeches on PKI in the period of the national united front.

The three-year plan also called for increased publishing activity by the Party's regional organizations. Several local Party periodicals appeared, including the semimonthly *Suara Ibukota (Voice of the Capital)* published by PKI in Djakarta Raja from the middle of March 1959, *Warta Sunda (Sunda News)* published in Bandung, *Suara Persatuan (The Voice of Unity)* published in Semarang, *Buletin PKI Djawa Timur (East Java PKI Bulletin)* published in Surabaja, and *Lombok Bangun (Lombok Awakes)* published in Mataram, Lombok. At the time of the 1957 and 1958 local elections in Java, South Sumatra, Riau, and Kalimantan, election programs were published in booklet form by the Party organizations in at least the five province-level regions of Java (that is, Djakarta Raja, West Java, Central Java, the special territory of Jogjakarta, and East Java), and also in some of the cities, such as Surabaja and Jogjakarta. The Party organizations at the *kabupaten* level also issued election programs, but these were mostly mimeographed. A little work was done in publishing in the regional languages. In 1957, for example, there was mention of a work by Mao Tse-tung translated into Sundanese, and one by Stalin into Javanese.[109]

Because in Indonesia wages for workers are low and the price of printed materials relatively very high, PKI faced the problem of how to make its publications available to the large number of cadres, members, and sympathizers who could not afford to buy them.[110] As a partial solution to the problem, the plan aimed to establish a library in every committee. To what extent the plan has been successful in this sphere has not been disclosed publicly, but the work has been taken seriously.[111] The value of the libraries was, however, limited by the illiteracy widespread among the ordinary members and lower cadres and by the "very limited desire to read" among those who were literate.[112]

The final objective of the three-year plan in the field of education was the creation of educational institutions for non-Party progressives,

especially the creation of a people's university. A committee to organize
the Universitas Rakjat (UNRA, People's University) was established
on September 19, 1958, on the initiative of PKI leaders and well-known
fellow travelers.[113] Siswojo, a member of the PKI Central Committee,
became its chairman.[114] On October 31, a 21-person council of curators
was formed and included Aidit, Sakirman, and Njono, the chairman of
SOBSI.[115] Aidit was elected chairman of the council on January 17,
1959.[116]

When the UNRA committee was first established, it announced that
the objective of the university was "to develop scientific knowledge
among the people."[117] Aidit, however, revealed the true objective in an
article in *World Marxist Review*.[118] He wrote that UNRA was intended
for those Party members and other progressives who were unable to
attend the national or regional Party schools for lack of places or
because their daily occupations did not afford them the opportunity.
He further noted that:

The curriculum of the University is closely linked with the urgent tasks of the
Party, namely the building of a national front and the Party. The education is aimed
at eliminating ideological confusion, at deepening the understanding of present and
future tasks.

UNRA courses opened in Djakarta and Jogjakarta in December
1958.[119] Within a year there were branches in eight other towns: Keba-
joran Baru, Bandung, Surakarta, Semarang, Surabaja, Malang, Palem-
bang, and Medan. By mid-1963 UNRA was functioning in at least
seventeen towns. Assistance in equipping UNRA was asked of foreign
diplomatic representatives in Indonesia. They gave "much assistance."
For example, the East German International Relations Bureau and the
Indonesia-Soviet Friendship Association gave books and film projectors.

Students are admitted to UNRA if they have a junior high school
level of education or the equivalent or if they are capable but have not
had the opportunity to study. UNRA, in spite of its name, is not for
the people. The fees are too high to permit workers or peasants to
attend.[120] The UNRA leaders said in interview that their students consisted of lower civil servants, a few teachers, and cadres and activists
from the trade unions, youth, women, and other mass organizations. In
at least some cases the mass organizations pay the fees for their
members.

It is difficult to estimate the number of students in UNRA. In September 1959 the UNRA chairman claimed 2,816 enrolled students, but
this figure has to be qualified, and the qualification throws some light
on the difficulty faced by PKI in obtaining sustained activity from its

members. In Surabaja 600 students began the courses, but within a year only 300 were left; in Jogjakarta 350 started, but a year later only between 100 and 150 were left. Of the students who continued the courses "very few indeed," according to the UNRA national secretary, attended every class. So many dropped out because they lost interest, or because it was too much effort to attend, or they found the fees too high. The reasons for absenteeism among those who continued were several: the wet season, many people had to work overtime or at two jobs and so had little time or inclination to attend night classes, and the cadres of the Party and the mass organizations were often sent out of town for days or weeks.

In May 1960, the permanent staff of UNRA included seven at the center, and five in Surabaja. I did not find the numbers elsewhere. At the end of 1959 there were 250 UNRA teachers throughout Indonesia. They received no pay, only transport costs. The UNRA headquarters issues mimeographed monthly course guides, which the students must buy for two rupiahs each month. UNRA possessed no buildings of its own by the middle of 1960, and had to rent premises. In 1959 UNRA also began to publish booklets containing UNRA lectures delivered by Communist leaders. Their subjects range from the question of race and racialism to discussions of economic and financial policy.

As of May 1960, UNRA offered five courses, each lasting two years. The one taken by the great majority of students was political science, which covered seven subjects: Marxist political science, the Indonesian independence movement, Indonesian society and economy, the history of Indonesia, constitutional law, geography, and the history of the world. Political science was taught in all UNRA branches. The second most important course was English, taught in eight branches, with an emphasis on translation from English to Indonesian, "because many published materials arrive in English," and on conversation, "because many foreign guests come to Indonesia." Journalism was taught in two branches, its importance for PKI being obvious.[121] In the art course, which was taught in two branches, UNRA endeavored to teach the students to see society and to portray a situation from it. The national secretary pointed out that pictures and caricatures are very important in Indonesia where a high percentage of the population is illiterate. Indonesian language and literature were taught in Djakarta.

One day before the first three-year plan ended on August 17, 1959, the Central Committee established two new educational institutions in Djakarta.[122] A campaign to raise funds for a Central Committee house of culture was opened in August 1956, and raised 4 million rupiahs. The house was finally opened on August 16, 1959, with Njoto as chairman of the supervising committee. At the same time, Aidit proclaimed the establishment of the Aliarcham Academy of Social Sciences, which was to teach Marxism-Leninism and also to study the social sciences from the Marxist-Leninist viewpoint.

The preparations for the Sixth National Congress were used as a stimulus to the completion of the three-year plan, and a means of heightening Party activity in general and strengthening the ties of the Party with the masses.

On January 5, 1959, the Politbureau called for a nationwide competition in four fields: services to the people, promotion of the people's culture, education work within the Party, and the expansion of the Party organization.[123]

The most spectacular activity in the preparation for the Sixth Congress was the formation of voluntary work brigades of Party members. These served a triple purpose: to raise the work enthusiasm of ordinary members and candidate members, to bring the cadres into closer contact with the people, and to increase the people's support for the Party. The incomplete list of work done by the brigades included the repair or construction of 3,249 kilometers of roads, 985 kilometers of drains, 2,280 houses, 80 school buildings, 5,119 public lavatories, 3,133 public bathing places, and 1,477 bridges; the construction of 139 dams; the establishment of 351 anti-illiteracy centers; and the killing of 186,698 field mice.[124]

But probably the most important result for the Party of the congress preparations was the intensive discussion in all levels of the Party of the draft constitution, draft program, and draft Central Committee general report which had been published in December 1958.[125]

After 1956 the former heated attacks on the ideological deviations and the heinous "isms" that could arise during the implementation of the national united front gave way to far more gentle reminders that these dangers still existed. The draft of the Central Committee report to be presented to the Sixth Congress, which was published in December 1958, reiterated the need to wage ceaseless war against subjectivism. But although the report as finally presented to the congress retained an outline of methods for combating subjectivism, it dropped the sentence which had stated that "subjectivism still exists up to the present." That the Aidit leadership considered ideological deviation to have become a minor problem was shown markedly in Aidit's speech in May 1959, "Building the Organization is Important, but Building Ideology is Even More Important." [126] Instead of attacking a long list of deviations and errors, Aidit merely stressed the need to study the philosophy of Marxism-Leninism in order to avoid the errors caused by bourgeois ways of thinking.

When the second break occurred between the Soviet Union and Yugoslavia, the PKI leaders dutifully warned against "modern revisionism." Its manifestations, the PKI leaders declared, were self-satisfaction, chauvinism, and slanders against the socialist peace camp, the Soviet Union, and the Soviet Communist Party.[127] But although Aidit told the Sixth Congress of the continuing danger of modern revisionism,[128] he boasted in February 1960 to the world Communist parties that "the Tito brand of revisionism has not found the slightest response in the Communist Party of Indonesia." [129]

In order to explain why, during the first three-year plan, the Aidit leadership ceased its violent attacks on errors of ideology and methods of work, it is necessary to note the changes that had taken place within the Party. In brief, before 1956, and especially in the first years after January 1951, the Aidit leadership used strident campaigns in order to justify the removal of the "old" leaders, and to frighten any of their real or supposed followers into acquiescence to the new policies. Furthermore, the new Party leadership had neither the material nor human resources to conduct a large-scale educational campaign within the Party, and made the attacks on the various erroneous "isms" in order to pinpoint those errors which, after a reading of the history of PKI and foreign Communist parties, were deemed most likely to occur during a period of the national united front.

By the time the three-year plan was put into operation, the need for strident anti-error campaigns was removed. Firstly, the Aidit leadership was secure in its control over the Party and in the loyalty of its members. The "old" leaders had long since been removed, there had been no signs of significant support for them, the new leadership showed no signs of division, and the large Party that had been built since January 1951 demonstrated a surprising solidarity.[130] Secondly, those cadres who had earlier exhibited error or tendency to error had been weeded out or corrected. And thirdly, the Party now had sufficient teachers, funds, and translated literature to permit the launching of a massive political education campaign which could tackle political education systematically and so remove the need for particular anti-"isms" campaigns.

5. THE SECOND 3-YEAR PLAN, 1960-1963

By the time of the PKI Sixth National Congress in September 1959, political freedom in Indonesia was gravely threatened. On June 4 a temporary ban had been imposed on all political activities. From August 1, closed meetings were again permitted, but only if the military authorities had been given prior notice. A ban was temporarily retained on public meetings and demonstrations, and on all political activities in those areas where military operations were in progress against the rebels. These latter areas included West Sumatra, parts of West Java, and parts of Sulawesi. It was widely rumored that the military authorities at first refused permission for the Sixth Congress. They retracted only after Sukarno intervened.

Despite, and probably stimulated by, the growing threat to political activity, the PKI leaders expressed to the Sixth Congress their determination to draw up and execute a second three-year plan of organization and education. The plan went into effect in April 1960. Quotas were set in eleven main fields.[131] Four concerned education: cadre schools at the national, provincial, and *kabupaten* levels; the operation of political schools, presumably at the *ketjamatan* (subsection) level; people's political courses at the branch level; and anti-illiteracy courses, presumably at the group level. Five concerned organizational matters: the extended use of *Harian Rakjat,* the promotion of candidates to full membership, the collection of membership dues, the organization of ordinary members into groups, and the expansion of membership. Two were miscellaneous: research in the villages, and the creation of coöperatives.

Information is sparse on the details of the second three-year plan, on its actual goals and on actual implementation of them. This is partly a result of the government's suspension of all PKI Central Committee journals in October 1960. It may also be an indication of increased secrecy on the part of the PKI leaders in view of the threat to political parties in the period of Guided Democracy after July 1959.

In April 1962, Aidit told a Central Committee plenary meeting that "Despite many difficulties, our second three-year plan fundamentally is proceeding well." [132] But to ensure success in the more important fields, activities in the final twelve months were canalized into a "four increases movement": increase political schools and people's courses; increase the membership of the Party and the mass organizations (this was perhaps the first time that PKI publicly acknowledged its direct involvement in those ostensibly non-Party organizations); promote candidate members; and increase the inflow of membership dues. Of these four, education was pointed out as the most important. Stress was retained on the need for higher cadres to "go down" in order to assist the lower levels of the Party in implementing the plan.

As of February 1963, with two months still left, the unannounced quotas in the eleven main fields had been implemented on average 100 per cent.[133] The highest achievements were in the extended use of *Harian Rakjat* (180 per cent fulfillment of the plan quota),[134] the Party central school (150 per cent), and people's courses, coöperatives, and village research (128 per cent each). Least success was gained with political schools (47 percent), the collection of dues (50 per cent), and the promotion of candidates to full membership (65 per cent). These last two items continued to be unsolved problems. In the field of education, however, some 82 per cent of cadres and a majority of members had already "tasted" education in Marxism-Leninism and the basic problems of the Indonesian revolution. Party membership passed two millions in the second half of 1962 and PKI became undisputably the largest Communist party outside the Sino-Soviet bloc. As of July 1962, Aidit stated that 60 per cent of members were of peasant origin.[135] But no announcement has been made as to the success of the Party's efforts to increase the proportion of members from the proletarian sections of the rural and urban populations.[136]

During the period of the second three-year plan, the Party continued to organize seminars and conferences on particular topics. At the national level, an education seminar was held in July 1960 to discuss Indonesian education in general,[137] and in July 1961 PKI held its second national peasants' conference.[138] The PKI Seventh (Extraordinary) National Congress was held in April 1962. Its purpose was primarily to adapt the Party constitution and program to official regulations governing the stated objectives, body of doctrine, and methods of work of all political parties.[139] At the provincial and lower levels, conferences and seminars were held to discuss such matters as the economic situation, Party work among women, the establishment of coöperatives, and Party work among fishermen.

By the time of the Central Committee plenary meeting in February 1963, Party leaders were already discussing the period after the completion of the second plan in April.[140] A new, four-year plan of culture, ideology, and organization was to be instituted in mid-1963. The essentials of the plan already had been drawn up by the Central Committee and discussed by "almost all" central and provincial bodies. Previous activities were to be continued, but a new goal was added: cadres were to be both "Communist and expert." All Central Committee and province-level cadres would be required to complete three years in a Party academy; *kabupaten*-level cadres were to attend UNRA and receive general and specialized education equivalent to the com-

pletion of high school; and institutions were to be established to
provide general education to lower cadres. Special courses would be
created to train the large number of teachers required. In Aidit's
words, "The present stage of struggle demands of our Party that we
must now also educate communist cadres with general and special
knowledge (to have specialized expertise), educate cadres to be 'communist and expert.' " [141] Some of the academies had already been
founded: in August 1959 a social science academy, during 1962
academies for political science, economics, technology, and journalism,
and in January 1963 for language and literature (Indonesian, English,
Russian, and Chinese). These were to be added to during the four-
year plan, and branches established at the province level.

It is interesting to speculate on this latest emphasis in the Aidit
leadership's efforts to educate the Party cadres. Perhaps greater
knowledge combined with specific expertise was necessary so that
PKI could play a more informed and therefore influential role in the
many top-level advisory bodies being established by Sukarno as
President/Prime Minister. Perhaps the Aidit leadership looked forward to an imminent assumption of power, in which case they would
need cadres well educated in more than Marxism-Leninism and
current Party strategy and tactics—or perhaps the leaders needed to
give their cadres a sense of imminent victory after twelve years of hard
work. Perhaps the leadership sought to create a large number of
"experts" who could then infiltrate the intelligentsia and educated
middle classes which continued to prove unresponsive to Party
blandishments. Or perhaps the leaders merely sought to keep the
cadres active and enthusiastic while waiting for the Indonesian political situation to move in a direction more propitious for direct political action by the Party.

By unrelenting perseverance the Aidit leadership has built not only
a mass party but also a party free from overt factionalism and dispute.
Most of the members entered the Party as illiterates or semiliterates,
with little political consciousness. Almost all have been given basic
political education, and several hundred thousand are now cadres, the
product of intensive training in ideological, political, and organizational matters. PKI has become a major star in the Communist international constellation; at home it is by far the largest, the most disciplined, and the most efficient of Indonesian parties.

The Aidit leadership has been patiently preparing for an irreversible
assumption of power. Meanwhile, the leaders of the other parties have,
in general, been unconcerned with the masses, except to use traditional

civil and religious authorities to mobilize mass support when regrettably necessary for occasions such as elections. They have been preoccupied with the intrigue and maneuvering within the polite elite. Their goal is government office, which they are so eager to use for their own short-sighted interests. As a result, their parties are hollow shells, rent by factionalism, and blissfully devoid of the educational effort so patiently performed within PKI.

The successful construction of a mass party has been closely bound to the implementation of the second major task of the national united front strategy: attracting and organizing broad support among the poorer sections of society. The mass party is dependent for its existence on good will and support won among the masses. And in turn, the large, disciplined party has effectively extended good will and organization far beyond the confines of the Party itself.

6. SOLIDARITY WITHIN PKI UNDER THE AIDIT LEADERSHIP

Since the Aidit leadership assumed full control of PKI in January 1951, there has been only one overt challenge, by Alimin in 1956, to the wisdom of the leadership's policies. Ten years free from "Mensheviks," "Trotskyites," "Titoists" and other "traitors" puts PKI into a special category among Communist parties.[142] This solidarity requires explanation. The following explanation is concerned with only the cadres of the Party, that is the committee members and other functionaries, from whom any revolt against the Party leadership would be expected. It is concerned with the reasons for the solidarity that exists among two groups of cadres: the middle and lower cadres, and the leaders at the national level.

The structure of the Party is the first, and most obvious, factor contributing to the solidarity with the central leadership that is found among the middle and lower cadres. All but four or five thousand of the more than 2 million present members of PKI have entered the Party since January 1951. The Aidit leadership has therefore been able to use the technique of democratic centralism to prevent the rise of elements considered hostile or potentially hostile to itself. Any person wishing to enter PKI is first thoroughly scrutinized and then must spend a period of six months to five years of candidacy, depending upon his social and political background, during which he is closely watched. Then, if he is accepted as a full member, his election to a committee post requires the endorsement of a higher committee. Should he become a full-time cadre, he can gain promotion only if he proves fully satisfactory to the leadership. Therefore, because the Aidit leadership has used great care in supervising the promotion of committee members and full-time cadres, there has been little chance that elements hostile to the central leadership could rise far within the Party.

At the same time as exercising this control, the central leadership has constantly stressed that "there must be democratic life within the Party." [143] It has encouraged cadres and ordinary members to air grievances, criticisms, and queries within the privacy of Party meetings, and has worked to remove them by patient explanations and education. Errors committed by cadres have been met, since 1951, not by vituperation or expulsion but again by patient correction and education. This method has meant that any nascent opposition to the central leadership has been aired, discussed, and removed before it reaches the point of deep dissatisfaction or expulsion or withdrawal from the Party.

The Aidit leadership has exerted considerable effort to provide political education for its cadres. The political schools and courses have been taught by higher cadres loyal to the central leadership, and they have used only materials which the leadership considers to justify its own policies and tactics. This education has been doubly effective due to the social and political origins of the cadres. Most cadres entered the Party after the Aidit leadership had won control, and have no first-hand experience of the older ideological or personal disputes within PKI or the international Communist movement. Most cadres entered the Party either illiterate or semiliterate and with no previous political experience. Their political education has come solely from what might be termed Aidit channels, and they have no access to Communist literature other than that which the central leadership writes or translates from foreign sources.[144]

Another significant factor in maintaining the solidarity of the middle and lower cadres with the central leadership has been the ability of the leadership to distribute rewards and provide means for status advancement to loyal Party workers. The patronage at the disposal of the Party leaders includes positions in the Party itself and in the many Communist-led mass organizations, all of which have been expanding rapidly and thereby providing wide promotion possibilities. It includes also positions in governmental bodies at the national and local levels,[145] and in *kampong* associations, elected village governments, and coöperatives. The Party leaders also decide which cadres shall participate in the many delegations invited to the Communist countries.

The apparent validity of the policies and tactics of the Aidit leadership is also a factor which operates to maintain the cadres' loyalty to the leadership. Under Aidit's direction, PKI has grown from insignificance to being by far the largest and best-organized party in the country and the leader of mass organizations embracing over 12 million members. Under his care, PKI has approached, in the eyes of its members, steadily closer to government power. Aidit is not only honored in his own country by President Sukarno, but also abroad by the leaders of two of the world's most powerful countries, the Soviet Union and China. In such a situation it is not surprising that his leadership has been virtually unchallenged—especially if victory and the distribution of far greater rewards (in status if not in material wealth) appear imminent.

An important factor which strengthens the solidarity of PKI as a whole, and of the cadres in particular, is the existence of a Party-centered community. We have seen how the Party can provide routes for status advancement. The Party and its mass organizations also provide a defense against hostile or potentially hostile forces, such as the landlord, the employer, the village head, or a government official. They provide assistance in times of material need, such as when there are births, illness, or death in the family. When cadres travel away from their homes, their families are looked after. The Party and its mass organizations give education, both political and basic literacy, they organize sports, provide kindergartens, establish coöperatives. They not only provide employment to many cadres but also come to furnish them with their circle of friends. In short, a community is established within the general community—and the Aidit leadership has taken care that the cadres benefit most from the Party-centered community. Because serious opposition to the central leadership might lead to expulsion from the Party community, such opposition cannot be engaged in lightly.

A final factor, and a nebulous one, is the tradition of authoritarianism that is strong within especially Javanese society, from which the great majority of PKI cadres are derived. One does not openly disagree with one's "superiors." The most one does is to give public agreement and then quietly disregard what the "superiors" have said or ordered.[146] This tradition operates in favor of overt obedience to the leaders of any organization, as long as the leaders are still recognized as leaders or superiors. Because the Aidit leadership has so far proved successful, it retains the overt loyalty and obedience of the cadres as well as of the ordinary members. But this tradition does not operate among those who regard themselves as national leaders, and the phenomenon of more than a decade of solidarity among the central leadership requires additional explanation to the one already given above.

Of the fourteen members of the Central Committee in January 1951, only three have been removed for political reasons: Tan Ling Djie, Alimin, and Wikana. But all three were elected on the PKI list to the Constituent Assembly in December 1955, and Wikana was returned to the Central Committee in September 1959. Tan Ling Djie fully confessed his errors by the time of the Fifth Congress in March 1954, Wikana was not publicly chastised after 1951, and only Alimin has publicly opposed the Aidit leadership. Nor have any of the other members of the Central Committee, including those who have entered since 1951, opposed the Aidit leadership—either publicly or, if the lack of rumors is any evidence, within the Party. This is an unusual record of solidarity for the central leadership of any Communist party.

Apart from the factors discussed above as operating among the middle and lower cadres which also affect those above them, the explanation of this solidarity at the national level is to be found in an examination of the two groups that constitute the central leadership: the group which has entered the central leadership since January 1951, and the group which formed the Central Committee in 1951. The new group has been promoted by the Aidit leadership for ability but also for loyalty to the leadership. While the Party continues to grow stronger, and the leadership's policies thereby vindicated, it is not to be expected that this group of hand-picked, mostly very young Communists who have received their only political education from the Aidit leadership, will give rise to an opposition to the Aidit-Lukman-Njoto triumvirate.

The 1951 group in the Central Committee has also accepted the leadership of the triumvirate with very few public signs of resentment or disagreement. This is due to the personalities of the triumvirate, and especially to their success in guiding the Party. Aidit, Lukman, and Njoto have maintained their unity, and only unsubstantiated anti-Communist rumors have at any time indicated disagreement between them. Not only have these three worked together in a collective and amicable manner, but they have apparently succeeded in achieving the same result with the other members of the central leadership.

But of far greater importance in maintaining the solidarity of the central leadership had been the success achieved under the guidance of Aidit, Lukman, and Njoto. This success has strengthened the triumvirate's position in four ways. First, it has increased the stature of the triumvirate vis-à-vis the other members of the central leadership. Second, with the enormous increase in the size of the Party, the overwhelming majority of members and noncentral leaders know only the triumvirate as the legitimate Party leaders, have been subjected to their system of political education, and have no old loyalties or particular reasons for new ones toward the other members of the central leadership. Third, the unbroken and continuing success of the triumvirate's policies and tactics removes both grounds for opposition or grounds that might gain much support within the Party. Fourth, when final success seems close because of the Aidit leadership's guidance, why risk total defeat by attacking the triumvirate?

The only public challenge to the wisdom of the Aidit leadership's policies has come from Alimin, the only veteran Communist of any note to survive the Madiun rebellion. While Aidit was attending the Twentieth Congress of the Communist Party of the Soviet Union, Alimin on March 26, 1956, circulated among the remaining leaders of PKI a statement in which he strongly denounced the leadership of the Party and the policies it was pursuing.[147]

Alimin claimed that an "opportunist group or soft group" had taken over the leadership of the Party, and had then practiced class collaboration, stifled democracy within the Party, neglected the revolutionary ideological education of its members, and brought the Party to the level of "an ordinary bourgeois party that no longer teaches class consciousness." The Party had grown quantitatively, but was now weak in quality. Alimin expressed "disappointment, concern and anxiety" at the "increasingly unclear" political leadership given to the Party. Finally, he warned of the great danger that the "ideological and political deviation" being followed by the Party would not bring the Party to victory. To cleanse the Party, he pleaded for "The broadest self-criticism and criticism . . . freely or without fear . . . and against anyone."

Alimin's criticisms would have been comprehensible to the old guard of PKI who had studied Marxist-Leninist literature widely and which still remembered the militant extremism that led to the 1926 Communist rebellion in Indonesia. But almost all the old guard had died or had been killed or had left the Party. For the reasons that have been outlined above, Alimin's statement fell on barren ground and received no overt support within the Party. After confession of error on May 10, 1956, he was again obstinate and left the Party on August 8, 1956.[148]

In November 1958 and September 1959, although he had reëstablished contact with the Party headquarters, Alimin published booklets which conflicted with Party policy,[149] but which produced no ripple within the Party. When I met him in May 1960 he was old, senile, ailing, lonely, no longer visited by Party members, and obsessed with what he considered to be the Party leadership's flouting of the elementary principles of Marxism-Leninism. He confirmed that his opposition to the Aidit leadership evoked no response in the Party. The solitary nature of his opposition only illustrated the solidarity among the post-1951 leadership.[150]

From the available evidence, it appears that while the Aidit-Lukman-Njoto triumvirate retains its solidarity, and while the triumvirate's policies and tactics lead to continued PKI advances, there is little possibility of a breakdown in the twelve-year cohesion of Party cadres.

7. AN "ILLEGAL PKI"?

PKI claims to have maintained an "illegal PKI" from the end of the Communist rebellion of 1926-1927 to the return of Musso in August 1948.[151] With the outbreak of the Madiun rebellion in September 1948 and the Dutch occupation of the remaining Republican territory in Java in December, PKI was forced to go underground again. An "illegal PKI" was retained throughout 1950 to guide the legal PKI, the Indonesian Labor Party, and the Socialist Party. In other words, an "illegal PKI" had existed for all but one month of the 25 years preceding the January 1951 change in the PKI leadership. Since then there have been reports and rumors of two kinds of illegal PKI: active guerrilla bands, and secret groups which prepare for an eventual revolutionary situation. The purpose of the following paragraphs is to examine the scanty available evidence in order to estimate whether the Aidit leadership has undertaken the organization of one kind or both kinds of illegal PKI.

There is no doubt that armed bands were active in East Java during the first half of 1951. Feith and Kahin describe them as PKI-connected or PKI-financed.[152] These groups in East Java mostly ceased operations before the end of 1951, but an armed force in Central Java, known as the MMC,[153] carried out armed attacks until as late as 1955. Kahin goes so far as to claim that in 1952 the PKI leaders concentrated their armed bands into the MMC area "and gave intensive military and political training to youths brought in from East and Central Java for short periods on a rotating basis." [154] Some slight confirmation that the Aidit leadership was at least contemplating guerrilla warfare (and Aidit and Lukman had returned in July 1950 after eighteen months in China and with the Viet Minh) is given by the translation by PKI late in 1950 and early in 1951 of two foreign works on guerrilla warfare.[155]

The Communist leaders denied publicly any connection with the MMC,[156] and as early as May 1951 blamed the imperialists for the terrorism which was labelled Communist by the anti-Communists.[157] Furthermore, in an article intended for internal Party consumption only, the PKI leaders in July 1951 condemned the plundering of peasant property in the MMC area.[158] These protestations of innocence do not of themselves prove innocence. However, non-Communist political and government officials I spoke with in the Merbabu-Merapi area viewed the MMC as remnants of the Madiun rebels who held out for a while until their leaders were killed by the army or police. And it would be surprising if PKI could have brought many youths into the MMC area, trained them there, and then returned them to their home areas, without detection by the authorities or anti-Communists.

From the limited information available to me, it would appear that the Aidit leadership did not encourage the formation of PKI armed bands. Those that existed in East Java in the first half of 1951 quickly ceased operations, though it is not known if this was on instruction from the Party leaders or as a result of military pressure against them. The MMC is a separate and so far unsolved problem. Its leaders were Communists from before the Madiun rebellion who fled to the mountains when the rebellion failed. They apparently gained some adherents from poor peasants and demobilized troops, and operated more as bandits than the creators of a small liberation base. Due to army and police attacks the MMC mostly ceased operations by the end of 1952, and completely by the end of 1955. As yet I have obtained no concrete evidence of a command link between the Aidit leadership and the MMC leaders, or of Kahin's report that the MMC area was used to train numbers of Communist youths in political and military matters.

When viewed in the wider context of the national united front policy which the Aidit leadership pursued from about the end of 1951, it seems highly unlikely that the PKI leaders would have encouraged the MMC. The advantages were too small, the disadvantages too great. The MMC area was restricted, and could have been, and was, eradicated by relatively small numbers of troops. Furthermore, the PKI leaders could not risk the exposure of their part in the MMC terrorism, for this might have negated the painstaking work to create the image of PKI as respectable, democracy-loving, antiterrorist.[159]

The second kind of "illegal PKI" that has been persistently rumored since January 1951 is that of a network of secret groups preparing for an eventual revolutionary situation. Several newspaper reports seem to confirm the rumors. In November 1954, sixteen PKI members from Temanggung, Central Java, were imprisoned for recruiting a secret section of the Party which was to organize a "liberation army" to be used if PKI fared badly in the 1955 general elections.[160] The Djakarta weekly newspaper *Geledek* reported on May 31, 1959, that the headquarters of a "PKI-Malam" (Night PKI) had been raided by the authorities in Rembang, Central Java, and a number of weapons seized.[161] PKI-Malam was reported to have branches in Central and East Java and to be preparing for a rebellion to establish a people's democracy. The Jogjakarta newspaper *Nasional* carried a report on April 11, 1960, of the arrest and imprisonment in Pati (incidentally only some 25 miles from Rembang) of six persons, including five members of the Pati representative council, for holding a subversive meeting.[162] Materials confiscated at the meeting included notes and letters on "How PKI can carry out an armed movement in 1960," and a "3-day plan to replace the *bupati* and *pamong pradja.*"[163]

Many factors must be considered in attempting to unravel the rumors and reports of an illegal PKI that is preparing for eventual rebellion. First, it is logical that the PKI leaders should have prepared plans for the eventuality of being forced underground by government repression, and that it has at least a skeleton underground organization even if its projected members are at present working above ground. Second, the Sukiman government was unable to substantiate the charge of plotting to overthrow the government on which it arrested 2,000 Communists and Communist-supporters in August 1951. Nor have later governments or even anti-Communists revealed concrete evidence to support such a charge against PKI. Third, the creation of a PKI-Malam by PKI before legal political activity was repressed would destroy much of the image PKI has built of itself as an essential part of the national united front policy. On the other hand, if the possibility of severe repression seemed great the PKI leaders might consider the risk of establishing an underground PKI worth taking. But such a possibility did not loom large after 1951, with the doubtful exception of the brief period of the Masjumi-led Burhanudin Harahap cabinet. Fourth, the PKI-Malam as reported in *Geledek* could be comprised of members of the small groups of extremist, self-styled Communists such as belong to Ibnu Parna's Acoma. And, fifth, it is possible that PKI contains extremists, militant elements, who are dissatisfied with the national united front policy and have, without the sanction of the central leadership, established their own minor underground organizations.

In short, there is no concrete evidence that the Aidit leadership has organized an underground section of the Party which is preparing for the eventuality of revolution. Rather, the leadership will have made preparations for important cadres and for a skeleton force of middle and lower cadres to go underground in the event of severe government repression. Reports of PKI-Malam and similar organizations probably stem from the activities of non-PKI extreme leftists or of a small number of PKI members acting without the authorization of the central Party leadership.

COMMUNIST FUNDS IN INDONESIA

PKI is indisputably the wealthiest political party in Indonesia. It can afford to maintain more full-time organizers, publish more literature, and run more costly election campaigns than any other party. The purpose of this section is to examine the limited available material concerning PKI's income and expenditures. The income and expenditure of PKI in this analysis refers not only to the Party but also to the many Communist-led mass organizations, because together they constitute a financial as well as political unit.

PKI has been unable to tap those direct or indirect government sources which have provided most income for at least PNI and NU of the other major parties. The openly acknowledged sources of income for the Party and its mass organizations fall into five categories: Party membership dues, the membership dues of the mass organizations, donations, special fund-raising campaigns, and the wages of representatives in governmental bodies.

Under the April 1951 PKI constitution, membership dues were fixed on a sliding scale varying from about 0.33 per cent of income for the lower income brackets, to a minimum of 1.5 per cent for higher incomes.[1] This rate was reduced in the September 1959 constitution to 0.2 per cent for members in the lowest incomes, and a minimum of 1 per cent for those in the highest.[2] The entrance fee has remained unchanged as the equivalent of one month's membership dues. If the dues were collected regularly and fully, they would be an enormous source of income, especially after claimed Party membership passed the one million mark by the beginning of 1956. Various pieces of evidence would indicate, however, that the payment of dues is at a low rate and that those collected by the lower Party organizations are not forwarded in stipulated percentages to the higher committees.

An article by Anwar Sanusi in October 1956 shed light on the efficacy of the collection of dues in West Java.[3] Sanusi stated that the work of the West Java provincial committee was not being performed as well as it should, because not enough money was coming in. Of the 22 section committees in West Java at that time

only a few send money to the provincial committee every month or occasionally. The average amount that enters each month from the section committees does not reach 20 per cent of the amount that is really needed for the varied work of the provincial committee to be done well.

He added:

From some *kabupatens* and large towns, subscription money does not reach the higher committees, especially the provincial committee and central committee, or does so only in very small amounts, because . . . it is used up by the lower committees.

An article the following month by Isk of the Djakarta Raja committee[4] reported that "the Party in Djakarta Raja experiences almost the same situation" as that described by Sanusi. Isk complained of the belief, widely held within PKI, that members and candidate members need not pay membership and entrance dues because the Party could always receive money from people outside the Party. He also complained that some section committees and subsection committees considered it unimportant to forward membership fees to the higher committees.

Party leaders have continued to criticize deficiencies in the collection of membership dues,[5] and when I was in Java in 1959 and 1960 Party cadres indicated to me that the inflow of dues was still low.

The articles on West Java and Djakarta Raja touched upon a problem which has been serious in PKI: that the lower committees which collect the dues keep more than their share and pass on little or nothing to the higher committees. In order to eliminate this "wastage," the Central Committee issued an order at about the end of July 1956 that the 10 per cent of membership dues allotted for the Central Committee henceforth be forwarded directly by the subsection to the Central Committee instead of trickling upward via the section committees and provincial committees as formerly.[6] A Central Committee circular to all subsection committees in April 1958 stated clearly that not all subsections were fulfilling the earlier instruction.[7]

While the above information gives evidence of a certain weakness in Party discipline, it also indicates that the higher Party committees were not receiving from membership dues sufficient funds to operate properly.

In mid-1963 the Communist-led mass organizations for workers, peasants, youth, women, village officials, artists, and students claimed a combined membership of over twelve millions. Their membership dues constitute the second source of funds for the Indonesian Communist movement. But the difficulties experienced by PKI in collecting dues have been multiplied and magnified in the case of mass organizations. National, provincial, and local leaders of these organizations complained to me in 1959 and 1960 of the impossibility of collecting more than a tiny percentage of dues. This verbal generalization has been documented.[8] Some middle and lower cadres unwarily admitted in interview that the dues they collected covered but a minor part of the cost of operating their organizations at those levels. They certainly had little left to pass on to higher levels. From the available evidence, then, it appears certain that none of the Communist-led mass organizations receive even an important percentage of their operational costs from membership dues.

The third acknowledged source of funds for the Communist movement is donations. The 1951 PKI constitution lists among the sources of Party finances, "contributions from non-Party persons and groups." [9] This the September 1959 constitution reworded as "nonbinding contributions." [10] Similar clauses are contained in the constitutions of the mass organizations. Leaders of Pemuda Rakjat in East Java said in interview on May 9, 1960, that their four province-level full-timers relied on money and other help from "sympathizers" outside the organization. But although the constitutions and members of PKI and its mass organizations acknowledge contributions from sources outside their organizations, these sources and the amounts received from them have not been disclosed. It is on these points that the interested non-Communists do most speculation.

The fourth acknowledged source of funds, and an important one, is that of special fund-raising campaigns. Two kinds of fund-raising methods are used, although any one campaign may use both: the direct collection of money, and the collection of materials that can be converted into money.

Examples of the direct collection of money include the campaigns to finance the March 1954 Party congress, to build a permanent headquarters for the Central Committee, and to build PKI's house of culture. In order to finance the 1954 congress, Aidit ordered every Party member and candidate member to contribute at least one rupiah.[11] On December 11, 1953, the Central Committee Secretariat issued a further order that each Party member and candidate member give three rupiahs during a three-and-a-half-month period in order to finance a Central Committee building.[12] The Central Committee decided in August 1956 to collect funds for a PKI house of culture, and later claimed that four million rupiahs had been collected.[13] From the published information, however, it is not possible to ascertain how much of the funds raised in the campaigns were from Party members or should be placed in the category of donations from non-Party persons. But if the Party has found great difficulty in persuading its members to pay membership dues or its lower committees to forward those dues collected to higher committees, it seems fair to assume that similar difficulties are faced in the special fund-raising campaigns, and that donations from outside the Party constitute a sizable element. As part of its campaign to raise funds for the 1957 local elections, at least the East Java provincial committee obliged each member and candidate member to collect money or produce, such as rice, bananas, coconuts, and cassava, from persons outside the Party.[14]

Most PKI members and sympathizers are poor and unable or unwilling to give money to the Party. Fund-raising has therefore had to take on special forms. In order to help finance the 1955 and 1957 election campaigns, members collected old sacks, oil bottles, old newspapers, ink bottles, stamps, old clothes, old tins, as well as produce; and groups were organized to catch fish and green frogs, collect sand and stones from the rivers, and gather banana leaves. The results of their labor were sold to the benefit of the Party.[15] The PKI also instituted the "Party tree," "Party hen," "Party sheep," and so on, system under which Party members plant a fruit tree or coconut tree or raise a bird or animal for the Party, and give the produce to the Party for sale [16]—a system also used by BTI.[17]

The best-documented PKI fund-raising campaign was that for the September 1959 national congress,[18] though again it is impossible to ascertain how much was raised from the Party and how much from outside. Not only were 3.5 million rupiahs in cash collected, but the delegates were provisioned, at least in part, by produce gathered by the Party and its mass organizations.[19] When the congress was concluded, over 2.5 million rupiahs surplus remained, which was then used to extend the Central Committee building and help finance the Party house of culture.[20] Although less produce was collected for the

Seventh National Congress in April 1963, over 5.5 million rupiahs were gathered. Five million of these were surplus to the cost of the congress and went into the fund for a new Central Committee building.[21]

Each of the Communist-led mass organizations also holds special fund-raising campaigns for conferences and congresses, and, from its own evidence, finds it far easier to obtain money for specific and only occasional purposes than for regular membership dues. These special campaigns, however, are not always successful. For example, the BTI leaders complained in March 1957 that the debts incurred for its September 1953 congress were still not settled.[22] And in August 1960, the PKI leadership sent out urgent instructions to all Party committees to assist Pemuda Rakjat in raising funds for its forthcoming congress.[23]

A fifth source of funds for the Communist movement in Indonesia is the wages of the PKI and mass organization representatives in parliament, in the Constituent Assembly, in local representative councils, and now in the Supreme Advisory Council, the National Planning Council, and the People's Consultative Assembly.[24] All PKI members who hold positions in the name of the Party must hand their wages to the Party and receive in return an honorarium.[25] Members of local representative councils are paid according to the number of meetings they attend, but in 1960 averaged about 400 to 500 rupiahs per month. This amount was the bare minimum required outside Djakarta to maintain a full-time middle or lower cadre. Members of the councils' executive committees earned much more. Because council work takes only a small amount of time, PKI full-time cadres who are also members of councils are in fact financed by the councils, and those council members with other jobs can hand over all their council wages to the Party.

The three main fields of expenditure for the Communist movement in Indonesia are: the routine work of running the Party and the mass organizations; special activities such as congresses, conferences, and the celebration of national and international anniversaries; and election campaigns.

One of the major items in the cost of the routine work of the Party and its mass organizations is the full-time personnel. The size of this personnel is a closely guarded secret, and any estimates are necessarily tentative in the extreme. In September 1959, PKI claimed to have in Java alone an organization in 18,722 villages and 1,430 *ketjamatans*.[26] At higher levels, the Party constitution provides for section committees in each *kabupaten* and municipality, of which there are 99 in

Java and 256 in all Indonesia. In Djakarta Raja in mid-1957 there were 19 section committees,[27] and the larger towns of Java each have several. At the time of the Sixth Congress in September 1959, there were about 22 major district and island committees. The number of full-timers in the different committees varies widely from area to area. In some areas each village committee has a full-timer, but in others even the section committees are without one. It would probably be close to the truth to say that there are between two and five thousand full-time Party workers, including cadres and typists.

Parallel to the Party full-timers, and often interwoven with them because cadres are often full-timers for the Party and one or more of the mass organizations, are the full-time workers of the mass organizations, numbering probably several thousands.

I was told by many non-Communists wherever I traveled in Java that a PKI full-time worker at the village or urban neighborhood level received between 500 and 1,000 rupiahs per month.[28] Observation of the clothes and homes of some of the medium-level full-timers of the Party and its mass organizations showed that they were far below middle-class standards, and indicated a monthly income of perhaps 500 rupiahs. To the cost of the full-timers' wages must also be added their travel expenses and also the cost of maintaining and equipping offices. The total in 1960 must have been at the very least two million rupiahs per month, remembering that some full-time Party workers received wages from the governmental bodies.

Within what might be termed routine expenditure is the financing of national and local schools and courses.[29] Some indication of the cost incurred in the field of education is given by examples from SOBSI. At the beginning of January 1957, the SOBSI national council announced that a campaign was to be completed by the end of February to collect the 1 to 2 million rupiahs necessary to open SOBSI's cadre school.[30] In 1958 and 1959 the SOBSI headquarters held twelve shifts of the national school, training in all about three hundred cadres who stayed in Djakarta for the month's duration of a shift.[31] The cost of the national school was not disclosed, but the total cost of the education program for SOBSI alone is indicated by figures for East Java.[32] From 1958 to May 1960, the East Java SOBSI provincial council organized 7 cadre courses of one month's duration. The cost averaged 25,000 rupiahs for each course (or 833 rupiahs per course member), of which the Ministry of Labor paid 10 per cent.[33] These scraps of information give some indication of how great must be the total cost of the schools and courses organized by PKI and its mass organizations at several levels of the organizations.

A second major item of expenditure is publishing. PKI came to publish a vast array of periodicals, booklets, and pamphlets besides the daily newspaper. Most of the mass organizations published at least a periodical and occasional booklets and pamphlets.[34] What evidence there is on the financing of the publications indicates that income has trailed far behind costs. The PKI monthly *Bintang Merah* was forced to cease operations from December 1951 to August 1952 with a debt of 20,000 rupiahs; and in January 1953 the Central Committee published a list of thirty Party committees with debts to *Bintang Merah* and thirty-six to *PKI-Buletin*.[35] The Indonesian Peace Committee's periodical *Damai* (*Peace*) incurred a deficit of 8,077 rupiahs in the first five months of existence from November 1952 to March 1953, with total income only 650 rupiahs.[36] The national council of SOBSI revealed that from January to October 1955 it had expended 100,603 rupiahs on publications but received only 60,731 rupiahs from them, while the national council of its estate workers' union had spent 105,772 rupiahs and received 29,381.[37] It also revealed that during 1955 the national council of its railways workers' union on average each month had spent 27,000 rupiahs and received 17,000 rupiahs for publications. Before January 1955 the average income of the SOBSI national council for publications had been only 10 per cent of the expenditure. In March 1957 the income for the SOBSI periodical *Bendera Buruh* was only 40 per cent of its cost.[38] In December 1957 Gerwani declared that it had a debt of "tens of thousands of rupiahs" to the printers.[39] Pemuda Rakjat was forced by financial difficulties to cease the publication of its chief periodical.

Only two figures are available as to the cost of the various congresses or conferences: BTI estimated before its September 1957 congress that it would cost 200,000 rupiahs, and the 1959 and 1962 PKI congresses cost 500,000 rupiahs each.[40] The Communist movement in Indonesia celebrates with much show several national and international anniversaries, including May Day, May 20 (the Day of National Awakening), May 23 (foundation of PKI), August 17 (national independence day) and November 12 (the outbreak of the 1926 Communist rebellion). The cost of the celebrations has not been published, but must be considerable for the often lavish decorations and receptions.

No figures have been published on the cost to PKI of the 1955 and 1957 election campaigns. In 1955 PKI spent far more than any other party on such items as large billboards and small cards showing the Party symbol, on travel expenses for the Party leaders, on carnival-like "peoples festivals" and the celebration of anniversaries, on the printing of pamphlets and brochures, and on the large-scale use of full-time paid election workers.[41] The Socialist Party leader Sjahrir estimated that PKI probably spent 200 million rupiahs on the 1955 campaigns.[42] PKI spent even more proportionately than the other parties in the 1957 local elections. One astute non-Communist in Jogjakarta told me that he had heard that PKI spent five million rupiahs in the Jogjakarta Special District—an area with only 976,948 of the 27,130,661 voters in Java.

Although the evidence is sketchy, it seems that PKI must have spent at least 200 million rupiahs on the 1955 and 1957 election campaigns. This figure might be reduced if one takes into account the large amount of voluntary and free labor that could be mobilized by PKI and its mass organizations. But it remains a substantial figure and one which, in the opinion of non-Communist Indonesians and foreign observers, could not possibly be extracted from members of the Party and its mass organizations who are for the most part poor peasants and town dwellers for whom 6 to 12 rupiahs was a day's wage.

After the above examination of the limited information on the sources of income and items of expenditure of PKI and its mass organizations, it would appear correct to state that the Indonesian Communists rely on "contributions from non-Party persons and groups," on "nonbinding contributions," for a sizable proportion of their income. The other sources do not appear to provide even half of what is expended. Who, then, are these non-Party donors? Visible, but limited, assistance is given by the Soviet Union, China, and other Soviet bloc countries whose books, periodicals, and pamphlets, usually in Indonesian, are sold in all Communist bookshops. Presumably the bookshops are given a good profit margin on this literature. Another way the Soviet bloc countries assist the Indonesian Communists is by financing delegations to visit the Soviet bloc. But the main source of non-Party contributions appears to be the more than 3 million Chinese (mostly Indonesian nationals) living in Indonesia.

Kahin states that PKI taps the Chinese business community for "substantial funds." [43] Some Chinese pay willingly, he writes, but "undoubtedly they usually do so because of persuasion or pressure from the Chinese embassy or pressure from the Communist-controlled labor unions and the threat of retaliatory action in case of noncompliance." Feith believes that the greater part of PKI's 1955 election campaign funds came "from individual Chinese businessmen resident in Indonesia, and very possibly also from overseas Communist governments through their consular and business representatives in Djakarta." [44] Doak Barnett reported in 1955 the generally held belief in Indonesia that the contributions from Chinese businessmen "make up a significant source of its [PKI's] ample political funds." [45] In Djakarta, Jogjakarta, Surakarta, and Surabaja, the information I received from non-Communists confirmed what Kahin, Feith, and Barnett had written.

The Chinese business community in Indonesia is large, far wealthier than the native Indonesians, but it is treated as alien by Indonesians in general, discriminated against by the Indonesian government, and would be unable to obtain police protection against, say, extortionary threats by a trade-union. At the same time, some Chinese youngsters are full of enthusiasm for the new China and Communism. It would be most surprising if PKI did not exploit this source of funds. The non-Communist parties have been financed, in general, from the proceeds of government corruption and from large individual donations, and are therefore in no position to criticize PKI for tapping the Chinese businessmen.

I know of no concrete evidence of PKI's receiving funds from the Communist embassies, legations, and trade missions. Feith, however, did report that in 1952 the Chinese embassy gave both money and literature to the Party;[46] and in 1960 a Russian Intourist agent was arrested on the charge of smuggling several million rupiahs *into* Indonesia for purposes unknown.

To summarize, PKI and its mass organizations incur, for routine and occasional matters, an expenditure far exceeding the expenditure of any other political party in Indonesia. But although PKI and its mass organizations have succeeded in extracting from their members some membership dues and perhaps more funds for special purposes, the total income from these sources is far below total expenditures. The deficit is made up by donors, mostly non-Party persons as few Communists are wealthy. PKI cannot tap government sources of wealth, and it seems reasonable to believe that a substantial part of Indonesian Communist funds is derived from the large Chinese business community and also possibly from the foreign Communist missions in Indonesia.

Part four
BUILDING MASS SUPPORT

XI

THE CULTIVATION
OF GENERAL APPEALS

As the Aidit leadership embarked on the implementation of the national united front policy, it hoped to win mass support primarily among the workers, the peasants, and the petty bourgeoisie. Winning this support would depend ultimately on the Party's ability to represent effectively the specific material interests of these groups, and much of the Party's efforts, especially through its mass organizations, have been directed toward such representation. But the Aidit leadership had a prior task: to make the Party generally acceptable to the potential Communist supporters, and to the leaders of the non-Communist forces whose toleration and alliance were deemed necessary if PKI was to accomplish its organizational and political goals. The potential supporters were, in general, the poorer Indonesians, imbued with nationalism and with the value of discussion and consensus, as opposed to conflict and division, while many of them were religious. The potential political allies were strongly nationalist, and some were strongly Moslem. From 1951, then, the Aidit leadership directed much of the Party's propaganda and activities to building a favorable image of PKI as a nationalist, anticolonial party, as a party sympathetic to religion, as a responsible party, opposed to the use of violence in the pursuit of political objectives, and as the resolute defender of democracy. That PKI lacked this image at the beginning of 1951 was partly the result of the Madiun rebellion, in which the Communists had attacked the central government during the war against the Dutch, and in which they had murdered many *santris*. In short, without this favorable image it would have been very difficult, probably impossible, to win mass support, and from this to build a mass party, and it would have been impossible to win the alliance of the non-Communist political forces.

The first task of the Aidit leadership was to disprove the accusations that the Madiun rebellion had been an antinational insurrection. In September 1950, shortly after the return of Aidit and Lukman to the Party leadership, PKI published an account of Madiun which set the lines for a new, patriotic interpretation.[1] It denied that a rival Republican government had been formed at Madiun, that the national flag had been lowered, and the national anthem banned. The "affair" had become bloody only when President Sukarno ordered the elimination of the Communists and their allies, who then fought in self defense. In later years, refinements were added to the new version of the "affair."[2] At Madiun anti-imperialists and true patriots were mercilessly butchered by those ready to treat with the imperialist enemy; American imperialists had planned the provocation which forced the heroes of Madiun to fight in self defense; and the real Indonesian instigators of the provocation turned out to be Hatta, Sukiman, and Natsir, and not Sukarno, whose name was omitted from post-1951 versions of the "affair."

The evidence suggests that the PKI leaders were pleading their case before a largely sympathetic public. It was easy to establish the Party's anti-Dutch character, which had been demonstrated on many occasions since 1920. Many non-Communist political leaders believed that there certainly had been provocation before the rebellion began. And most Indonesians, especially those in the groups PKI has sought to attract, had little access to news at the time of the rebellion, so that, except among the more *santri* population, the anti-Communist version of the rebellion would not have been heard or, if heard, not given much credence. It is important to note that the Madiun area remains a Communist stronghold, that is, that the peasants and workers in the area of the rebellion itself did not consider the "affair" an antinational insurrection. But the Communist leaders still felt the need to present their version of Madiun in a manner that would free them from any taint of antinational activity.

The revamping of Madiun was the logical prelude to the Aidit leadership's attempt to portray PKI as the most patriotic of parties. After the revolution against the Dutch, which ended only in December 1949, the level of Indonesian nationalism ran high. Most politically-aware Indonesians still considered their country's sovereignty to be restricted or threatened by the remnants of Dutch power, whether in the form of economic power or in the form of the continued occupation of West Irian. PKI was obliged to identify itself with the popular mood. In a speech of May 23, 1952, Aidit declared:

For the Communists, service to the Party, to the national interest, to the interests of the homeland and to its people is one and indivisible. If a Communist does not serve the interests of the nation, of the homeland and of the people, it means that he does not serve the interests of the Party and that he is not a good Communist. . . .

Every Communist is a patriot, and if there is a patriot who is not a Communist then the door of PKI is always open to receive him as a member.[3]

As positive proof of its patriotism, PKI has paid warm respect to the symbols of Indonesian nationalism: the national anthem, the national flag, the national language, nationalist anniversaries, the honoring of nationalist heroes, Pantjasila,[4] and the Proclamation Republic founded on August 17, 1945.[5] Beginning with the celebration of National Awakening Day on May 20, 1952, PKI joined with other political groups in organizing nationalist celebrations.[6] This coöperation has been maintained in succeeding years.

In keeping with their new-found nationalism, the PKI leaders during 1952 gradually reduced their attacks on President Sukarno. This change was inspired partly by the recognition that for the great majority of at least the Javanese, Sukarno enjoyed great personal popularity as a nationalist hero; and partly by the realization that, unlike Vice-President Hatta, he was not avowedly anti-Communist but was, if anything, opposed to the extreme anti-Communist forces. By the time of the 1955 election campaigns, PKI was even attempting to link the name of the great nationalist leader with itself. The need to effect the link increased after 1955 as Sukarno's power increased and as he became the major barrier to an assumption of power by the largely anti-Communist army leaders.

The Aidit leadership, despite its preference for denunciation of American imperialism, publicly accepted the popular estimate of what was the major imperialist threat to the country. Although attacks on the American imperialists were not halted, Aidit conceded in March 1954:

The first enemy of the Indonesian people, from the viewpoint of its great power in several spheres, particularly in the economic sphere, is Dutch imperialism. Therefore the national united front must be aimed in the first place at the liquidation of Dutch imperialism, and not at the liquidation of all foreign imperialism in Indonesia.[7]

Even as late as September 1959, after all Dutch enterprises had been seized by the Indonesian government, Aidit, while describing American imperialism as "the most dangerous enemy of the Indonesian people," nevertheless conceded to Indonesian nationalist feeling that "Dutch imperialism still constitutes the first enemy of the Indonesian people." [8]

The Communists' anti-Western position has stood them in good stead in their effort to demonstrate their nationalist fervor. For example, they attacked the Round Table Conference agreement from the first as a grave restriction on Indonesia's sovereignty, they accused the imperialists of aiding the anti-Republic Moslem rebels in West Java and Atjeh, and they heatedly denounced the alleged American, SEATO, and Kuomintang assistance to the PRRI-Permesta rebels from 1958 to 1961 as an attempt to overthrow the legitimate government and replace it by one subservient to the imperialists' interests. Toward the end of 1962 and in the early part of 1963, the plan to create a Malaysian Federation came under strong Indonesian attack. PKI was well to the fore in denouncing it as a British neocolonialist plot.

To prove to Indonesians in general that PKI shared Indonesian nationalism was a relatively easy task, but the Aidit leadership was faced with the much more complex problem of proving to the religious that PKI was sympathetic to religion. As early as May 1951, Aidit, speaking in Bogor, a heavily Moslem town, stressed that under communism religion would not be suppressed but would thrive, and that PKI certainly would not refuse to admit religious people into the Party.[9] From 1952 onward, PKI and its mass organizations have publicized annually their greetings for Idul Fitri, the Moslem feast marking the end of the Ramadan fast. At the same time, the PKI leaders have had to make it clear that they opposed Masjumi and the Darul Islam rebels not because they were Moslem, but because they were antinational and serving the interests of Indonesia's external enemies. In August 1953, for example, after PKI had attacked Masjumi and the Darul Islam rebels during the period of discussions that preceded the formation of the first Ali Sastroamidjojo cabinet, Aidit explained:

The accusation that PKI's anti-DI [Darul Islam] policy is the same as anti-Islam is a very dirty and a very stupid slander. In its statements PKI does not urge the disturbance of the Moslem religion, nor does it even oppose Masjumi people. PKI always urges its members to hold high freedom of religion, including the Moslem religion, and to coöperate with the members of all parties including Masjumi. . . .

Contrary to Masjumi, PKI clearly and resolutely defends freedom of religion, including the Moslem religion, because PKI's anti-DI policy is a policy of fighting the
groups that dishonor religion.[10]

During the 1955 general election campaign, in particular, Aidit urged
Party members to explain that PKI attacked Masjumi because it was
anti-Communist, not because it was a Moslem party.[11]

Besides proclaiming that they were not hostile to religion, the Communists actively sought to win the support of the religious people. It
was obvious that their efforts to do so would be hampered until they
could win the neutrality, or sympathy, of the *kiajis,* the Islamic religious teachers who held great authority among the Moslem masses.
There are some indications that PKI went out of its way to influence
kiajis. For example, a member of the South Kalimantan provincial
committee has described in an article how PKI in his region set about
winning over the local *kiajis.*[12] Party workers would send Communist
literature to those *kiajis* who like to read, they would deferentially
discuss political subjects with *kiajis* who like to talk and discuss, they
would join the *kiajis'* religious instruction classes and there politely
but skillfully propound the virtues of PKI, and they would participate
in social work of a religious nature (such as cleaning graves and repairing mosques and prayer houses) in order to consolidate the *kiajis'*
sympathy for PKI. In August 1957, it was claimed that such patient
work was producing results among the *kiajis.* "They are beginning to
say that PKI is good, and that this or that religious party is not good
and only uses religion as a mask, and so on." Some were already
disposed to vote for PKI.[13]

The Christian minority, which remains small and tightly integrated,
has not been an object of PKI recruitment to any extent, although
occasional efforts have been made to prove that "the aims and teachings of the Communists are in accord with the Bible's directives." [14]
But the Party leaders remain alert to the need to appear sympathetic to
religion, especially Islam. Lukman, speaking at the Sixth PKI Congress
in September 1959, reminded delegates that without a correct attitude
on the religious question, "the Party's united front work would face
more difficulties and obstacles and could even experience defeat." [15]

The same skill which the Aidit leadership employed in presenting
PKI as a staunchly patriotic party and one sympathetic toward religion,
was also employed to convey the impression that PKI was a fully
responsible party, ready to take its place in the building of a united
and nationalist Indonesia. The Party leaders have been concerned to
stress that PKI places the national good before its own interests as a
party, and that it therefore shuns the voluntary use of force as a politi-

cal instrument and welcomes the opportunity to work with the other
political forces, even with the "reactionary" parties if to do so would
benefit the nation. This professed concern for the good of the people
and nation as a whole has been the basis of the Party's appeals for all-
embracing governments of national unity. And as the PKI Central
Committee concluded in December 1960:

... in carrying out the national struggle we must hold firmly to the basic principle:
place the interests of class and of the Party below the national interest, or place
the national interest above the interests of class and of the Party.[16]

It has been easier for the PKI leaders to create the image of PKI
as "the party of the people" [17] because the Party has been excluded
from cabinet office since 1948.[18] They have been able to take up popular demands without the worry of having to implement them. As the
self-appointed spokesman of the people, PKI has advanced such demands as reductions in food prices, general increases in wages, the
adequate provision of basic consumer articles, increased educational
and health facilities, and a progressive taxation system directed against
foreign companies. It is important to note that each demand has been
presented as reasonable, and often has been accompanied by an outline of how it may be met. At another level, PKI has put forward proposals for improving Indonesia's economic policies. In March 1957,
to take an example, the economic department of the PKI Central Committee published a study to show how economic development could
be undertaken without calling on private foreign capital.[19] In November 1957, Runturambi of SOBSI and Aidit took part in a national
consultative conference on reconstruction,[20] while since the creation
in August 1959 of the National Planning Council, to which Communist
representatives were appointed, PKI has taken an important part in
the discussion of longterm national economic policies. The demands
and proposals put forward by PKI are contrived proof that PKI has
the interests of the whole people at heart, that it promotes these
interests in a responsible manner, not seeking merely to embarrass governments and ministers, and that PKI is ready and able to accept
responsibility in national administration. In short, PKI wants to be
respected as a responsible and restrained party, imbued with a strong
sense of the welfare of the people and of the nation as a whole.

The Aidit leadership has been at pains to explain that PKI, providing it is not attacked first, will never resort to violence to realize
its goals. As the leaders pledged in 1951, when several thousand Communists and Communist sympathizers had been arrested on an (unsubstantiated) charge of plotting to overthrow the government:

In the struggle to realize their political convictions, the communists will not use force while the ruling class still leaves the peaceful, the parliamentary way open. If there is the use of force, the spilling of blood, a civil war, it will not be the Communists who start them but the ruling class itself.[21]

These sentiments have been repeated down to the present,[22] and the PKI leaders have even eschewed the use of force in disputes between labor and management, peasants and landlords, and between itself and other political groups.[23]

Indeed, the Aidit leadership has tried not only to present PKI as a party willing to work within a parliamentary regime, but also as a protagonist of that regime, in fact, as a tireless defender of democracy. In October 1951, for example, PKI claimed that it was "the foremost defender of parliament's prestige, and always will be so," [24] while in May 1953, Aidit declared that "the Communist parties and the democratic parties can gather the masses around them only if the Party honors the banner of bourgeois democratic freedom that has been discarded by the bourgeoisie." [25] During 1951 PKI was one of the groups most vocal in calling for full democratic freedoms, and at the time of the October 17, 1952, "affair," it defended the parliamentary system as being "far better than the fascist military dictatorship system." [26] The defense of democratic liberties was an important theme in PKI propaganda during the 1955 election campaigns. Since 1956, with the rise of Sukarno and the army to dominant political position, there has been a gradual constriction of democratic liberties and of the power of parliament. PKI could not spring militantly to the defense of democracy because the Party was dependent upon its alliance with Sukarno in order to prevent stern anti-Communist measures that the army was believed to advocate. PKI has protested loudly and often, however, against the most flagrant infringements of democratic rights, and if its protests are more subdued than in previous years, they are still far more numerous and courageous than the protests expressed by PNI and NU leaders.[27] As a result, many millions of Indonesians have come to regard PKI as the most sincere and courageous defender of democratic liberties in general, and of the parliamentary system in particular.

XII

APPEALS TO SPECIFIC
SECTIONS OF SOCIETY

The winning of mass support involved the Aidit leadership in two basic tasks. I have discussed in the preceding section how the Aidit leadership endeavored to create among the social groups most likely to support the Party, an image of PKI as patriotic, as tolerant of and even sympathetic to religion, and as a responsible, peaceable party working within and defending parliamentary democracy. Such an image was designed to create a climate of opinion in which PKI could pursue with relative ease its second task, that of attracting and organizing mass support by representing the material interests of the different sections of "the people." The Party itself remained the focal organization, assimilating members and extending its organizational network as fast as possible. But because of the low level of political awareness of the Indonesian urban and rural poor in general, the Aidit leadership built nominally independent mass organizations as a means of mobilizing, if only for simple action, a vast body of sympathizers who would otherwise remain beyond the Party's influence. The mass organizations could also be relied upon to tap hitherto inaccessible resources of member and cadre talent for PKI itself, and apparently they became the chief source of new recruits for the Party.

Lukman made clear his party's concept of mass organizations in an article he wrote early in 1951:[1]

By mass organization we mean a non-political organization of the masses, of the people. A mass organization binds together several groups of the people according to their social position, for example: a workers' organization (trade-union), peasants' organization, youth organization, women's organization, and so on. Also included in the mass organizations are various social and cultural organizations. The mass organizations arise on the basis and stimulus of the most simple and direct interests of the respective groups of the masses. Thus a trade-union organization arises on the basis and stimulus of the simple and direct interests of its members . . . , and so on.

Lukman went on to declare that a mass organization should not have the same basis as the Party, that is, Marxism-Leninism, but

must be based on the ties of everyday social-economic needs and must be broad in nature. In order to meet these conditions, the most simple consciousness of the masses of the need to organize is sufficient to be the condition of membership of the respective mass organizations.

If Marxism-Leninism was maintained as a basis, two dangers would arise: either membership would be restricted to those who first agreed with and worked hard to understand Marxism, which would prevent mass membership; or Marxism-Leninism would not be maintained as a fighting faith, in which case its meaning "would become merely an empty slogan" and the working-class struggle led by PKI would be harmed. The purpose of the mass organizations, Lukman declared, was to make the masses aware of the importance of organization, "Even though it is the simplest awareness and based only on their own direct interests."

Lukman also defined the role of the Party vis-à-vis mass organizations. The Party must

give leadership to the mass organizations in their actions, which means to train and raise the awareness of their members. This is the task, the duty of the Party fractions in the mass organizations. The broader the mass organization, the more the masses can be united, the broader the masses we can influence and give leadership to. That is why every Communist must fight hard for the unity of each kind of mass organization. Splitting a mass organization is not the work of Communists but of Trotskyites and social democrats (socialists). Communists in mass organizations led by Trotskyites and social democrats . . . may not leave the mass organization because that would mean allowing the masses to continue under the leadership of persons who are truly the enemies of the people. We Communists must have the slogan: where the masses are, that is our place! Therefore we Communists cannot refuse to work in a mass organization, however reactionary it may be.

Finally, Lukman emphasized that although mass organizations should be nonpolitical, in fascist or colonial or semicolonial countries their struggle to achieve social-economic goals necessarily involved them in politics. Therefore:

. . . it is the Communists' basic responsibility gradually to train and to give progressive political leadership to all mass organizations. Therefore those persons are
clearly wrong who believe that the mass organizations cannot give "satisfaction"
to people who wish to participate in political action but are still unable to fulfil
the conditions for entering PKI.

Analysis of the activities of the Communist-led mass organizations
during the first twelve years of the Aidit leadership shows that their
political role has been broadly fourfold:

1. To gather the widest possible sections of society into organizations led by PKI, to arouse in them an awareness of the importance
of organization, to give them basic political education, and gradually
to discipline them.

2. To open new social and geographic areas to PKI penetration. One
or more mass organizations have been established where it would have
been impossible to establish PKI directly because of political ignorance
or opposition to communism. Their basic education in organizational
and political matters has then created a favorable environment for the
establishment of the Party itself.

3. To provide a source of Party members and cadres. The leaders
and cadres of the mass organizations are open or covert Party members;
they watch to see which of their activists are most susceptible to political education, and then gradually draw them into the Party.

4. To assist PKI in its political struggle. The mass organizations
have been used, for example, to gather votes for PKI by assisting in
the work of propaganda, organizing meetings, and mobilizing people
to go to the polls; to render support to PKI's position on various
matters or to PKI demands by petitions, demonstrations, telegrams,
letters, delegations, and the threat of strike action or general unrest;
and to impress and woo Sukarno by gathering large crowds for his
meetings, mobilizing large contingents for independence day parades,
and so on. The mass organizations are also expected to provide a
major source of strength for PKI in case the Party ever has to use force
in order to resist repression or bid for power.

The Party and its mass organizations work closely together in mutual
assistance. It is quite common for a cadre or activist to work for the
Party and for one or more mass organizations. In some areas the Party
organization has been established first, and has then used its cadres to
create mass organizations that widen the PKI sphere of influence and
control and that prepare the way for a further expansion of the Party
itself. In other areas, if the time is not yet ripe for the establishment
of the Party, the cadres have first set up one or more mass organizations that then prepare the ground for the Party organization. Not

enough information is available to estimate which is usually established first, the Party or the mass organization. It would appear, however, that in the first years of the Aidit leadership, when the Party feared government repression and had not achieved the respectability, association with Sukarno, and physical size (with a large number of trained Party cadres available) which it had by 1955, it was more usual for mass organizations to be established first. This was more especially so in the rural areas, where PKI had little organization before mid-1954. I received some information to indicate that in more recent years, in some areas where PKI and the mass organizations have been established for some time, the Party has taken over the work formerly done by its least efficient mass organizations such as BTI, the peasant organization.

The obligation has not been taken lightly for every Party member: "To serve the people, to consolidate the Party's connections with them, to study their wishes and correctly report these to the Party in time, and to explain Party policy to them." [2] The Aidit leadership has made great efforts to learn the desires and hopes of each section of society, the pressing problems they face in their daily lives. And it has created an extensive network of Party and mass organizations which can present organization, program, and course of action that seem capable of fulfilling the desires and hopes, of tackling the problems. The work of PKI and its mass organizations does not, however, give a full explanation of the success achieved in winning and organizing the support of many millions of Indonesians. The expansion of the Party organization has been facilitated by the apathy of the other parties toward organizational work at the grass roots. This apathy has been even more marked in their work of building mass organizations.

The following sections deal with the activities of PKI and its mass organizations designed to attract and organize support among the different sections of the Indonesian "people": workers, peasants, the petty bourgeoisie, youth, women, the ethnic groups and ethnic minorities, and the veterans of the revolution.

XIII

THE WORKERS

Communist leaders believe that the workers constitute the most revolutionary, the most reliable, and the most easily organized social basis of Communist support. In Indonesia after independence, unlike in China after 1927, no major barriers were placed between the Communist leaders and the workers. Therefore the Aidit leadership has given first priority to organizing the workers. As the PKI leaders acknowledged in their May Day message of 1958:

Since the source of the strength and of the cadres of the Communist Party lies primarily in the trade-union movement, it goes without saying that the foremost task of the Communists is to work in the trade-unions.[1]

The trade-union federation, SOBSI, has been built as the chief means of attracting and organizing the workers, and the following section is concerned largely with SOBSI and its member unions. Mention is also made of other means employed by the Aidit leadership to win the allegiance of the urban poor in general.

1. SOBSI

The Consolidation of PKI Control Over SOBSI

SOBSI had been founded in November 1946 as an all-embracing trade-union federation with the basic task of mobilizing the workers for the defense of the Republic. Before the Madiun rebellion it had a virtual monopoly in the field of organized labor within the Republic. Communists and non-Communists had been about evenly divided in its leadership, but no disputes had arisen between the two groups who were united by a feeling of leftist solidarity in the struggle to defeat the Dutch and to create a socialist Indonesia. This solidarity was broken by the rebellion, but Communists remained in control of the major part of the organization. Hence the problem for the PKI leaders after Madiun was not to establish a new trade-union federation, but to consolidate their position in SOBSI, to shape SOBSI into an efficient organization under complete Party control, and to extend its membership and organization.

When the rebellion broke out in September 1948, many of the Communist leaders in SOBSI either went into hiding or made their way to Madiun. Harjono, chairman of SOBSI, and Maruto Darusman, chairman of the largest member union, the estate workers' Sarbupri, were killed along with many other Communist trade-union cadres. But because SOBSI as an organization did not participate in the rebellion it was not declared illegal. Nineteen of the 34 member unions withdrew from the federation in protest against the involvement of some of its Communist leaders in the rebellion.

Discussions to reunite the unions were in progress when the Dutch attack on the Republic in December 1948 temporarily stopped all trade-union activity. In May 1949 efforts were resumed toward the creation of a single all-Indonesia trade-union federation. By the end of October 1949 SOBSI was again functioning. The newly reorganized leadership was already clearly PKI-dominated and the non-Communist acting chairman, Asrarudin, left the organization. In attempting to explain the Communist domination of SOBSI so soon after Madiun, Asrarudin has suggested two reasons: that many of the non-Communist individuals and trade-unions had withdrawn from SOBSI at the time of the rebellion and thereby increased the already high proportion of Communists in the SOBSI leadership; and that PKI won the allegiance of many trade-union cadres and activists by its ability to pay regular wages and to provide trips abroad as rewards for good service.[2] Other reasons must include the concentration of PKI efforts and personnel in SOBSI, in contrast with the other parties' lack of interest in trade-union work; and that PKI was the only party which appeared to be truly concerned with the interests of the workers and their activists.

On January 5, 1950, a nine-man SOBSI delegation, headed by Njono, left for China to study the workers' struggle there. It was not until November 19 that four of the delegates, including Njono, returned.[3]

The other five members remained longer. Presumably the members of the delegation underwent education in political and trade-union matters while in China, and on their return provided PKI with a well-trained leadership for SOBSI. Njono, 28 years old when he returned, took over the leading position in SOBSI and has retained it until the present.[4]

According to Kahin's analysis, by mid-1951 almost the entire membership of SOBSI looked to PKI for leadership, while most of the member unions were PKI-dominated, and the remainder PKI-influenced.[5] A few leaders refused to recognize the leadership of PKI, but they were quickly ousted.

SOBSI claims that some 3,000 of its cadres and members were imprisoned during the August 1951 arrests of government opponents.[6] But despite the arrest of PKI and SOBSI leaders, few branches of SOBSI or its member unions took protest action. This warned the PKI leaders that their control over SOBSI was not deeply rooted. Control of the top leadership was already fairly effective, but not yet of the middle and lower cadres. As a result, the PKI membership drive which began in March 1952 had as one of its major aims to bring under Party discipline a greater number of the middle and lower level cadres and activists of SOBSI and its member unions.[7] By November 1954, in the judgment of Boyd Compton, SOBSI's "top leadership is communist, its second-echelon leaders are communist or communist-dominated, and its rank and file are generally communist-directed."[8]

In the middle of 1960, when I was in Indonesia, it appeared that virtually all cadres of SOBSI and its unions were members of PKI, or, if not actually Party members, had been subjected to schools and courses arranged and taught by the Communist leaders. Communist control of the leadership of SOBSI had ensured that only persons who were Party members or had proved themselves amenable to PKI control were chosen as cadres and received promotion within the unions. For all others the channels of promotion were closed.

At the same time as being completely controlled by PKI, SOBSI maintains the fiction of being tied to no political party. However, of the 61 persons elected to the national council at the SOBSI congress of January 1955, over half were known to be members of the Party. In the September 1955 parliamentary elections eight members of the national council were elected on the "PKI and non-party" list, six as PKI members, and two as so-called nonparty men. The nine-man SOBSI central bureau elected in 1956 consisted of these eight members of parliament in addition to a well-known fellow traveler.

PKI has had to pay a price for the consolidation of its hold on

SOBSI. As Communist control became increasingly evident, many non-Communists withdrew, others were forced out, and the non-Communist parties began to establish their own trade-union organizations. The non-Communist unions are still disunited and organizationally weak, but the system of labor-dispute arbitration enforced by the government has permitted them to survive, and their effect of breaking the former SOBSI monopoly in the various labor fields seriously weakens the political usefulness of SOBSI—a question that will be discussed below.

THE GROWTH OF SOBSI

The official SOBSI claim is that as soon as the Round Table Conference agreement was signed in November 1949, SOBSI began a rapid expansion.[9] With the slogan "cancel the Round Table Conference agreement" and the basic demand for Lebaran bonus,[10] SOBSI won much support. Furthermore, many new unions sprang up in the former Dutch-occupied areas and then affiliated themselves with SOBSI. SOBSI branch offices were opened in virtually every *kabupaten* capital, and within a year of its reëstablishment in September 1949, SOBSI claimed to contain 25 vertical trade-unions, many local unions, and 2.5 million members. From 1950 until 1955 SOBSI continued to claim 2.5 million members, but the number of SOBSI branch offices increased from 117 in November 1951 to 125 two years later.[11] At the Second National Congress in January 1955 a membership of 2,661,970 was claimed, and 128 branch offices.[12] In September 1957 the central bureau announced that after the simplification of trade-unions, SOBSI now included 31 national unions; there were eight SOBSI regional offices and 150 branches.[13] As of November 1960, SOBSI claimed 2,732,-909 members, 165 branches, and 5 preparatory branches.[14] At the end of 1962, SOBSI claimed 3,277,032 members.[15]

The official SOBSI picture has been a total membership since 1950 of between 2.5 and 3.3 millions, virtually static, but a steady increase in the number of SOBSI regional and branch offices. The figures for the number of offices are presumably correct as they can be readily checked, but the membership claims have been widely challenged by non-Communist Indonesian and foreign observers. It is extremely difficult for an outsider to judge whether or not total SOBSI membership has declined since about 1951 due to the establishment of competing non-SOBSI unions in many fields, or if SOBSI membership has remained more or less static, advances among formerly unorganized workers balancing losses to the new non-Communist unions.[16]

In the early part of 1952, Goldberg estimated the total number of organized workers in Indonesia to be far less than 2 millions, with SOBSI's share 800,000 to 850,000.[17] Tedjasukmana, a former Minister of Labor, estimated in 1958 that some 3 to 4 million workers were organized, of which SOBSI accounted for more than 60 per cent,[18] or for at least 1.8-2.4 millions. Richardson, writing in October 1958, however, reported the estimate of "experienced observers" that the total number of organized workers may well have been below two millions.[19] Both Goldberg and Tedjasukmana had access to government and other materials, and their evidence would suggest a considerable increase in SOBSI membership between 1952 and 1958, and would indicate that SOBSI's earlier claims to large membership were bluff to lend weight to SOBSI's demands and PKI's political bargaining position. But, as Richardson's evidence indicates, much research is still required before any fairly accurate estimate can be made of trade-union membership.

STRENGTHENING SOBSI

Although SOBSI is a federation of national and local trade-unions, it endeavors not only to coördinate the policies of its member unions but also, through the SOBSI regional and branch offices, to coördinate, control and assist trade-union activities down to the local level.

All workers belonging to member unions are also considered as direct members of SOBSI. Ordinary members participate in the "basic organizations" of the trade-unions, and wherever there is more than one basic organization in one field of work, a coördinating committee is established. The ordinary trade-union members "in the various fields of work are coördinated and led by the SOBSI branch whose area is determined by the SOBSI regional council."[20] The regional councils have the dual task of coördinating and leading the member unions at the regional level, and of supervising the work of the SOBSI branches.[21] Among other duties, the national council assists in the simplification of member unions, assists and coördinates the central leadership bodies of the member unions, and gives leadership to the lower levels of the SOBSI organization in the implementation of the decisions of the national congress.[22] Both the SOBSI regional councils and branches also coördinate and assist the lower levels of the member unions in implementing SOBSI decisions.

In short, SOBSI is more than an ordinary federation of trade-unions, especially as the leadership of SOBSI and the member unions is unchallengeably in Communist hands. Major policy decisions are taken by the central leadership, which is part of the PKI leadership, and the SOBSI machinery is used to ensure the correct implementation of policy right down to the places of work. What might be termed the leadership role of SOBSI is balanced by the assistance SOBSI gives to the member unions in their everyday work—in such matters as administration, the creation and training of cadres, the maintenance and expansion of membership, the methods of solving labor disputes— while SOBSI by its very size can add weight to their demands and can also, presumably, assist those in financial need. The following paragraphs deal with the effort made to strengthen the SOBSI organization, which is also the effort to strengthen PKI's control over SOBSI and thereby over the SOBSI members.

A large number of cadres and activists of SOBSI and its member unions were brought into PKI during the first PKI membership drive which began in March 1952. Before 1956 the only thorough political and organizational training they received was from PKI itself; SOBSI and its member unions did no more than give their cadres organizational training in an incidental manner.

It was only in February 1956, when SOBSI was freed from the hectic work of the general election campaigns, that the national council decided that SOBSI should establish an education system reaching from the center to the branches.[23] The intention was to set up a SOBSI central school for cadres of the SOBSI regional councils and the national councils of member unions; SOBSI regional schools for cadres of the SOBSI branches and the member unions' regional councils; SOBSI branch courses for cadres of the member unions' branch councils and for leaders of the member unions' basic organizations; and schools organized by the national councils of the member unions for their own cadres.[24] On October 23, 1956, the central bureau, adapting for SOBSI the educational program drawn up in July for PKI, decided that the SOBSI schools and courses would teach four main subjects: the history of the labor movement, SOBSI's social and economic program, the national united front strategy, and problems of organization.[25]

In mid-November 1956 the SOBSI region council in Central Java opened its first cadre school. The central school went into operation in the first quarter of 1958. By the end of 1958, 133 students had received training in six "shifts" of the central school—each shift lasting one month, the students living in a hostel together and undertaking full-

138

time study during their shift.[26] A total of 21 school shifts had been held
at the regional level, branch courses had been begun in November and
December, a seminar on education had been arranged, and Sarbupri
and the railway workers' union had each held one shift of their central
schools. During 1959 the SOBSI central school held six more shifts,
bringing the total number of "graduates" to about 300.[27] The regional
and branch schools and courses were running smoothly.[28] Besides the
four main subjects, cadres and activists were also being taught Indonesian language and history, and general knowledge.[29]

This scale of cadre education must ensure not only considerable
PKI control or influence over the cadres of SOBSI and its member
unions, especially when the SOBSI education system is bolstered by the
PKI educational program for Party members, but also a considerable
increase in the skill of the cadres in their everyday work of attracting
and organizing the workers.[30] The massive SOBSI education program
also provides the means of creating new cadres from the rank and file:

For the rank and file there are opportunities to be acquainted with the basic
problems of the labor movement and with elementary rules of trade unionism. The
best among the membership are then given the chance to qualify themselves for
union posts. In this way talents are discovered and prospective cadres and leaders
are recruited from the rank and file.[31]

It goes almost without saying that no other Indonesian trade-union
organization has an educational program of any scale. Nor can any
other trade-union organization offer the reward and political indoctrination of the free trips to the Soviet bloc countries that have been
enjoyed by many tens of SOBSI cadres.

As part of the education program was the attempt to increase the
circulation of the SOBSI periodical *Bendera Buruh (Workers' Flag)*.[32]
In May 1957 circulation was only 5,500; this increased only slightly to
5,750 in April 1958, not a large number among a claimed membership
of 2.6 millions. A plan to have *Bendura Buruh* received in every basic
organization of the member unions by the end of 1958 was not fulfilled,[33] but it was claimed that during 1959 circulation was raised to
15,000.[34] In October 1960, *Bendera Buruh* suffered the fate of most
party and mass organization journals. It was suspended indefinitely.

The first comprehensive attempt to improve the SOBSI organization
was a one-year plan drawn up in September 1957 and implemented
during 1958.[35] It dealt with such matters as organizing ordinary members into groups, opening new SOBSI regional and *kabupaten* offices,
increasing the number of full-time cadres, and improving the collection of membership dues. By the end of 1958 it was clear that the

SOBSI leaders had grossly overestimated the efficiency of their organization and its ability to make rapid improvements.[36]

The formation of groups of ordinary members, begun with intensity in 1958, could be of great significance in binding the ordinary members to the union leadership and in increasing the participation of ordinary members in union activities. Group leaders are brought into the activities of the leadership of the basic organization: they participate in delegations to meet employers, they gather members to give explanations of union policy, to collect fees, and to read SOBSI publications and *Harian Rakjat* together, and they organize assistance to work comrades in times of need, such as deaths, marriages, and births.[37] But to what extent the groups of ordinary members have been formed and are active has not been revealed.

In the latter half of 1958, SOBSI, when PKI was doing the same in preparation for the First National Conference of Peasants and Fishermen, first undertook a "go down" campaign

in order to further strengthen the relations between the organization and the masses and between the higher and lower levels of the organization, as well as to avoid subjective methods of leadership not in accordance with the objective facts.[38]

One-year plans of organization were implemented in 1959 and 1960. On January 1, 1961, SOBSI launched its own three-year plan of organization, education, and culture. In the field of organization, the plan sought to consolidate SOBSI control of transport and agrarian workers, to extend membership among *betjak* drivers, fisherman laborers, and workers in trade, to improve finances, to effect a "go down" movement among cadres, and to increase the efficient functioning of the organization.[39] The plan also called for the "mass political education" of 150,000 activists in the basic union organizations; the goal was for them to "know action, know production, know organization, and know the revolution." [40] Choirs and sports teams were to be formed, the former to sing revolutionary songs.

Considerable progress was made on the plan during 1961 and 1962.[41] In these first two years membership of SOBSI unions was increased by 544,123 to a total of 3,277,032. In the basic union organizations 30,703 activists had been given education, and 5,278 teachers had been trained for education work at this basic level. In 1962, 19,964 workers completed SOBSI anti-illiteracy courses; eleven new choirs were formed, and 145 new sports teams. For 1963, SOBSI leaders intended to intensify the political education of activists, and to provide cadres with special training in business economics.

Finally, it is important to make some estimate of the full-timers working for SOBSI and its member unions because it is the existence of a large body of relatively well-paid and well-trained full-timers enjoying adequate promotion possibilities that distinguishes SOBSI from the other trade-union organizations and that greatly facilitates SOBSI's work of organizing the masses and attracting potential cadre material. The evidence is fragmentary, but less so than that for PKI or the other Communist-led mass organizations.

In the SOBSI headquarters in Djakarta there were, in the early part of 1960, 50 full-timers including the odd-job men, the women cleaners and cooks, and the chauffeurs for the two cars.[42] The number of full-timers at the regional and branch levels varied greatly because, in general, the SOBSI regions and branches parallel the government administrative divisions which embrace widely different total populations and numbers of workers. In East Java, a relatively well-organized region with claimed total of 510,000 SOBSI members, in mid-1960 there were 9 full-timers in the provincial office, and 15 in the Surabaja city office; in each of the 29 branch offices there was an average of two full-timers.[43] In the Jogjakarta Special District, with a larger population than Surabaja but far fewer trade-union members, the SOBSI branch office had 9 full-timers,[44] while a visual examination of the office showed that several of these were female clerical staff. Evidence supplied by SOBSI leader Munir suggests that the number of full-timers in the member unions is high.[45] In December 1958 he reported that the basic organizations of government trade-unions and small unions in private concerns had no full-timers, but that those in large private concerns, such as estates, and the sugar and oil industries, in general had them; the coördinating committees for the basic organizations in unions in private concerns generally had at least one full-timer. In November 1960 there were "about 7,000 basic organizations." [46]

Thus, within Java SOBSI itself maintains a large staff at the center and in the large cities, and an average of perhaps two full-timers for each of the approximately 100 to 130 branches in the island. This would mean about 300 SOBSI full-timers in Java alone, added to which is the number of full-timers of the member unions which must reach well over 1,000 and probably much higher. With this now well-trained and indoctrinated cadre force, SOBSI, and therefore PKI, is able to organize over 50 per cent of the unionized Indonesian workers and mobilize them for PKI's political advantage. But before examining the work SOBSI and its member unions have done in order to win their members, a brief section will indicate the major SOBSI unions so as to show where SOBSI and PKI have their greatest strength among the workers.

THE SOBSI MEMBER UNIONS

The SOBSI unions are not restricted to the towns. Some of the largest unions "are composed of people who are still bound to village and country life with its traditional social ties": [47] Sarbupri, the estate workers' union, SBG, the sugar workers' union, and Sarbuksi, the forestry workers' union. In the first years after 1950, when Sarbupri was still the only important estate workers' union, membership claims of 700,000 were made. More reasonable were those for 370,000 and 390,000 made in October 1956.[48] The SBG, founded on March 3, 1946, claimed 305,000 members in 1957, including seasonal and nonactive workers; [49] Sarbuksi in January 1962 claimed 250,000 members,[50] but many of these too would be seasonal workers. Other SOBSI unions with large memberships that include a high number of seasonal and rural workers are: SEPDA, founded in June 1947 for workers and employees of local government at the *kabupaten* and municipality level, with a claimed membership of 99,000 in March 1963; and SBPU, for construction and general workers, with 51,000 in April 1963.[51] All of the above five unions have proved important channels by which Communist cadres and sympathies as well as the rudimentary consciousness of class and of the importance of organization have entered the rural areas.

Control of transportation would be a vital weapon in the event of a political crisis in Indonesia, and with the trend toward a possible showdown between PKI and the army, the PKI Sixth National Congress in September 1959 called for improved work among the transport workers.[52] The largest of the SOBSI transport workers' unions is that for railwaymen, SBKA, founded in March 1946, and claiming 70,000 members in March 1962.[53] About the same size is SBPP, formed in 1950 as a merger of several seamen's and harbor workers' unions, and in December 1962 claiming 70,000 members.[54] SBKB, for chauffeurs, truck drivers, and other workers in motor transport, claimed 40,000 members in 1962. In 1955 the SOBSI post, telegraph, and telephone workers' union claimed 50,000 members, but lost most of these when a rival non-Communist union was established in 1956. SERBAUD, for workers and employees in air transport, has less than 3,000 members.

In the industrial sphere, SOBSI unions are strong among textile workers, oil workers, miners, cigarette workers, and metal industry workers. The textile and clothing workers' union, including *batik* workers, claimed 94,000 members in April 1963.[55] The oil workers' union claimed 60,000 members in July 1950 when it was formed as a merger of four vertical and two local unions; in 1963 it claimed only 30,000.[56] The miners' union claimed 19,570 members in 1956, the cigarette workers' union 70,000 in 1962, and the metal industry workers' union 10,190 in 1960.[57]

Of the approximately 800,000 government officials and employees, not including "workers," SOBSI claims that 531,946 are members of 40 SOBSI unions.[58] Among the more important SOBSI unions of government employees is the union for Ministry of Defense employees, with a claimed membership of 80,000.[59] A small but perhaps in the long run politically important union is the SB Kependjaraan of prison workers and employees. This union has no competitor. In April 1958 it claimed 8,736 members in 217 prisons, out of a total of 10,500 employees in 344 prisons and prison offices. Three years later it claimed 10,000 members.[60]

Another SOBSI union worthy of note is Sarbufis, for film and stage workers, with a claimed membership of 6,000 in 1960.[61] Included in Sarbufis are actors of *ketoprak*,[62] a popular traditional Javanese drama form which is often given contemporary political content.

THE "MODERATE" SOBSI POLICY [63]

During 1950, 1951, and the early part of 1952 the SOBSI leaders sought to foment militant action against the employers through the exploitation of the workers' genuine grievances at miserably low wages and gravely deficient work conditions and social security. A halt to this "sectarianism" was called in a PKI Central Committee resolution of March 1, 1952, which elaborated the role SOBSI was to play in the newly evolved national united front policy.[64] The halt was consistent with the Aidit leadership's conclusion that it must discard its radical character in order to attract wide support among the politically quiescent masses and to win the toleration or alliance of the relatively far stronger non-Communist political forces in Indonesia. SOBSI was to organize the broadest possible section of the workers, coöperate with the non-SOBSI unions, and even maintain friendly relations with other social classes.

According to the Central Committee resolution, "The workers' front must constitute the strongest, most united, most progressive, and most conscious front in the broad national united front." [65] In order to attract the mass of workers and also establish good relations with other trade-unions and the employers,

the sections of the working class that are already militant must purge themselves of sectarian diseases and of empty "left" slogans. . . . Sectarianism is a disease that must be ceaselessly and violently eradicated. Only by the removal of sectarianism can the sections of the working class who are already militant attract the mass of workers who are still backward, and draw the entire people into the struggle for peace and national independence.[66]

Even a strong workers' united front, including a large number of militant workers and coöperation toward common goals between SOBSI and non-SOBSI unions, would not be sufficiently strong, so the PKI Central Committee resolution claimed, to withstand the imperialists and internal reactionaries. Therefore the workers' front (which in fact meant SOBSI and any alliance between SOBSI and other unions) had to establish and maintain good relations with other classes. This could only be done by toning down the workers' actions, by union support for the demands of other classes, and by winning the friendship of the national employers.

The Central Committee called on the workers to ensure that any action they took fulfilled three conditions: that it was considered correct and just by the majority of the people and so received their sympathy and support; that it was begun where the possibility of success was great; and that it was begun and concluded at the correct time. But at the same time as limiting their own demands and the militancy of their actions, the workers had to lend support to the demands of other classes who should be included in the national united front:

Through actions of solidarity, through sympathy strikes and other forms of political action that are intelligible, that can receive the sympathy of and be supported by the broad masses, the Indonesian workers will steel the fighting unity of the masses, and will gradually emerge to the fore as the defender of democratic rights and freedom, the champion of peace, the leader, the uniter of all groups of the people and the builder of the national united front.[67]

The workers, as an instrument of the Party's national united front policy, were even instructed by the Central Committee resolution to strive to remove any hostility felt toward them by the national industrialists. The workers had to explain that sometimes they would demand improvements, but at the same time they would assist the national industrialists in their struggle against imperialist monopoly and explain that a people's democracy, the workers' political goal, would guarantee the existence of the national industrialists.

A SOBSI national conference from September 27 to October 12, 1952, accepted the role of SOBSI within the national united front policy. "Sectarianism and the 'closed-door' policy were thrown far away." [68] A new constitution was adopted, to be endorsed by the Second National Congress in January 1955, which deleted all terms that sounded communistic, such as "socialism," "democratic centralism," "people's democracy," and "class struggle," "because they have created a division between the SOBSI unions and those who belong to no trade-union federation." [69] The SOBSI central bureau explained that the 1947 constitution had stated SOBSI's intention "to mobilize all workers to achieve a socialist society," but because the revolution had failed,

the duty of the Indonesian workers now is not to oppose capitalism and build a socialist society, but, together with the peasants, the petty bourgeoisie and the non-compradore national bourgoisie, to oppose imperialism and build a people's democratic society as the first step . . . towards a socialist society.[70]

B. O. Hutapea, prominent in both PKI and SOBSI, wrote an article in September 1952 which explained the new line taken toward the national industrialists.[71] He repeated the PKI argument that small and medium capital, which is usually Indonesian, developed an opposition to giant capital and could therefore side with the anti-imperialists.

The proletariat must be able to mobilize this strength [of the small and medium capitalists], not only by supporting the economic and social demands of the national industrialists . . . but also by limiting the demands of the workers who work in their enterprises, though without neglecting the workers.

Under the new constitution drawn up by the 1952 conference, membership of SOBSI was opened to "all organized workers, through their respective trade-unions, . . . irrespective of ethnic origin, descent, sex, religion and political conviction." [72] The fiction of SOBSI's political independence has been meticulously maintained down to the present. In November 1957, for example, the SOBSI leaders claimed that in SOBSI "we see each person is free to choose the party he likes. We have persons from Masjumi, PKI, PNI and so on, and a large part are non-party persons." [73] At the same time the leaders further claim:

The attitude of SOBSI towards the parties is determined by the political activities of the parties for the interests of the workers in general. . . . The sympathy of SOBSI and the workers for PKI is because PKI in words and deeds is always active in fighting for the workers' interests. This attitude of SOBSI is also held towards other parties that carry out a program that benefits the workers.[74]

Presumably this fiction of political independence must be aimed to deceive the rank and file members and potential members who are non-Communist but not politically conscious. It could hardly be expected to deceive non-Communist politicians and trade-unionists. Probably another purpose of this fiction is officially to dissociate SOBSI from PKI so that if the latter were to be subjected to repression, SOBSI could claim immunity as a politically independent organization.[75]

Since 1952 the SOBSI leaders, implementing the national united front policy, have been unwilling to antagonize either the government or the national employers. In the words of the central bureau report to the September 1957 national conference:

All persons and groups, irrespective of political affiliation, religious conviction, ethnic group, and party, who are not proved to be agents of Dutch monopoly and who are not proved to be agents of the warmongers, are the friends of the workers.[76]

Only those who had proved themselves to be "very reactionary" were to be combated, while toward others "we must avoid excessive demands" in the interests of the broadest possible unity. Njono, speaking to the national council at the end of December 1958, elaborated on the theme of different categories of antagonism within society and the different methods to be employed for their solution: contradictions that arose between the workers and the armed forces, the current cabinet, and the national businessmen, were not major ones.[77] They should be solved by "democratic means" in order to strengthen the national unity required to solve the most fundamental contradiction, that between the Indonesian people and imperialism.

From the formation of the first Ali Sastroamidjojo cabinet on August 1, 1953, until the end of 1959, with the exception of the brief period of the Masjumi-led Burhanudin Harahap cabinet, SOBSI carefully avoided blaming the government for the deteriorating economic situation, instead blaming the imperialists and their agents. What is more, the SOBSI leaders frequently stated their desire to assist in the economic development of the country. In November 1957 the SOBSI national conference declared of the government's five-year plan that "the trade-unions must assist in its accomplishment," and stated SOBSI's policy to be that of "struggle within the framework of the country's economic development"; [78] in the same month a SOBSI representative participated in the government-sponsored national consultative conference on reconstruction; [79] and in August 1959 a SOBSI representative took his place on the Sukarno-appointed National Planning Council entrusted with the task of formulating a comprehensive plan for national development. After the government take-over of Dutch enterprises in December 1957, both SOBSI and PKI pledged their support to the efforts to keep them running.

Concerning the nongovernment Indonesian employers, SOBSI has not only limited its demands upon them, but has continued to declare that its unions "always assist the national industrialists to overcome the difficulties facing them." [80] SOBSI even has stated its desire to raise productivity and efficiency in their enterprises on the basis of mutual profit.[81] Such magnanimity could be carried too far, however, and the PKI leaders rejected the idea of an increase-production movement to welcome the Sixth Party Congress on the grounds that such a movement "could even be a good deed for the bourgeoisie or for the enemies of the people, so that it could harm the people." [82]

At the PKI congress in September 1959 Aidit once again expressed concern at the danger of radical labor action.[83] He said that economic instability, a decline in the people's standard of living, the threat of mass dismissals, and efforts to reduce trade-union rights had caused "unrest among the working masses and may result in desperate or extremely radical measures if they are not given correct leadership. That is why greater attention must be given to improving work in the basic organizations." In other words, PKI, and therefore SOBSI, was not only *not* inciting the workers to militant action, but, for the sake of the national united front policy, was preparing to restrain them from radical measures provoked by the worsening economic situation.

Since the beginning of 1952, then, SOBSI and its unions have moderated their demands and actions for the sake of PKI's national united front. The emphasis has been on "reasonable and just" demands,[84] on the solution of disputes between the workers and national employers, governmental and private, by friendly means. This has not decreased SOBSI's attractiveness for the Indonesian workers for four reasons. First, SOBSI has far greater finances, personnel, and zeal with which to make its presence felt among the workers. Second, almost all other trade-union organizations are either tied to political parties associated with one or more cabinet—and therefore strictly limited in the militancy they could show and associated with the government's failure to improve the condition of the workers—or they are specifically religious groupings with a severely limited potential membership among the largely *abangan* workers. Third, the great majority of Indonesian workers, as the PKI Central Committee resolution of March 1, 1952, indicated, are loath to take radical action. And, fourth, SOBSI has been, despite its moderation and reasonableness, the most effective defender of the workers' interests, the most courageous in pressing for improvements in wages and working conditions.

The following section deals with SOBSI's work in defense of the workers' interests, that is, SOBSI's basic trade-union work by which it has won the allegiance of over 50 per cent of organized workers in Indonesia.

SOBSI's DEFENSE OF THE WORKERS' INTERESTS

It is outside the scope of this study to make a detailed analysis of all the work undertaken by SOBSI and its member unions in the promotion of the workers' interests, but this section discusses some aspects of this work, namely, the struggle for trade-union freedoms, the formulation of comprehensive and popular programs of demands, and some examples of large and small successes achieved by SOBSI unions for their members.

SOBSI protests were in part instrumental in ending the prohibition of strikes in "vital" industries issued first by some regional army commanders in the latter half of 1950 and then by the Natsir government at the beginning of 1951.[85] The emergency law which replaced it in September 1951 removed the prohibition but established a compulsory labor disputes arbitration system and laid down rules which in effect greatly restricted the opportunity for strikes or lockouts.[86] This also drew SOBSI criticism, but it became less raucous when the national united front policy was put into practice. Partly as a result of SOBSI and PKI demands, the September 1951 regulation was replaced by a new law in June 1958 which brought trade-union representatives into the arbitration committees.[87] Meanwhile, however, the state of emergency decreed in March 1957 had placed far greater restrictions on trade-union freedom. Because the PKI wished to antagonize neither Sukarno, who had issued the decree, nor the army, which played a major administrative role under the decree, SOBSI made few open protests at the infringement of trade-union freedom—though it did protest vehemently when, on August 24, 1957, strikes were prohibited in "vital" enterprises, which meant that virtually all strikes would be illegal.

With the general economic deterioration, in which continuous and sometimes rapid inflation has constantly reduced the already low real value of wages, SOBSI has found no difficulty in discovering grievances to represent. More or less comprehensive lists of demands have been presented to the government on each May Day and New Year, by each SOBSI congress, conference, and national council meeting, and during periods of cabinet formation. SOBSI has gained popularity by its repeated demands for wages to be adjusted in line with price increases, for the provision of essential commodities at low prices, for a Lebaran bonus equal to one month's pay, for the provision of increased job opportunities, and for the prohibition of mass dismissals.

The scope of the SOBSI programs of demands is illustrated by those drawn up by the SOBSI leadership for endorsement by the August 1960 national congress.[88] Within the draft "Program of Demands for National Economic Development," designed to appeal to all sections of workers, were 80 points grouped under the headings "lower prices and speed up production," "nationalize Dutch enterprises and strengthen the state's sector of the economy," "increase internal production and implement foreign economic relations of benefit to Indonesia," measures for increasing the production of rice, textiles, oil, sugar, and fish, and measures for improving communications.[89] The draft program of social and economic demands was divided into six categories: a general category dealing with trade-union rights and democracy; 44 demands for government employees; four demands for workers in the former Dutch enterprises; 37 demands for workers in private enterprises, with special subheadings for workers in large foreign enterprises, in national enterprises, and in small enterprises; two demands for young workers; and six "for the rights and interests of women workers." [90] Thus the SOBSI leaders try to appeal to the working class as a whole and to each worker in his particular employment.

Obviously lists of demands without concrete results would hardly serve to maintain SOBSI membership. Examples of some of the major successes achieved by SOBSI since 1949 are given.

The first major SOBSI success was the Sarbupri strike of August and September 1950 when work was brought to a halt on virtually all private estates.[91] The government finally intervened and established a minimum wage for estate workers that was far higher than the previous average wage rate.[92] Also in 1950 the oil workers successfully struck against dismissals and for workers' compensation and a noncontributory pension.[93] In September 1953 Sarbupri strike action forced the government to alter a decision of the arbitration committee and grant a 30 per cent wage increase at a time of stable prices.[94] SOBSI successes during 1955 included general victory of the demand for Lebaran bonuses, wage increases of 10 to 20 per cent for workers in private industry, the free or cheap distribution of essential commodities in some enterprises, a new wage scale for government employees and workers, and considerable increases in wages and benefits for workers in the Shell and Standard Vacuum oil companies.[95] In 1956 strong SOBSI and PKI opposition was in part responsible for the failure of the plan of the minister of finance to cut drastically the number of government employees.

During 1957 SOBSI claimed as successful its efforts to obtain a provisional wage increase for government workers.[96] In the latter half of 1958 all trade-unions of government workers jointly raised the demand for a minimum wage of 135 rupiahs per month, a demand previously raised only by SOBSI; in December a resolution incorporating this demand was tabled by PKI and SOBSI members of parliament, and was carried unanimously, accepted by the government, and put into effect as of January 1, 1959.[97] When the government took over the Dutch enterprises in December 1957, a grave dislocation of interisland shipping occurred and at the end of 1958 several tens of thousands of harbor workers and seamen were still fully unemployed. SOBSI then proposed that seamen of the former Dutch shipping company who were still unemployed should receive full pay until they found work; the government agreed to give full pay until the middle of 1959.[98] In the period 1960 to 1963 inflation was particularly rapid and the government and private employers gave frequent wage increases. SOBSI and its member unions claimed that the increases were the result of their demands and actions.

Most of SOBSI's social-economic successes have not, however, been in the spectacular category. They have been won under the slogan formulated at the end of 1951, "small but successful," as opposed to "large but failed." [99] Within the scope of such "small but successful" actions are demands for small wage increases, the issue of work clothes, the issue of a trade-union room, sports facilities, meal breaks, and increased distribution of essential commodities free or at low prices.

The above scattered examples of successful SOBSI action in the promotion of the workers' interests indicate that SOBSI has effectively proved its worth as an efficient industrial organization. A comparison of the socioeconomic gains won by SOBSI through the use of all means at its disposal with those won by other trade-union organizations, suggests that SOBSI has been far more active and successful in the basic trade-union work which attracts members and binds them to a trade-union.[100]

SOBSI's Relations with Other Trade-Unions

A PKI Central Committee resolution of March 1, 1952, viciously attacked the non-SOBSI unions but expressed nonetheless the need to coöperate with them.[101] SOBSI was slow to seek unity with the competing unions it had been denouncing as imperialist agents, but gradually developed an increasing enthusiasm for this work. The main fields of coöperation have been three: joint committees of trade-unions in particular fields of work, joint committees for national celebrations, particularly for May Day, and joint trade-union delegations to fill invitations to the Soviet bloc countries.

What is called the coöperation meeting of government employees' trade-unions was established in 1953 with originally 32 members, and grew to include 71 unions and 90 per cent of all government workers by July 1959.[102] The coöperation meeting of trade-unions in foreign enterprises was established in 1955, and by January 1960 was reported to include 40 unions with 1.5 million members.[103] The coöperation body of estate workers' organizations was formed in 1957 and included Sarbupri plus seven major non-SOBSI unions.[104] By September 1957, a coöperation meeting of oil workers' unions had also begun to function.[105]

The first joint May Day committee was formed in 1953 when SOBSI and five other trade-union federations, including PNI's KBKI, established a central committee.[106] Joint May Day celebrations have been held in succeeding years.[107] The countries of the Soviet bloc early invited the Indonesian trade-unions to send joint delegations on free visits. One of the earliest reported joint delegations attended the 1953 May Day celebrations in Peking and the Seventh All-China Congress of Trade-unions, and then went on a tour from Mukden to Canton.[108] Since 1953 the flow of joint trade-union delegations to the Soviet bloc has been considerable.[109]

The question arises, have the joint actions benefited SOBSI? And the answer would appear to be negative. Joint meetings have provided SOBSI leaders with broader audiences, but they have also presented the SOBSI rank and file as an audience for the non-SOBSI leaders. Joint actions, especially through the various coöperation meetings and bodies, have apparently brought the unions greater success than individual action would have achieved, but all unions benefit from them and especially the smaller unions, usually non-SOBSI, whose bargaining position would otherwise be much weaker.

In other words, SOBSI's friendship toward and coöperation with the non-SOBSI trade-union federations and nonfederated unions have not been of direct benefit to SOBSI itself.[110] The policy has been dictated by PKI's overriding concern to pursue the national united front policy at the level of national politics.

SOBSI's POLITICAL USEFULNESS TO PKI

Efficient trade-union work in the defense of the workers' interests is not the primary purpose of SOBSI under the guidance of the Aidit leadership. That work is necessary in order to attract the broad mass of the workers, but the primary goal of the PKI leaders is to create in SOBSI as in every mass organization, an organization that can lend support to the Party's political struggle. Until the present, SOBSI has proved politically useful in a number of related ways: it has provided a source of Party cadres and members, it has provided a platform for pro-Communist propaganda, and it has been a valuable assistant in supporting and strengthening the Party in its relations with the other political forces. The Aidit leadership also has endeavored to create in SOBSI a major source of strength that could prove decisive in the event of a political showdown.

The Communist leaders of SOBSI and its member unions are constantly searching for potential Party cadres and activists among their members, and use the SOBSI educational machinery, both formal and informal, to raise and guide the political consciousness of their own cadres and activists to the point where they voluntarily enter PKI. Through their publications, bulletin boards, and cadres, SOBSI and its unions have faithfully publicized the current PKI line and PKI's defense of the workers' interests. And SOBSI, like the other Communist-led mass organizations, has been an important vehicle for preparing the way for the geographical spread of the Party.

The assistance SOBSI has given PKI in the latter's political struggle is far more complex, and can be considered under four headings: the mobilization of electoral support, assistance in creating a favorable atmosphere for the development of the national united front policy, direct pressure to assist PKI on particular issues, and additional support for PKI in conferences and governmental bodies.

In the two national elections of 1955 and the local elections of 1957-1958, SOBSI played a significant part in mobilizing votes for PKI. Before the 1955 elections, SOBSI appointed, at all levels down to the basic organization, general election action committees or special cadres with the task of assisting in the election campaigns;[111] and on July 15, 1955, the SOBSI secretariat issued a call to all member unions and all SOBSI regional committees and branches to prepare the workers for voting by showing them how to punch the hole through the appropriate symbol on the voting paper.[112] SOBSI was also used to distribute PKI literature and mobilize crowds for Party meetings.

We have seen how SOBSI has adopted a moderate pose in its dealings with the government and Indonesian employers, and how it has sought coöperation with non-SOBSI unions—all in order to create the impression that Communists are reasonable, responsible persons, and worthwhile allies. SOBSI's moderation and even friendliness were perhaps calculated to allay any fears and suspicions which the non-Communists may have harbored regarding the disruptive and aggressive nature of the Indonesian Communists. The ability of SOBSI to work amicably with the non-SOBSI unions for their mutual benefit, and perhaps even for the greater benefit of the non-SOBSI unions, should be a lesson to the non-Communist politicians that coöperation with PKI at the political level could be beneficial. And if PKI and its mass organizations are in fact reasonable and well meaning, how then can they be regarded as dangerous? Why should their repression be considered necessary?

The positive pressure that SOBSI, like the other Communist-led mass organizations, has applied in support of PKI has been in the form of statements and resolutions, mass meetings and demonstrations, posters and banners, letters, cables, petitions, and delegations to the president, to cabinet ministers, speakers of parliament, the president of the supreme court, the attorney-general, the army chief, and any other conceivable government authority, and the use or threat of political strikes. Two major examples of SOBSI's use of or threat of political strike action occurred in March 1957. On March 18, SOBSI in South Sumatra held a 24-hour general strike to protest the seizure of power by the regional army commander and to demand the restoration of civil government; and on March 19 a SOBSI delegation warned Suwirjo, the cabinet formateur, that if a cabinet was formed with Masjumi but without PKI, "SOBSI will not hesitate and is always in readiness to lead a total strike action all over Indonesia." [113]

On July 12, 1957, a 45-member National Council was installed by Sukarno to assist the cabinet, and for the first time the president included "functional groups" in governmental bodies. SOBSI received one seat on the National Council, one on the 45-member National Advisory Council appointed on August 15, 1959, one on the 77-member National Planning Council appointed on the same day, and about eight in the appointed parliament installed on June 25, 1960. SOBSI also received representation as a "functional group" in the Provisional People's Consultative Assembly, the local and provincial councils, and the National Council of the National Front, all of which were appointed by President Sukarno after July 1959 within the framework of Guided Democracy. The SOBSI seats by themselves are not significant, but when added to those of the other Communist-led mass organizations they do give considerable additional representation to PKI.

If the national united front policy fails to enable PKI to take power by peaceful means, then SOBSI might be of crucial importance in any possible show of strength between the political forces. In SOBSI, PKI has an organization that reaches into government ministries, that might be able to bring the economy to a standstill, and that might be able to mobilize large numbers of workers to the side of PKI. Perhaps the threat, spoken or implied, of the use of the massive PKI network given at a time of major political crisis might be able to bring PKI to power. The fundamental question, the real strength of PKI vis-à-vis the other political forces, will be dealt with in Part Five, XXII, below. But some examination needs to be made here of SOBSI's real strength in the labor field because SOBSI is PKI's most important mass organization, well supplied with funds and cadres, and organized in vital sectors of the economy among those who should be, according to PKI's Marxist analysis, the most militant and politically conscious of the Party's supporters.

The strength SOBSI could exert in the event of a political crisis depends not only on the size of its own membership and body of well-trained cadres but also on other factors: the size, and occupational and regional distribution of the non-SOBSI unions and of the unorganized workers, and what might be termed the character of the SOBSI membership.

Until the Madiun rebellion, SOBSI and its member unions had a virtual monopoly of trade-union activities within the Republic. But, as has been seen, the rebellion and the later tightening of PKI control over SOBSI led many trade-unions and unionists to leave. The history of the appearance, disappearance, fragmentation, and growth of the non-SOBSI unions since Madiun is most complicated, but the general outline indicates a steady increase in the combined size of the non-SOBSI unions.[114] The following paragraphs are concerned only with indicating the relative sizes of the non-SOBSI unions in 1960.

Several trade-union federations exist that are tied to particular political parties. The largest, PNI's KBKI, was founded in December 1952 and by 1958 claimed over one million members; at the beginning of 1960 it claimed 143 branches with at least one full-timer in each branch.[115] The Socialist Party's KBSI in March 1958 claimed 376,000 members,[116] and contained three important unions: the railway workers' PBKA with a claimed membership of 32,000 at the end of 1959, the estate workers' Perbupri with 120,000, and a union of civil aviation workers which claimed 60 per cent of all workers in that field.[117] The Labor Party runs a small federation with perhaps 30,000 members. Among the trade-union federations based on religion, the

largest is the Masjumi-inclined SBII, now called Gasbiindo, founded
at the end of 1947 and hopefully claiming 850,000 members at the end
of 1959.[118] Three other Islamic trade-union federations existed in 1960,
but their combined size could not be above 100,000 members. Both
Christian Protestants and Roman Catholics also have their own small
federations. In 1962 and 1963 SOBSI was also faced with trade-unions
sponsored and assisted by officials in government estates, factories, and
trading concerns. Some of them were affiliated with a new federation
with the title SOKSI, Sentral Organisasi Karjawan Sosialis Indonesia
(Indonesian Socialist Workers' Organization Central). The vehemence
of SOBSI attacks on these "company unions" indicated that they were
eating into SOBSI's membership.[119]

In 1954 there were about 980 unaffiliated trade-union organizations,
with a total claimed membership of 711,000. They included many of
the trade-unions for white-collar workers in banks, air transport, the
police, government ministries, and public services.[120] Among the more
important nonfederated unions is the teachers' union, with 128,000
members, and a North Sumatra estate workers' union with up to
100,000 members.[121]

The rise of the non-SOBSI unions has broken the monopoly of almost
every SOBSI union in its particular sphere.[122] SOBSI leaders, non-
SOBSI unionists, and Ministry of Labor officials alike estimate that
SOBSI now includes perhaps 50 to 60 per cent of all organized labor.
But the collapse of the SOBSI monopoly means that there is now
virtually no labor area in which SOBSI could cause a complete stop-
page without the support of the non-SOBSI unions. Furthermore, the
reservoir of unemployed and nonunionized workers[123] faces any go-it-
alone strike by SOBSI with the possibility of defeat—unless it were in
a highly skilled field.

The second major factor involved in any estimate of SOBSI's real
strength in the labor field is the character of the SOBSI membership.
In other words, how militant are the SOBSI members? How far would
they follow the SOBSI leaders, in the event of a political crisis, in
militant action that would be clearly pro-PKI? The answers given in
1960 by non-Communist trade-union leaders, security police officers,
and Ministry of Labor officials were fairly uniform:

I do not believe that PKI could lead the workers in political strikes, . . .

SOBSI no longer dare start a strike alone; it could not, alone, lead strikes, especially
of a political nature, . . .

The SOBSI members have a strong attachment to their trade-union leaders, but I am not at all convinced that in a political crisis many would follow PKI against the government for clearly political purposes, . . .

If there was a grave political crisis, the SOBSI workers would say, "go fight for yourself" and then go home.[124]

The extent to which the SOBSI members would follow their leaders in clearly political action would depend, of course, on where the lines of political division were drawn. But if PKI were opposed to the government and without a powerful ally such as the president, it is very doubtful indeed whether the SOBSI members, with some few exceptions, would militantly support PKI. This relative passivity requires some explanation.

Four factors mentioned in the Introduction help explain the passivity of the Indonesian workers. First, the majority of workers are in small enterprises, which an any country are the most difficult for trade-unions to organize for militant action. Second, the small employers still accept, in general, a certain fatherly responsibility toward their workers, which helps prevent the growth of antagonistic labor relations. Third, about 35 per cent of the workers are women, and more in some of the large-scale industries, who also constitute an obstacle to the development of militant trade-unionism, the more so in a country where women are traditionally "malu," shy. Fourth, and most important, the Indonesian workers are usually not far removed in time or family connections from the peasantry, and retain a strong sense of acceptance of authority or the tradition of open obedience. Certainly the ingrained behavioral patterns of the village have undergone change with the migration to the cities, especially among the literate and skilled workers and among those who have lived in the towns for a long time; but the patterns do not appear to have changed so much among most workers.

Throughout their history, moreover, Indonesian trade-unions have been sternly discouraged from militant action. The workers have received neither the leadership nor the experience in industrial action necessary to rid them of their obedience to established authority and to develop the traits of solidarity in action and aggressiveness in politics. During the Dutch and Japanese rule the growth of trade-unions was severely curtailed,[125] and the few strikes were quickly suppressed.[126] When trade-unions were formed after the proclamation of independence, they were not the spontaneous creation of the workers but the fabrication of literate middle-class persons. Even today, the national and regional leadership of SOBSI and its member unions contains hardly a single cadre of other than white-collar origin, and the SOBSI leaders complain in private of the great difficulty of finding workers who can be trained as trade-union cadres. During the revolution strikes were antipatriotic and reduced to a minimum, and from the end of 1950 military and government regulations as well as PKI's national united front policy have also reduced the number of strikes. There have been very few strikes since 1956.

When an ordinary worker enters a trade-union, what does he expect to put into it, and to receive from it? He joins because the union offers to help him face problems raised by his employment, and more often than not he joins a SOBSI union because it is the largest, the best organized, and the most successful. His membership is, however, largely passive. Under the labor disputes arbitration and conciliation system established in 1951, when the worker has a complaint or a problem he takes it to the trade-union cadre, usually a person of higher, "superior" social status, who then takes it to the employer or a government committee for solution. The worker himself rarely participates in direct action. Whereas in the village the peasant traditionally has taken problems to the "bapak" (father) *lurah* or government official, the urban worker takes his problems to a new "bapak" who then negotiates with "the authorities" on his behalf.

If the above general picture is correct, the workers have no or very little experience in methods of direct action (and SOBSI still strives to suppress the occasional outburst of "radical" action), they are not conscious of the power they could exert by such action, and they look upon the union as a sort of "bapak" who mediates between themselves and the more-or-less incomprehensible forces that weigh upon them. Such a picture is oversimplified and certainly would not apply to some of the SOBSI unionists, perhaps, for example, the more skilled railway workers. But it does seem to have wide validity. And if it does, then it means that SOBSI could not be of the importance its numbers indicate were PKI to face a show of strength with its political enemies. The workers do not have the militancy, the unity, the training in direct action, or even the belief in their own strength, to follow SOBSI and PKI against "the authorities" if "the authorities" were to demonstrate their determined opposition.[127]

2. DIRECT PARTY WORK

Although the Aidit leadership has used the mass organizations to gather support and potential members, it has been careful not to obscure PKI's primary position as the militant defender of the working class. The mass organizations swell the vociferous campaigns for popular demands, such as the provision of essential commodities at low prices, but PKI is pointed to as the clear leader of the campaigns. At one level, PKI is presented to the workers as the party most able in representing their material demands, but at another level PKI is presented as the champion of a political system which will ensure social and economic justice for the masses.

At the present stage of the Indonesian revolution, PKI offers a people's democracy. The PKI program endorsed in March 1954 promised that for the workers, people's democracy would mean industrial expansion, a minimum wage, an annual holiday of at least two weeks with full pay, a social security system paid for by the state and the capitalists, price controls, a six-hour work day in mines and other unhealthy employment, the abolition of "semifeudal exploitation of work," such as contract labor, the prohibition of female, child, and youth labor in unhealthy work, the free development of trade-unions, and the right of labor to make collective agreements.[128] In the election manifesto endorsed at the same time, the PKI promise was contained in a single sentence: "For the workers, to vote PKI means rice, fair wages, and just social security." [129]

For the 1957–1958 regional and local elections, PKI issued election programs for each province and for each *kabupaten* and municipality. The PKI election program for Surabaja illustrates the promises PKI has made to the workers.[130] Apart from promises of a general appeal, such as improved educational and medical facilities, those designed particularly for the urban worker included the following:

1. to fight for a minimum daily wage of seven rupiahs for municipal workers;
2. to increase the supply of water;
3. to endeavor to increase the supply of electricity to the *kampongs*;
4. to build and repair alleys, roads, and bridges;
5. to fight for the immediate legalization of houses built by squatters on disputed land;
6. to make more land available for *kampongs* and industry;
7. to fight for the removal of discrimination against women in the spheres of wages and jobs; and
8. to increase the number of courses for teaching the various trades.

The PKI slogan to attact the Surabaja workers was: "For the workers and government employees, to vote PKI means proper wages, housing, social security, and work conditions."

Besides promises of a better life, and its work in the mass organizations, PKI has also undertaken a variety of tasks aimed at winning the support of the urban population. The Party and its mass organizations have collected relief for victims of floods and *kampong* fires,[131] and some Party committees have formed local fire brigades to assist the municipal brigades.[132] PKI work brigades have also helped to clean *kampong* gutters, and to build and repair *kampong* houses, public lavatories and bathing places, and gutters. So far, however, PKI and its mass organizations have been unable to inspire any large number of their members to join such brigades.

An important function filled by PKI and its mass organizations among the poor sections of society, both urban and rural, is the provision of mutual assistance in times of need, such as deaths, marriages, births, and illness, a valuable service to people near or at subsistence level and with no or few social security services. Since 1958 PKI has written and talked much on the need to establish coöperatives, including consumer coöperatives which would free especially the workers from the speculative practices of the shopkeepers. As yet, however, concrete results have not been announced, and as the emphasis of the coöperative campaign has been in the rural areas, the campaign will be dealt with more fully in the section on the peasantry.

In many cities of Java a system of *kampong* government has been established distinct from the municipal and national government structure. *Rukun-rukun tetangga* (associations of neighbors) are united in *rukun-rukun kampong* (*kampong* associations) which in turn are united in an all-city federation. The strength and sphere of activities of the *kampong* government systems vary from city to city and they have disappeared altogether in some, such as Malang,[133] but in Surabaja, the second largest town in Indonesia and the most important industrially, PKI built the RKKS (Rukun Kampong Kota Surabaja, Surabaja City Kampong Association) into "a system of community organizations . . . strong enough to compete with the official local administrative system." [134]

The Japanese had originally established the *rukun kampong* system in Surabaja during their occupation as a distribution network for scarce commodities, as a mutual surveillance system, and as a means of mobilizing forced labor and semimilitary guard units.[135] In January 1950 the RKKS was established under PKI direction. In the absence of a government structure below the level of the *lingkungan*, of which there are 37 in Surabaja, the RKKS became the effective government in the *kampongs*. When, in the second half of 1950, the government appointed officials for the *lingkungans*, they were mostly the candidates proposed by the RKKS branches. "During the succeeding years, it was difficult to distinguish between the functioning of the R.K.K.S. branch at the ward level and the ward government itself." [136] The RKKS collects fees from each household, builds schools, organizes community work to clean gutters and repair alleys, subsidizes burials, and arranges for the night guards that are usually led by a member of Pemuda Rakjat.

The political usefulness of the RKKS to PKI has been considerable: it has mobilized people for rallies and demonstrations, mobilized voters in elections, and has served to bring those *kampong* dwellers with greater initiative into the PKI orbit and then into the Party itself. Although the local army commander in April 1958 issued a regulation forbidding the RKKS to engage openly in politics, the RKKS could not be banned because, in the absence of a government structure below the *lingkungan* level, it was needed to perform the government duties of census-taking, *kampong* cleaning and security, and the distribution of coupons for essential commodities. As of May 1960, PKI members or sympathizers still controlled 26 of the 27 *lingkungan* offices.

The importance of the *rukun kampong* system in other Javanese towns is not comparable to that of the RKKS, but the PKI exploitation of the system outside Surabaja still awaits research.

XIV

THE PEASANTS

1. THE PKI ATTITUDE TO THE PEASANTS

During the revolution PKI had largely ignored the peasantry. Then, in August 1948, the Politbureau admitted past errors and declared that "Without the active support of the peasants, the national revolution will certainly be defeated." [1] One of the main tasks of the Fifth National Congress scheduled for October 1948 was to formulate an agrarian program that could unite the poor, small, and medium peasants with the workers, that is, with the Party.[2] The congress was not held nor the program formulated because in September the Madiun rebellion broke out and in December the Dutch launched their second attack on the Republic. For almost five years after Madiun the PKI leaders devoted their resources to reconstructing and expanding support in the towns and in the trade-unions. Some work was done in analyzing rural conditions,[3] but it was not translated into practical action. This phase came to an end in July 1953 when Aidit published an article which turned the major focus of Party activity onto the rural areas.[4]

Aidit stated that "The agrarian revolution is the essence of the people's democratic revolution in Indonesia." Therefore it was vital for the Party to win the allegiance of the peasants. He admitted that the peasant mass was indifferent to and not rarely suspicious of the

Party, and blamed this on several factors: first, "there is not yet a single Party member who thoroughly understands, and very few who know about, agrarian relations and the life and demands of the peasants"; second, the Communist-led peasant organizations had raised the slogans "the right of the state over all land" and "nationalization of all land," which made the peasants suspicious because they did not understand them; and third, the Party did not yet have a "correct and revolutionary" agrarian program to attract the peasants. He called for an end to the "serious deficiency" in Party work among the peasants, and for an expansion of Party membership in the villages, especially among the laborers and poor peasants.

Aidit scornfully rejected the contention of some cadres in the rural areas that the peasants there had no problems which could be exploited in order to bind them to the forces of the revolution. All cadres must realize that the peasants had many demands, and that

For each demand a movement can be made based on a slogan, for example: "lower land rents," "lower the interest rate on loans," "lower state taxes," "cancel arrears in land tax," "abolish *setoran paksa*," "abolish *pologoro*," "abolish *rodi*," "don't touch the land that is worked by the peasants," "give unworked land to the peasants," "the peasants' right to determine the rent of the land leased to foreign estates," "arm the peasants in order to crush the DI, TII and other terrorist gangs," "assistance in seeds and tools for the peasants," "one agricultural school for each *ketjamatan*," "abolish the fee for permission to kill and sell livestock," "abolish the fee for identification papers," "improve the old irrigation and make new," "form a village government that defends the people," etc., etc. [*sic*]. These are not all the slogans of the peasants' everyday demands. There are too many to be included here.[5]

It was the duty of Party cadres and members, Aidit wrote, to decide, through discussion with the peasants, which was the most urgent demand in any place at a given time.

As the basic slogans with which the Party could attract the peasant masses, Aidit laid down "land for the peasants," "distribution of land to the peasants," and "peasant private ownership of land."

With these slogans the peasants will certainly have no doubts about our program, and they will even support it with all their strength. This is the guarantee for firm alliance between the workers and peasants, the guarantee for a strong national united front, the guarantee for our victory.[6]

Aidit was aware, however, of the danger of "adventurism," of trying to bring the peasants' struggle to a higher level without preparatory organizational and educational work, and he carefully laid down techniques by which the peasants could be brought by stages toward the point of implementing the "land for the peasants" slogan.

The March 1954 Party congress endorsed the new emphasis on the importance of peasant participation in the revolution, and clarified the basic and most immediate tasks of the Communist Party, that is, to mobilize the peasants and draw them into the struggle to eliminate the remnants of feudalism, and to develop the anti-feudal agrarian revolution.[7]

Since the Fifth Congress the Aidit leadership has continued to acknowledge the agrarian revolution as the essential element of the Indonesian revolution. In December 1960, for example, Aidit referred to "the emphasis on activities among the peasants within the framework of strengthening the national front." [8]

The Aidit leadership has classified the peasantry into several broad social divisions based on land ownership.[9] It has been aware that in order to mobilize the support of the nonlandlord elements, then it must first understand the specific interests and demands of the different social divisions. Because the conditions of the peasants vary widely from region to region, and even from village to village, and because so little information is available concerning agrarian relations in Indonesia, the Party leaders have endeavored to collect their own information. This task was begun systematically early in 1958. At the end of that year Party cadres were instructed to "go down to the villages," to live, eat, and work with the peasants, in order to gather first-hand information in preparation for the PKI First National Peasants' Conference in April 1959.[10] Since the conference, both PKI and BTI have continued to compile information from villages (especially in Java) on such matters as land tenure, interest rates charged by moneylenders, and the survival of feudal customs. Village research became an important part of the PKI second three-year plan initiated early in 1960. It was later hoped to amass concrete statistics on rural conditions in each region of Indonesia by the end of 1963.[11] The information collected is to enable PKI and its mass organizations to make more specific, and therefore more effective, appeals to the different sections of the peasantry and in the different regions of the country.

2. BUILDING AN ORGANIZATION AMONG THE PEASANTS

PKI

Prior to the March 1954 congress, PKI had made few direct inroads into the villages. At the congress it was announced that less than half of the 165,206 Party members were of peasant origin. It is reasonable to assume that a good proportion of those of peasant origin were in the estate, forestry, and sugar-mill areas where SOBSI unions had already been active for some years. The membership drive which followed the congress was aimed particularly at the peasants. Before the end of 1955 claimed Party membership had passed one million, and was given as one and a half millions at the beginning of 1959, at which figure it stayed until the Sixth Congress in September 1959. In December 1958 it was reported that peasants constituted over half the Party membership, while the Sixth Congress was informed that the proportion of peasant members was still increasing.[12] These official Party figures indicate that between March 1954 and December 1958 the number of peasant members increased from less than 80,000 to well over three-quarters of a million. Party membership passed two millions in the latter half of 1962, with peasants constituting over 60 per cent.

In his report to the Sixth Congress in September 1959, Anwar Sanusi presented statistics on the distribution of the Party organization in Java at that time which also can be used to visualize the situation in July 1956.[13] According to his figures, in July 1956 PKI had a branch in about 34 per cent of the 21,047 villages in Java, and increased this to 84.2 per cent in the next three years; in July 1956 PKI had a subsection in about 70 per cent of the 1,449 *ketjamatans*, and increased this to 98.7 per cent. From an analysis of the 1957 local election results, the "vacant" villages and *ketjamatans* would be in the strongly Moslem areas of West Java and East Java, including Madura.

Vital to strengthening the Party organization in the rural areas has been the creation of good cadres for work among the peasants. This has been difficult in the Javanese villages for a number of reasons.[14] First, the more literate and politically conscious peasants who tend to become cadres in both the Party and the mass organizations are often middle and rich peasants or even landlords, and retain the attitudes of their social position toward the poorer peasants. Second, in the relative social peace of the village, many cadres, themselves of peasant origin, are loath to create social disunity in the village or have failed to recognize the existence of landlord exploitation. Third, some PKI cadres have tended to become landlords once they become village officials, and to ignore the sufferings of the poorer peasants. Fourth, the educational level of peasant members is generally so low that they must be taught literary and basic general knowledge before they can receive political training. And, fifth, cadres from urban areas often do not know the regional language required, or are simply unwilling to engage in rural work.

The continuing low level of the quality of peasant cadres was admitted in "The Report on Party Work among the Peasants" submitted to the PKI First National Peasants' Conference in mid-April 1959:

The majority of Party cadres at the subsection and branch levels in the villages have not yet deeply studied the class divisions, the characteristics of each class and the class relations in the village. In general they are still unable to distinguish the landlord from the rich peasant, and still do not know the difference between the rich peasant and the medium peasant. This means that they do not yet thoroughly know who are the friends and who are the enemies of the revolution.[15]

Worse still, the cadres even up to the section level did not, in general, know

who constitute the landlord group and what is the history of their land ownership, the means by which the landlord steals the peasants' land, the forms of exploitation and the evil nature of the exploitation of the landlord and moneylender, the way the landlord and moneylender squeeze and deceive the peasants, the way the landlord uses government officials and thugs to oppress the peasants.[16]

The work of the Party in educating a body of cadres has been detailed in the section on building the Party. But special attention has had to be given to peasant cadres because of their generally lower quality. A report presented to the Central Committee in July 1957 proposed conferences between peasant activists as a means of improving their quality.[17] Before the 1959 National Peasants' Conference the Party launched its first "go down to the villages" and "three-to-gethers" movement, as has been described above, partly as a way to increase the middle and upper cadres' understanding of village life. In the conference itself, the Party leaders called for special schools for peasant cadres, and for the replacement of Party rural workers whose individual interests conflicted with those of the peasants.[18]

In short, by September 1959 the PKI organization had been extended into the great majority of Javanese villages and into virtually every village in the strongly PKI area of Central and East Java. An intensive effort in cadre education had greatly increased both the number and quality of rural cadres. Their quality still left much to be desired, but the Party leaders were aware of the deficiencies and were taking measures to eradicate them.

It should be noted here that the Aidit leadership in its work of attracting and mobilizing the peasants had used not only PKI and the specifically peasant mass organizations but also the youth organization and the women's organization, the majority of whose members are villagers.

BTI

When the Aidit leadership won control of PKI in January 1951, the Party had complete control of one national peasant organization, RTI (Rukun Tani Indonesia, Indonesian Peasants' Union), disguised control of BTI, and influence in a third, SAKTI (Sarekat Tani Indonesia, Indonesian Peasants' Association). On July 2, 1951, these three organizations established the FPT (Front Persatuan Tani, Peasants' United Front) with a joint program of demands.[19] For over two years the FPT operated as a fairly closely knit body, issuing statements and demands concerning the major peasant problems and political events. In December 1952 the FPT even organized a joint cadre course, using as study material what had been used in an RTI cadre course in June 1951, the first reported peasants' cadre course in Indonesia.[20] In December 1951, the FPT claimed half a million members,[21] the great majority of whom must have been in Java.

At the beginning of 1953 the Communist leaders of RTI proposed the fusion of BTI, SAKTI, and itself. The Communists in BTI had finally removed the remaining non-Communists from the leadership of the organization and readily agreed to the proposal. But although the SAKTI executive committee also agreed, an internal struggle with members of the small Trotskyite party, Acoma, prevented the fusion for over two more years.[22] From September 14 to 20, 1953, BTI and RTI held a fusion congress, the joint organization retaining the name BTI.[23] At the time of the fusion, BTI claimed 240,000 members, RTI 120,000.[24] Once the Communist wing in SAKTI was confident of its own control of the organization, a SAKTI congress was held in June 1955 which accepted fusion with BTI.[25]

By the time of the fusion between BTI and RTI, PKI was concentrating its efforts in the rural areas, and BTI began to grow rapidly. In March 1954 it claimed 800,000 members.[26] One year later it claimed 170 branches in 136 of the 162 *kabupatens* in Indonesia, subbranches in 7,638 of the 43,249 villages, and a total membership of 2,027,500.[27] When SAKTI fused with BTI in 1955 it claimed to have 42 branches, 378 subbranches, and 200,000 members.[28] At the end of 1955, after what must have been a massive membership drive parallel to the drives by PKI and its other mass organizations in preparation for the general elections, BTI claimed 3,315,820 members.[29] Thus, according to the figures issued by the peasant organizations, the number of peasants in the PKI-controlled organizations had risen from 360,000 in September 1953 when RTI fused with BTI, to over 3.3 millions at the end of 1955.

The BTI national council meeting from March 26 to 28, 1955, reviewed the work of the organization.[30] Until that time, BTI had been active principally in the areas of estate and forestry lands where BTI could easily exploit the problems of the peasant squatters who had occupied large tracts of land during the Japanese occupation and the revolution. The council decided that while consolidation was required in such areas, BTI had to extend its activities into the ordinary villages. This required cadre courses to explain the BTI constitution and the class divisions and forms of exploitation in the villages; the increased distribution of the periodical *Suara Tani (Voice of the Peasants)*; and improved methods of work, the implementation of collective leadership, and the activation of members' meetings. The question was also raised of purging those landlord elements in the organization, especially those in positions of leadership, who had entered in order to intimidate or persuade the peasants against resorting to "radical" action.[31]

In the BTI Fifth Congress, from September 5 to 12, 1957, Sardjono, who is reportedly a close associate of Alimin, was removed from the position of chairman and given the honorary post of third vice-chairman. The new leadership consisted entirely of persons of proved loyalty to the Aidit leadership.[32] It was claimed that BTI now had 201 branches, 1,323 *ketjamatan*-level organizations, 13,787 village-level subbranches, and 3,390,286 members.[33] The heavy concentration in Java is revealed in the figures in table 2 (see p. 167). The only significant membership claims outside Java were for North Sumatra, 152,094, and South Sumatra, 108,210, but there were already two province-level organizations in Kalimantan, "several" *kabupaten*-level branches in Sulawesi, and BTI organizations in many of the smaller islands of East Indonesia and Nusatenggara, from Bali to Halmahera and the Aru archipelago.[34]

Among the proposals contained in the executive council's report to the congress were: the further expansion of membership and easier conditions for acceptance of members; an extensive anti-illiteracy drive among BTI activists and the peasant masses; increased distribution of *Suara Tani* as a propaganda tool and a means of raising the cadres' political awareness; and regional conferences to discuss common experiences and problems.[35]

In April 1959 BTI claimed 3.5 million members, or 14 per cent of all adult peasants, branches in almost every *kabupaten*, organizations in 45 per cent of all *ketjamatans*, and subbranches in 35 per cent of all villages.[36] Growth since the Fifth Congress had been largely effected outside Java, especially in Atjeh, Bali, Sumba, Flores, and Timor. The

TABLE 2
BTI Organization and Membership, September 1957

Province	Kabupaten Organizations	Ketjamatan Organizations	Sub-branches	Members
Djakarta Raja	3	9	76	20,358
West Java	19	257	1,744	657,134
Central Java	38	416	4,533	1,160,654*
East Java	29	422	4,906	1,163,894
Total	89	1,104	11,259	3,002,040
Total outside Java	112	219	2,528	388,246

*BTI's membership claims have not been consistent. In April 1958, for example, BTI in Central Java claimed to have 37 branches and 600,000 members; *TI*, April 10, 1958. Sudisman, a member of the PKI Politbureau, stated in December, 1957 that: BTI . . . has 1.6 million members and is able to mobilize more than three million peasants in actions to demand that empty lands of the Dutch estates be distributed to the landless peasants . . .
Sudisman, "Semangat Bukit 1211 Membadjakan Rakjat Korea dalam Mengalahkan Agresi dan Membangun Sosialisme" ["The Spirit of Hill 1211 Steels the Korean People in Defeating Aggression and Developing Socialism"], *BM*, December 1957, p. 511.

national council which met in that month emphasized the need to adapt the form of organization at the village level to the local everyday needs of the peasants. Members should be organized not only in groups based on place of residence, but also in groups based on units of work, for example groups of renters of landlords' land. But, "besides BTI and coöperatives are also needed *arisan* and sports groups and various mutual assistance groups . . . , death associations, etc."[37]

Of the greatest long-term importance for BTI are its efforts to produce a large and capable cadre force. The generally poor quality of PKI's peasant cadres has already been referred to, but the cadre situation within BTI is far worse in terms of both numbers and quality. As late as April 1959, many BTI branches and even some regional committees were without full-time officials,[38] and although many cadres of PKI and the other mass organizations double as BTI cadres this means that BTI work does not receive the attention it should. In May 1957 *Suara Tani* commented that there were still many illiterate activists in the subbranches and *ketjamatan* committees, with some even holding the position of secretary-general at the latter level.[39] Work had already begun on the eradication of illiteracy among activists but had not advanced far. What PKI and BTI call the ideological shortcomings among their peasant cadres stem from the social origin of many of the cadres among the rich peasants and landlords.[40] Although efforts had been made since 1955 to remove these shortcomings by purges or education, they were still being referred to as an obstacle to correct work in 1959.[41] With the grave shortage of literate and capable cadres of reliable social origins, it has proved difficult to remove those with suspect backgrounds.

Before 1959 cadre education in BTI was unsystematic and on a small scale. Then the national council meeting of April 22 to 26, 1959, which met a few days after the PKI First National Peasants' Conference, drew up a second three-year plan of organization and education. The general outline of the plan was as follows:[42]

Organization:

1. To increase membership by 50 per cent in the first year, 75 per cent in the first two years, and 100 per cent in the three years, that is, to 7 millions;

2. to provide each branch with a typewriter, each subbranch with a name board.

Education:

1. To extend the circulation of *Suara Tani*. All BTI committees down to the *ketjamatan* level were required to subscribe to *Suara Tani*, and activists were obliged to write up their experiences for it;

2. to encourage the lower BTI committees to issue their own periodicals, however simple and in longhand if necessary, in the local languages;

3. to eradicate illiteracy speedily among activists at the *ketjamatan* level, and intensify anti-illiteracy courses for the peasant masses in seasons of least agricultural work;

4. to intensify cadre courses at the center and in the regions, and unify their education under four basic headings: the peasants' social and economic problems, BTI and other people's organizations in the villages, the birth and growth of the national peasant movement and the experience of peasant movements abroad, and the development of the nationalist movement. Education in agriculture was also to be given.

Each committee was set a target after discussions from the level of members' meetings upward. Some areas began work under the plan on November 25, 1959, the rest on May 1, 1960. In June 1960 the BTI leadership announced that in general the quotas had proved to be too low, and that some areas, such as Central Java, had already raised them.[43] An impression of what the plan meant for each region is given by the example of East Java.[44] There the goals of the first year of the plan included: to buy a mimeograph machine, a new typewriter and bicycle for the provincial office; to increase the number of full-time officials in the provincial office, and to prepare two cadres of the branch level and four of a lower level for sending outside Java; to establish a system of cadre courses, and to hold two courses at the province level; to increase the distribution of *Suara Tani* and to hold monthly discussions on its contents; to publish a newsletter; to hold a seminar on agriculture; to effect systematic control of the branch committees; to extend the organization into "vacant" areas; and to lead specified campaigns in the peasants' interests.

On November 12, 1959, a peasants' education building association was established with BTI's chairman as its chairman, and including leaders from Pemuda Rakjat, Gerwani, and SOBSI unions.[45] The declared aim of the association was to promote scientific knowledge among the peasants and to raise their spirit of patriotism "in the widest meaning." By July 1960 each BTI member was obliged to pay half a rupiah, part of the money for the new association (which was intended at least for the training of coöperative cadres), and part for BTI's own central office.[46]

By the time of the BTI Sixth National Congress in July 1962, further great gains were reported in the extension of the organization and its membership. There were now claimed to be 5,654,974 members (25 per cent of the adult peasant population), 18,784 subbranches (43 per cent of all peasant villages), 1,982 *ketjamatan*-level organizations (84 per cent of all *ketjamatans*), 254 *kabupaten*-level (virtually 100 per cent), and 21 province-level organizations.[47] The congress noted, however, that "Although BTI has achieved important advances, those advances in general are still below the quotas of the three-year plan." It is to be noted, also, that the congress was the occasion for the elevation of Asmu to the position of BTI general chairman. Asmu had already been for several years the chief PKI spokesman on agrarian affairs.

In short, BTI has built a mass membership and an extensive organizational network, especially in Java—and with even less competition from non-Communist organizations than either PKI or SOBSI has faced in its own work. For the non-Communist politicians, organizational work among the peasants is even less attractive than among the workers. But both BTI and PKI still experience a grave shortage of good peasant cadres. The great majority of peasants are poor, illiterate, parochial, unaware that their conditions can be changed by their own efforts, and they therefore constitute poor cadre material. The efforts of BTI itself and of PKI under their respective three-year plans have increased the number and quality of their peasant cadres, but both are still markedly deficient. BTI especially is faced with such grave and as yet unsolved financial difficulties,[48] that it is unable to appoint sufficient full-time cadres, whatever their quality.

PPDI [49]

The Persatuan Pamong Desa Indonesia (Indonesian Village Officials' Association) was founded on September 26, 1946, by the fusion of seven village officials' associations. After the transfer of sovereignty to Indonesia in December 1949, PPDI spread rapidly from the former areas of the Republic in Java, and by the time of its Third Congress in May 1951 had extended throughout Java and even into Sumatra. PKI control of the PPDI leadership by 1951 at the latest is indicated by the phraseology used in the statement made at that time of the basis and goals of PPDI's struggle.[50] The present leaders, all of whom are PKI members or sympathizers, were elected at the last congress in July 1955. Actual leadership is in the hands of Usman Muftiwidjaja who was elected on the PKI list to the Constituent Assembly and is now a member of the appointed parliament.

As of May 1960 the PPDI leaders claimed that there were 108 branches at the *kabupaten* level, and 350,000 members, of whom two-thirds were in Java and Madura.[51] In South Sumatra PPDI was also evenly spread, but elsewhere it had few members. There is no competing village officials' association.

PPDI's struggle for the interests of the village officials has been centered around three main matters.[52] The first is the status of village officials. PPDI demands that village officials be given the status of either local or central government officials, which would mean that they would be free from arbitrary dismissal and would receive regular wages and pension rights. This is the chief long-term demand. The second concerns the officials' income. Since 1951 the central government has subsidized the poorer villages to enable them to pay their officials stipulated minimum wages. But these minimums are far below minimum living requirements and PPDI urges the government to provide larger subsidies. The third concerns the situation of village officials in the disturbed areas. Partly because of PPDI demands, the government pays compensation to the families of village officials killed at their posts, and allowances to officials forced from their villages by terrorist or rebel activities. PPDI demands that the allowances be considerably increased.

PPDI is clearly the poorest of PKI's mass organizations. In 1960 the head office was a one-room affair up some very steep ladders in a small, run-down shop in Surakarta. At the center, there were two full-timers, both members of PKI, plus part-time help from those with other employment, for example from Usman and from the secretary-general who is a village head. Almost all PPDI functionaries in the regions are part-timers. In Surabaja I visited the home of the full-time secretary for East Java and found it to be a pantry-size, ramshackle addition to the side of a *kampong* house. But it is doubtful if even the low expenses of PPDI are met by subscriptions, for when I asked the three members of the Central Secretariat about membership fees, they all agreed that it was more or less impossible to collect them, but disagreed on what the fee was. They had to settle the resultant argument by consulting the constitution.

Apart from being the poorest of the PKI mass organizations, PPDI is also the least effective politically and has failed to develop a sympathetic attitude toward PKI and its policies among more than a very small section of its membership. A well-produced monthly periodical appeared at the beginning of 1957, but within two years had disappeared because of financial difficulties. As yet no cadre schools or classes have been held, but written courses on a small scale are organized "to give the cadres an understanding of the revolution."

Communists control PPDI at the center because no one else has cared to challenge them. But from information received from members of the central government's rural administrative service it would appear that PKI has little influence over the great majority of PPDI members. The members are, in general, more literate, wealthy, and politically conscious than the ordinary villagers, they tend to be supporters of PNI or of one of the Moslem parties, and they are members of PPDI for the sole purpose of promoting their own specific interests.

As in the case of the other PKI-led mass organizations, the PPDI central leadership frequently issues statements, in the name of the whole organization, in support of PKI policies and demands, thus adding numerical weight, or apparent weight, to PKI's position.

3. WORK AMONG THE PEASANTS

This section contains two main divisions: Communist work in the areas of easier access, namely, the estate, forestry, insecure, and transmigrant areas; and work in the ordinary villages.

WORK IN THE AREAS OF EASIER ACCESS

PKI first entered the villages in the estate and forestry areas. During the Japanese occupation and the revolution, tens of thousands of land-hungry peasants moved onto estate and forestry lands. Under the terms of the Round Table Conference agreement, the Indonesian government was obliged to restore estate lands to their former owners. At the same time the government's forestry service began evicting the squatters from its land. The result was a series of bitter clashes between the authorities and the peasants. In some areas peasants were shot, and in many more the squatters' homes were destroyed, their crops ploughed up.

PKI, the peasant organizations BTI, RTI and SAKTI, SOBSI unions such as the estate workers' and the forestry workers' unions, and other mass organizations, including Pemuda Rakjat, fought alongside the peasants, often successfully, to prevent eviction or to obtain compensation in the event of eviction. The climax to the attempts to dislodge the squatters from estate lands was reached on March 16, 1953, when five squatters were shot by police at Tandjung Morawa in North Sumatra. The FPT strongly denounced the shooting. On May 2 a SAKTI member of parliament introduced a motion demanding an immediate halt to antisquatter action in the area, and the creation of a committee, including peasant representatives, to settle the land problem there. This motion led to a division between PNI and Masjumi, and to the downfall of the Wilopo cabinet.

Sadjarwo, of BTI, sat as minister of agriculture in the next cabinet and was partly responsible for the emergency law of June 8, 1954, concerning the settlement of the question of the people's use of estate lands.[53] While PKI and its peasant organizations objected to some of the provisions of the new law, they welcomed its recognition of the squatters' right to appoint their representatives to negotiate with the estate owners, and its stipulation that any decision must consider the peasants' interests. In October 1956, the 1954 law was extended to include squatters on state forestry lands.[54] Despite the 1954 and 1956 laws, occasional violent disputes have continued between the squatters and the authorities, but BTI has usually succeeded in winning ultimate recognition of the peasants' interests in any land settlement.

The regions of sugar cane have also provided an easier point of entry into the rural areas for PKI and its peasant organizations. Since the transfer of sovereignty in December 1949, the government has fixed, at a level it deems reasonable, the rent of the land leased by the peasants to the sugar mills for cane-growing. This system has been strongly opposed by the peasants and BTI who demand that leasing of land be completely voluntary, and that the rent be fixed in discussions between the peasants or their representatives and the factories.[55]

PKI and its peasant organizations have also found a ready problem to exploit in the areas threatened by bandits and rebels. Such areas where they have made progress are parts of West Java, and, after February 1958, the rebel areas of Sumatra and North Sulawesi.[56] Since its November 1951 agrarian program, PKI has called for the confiscation of the land of prorebel and probandit landlords, and its distribution to the poor and landless peasants,[57] a demand strongly emphasized by PKI and BTI in West Java. PKI and its mass organizations have also been loud and persistent in their demand for government provision of weapons to enable the peasants to protect themselves. The Communist solicitude for the victims of armed bands is illustrated by a mass meeting in Bogor in 1954 where PKI distributed clothes and rice to peasants who had been robbed or burned out by Darul Islam gangs.[58]

Only about 25,000 persons per year have left Java for the outer islands since 1949, but they comprise a significant percentage of the population in South Sumatra where they also probably constitute a large proportion of BTI's September 1957 claim of 108,210 members in that region. Unhappily for the transmigrants, transport shortages cause bottlenecks at ports, thieves in the shape of shopkeepers, ticket sellers, and robbers strip them of their little wealth, and the areas they go to are often ill prepared. These conditions provide a source of discontent that PKI and BTI can exploit. Both PKI and BTI recognize the need for transmigration, but declare that it "must not be of the nature of moving poverty from Java to the other islands." [59] They demand adequate transportation, work tools, housing, medical facilities, and living expenses while the new land is being opened up.

Work in the Ordinary Villages

In the second half of 1953, PKI and its mass organizations began the immense task of organizing the great majority of Java's peasants who live in ordinary villages, villages where even PKI and BTI cadres often claimed that no peasant problems existed, that no landlords were to be found. The PKI leaders readily admit that "the task of cultivating the peasants' trust in the Party and of convincing the peasants of their own strength is a difficult one, especially if we bear in mind their backwardness." [60] Aidit recognized in July 1953, as the campaign to attract the peasant masses was begun:

Only by practical work among the peasants, only by leading the peasants in the struggle for their everyday demands, demands that seem small, insignificant, unimportant, only in this way can Party cadres and members have close relations with the peasants and receive their trust. Only by actions to demand things that seem small, insignificant, unimportant, can the peasants' organization grow stronger, wider and more solid.

Only through the work of organizing and educating the peasants can the peasants' struggle be raised to a higher level. Only through this work can the peasants be educated and mobilized so that the time will be ripe to carry out the slogans "land for the peasants," "distribution of land to the peasants," and "peasant private ownership of land."[61]

In order to strengthen the peasants' confidence in themselves and in PKI and BTI, the Aidit leadership has concentrated on "small but successful" actions. "Passionate and 'leftist' measures, not based on the true consciousness of the peasants, must not be taken. Measures of that kind confuse the peasants and retard their consciousness."[62] In each action, the peasants must be "convinced of its justice, correctness and benefit," and "the Party must always strive to be able to draw in and mobilize 90 per cent of the village inhabitants."[63]

The list of "small but successful" actions led by PKI and BTI among the peasants ranges from the most trifling to demands for rent reduction. In the words of a PKI guide for its peasant cadres:

After the peasant organization is formed, quickly undertake concrete activities in defense of the peasants' interests, such as the distribution of fertilizer, seedlings and tools at a cheap price, repairing the water channels, repairing the fish-ponds and distributing fish eggs, establishing coöperatives, sinking wells together, repairing the village bridges and roads, organizing a death association, general education and education of agrarian leaders, defense of people brought to court, eradication of illiteracy, organizing sports and cultural bodies, etc.[64]

And each activity is used to raise the peasants' class consciousness and militancy. As a leader of PKI and BTI reminded the peasant cadres:

In organizing mutual assistance when members suffer illness or death, do not forget to connect this activity with propaganda to the effect that the landlord's exploitation and oppression have caused the health of the peasant laborers and poor peasants to be very bad, their life in general to be shorter, many of their children to die in the womb or before reaching the age of six, many of their wives to die in childbirth . . . etc. In this way the peasants understand that the entire bad situation which befalls them is the result of the landlord's exploitation and oppression. In this way the peasants will gradually reach the conclusion that the landlord class is their first enemy, and by knowing the methods of exploitation used by the landlord the peasants will understand that the landlord's ownership of land is unjust and that the landlord must be opposed.[65]

Actions that directly affect the interests of the landlords, such as demands for joint land rent agreements, and demands for lowered interest rates on loans, higher wages for laborers, and lowered land rents, were not undertaken on any scale until after 1955. They are still limited in scope for three main reasons: first, in the present stage of the revolution the Aidit leadership seeks the broadest alliance in order to combat imperialism, and therefore does not want to alienate political forces containing landlord elements; [66] second, in the relative social peace of the Javanese village, the peasants need much preparatory work before they will take direct action against the local landlords; and, third, PKI and BTI are only now producing sufficient well-trained cadres willing and capable of directing antilandlord actions.

The April 1959 PKI First National Peasants' Conference formulated a new campaign slogan which could be the basis for arousing the poorer peasants against the landlords, and yet be sufficiently just to make opposition appear grossly unjust: the 6:4 slogan. That is, for the division of crops in the proportion of six parts for the sharecropper and four for the landlord, with the stipulation that if any landlords were already receiving less than four shares they should continue to do so, with a minimum of two and a half shares.[67] Communist and affiliated members of parliament put forward a motion in parliament for the 6:4 division of crops.[68] The government stepped in quickly with its own bill which, after some amendment, was adopted unanimously on November 20, 1959, and provided for a 5:5 division, though retaining agreements already more favorable to the tenants.[69]

Having won this parliamentary victory, PKI and BTI launched a campaign to acquaint the peasants with their rights under the new law. At the same time, the 6:4 demand has been extended gradually, but its implementation is slow and requires careful preparation because the

. . . 6:4 action and other actions against the landlords' exploitation are entirely new for the peasants and even for most BTI cadres. The existence of examples of successful action will facilitate *our work to convince the peasants of the justice of the 6:4 demand* and of the power of the peasants' unity. It also constitutes an important education for the local BTI cadres.[70]

Since 1957, but especially since 1959, PKI and BTI have been introducing a new form of peasant organization in the villages. Three types of *klompoks*, or groups, have been established alongside the existing village subbranches of the Party and BTI.[71] The subbranches are large and heterogeneous. The groups are kept small, and membership in them is open to peasants irrespective of political affiliation, religious belief, or membership in BTI. The first type are laborers' groups, embracing landless farm laborers as well as poor and middle peasants who must work for others to supplement their income. These are organized on the basis of type of work, such as hoeing, planting, and harvesting.

Groups of the second type are composed of tenant farmers, and the third type is for peasants who work their own land. The landholders' groups function, in effect, as mutual aid teams in the sphere of agricultural production. The groups as a whole are designed to broaden the influence of the Communist organizations, find potential member and cadre material, and press more effectively the demands of the different socioeconomic groups within the village.

Another important decision taken by the 1959 PKI peasants' conference was to discard the Party's previous antipathy to coöperatives.[72] The conference concluded that the formation of coöperatives would provide the Communists with an additional instrument for assisting the peasants and strengthening the Party's political influence and control over them. As the peasants still needed to be convinced of the benefit of the coöperatives, it was decided that the movement must advance "step by step." The first step would involve the formation of mutual aid teams in agricultural production, small savings-and-loan groups, and groups for the joint purchase of improved rice seed. Then, when the peasants were convinced that full-scale coöperatives would be to their advantage, these would be formed on the basis of "voluntary, democratic, open, mutually beneficial, self-established, and nonpolitical" principles. Both PKI and BTI have since been training cadres in the management of coöperatives, but the movement progresses slowly. As one BTI cadre reported in July 1961, "it is certainly not easy to speed up the coöperative movement among the peasants." [73]

An interesting feature of Communist work in the villages since the 1959 peasants' conference has been the assistance given to peasants in increasing farm production. Cadres have been active in popularizing eight principles for increasing rice yields: plough deeply, plant closely, improve seedlings, give more fertilizer, improve tools, weed the crops, combat diseases, and improve irrigation. BTI has also been instrumental in developing improved strains of rice and in distributing the new seed.

In 1959 and early 1960, Communist cadres confidently assured the author that the bourgeois government of Indonesia would never institute land reform. They were soon proved wrong. Between September and December of 1960, the government issued a land reform act which imposed severe limits on the maximum size of landholdings (plantations excluded) in each regional administrative unit.[74] Throughout most of Java the maximum holding per family is fixed at 5 hectares (12.4 acres) of irrigated land or 6 hectares (14.8 acres) of unirrigated fields. The law required land held in excess of the maximum to be redistributed to peasants owning little or no land, the beneficiaries to pay for their new land over a period of fifteen years. Given the rate of monetary inflation, the real price paid by the recipients could be very low. Due to the usual governmental inefficiency in Indonesia, the registration of excess lands proceeded slowly. By February 1963, only 1,500 hectares had been actually redistributed.[75]

PKI and BTI publicly welcomed the land reform law and promised assistance in its implementation. But they also maintained that both the 1959 crop division law and the land reform act "will not entirely eradicate imperialist and landlord power." [76] In a sense they were right. The law requiring a 5:5 division of crops is only a first step toward reducing farm rents. And land reform, in Java at least, cannot eradicate the land problem, which is basically one of land shortage rather than of landlords. According to official government statements, only approximately 200,000 hectares (about 500,000 acres) will be available for redistribution in Java.[77] This is an insignificant amount to divide among Java's approximately 45 million peasants, half of whom are estimated to be currently landless. In other words, despite the stringent land reform, the great majority of Javanese peasants will remain landless or poor peasants. They will still have to work as laborers or tenant farmers on the land of their neighbors. Thus the problems of farm laborers' wages and land rents will also remain, and in the absence of cheap government credit facilities the poorer peasants will continue to fall prey to moneylenders. Therefore the "everyday needs and demands" of most peasants, in Java at least, will not be altered radically by the "bourgeois" land reform program. Meanwhile, in order to retain the support of those who may rise to middle peasant status through the acquisition of redistributed land, the Communists are already organizing mutual aid teams, production-boosting campaigns, and people's coöperatives.

4. THE POLITICAL USEFULNESS OF COMMUNIST SUPPORT IN THE VILLAGES

Massive peasant support was essential to the Aidit leadership in order to bring about a Communist victory by either peaceful or forceful means.

With large-scale peasant electoral support, PKI could increase its parliamentary representation. This in turn could increase the Party's bargaining position in national politics, and bring about if not a Communist government or Communist participation in a coalition government, at least the alliance of important political forces among the divided revolutionary political elite. It was also possible, though this advantage was realized probably in retrospect, that massive popular support would reduce the possibility of governmental repression of the Party for two reasons. First, the government would be hesitant to repress a party with obvious popularity—especially PKI which, under the national united front policy, was careful to appear friendly to the nationalists and responsible in the exercise of its role as a non-government party. Second, the government might hesitate to attempt to repress a party with broad, organized support out of fear of the calamitous results such an attempt might bring.

The Aidit leadership may have hoped to win power by completely peaceful means, but it cannot have expected to. It needed to build organized mass support capable of neutralizing or defeating the forces which would be expected to oppose a Communist bid for power. With the effort to organize mass support in the countryside, the Aidit leadership must have aimed to develop a force which, in the event of a political crisis, could be a major weapon for one of two purposes: to be displayed so as to intimidate opponents and convince wavering allies, that is, to win power by the mere display of apparent strength; or, if the opposition could not be intimidated, to be used along with the other Communist organizations in order to destroy the Party's opponents.

Results have certainly been achieved toward what might be termed the peaceful use of peasant support. PKI's numerical size and apparent organizational ability helped encourage first PNI and then Sukarno to seek the alliance of the Communists—of course on mutually beneficial terms. It is also possible that the size of PKI's rural votes and therefore presumed rural strength and popularity has been a factor in deterring repressive measures against the Communists.

Peasant support was an important factor enabling PKI to win 16.4 per cent of the total votes cast in the September 1955 parliamentary elections. Peasant support, too, was largely instrumental in the Communists winning 27.4 per cent of the votes in the provincial and local elections held in Java in the second half of 1957. And if the second national general election had been held on schedule in September 1959, PKI was generally expected to gain 25 per cent of the votes, and therefore one quarter of the seats in parliament. Given Indonesia's multiparty system and the strong antagonisms among the non-Communist and anti-Communist political parties, PKI would then have been in a very strong position. It could well have meant an early Communist entry into a coalition government. But the second general elections were postponed indefinitely. The parliamentary system, that had been in operation since the end of 1945, was swept aside as President Sukarno and the armed forces established the semiauthoritarian system known as Guided Democracy. In these changed circumstances, the Aidit leadership had little maneuverability. It was forced to seek alliance with Sukarno, whom it privately detested, and to accept, with only restrained protest and often public avowals of support, the various governmental measures to restrict the freedom of parties and mass organizations. Why? The answer is rooted in the real power available to PKI through its mass support. We have seen how the workers, organized in SOBSI and PKI, are still far from the acceptance of militant action against "the authorities." The peasants who support PKI and BTI are even less inclined to militancy.

The real power that the Aidit leadership wields through its support among the peasants is determined largely by two factors: the authority and influence exercised by other forces in the villages, and the nature of the support given by the peasants to the Communists.

The unanimous opinion of those non-Communist politicians and government officials with whom I talked in 1959 and 1960 and who were concerned with the peasants was that as yet PKI had achieved little in building support that could openly oppose, let alone attack and destroy, "the authorities" in the countryside. The authority of the central government's rural civil service and of the village officials has certainly declined, but it is still sufficiently impressive to deter the great majority of peasants from open acts of defiance. Furthermore, while Communist organization has grown, so too has the strength and authority of the army and the police in the rural areas. Only in the rarest cases would the peasants, conditioned to obey, stand against a combination of "authorities." PKI and BTI have admitted publicly the great difficulty in making the peasants aware of their exploited position, and in arousing them to even mild actions against Indonesian landlords. The present slogan is "all roads lead to 6:4," but even these roads are long and difficult, and if successfully traversed lead only to the start of the fundamental task of building peasant support that can act in a disciplined and militant manner when called upon to do so.

As in their trade-union work, the Indonesian Communists have faced competition in their effort to win mass rural support. At the end of 1954, for example, there were 35 peasant organizations in Indonesia, 7 centralized and more or less nationwide, and 28 locally based.[78] Within Java, it would seem that BTI membership is larger than that of all other peasant organizations combined. Despite this, the Moslem STII and PNI's Petani have greater influence than their membership would suggest mainly because they contain persons who retain influence and authority in the villages. The former includes many wealthier *santris,* and the latter many government and village officials.

Of greatest importance in calculating the real power that the Communists obtain from their peasant support, is the character of that support. What might be termed the intellectual appeal of Communism has had little if any effect among the Indonesian peasants. The Communists have had to win sympathy by concrete work for the peasants' interests, and this has been done to a large extent in the non-*santri* areas of Java through PKI and a wide range of organizations from the mass organizations to coöperatives, savings associations, and cultural and sports groups which may or may not be openly linked with the Communist organizations. Some areas where traditional social patterns have been weakened have proved more ready to accept the support of PKI and its organizations. In the majority of villages, however, the Communists have had to tread warily, to conform to village modes of behavior, to work wherever possible through traditionally influential persons. Step by step PKI has sought to give the peasants an awareness of their exploited position, to lead them to actions of an increasing scope to the point where they will oppose the local landowners. But the peasants and even many cadres are still unwilling to oppose the local persons of status, let alone the government authorities.

The Indonesian peasants generally—and especially, perhaps, those of Java—are basically passive and conservative in their political outlook. They are not militant, nor are they revolutionary. Precisely by pursuing moderate, nonrevolutionary tactics since it gained control of PKI, the Aidit leadership has indeed succeeded in winning the support of a substantial segment of the peasantry. But by the same token it has failed so far to develop any significant degree of militancy among them. The peasants welcome Communist assistance in the solution of their small but urgent problems, and in return they are willing to join the Party, or its subordinate mass organizations, and to give PKI their votes—but little else. The Aidit leadership is cognizant of this situation and expects to take years to create a militant and revolutionary force from the peasantry. It appears doubtful if such a force can be created in the foreseeable future.

XV

THE PETTY BOURGEOISIE

Doubts expressed above as to the validity of the Aidit leadership's concept of the petty bourgeoisie as a sociopolitical category in Indonesia,[1] are strengthened by an analysis of the efforts made by PKI to attract and organize the groups listed as comprising the petty bourgeoisie. The groups are of such diverse interests, social status, and political awareness that the PKI leaders have been forced to use a wide variety of methods in order to seek their support—with a marked lack of success among several of the groups.

The Indonesian petty bourgeoisie, as defined by the Aidit leadership, is, in general (with the obvious exceptions of the urban poor and the fishermen), better educated than the workers and peasants, and better informed on the progress of other countries and therefore on the extent of the incapacity and corruption of the successive Indonesian governments. It also suffers, with the obvious exception of the doctors, the economic chaos, the inflation, and the shortage of consumer goods and raw materials. As a result, the petty bourgeoisie ought to be more sympathetic than most not only to PKI's vocal struggle to alleviate the misery of the people, but also to PKI's promise of a people's democracy.

The short-term, frequently repeated demands of PKI that should appeal to the petty bourgeoisie in general include: reduced prices and increased distribution of essential commodities, increased educational and health facilities, eradication of corruption, better balance of Indonesia's foreign trade between capitalist and socialist countries so as to ensure high prices for Indonesia's exports, and the import of adequate industrial raw materials and consumer goods, resistance to fascism and the guarantee of democratic rights, the rapid development of the national economy, and the eradication of imperialist power and influence. PKI's opposition to the "fanatical" Moslems of Masjumi and the Darul Islam has also appealed to the largely unreligious or *abangan* petty bourgeoisie. Furthermore, the literate petty bourgeoisie should be able to grasp the significance of PKI's long-term goal, a people's democracy, which is promised to bring full national independence, full democratic rights for the people, the eradication of feudalism, and rapid economic development.

From the limited evidence I obtained, however, it appears that the political or intellectual appeal of PKI has met with little response, even among the intellectuals. Members of the petty bourgeoisie have been attracted to the Party or one of its mass organizations by what the Communists do or promise to do to promote the specific sectional interests of the population. The Party has sought to attract the urban poor by its work in the *kampongs,* as has been seen above; [2] the women's organization, Gerwani, has sought primarily to attract the poorer women, including those who constitute a high proportion of the petty traders; [3] Communist-led student organizations have sought to attract students in high school and university; [4] and the youth organization, Pemuda Rakjat, has attracted youths from the poorer sections of the petty bourgeoisie. [5]

The Aidit leadership has made special efforts to attract and organize two of the groups included in the petty bourgeoisie: the fishermen, and the intellectuals.

1. THE FISHERMEN

In 1959 the Aidit leadership was increasingly aware that due to the atrophy of democracy and the increased power of the army, the Party would probably face an ultimate choice between suffering repressive measures and making a bid for power. If faced with this choice, the support of Indonesia's fishermen would be a valuable asset: in the absence of a sizable navy, they could run personnel and equipment into or out of Indonesia in general and each island in particular.

Mention of the need to organize the "millions" of fishermen [6] was made by the BTI and PKI leaders in 1957 and 1958. That conditions were ripe for Communist organization was confirmed by a 1959 PKI survey of 70,000 fishermen in seven districts of East Java.[7] Seventy per cent were found to be fishermen laborers; not uncommonly fifteen laborers shared half the catch while the boatowner received the other half. Fifteen per cent were poor fishermen. Both of these groups were subjected to other forms of exploitation, including interest rates on loans as high as 1,233 per cent per annum. The PKI First National Peasants' Conference of April 1959 made a detailed examination of the question of organizing fishermen.[8] An analysis was made of the social divisions among fishermen which closely paralleled the analysis of the peasantry, and which concluded that:

The fishermen-laborers and the poor fishermen together with the middle fishermen are moving forces of the revolution and must therefore be aroused, organized and mobilized in actions for improved conditions and democratic liberties, and in the struggle for complete national independence.

The conference called for the creation of fishermen's unions for the laborers, of coöperatives "serving, in the first place, the interests of the poor and middle fishermen," and of "other organizations serving general interests, such as cultural and sports clubs." On August 3, 1960, the PKI Central Committee issued a circular which admitted that "until now the work of the Party among fishermen has not been developed and in some places has not begun at all." [9] Section committees were ordered to appoint cadres to supervise the work among fishermen, and instructions were given for the creation of a multiplicity of organizations in the fishing villages. The PKI Second National Peasants' Conference in July 1961 initiated a campaign to have a harvest-division law enacted for fishermen.[10] And SOBSI subsequently lent its services in the formation of trade unions for fishermen laborers.

2. THE INTELLECTUALS

The Aidit leadership has been perplexed by the intellectuals. In April 1951 the intellectuals were confidently classified among the driving forces of the revolution, and in 1957 Aidit included them within the supposedly revolutionary petty bourgeoisie.[11] But when they continued to withstand the attractions of the Party, the leadership was forced into qualifications. In November 1952, the Party leaders drew a distinction between "the old-generation intellectuals, who in general can be at the most neutralized, especially in revolutionary times," and the younger intellectuals who could be made a real and active force in the revolution.[12] This distinction according to age was discarded in 1957 when Aidit declared that ". . . intellectuals and the student youth are not a class in society but their class position is determined by family origin, by their conditions of living and by their political outlook." [13] The PKI Sixth National Congress in September 1959 acknowledged the intellectuals to be "generally patriotic and strongly anti-imperialist," but explicitly divided them into two categories: those "born and created of Indonesian labor who are striving for the traditions of our people and of our intellectuals," and those with an inconsistent attitude to the revolution, the ideological representatives of the economically and politically insecure bourgeoisie.[14]

What accounts for PKI's continued failure to attract more than a handful of intellectuals? [15] A partial but complex answer revolves around the social origins, social status, and occupations of the intellectuals. The older intellectuals tend to come from aristocratic or wealthy families because such families were the only ones which, under Dutch rule, were able to give their children higher education, and even today very few university students have their origins in the poor sections of society.[16] At the same time, achievement in formal education is an important determinant of social status so that, by and large, a high level of formal education brings with it a high social status. And high-status Indonesians have shown, in general, little concern for the plight of their poorer countrymen.

It has also been the case since independence that Indonesia, unlike some countries, has had no group of unemployed intellectuals to form a reservoir of revolutionaries. Anyone with a fairly high level of formal education has found ready and prestigeful employment, especially in the growing bureaucracy and also in the expanding university system and the large, mostly foreign, private concerns. In order to obtain, retain, or advance their positions, the educated Indonesians have tended either to remain aloof from politics or to support the political parties of the persons in control of employment. And in no case, in government, university or private employment, have those in control been Communists.

Although PKI has failed to attract many intellectuals, it has built LEKRA, the only large, nationwide mass organization of cultural workers.

LEKRA

LEKRA was founded on August 17, 1950, with Njoto as the Party's guiding hand in the central secretariat. Special sections were set up for literature, the plastic arts, voice, drama and film, philosophy, and sports. Within a year, 21 branches had been established, sixteen in Java, three in Sumatra, one in Kalimantan, and one in Sulawesi.[17]

Major structural changes were made by the first LEKRA congress held in January 1959.[18] Before the congress the structure had been a simple one: at the center, the national council and the secretariat with the six special sections; a LEKRA organization at the regional level; and the local branches. The congress created a system of institutes which runs parallel to the old structure: institutes of literature, plastic arts, music, dance, drama, film, and science, with their own organizations reaching down to the branch level, and actually embracing ordinary members in their own cultural field. The ordinary branches now look after "general cultural matters." Under the new system, individual members receive better guidance and assistance in their own field. In July 1962 LEKRA leaders founded a "People's Art University" in Djakarta, containing an initial three academies: plastic arts, voice, and dance.[19]

In an interview, the LEKRA secretary-general claimed that as of May 1960 there were about 200 branches, each with two or three institute sections.[20] The most important and largest branches were in Jogjakarta, Surakarta, and Djakarta, while in Jogjakarta LEKRA was considerably strengthened by the *de facto* affiliation of a large group of young painters in the nominally independent People's Artists.[21] The LEKRA leaders overcame thirteen years of reticence to announce in May 1963 that their organization had 100,000 members.[22]

LEKRA, as the other mass organizations, has endeavored to attract membership by appealing to the interests of a specific section of society. As the only national cultural organization to have survived the last thirteen years, LEKRA has provided not only a place for discussion of common interests, but also some training in the different cultural fields. In a country almost devoid of facilities for the exhibition of works of art, LEKRA has provided them for any artist, irrespective of style. As an outlet for the work of both artists and writers, LEKRA publishes a periodical, *Zaman Baru*,[23] and since 1959 has begun to publish books and booklets. LEKRA artists are employed to create the decorations and posters for PKI and its mass organizations at times of celebrations, congresses, conferences, and elections,[24] and LEKRA members also provide talent for the cultural performances that are a popular feature of Communist meetings and election campaigns.

LEKRA claims to have had success in bringing together and organizing the *dalangs* in West and Central Java, the *ludruk* groups of East Java, and *gamelan* players, and to have been instrumental in the formation of BAKOKSI, a separate organization of *ketoprak* artists.[25] That is, it has acted as a sort of trade-union for the players in the traditional forms of Javanese entertainment.

LEKRA has been able to provide, thanks to its Communist connections, the reward of trips to Soviet-bloc countries for its most active members. The first LEKRA group to go abroad consisted of six persons who attended the 1951 Berlin youth festival. LEKRA members have attended all subsequent Communist international youth festivals, and have also participated in cultural delegations to several Communist countries.

Finally, in order to attract cultural workers by an appeal to their specific interests, LEKRA has formulated demands in their interest. For example, LEKRA's Second National Conference, held from October 28 to 30, 1957, demanded tax relief for artists, bigger subsidies for cultural organizations, lighter entertainment tax, protection and assistance for the national film industry, and the creation of a Ministry of Culture.[26] The national congress in January 1959 demanded reduced prices for cultural tools such as books, paints, canvas, and musical instruments.[27]

The political usefulness of LEKRA for PKI has been varied. Apart from adding its voice to those of the other mass organizations in support of PKI's position on particular issues, LEKRA has enhanced the attractiveness of PKI and the other mass organizations by making them more colorful with posters, banners and cultural entertainment. By organizing the artists in the traditional forms of entertainment, it has succeeded in infusing a pro-PKI political content into these tremendously popular art forms, and LEKRA has been the spearhead for the attack on Western "rock 'n' roll culture," with its "immoral," "sadistic," "war-thirsty" books, films, and music. This attack may have played a part in persuading the government to ban the "immorality" of Western music, Western dancing, and the hula-hoop.

LEKRA has tried to teach its members to portray the sufferings of the people in a realistic manner. But LEKRA is in no position to exact artistic discipline from its members who are in the organization for what it gives them and who still largely follow their own individualistic progress.[28] What LEKRA has done, as the only significant nationwide cultural organization in Indonesia, is to bring a wide range of cultural workers, from film actors and peasant entertainers to sophisticated poets and artists, into contact with PKI and into work of benefit of the Party.

XVI

YOUTH

The adult workers and peasants in Indonesia have been slow to discard the tradition of open obedience and to regard inequality as an injustice which they themselves can remove. As a result, they have not provided a fully satisfactory source of cadre material for PKI and its mass organizations. The Aidit leadership has spent, therefore, much effort in order to attract and organize the youth, to mold them politically before the dead weight of traditional values and behavior is placed upon them.

As youth is differentiated according to age and education, several mass organizations have been established for it. The largest and most important is Pemuda Rakjat, the continuation under a new name of Pemuda Sosialis Indonesia of the revolution. Pemuda Rakjat is the only mass organization which has formal ties with the Party, and which receives open assistance from the Party. It is aimed primarily at the urban and rural poor with little or no education. For high-school students there is IPPI, and for students of institutes of higher education, including universities, there is CGMI. Youngsters below high-school age have been provided with a Communist-led scout association and a young pioneer movement.

1. PEMUDA RAKJAT

THE GROWTH OF THE ORGANIZATION

During the revolution the Socialist Party included many shades of
leftists from the Sjahrir Socialists to covert Communists. Its youth
organization, Pemuda Sosialis Indonesia, played an important role in
mobilizing youth to the defense of the Republic, and organized its
own armed groups. The highest membership reached was about 50,000
to 100,000.[1] At the beginning of 1948 the Sjahrir Socialists broke away
from the Socialist Party to form the PSI, but they did not establish
their own youth organization until the end of 1954. Many of the
leaders and members of Pemuda Sosialis Indonesia were involved in
the Madiun rebellion, and the organization later claimed that one
thousand of its leaders were killed.[2]

The rebellion did not result in the proscription of the organization,
and its Third Congress was held in Djakarta from November 4 to 12,
1950. Total membership had fallen to 30,000, and the number of
branches to 149.[3] Perhaps indicative of an attempt to reëstablish the
organization's good character was the large photograph of President
Sukarno which, side by side with one of Mao Tse-tung, watched over
the congress. The congress was a victory for the Aidit group which
was then struggling to capture complete control of PKI. In line with
the thinking of the Aidit group, the old name of the organization was
discarded as one which would turn away prospective members. It was
replaced by Pemuda Rakjat. The declared objective of the organization
was altered from a socialist state to a people's democracy. Wikana, an
opponent of the Aidit group, was removed from the leadership. And
at a time when the Aidit group was struggling against Tan Ling
Djie's concept of more than one Marxist-Leninist party, the congress
promised to assist in the creation of a single Marxist-Leninist party,
PKI, as the leader of the revolution. During 1950 Pemuda Rakjat
joined the World Federation of Democratic Youth, and since then one
or other leader of Pemuda Rakjat has been a vice-president of the
WFDY.

During the first two years or so after the November 1950 congress,
Pemuda Rakjat, like the other PKI-led mass organizations, continued
to show a "sectarian" character despite its verbal rejection of sectarianism. From the little information that remains of its activities prior to
about 1954, it would appear that they were mainly complementary to
PKI's political agitation for a people's democracy, against colonialism,
against the Round Table Conference agreement, against the August

1951 mass arrests, against the state of war and siege regulations, and against PKI's political opponents. The first signs that sectarianism was being abandoned appeared only when the Aidit leadership was formulating its concept of a broad national united front.[4]

The Pemuda Rakjat Fourth Congress was held in November 1952, attended by about 300 delegates representing the 118 branches and 46,598 members.[5] The general report to the congress noted that 129 leaders had been imprisoned during the August 1951 arrests,[6] and contained a further strong attack on sectarianism. The constitution adopted by the congress opened Pemuda Rakjat to all young people, aged 14 to 30, who were Indonesian citizens and who agreed to the organization's constitution. Both entrance and membership fees were set so low that even if collected they would not exclude any potential member, however poor.[7]

Following the congress, membership began to rise slowly, and in June 1953 the national council issued the first plan for expansion of membership.[8] The goal was an increase from 70,319 to 150,000 by the end of 1953. By the time of the First National Conference in July 1954, Pemuda Rakjat claimed 281 branches and 202,605 members, of which 180 branches and 166,631 members were in Java, and 81 branches and 29,974 members in Sumatra.[9] The conference launched an ambitious plan to raise membership to 500,000 by the end of the year, with the emphasis on moving out of the towns into the rural areas. This goal was not reached, but in June 1955 Pemuda Rakjat claimed 458 branches and 450,000 members, and 601 branches and 616,605 members at the end of 1955.[10] Apparently the movement into the villages was successful, for it was claimed that about 75 per cent of the members in June 1955 were poor peasants.[11] By the end of 1955, 80 per cent of members were peasants, 15 per cent workers and office workers, 5 per cent students of high school and university, and 1 per cent "others," including small tradesmen and fishermen.[12] The secretary-general even complained that the number of young workers was now too low. Only about 5 per cent of members were girls.

The problem of cadre education was raised in the Pemuda Rakjat Fifth Congress held in July 1956. Some attempt had already been made at publication in order to provide material of use for cadres, but with indifferent success.[13] During the election campaign for the Constituent Assembly, the Pemuda Rakjat executive committee had instructed members to study Aidit's *For the Victory of the National United Front in the General Elections* as well as the committee's report to the fourth national council plenum.[14] The congress was told that in future education would be concentrated at the center and provincial

and *kabupaten* level for cadres, with collective discussions in all leadership bodies and members' groups.[15] In order to implement Marxist-
Leninist education, proper relations had to be arranged with PKI and
the Party's directives carried out. Visits to the Soviet bloc have been
of importance as political education as well as rewards. It was not
divulged what percentage of youth delegations abroad have been
Pemuda Rakjat members, but large delegations have attended, for
example, the Communist international youth festivals: 63 Indonesians
went to Berlin in 1951, about 100 went to Bucharest in 1953 (61
spending an extra three months in Eastern Europe, the USSR, and
China), 37 to Warsaw in 1955, about 200 to Moscow in 1957 (of whom
some also visited China and North Korea), and 136 to Helsinki in
1962.[16]

During 1958 Pemuda Rakjat formulated a plan of organization and
education to be completed before the Sixth Congress scheduled for the
beginning of 1960.[17] The important goals for the plan were four:

1. To increase membership to one million.

2. To extend organization into new areas, especially outside Java.

3. With regard to cadres: (a) to arrange the movement of cadres
from the better-established to the newer areas; (b) to arrange for every
province or province-level region[18] in Java and Sumatra (except
Djambi and Riau) to have two full-timers, and each similar area outside Java and Sumatra one each; (c) to arrange for every commissariat
in Java and Sumatra (except Djambi and Riau) to have at least one
full-timer, and outside Java and Sumatra one half-timer; and (d) to
arrange for every branch to have at least one mobile activist readily
available for work.

4. To implement the following education program: (a) at the center,
"shifts" of one month each in a central school to teach the history of
social development, the basic problems of the revolution, the Indonesian youth movement, and problems of Pemuda Rakjat organization; (b) at the province level, "shifts" of half a month to teach *How
Society Develops*, the *ABC of the Indonesian Revolution* (both of
which are study guides issued by PKI for use in its section and subsection schools), the Indonesian and international youth movements,
and problems of Pemuda Rakjat organization; (c) at the commissariat
level, schools and courses to study the Indonesian and international
youth movements, to give an understanding of the role of Pemuda
Rakjat, and to give general knowledge; (d) in the branches, discussions
on theory, using material from *Harian Rakjat* as well as the Pemuda
Rakjat constitution; and (e) in the subbranches, political lectures given

by leaders of the branch and by members of the local PKI subsection. Students in the schools were to live in hostels, and to work similarly to students in PKI schools. The general plan was that the schools at each level would educate cadres and activists from the immediately lower level, while the political lectures in the subbranches would be for both members and nonmembers.

At the end of 1957 there had been 802 branches and a claimed membership of 800,000.[19] In July 1958, the national council raised the membership goal to 1,200,000, and asked the urban sections of the organization to give attention not only to workers and girls, but also to high-school and university students.[20] The executive committee's report to the council indicated, however, that in fields other than membership expansion difficulties were being faced.[21] The periodical *Generasi Baru* could not be published due to a shortage of funds; the education system was not yet in operation; [22] and the losses suffered by Pemuda Rakjat at the hand of PRRI-Permesta rebels forced the organization to give the areas outside Java a prior claim on cadres.[23]

In 1959 "cadre education was begun on a nationwide scale and in a carefully organized fashion." [24] The central school began its first "shift" in January 1959,[25] and was soon followed by schools and courses at the lower levels as laid down in the 1958 plan. The central school held two shifts each year, each shift lasting one and a half months and taking 30 to 40 cadres. In the provincial and commissariat schools the courses lasted from one to three weeks depending partly on how often the students could meet.[26] Subjects taught were in line with the plan. Publishing efforts were not so successful, but in 1960 the small newssheet *Buletin Pemuda Rakjat* was still being published, at a rate of 10,000 copies per month, and was being distributed to each subbranch where it served as material for discussion, lectures, and for improving the organization.

At the time of the Pemuda Rakjat Sixth National Congress in September 1961, there were 1,250,000 members.[27] Seven per cent, or 87,500, were girls. There were now 172 *kabupaten*-level offices, 1,416 *ketjamaten*-level offices, and 10,798 subbranches. Claimed membership reached 1.5 millions in the early months of 1963.

It is difficult to estimate the number of full-time cadres in the Communist youth organization especially as many cadres often double as cadres for PKI and for one or more of the other mass organizations. From personal observation and from the sparse hints contained in speeches and published documents, it would appear that Pemuda Rakjat probably has at its disposal a few hundred full-timers or part-timers.

This is incomparably more than any other youth organization. Futhermore, Pemuda Rakjat receives constant assistance from PKI and the other Communist-led mass organizations.

THE ACTIVITIES OF PEMUDA RAKJAT

As has been seen, Pemuda Rakjat in the first two years or so after the November 1950 congress concentrated on directly political action. Since 1952 or 1953 political action has not been abandoned, but it has been concerned largely with building the image of the Communist group as the militant defender of Indonesian sovereignty, the patriotic bearer of the sacred flame of the 1945 revolution. Vociferous denunciation has been made of colonialism and imperialism, of any real or imaginary interference in Indonesia's internal affairs, of "Western culture" (including the "immoral" films and dances which offend a large number of Indonesians, especially the less educated and the more tradition-bound), and of "subversion," ranging from Dutch assistance to the Darul Islam rebels to Kuomintang and Western assistance to the PRRI-Permesta rebels.[28] The demand for the return of West Irian was regularly reiterated, and when PKI after 1955 began to move closer to Sukarno, Pemuda Rakjat organized campaigns in support of his concept of Guided Democracy. More recently, it drew attention to those contents of his Political Manifesto of August 17, 1959, which were of benefit to PKI. In a different vein, Pemuda Rakjat instructed its members to vote Communist in the 1955 and 1957 elections, and also organized brigades to campaign for PKI.

Pemuda Rakjat's political activities have been of considerable assistance to PKI. They also have attracted a few members and they have served to raise the political consciousness of cadres and activists. They have not been, however, a chief means by which Pemuda Rakjat has attracted over 1.5 million members. Sukatno, the secretary-general, wrote in 1955 that the way to attract mass membership was for Pemuda Rakjat to truly know the hopes of youth, for Pemuda Rakjat as a whole to fight for youth's "everyday interests," and for the subbranches to answer "the everyday needs of every section of youth, in workshops, factories, offices, harbors, urban *kampongs,* villages, estates, schools, etc." [29] Work toward this end has been twofold: the formulation of programs of demands aimed at each major section of youth, and the social and economic activities of the subbranches and groups.

An example of the comprehensive programs of demands drawn up by Pemuda Rakjat is that put forward by the Fifth Congress in July

1956.[30] It contained twenty general demands, seven demands specifically for young workers, eleven for young peasants, and fifteen for high-school and university students. The scope of the demands ranged widely: in the case of young workers, for example, from improved wages, social security, and work conditions, to the abolition of wage differences because of sex or age, the distribution of essential commodities at low prices, and technical education with scholarships from the employers and the government.

Political action and published programs of demands have meant little to the ordinary young worker or peasant. The great appeal of Pemuda Rakjat lies in its social and economic activities, and Pemuda Rakjat did not achieve mass membership until these were given priority.

The organization secretary told the First National Conference in July 1954:

In seeking for the *object of activity* of the organization to defend the rights of the various groups of youth in the various fields, *urgent* demands should be chosen which can be felt every day and *can* be carried out successfully, for example: abolition of *pologoro*, reduction of land rent, village democratization, higher wages, lower book prices, and so on.... In order to carry out demands as well as possible, we must coöperate with youth organizations, other mass organizations concerned, and with the mass of youth that is not yet organized ... what is especially important is to carry out concrete and continuous activity until the demands are successful. Once a demand is successful, then another object of activity must be sought with the goal of further raising the political and organizational consciousness as well as the militancy of the mass of youth, of the members and functionaries of Pemuda Rakjat.[31]

Urgent economic demands have sometimes been pressed by Pemuda Rakjat alone,[32] but usually Pemuda Rakjat has worked in conjunction with PKI and/or one or more of the other Communist-led mass organizations.

Like PKI and the other mass organizations, Pemuda Rakjat has also organized mutual-aid activities. They are of two kinds. The first is the organization of teams to build and repair roads and paths, bridges, houses, irrigation ditches, and gutters. The second is giving assistance to members in times of need or illness, which, among youth who are poor and without social services, is a valuable way of winning support. A member would be reluctant to leave Pemuda Rakjat and thereby forfeit the minimum security it affords him.[33] Pemuda Rakjat also helps its members by the provision of anti-illiteracy and general knowledge courses.

Professor A. G. Pringgodigdo, president of Airlangga University in Surabaja, told me that when he returned to Java after a visit to the

United States he was greatly impressed by the silence and darkness of the villages and urban *kampongs* once the sun had set, which at that latitude is always about 6 P.M. Few villagers or *kampong* dwellers can afford any but the weakest kerosene or candle light, and the atmosphere, in the absence of organized entertainment at a low price, is usually one of deep boredom. This is a clue to the main reason for Pemuda Rakjat's success in attracting a large membership.

Pemuda Rakjat provides the young members and peasants with something to do, something to relieve the darkness and boredom. The value of sports and cultural activities was recognized by Sukatno in November 1959 when he called for Pemuda Rakjat cadres to attract even greater numbers of workers and peasants by organizing all kinds of sports and cultural groups.[34] Volleyball, badminton, football, table tennis, and even chess clubs are organized under the leadership of the commissariats.[35] Physical-training groups have been established. The extent of the work in the sports field was indicated by the organization in November 1958 of a national sports festival, the first to be held by a youth organization in Indonesia.[36] Cultural activities vary widely, often in accord with the traditional forms of entertainment in the different regions, and include mixed choirs, many types of musical groups, and drama and music-drama groups.

An obvious failure in Pemuda Rakjat's work has been its attempt to attract girls into the organization. The leaders feel that the causes of this failure cannot be easily overcome: first, girls usually marry between the ages of 15 and 16 in the villages and by 20 at the latest in the towns, and once they are married they should enter the women's mass organization, not Pemuda Rakjat; and second, there is a strongly ingrained tradition that girls should not mix in public with young men. An effort has been made to overcome this second difficulty by creating special groups solely for girls and by experimenting with all-girl subbranches. Activities specifically for girls include classes in handicrafts such as raffia work, in how to raise fish, and in household skills such as sewing and cooking, but they are not yet widely developed.

Since the November 1950 congress, Pemuda Rakjat has proved a valuable assistant to PKI. It has attracted 1.5 million young workers, peasants, and students into an organization controlled by PKI; it has used them to add weight to the struggle of PKI and the other mass organizations; it has drawn from them cadres and activists who pass on to become cadres and activists of PKI and the other mass organizations; and it has endeavored to arouse in its ordinary members a sympathy for PKI and its general objectives. Through Pemuda Rakjat young people may acquire social, political, and educational values which will

predispose them as adults to vote for PKI and to enter PKI and/or
one of the other mass organizations.

2. STUDENT ORGANIZATIONS: IPPI AND CGMI

IPPI [37]

The Ikatan Peladjar Indonesia (League of Indonesian High School
Students) was formed in Jogjakarta in September 1945 and included
high-school students and a few university students. In February 1948
it merged with the Sarekat Mahasiswa Indonesia (Indonesian University Student Association) to form IPPI. During the revolution IPPI
and its predecessors were active chiefly in mobilizing students for the
struggle against the Dutch. The leadership consisted of socialists and
Communists, with no friction between the two. At the time of the
Madiun rebellion many of the Communist-inclined leaders in Java
went into hiding, but those in Sumatra remained in their posts. After
the second Dutch attack in December 1948 IPPI activists passed into
Dutch-occupied areas and helped establish a high-school student association which joined IPPI in 1950.

A covert Communist, Sujono Atmo, was elected to the IPPI leadership at the 1950 and 1951 congresses, and in the early 1950's the Communists won control of most branches in Central and East Java. The
non-Communists became aware of the attempt to capture IPPI and
united in 1954 to elect a central board free from Communists. Soon
afterward a split occurred in the Djakarta IPPI, rival Communist and
non-Communist sections competing. In 1957, because the central board
would not call a new congress, presumably because it was afraid of
losing control to the Communists, the Communist-led Bandung regional committee took the initiative of inviting the other Communist-
led sections to hold a congress. The congress was held, a new central
board elected, and two IPPI's existed, each claiming to be the only
legitimate one.

Since 1950 IPPI has declined in relative strength. Its membership
then was about 300,000. In 1960 it was still 300,000, despite a tremendous increase in the number of high-school students, and its organization was split in two. At the time of the split in 1957, the Communist-controlled branches, mainly in Java, contained a majority of
the membership. The decline in relative strength has been due to the
struggle between the Communists and non-Communists, to the de-
creasing attraction for university students who formed their own organizations and so removed what had been IPPI's source of leaders, to the

age (mostly over 30) of the present IPPI leaders, which increases the high-school students' apathy toward the organization, and to the refusal of many private schools, religious and secular, to permit their students to join IPPI because the organization includes many Communists.

The Communist-led IPPI concentrates its activities mainly on sports, social, and cultural activities in which it receives support from Pemuda Rakjat. Under its constitution IPPI is nonpolitical, and the Communists do not openly attempt to indoctrinate its members.[38] IPPI is used politically, in the short run, to mobilize students to support PKI-led rallies, demonstrations, and protests, and in the long run to plant the seeds of pro-PKI sympathies and to find a few promising students who can be trained to become Communist cadres and activists.

CGMI [39]

PKI has had indifferent success among the intellectuals as a whole, and very few university students have been won over. As an article in *Bintang Merah* of February 1958 [40] declared:

... up till now, bourgeois ideology and ways, that is, idealism and individualism, are still dominant in our universities. We see that the youths who graduate from high school with pure spirits and who form progressive elements, fall prey to bourgeois ideology and ways after entering university.

The article said that a Party seminar on work among students had just concluded that the Party must give "leadership and assistance to the students, both in fighting for economic and cultural improvements, especially improvements in their studies, and in raising their still far from adequate political consciousness"; and that the Communist-led student organizations must be broadly based on patriotism and unity.

Communist-led local university student associations were established in about 1950 in Bandung, Bogor, and Jogjakarta. They fused in November 1956 to form CGMI which initially claimed about 1,180 members. By early 1960 CGMI claimed 7,000 members in sixteen towns with institutions of higher learning,[41] the largest branches being Bandung and Jogjakarta with 1,750 members each, Surabaja with 500 members, Malang with 400, and the University of Indonesia in Djakarta with 300. These figures were hotly denied by the leaders of the other student organizations who estimated that CGMI had perhaps 4,000 members—compared with over 10,000 in the Masjumi-oriented HMI, about 10,000 in the PNI-oriented GMNI, and about 6,000 evenly divided between the Protestant and Roman Catholic student associations. At the beginning of 1963, CGMI claimed 17,000 members.[42] The rapid increase may be explained largely by the recruitment into CGMI of students of UNRA and the several PKI-organized academies. These new members are not true *mahasiswa*.

CGMI claims to be nonpolitical and nonreligious, and seeks to attract new members by a variety of activities such as:

1. strong opposition to the often sadistic initiation rites inflicted on new students;

2. waging a struggle for students' interests, for example organizing a delegation to the minister of education in January 1960 to demand reduced prices for books, increased budgets for the Ministry of Education, and increased students' allowances;

3. social events, such as excursions, badminton, and table tennis;

4. active propaganda in support of President Sukarno's political lines, and opposition to the PRRI-Permesta rebellion, and to all imperialist (Dutch, American, British, and SEATO) real and imaginary infringements of Indonesian sovereignty; and

5. opposition to "rock 'n' roll culture," and appeals for a culture based on "the Indonesian personality."

In 1959 CGMI also began to organize study groups for its own members, with the more advanced students helping the less advanced.

Apart from its own activities, CGMI attracts many new students because of its unique character. All other national student organizations are either openly tied to a political party or to a religion. For young students without political affiliation or strong religious feelings but who wish to join a national student organization, CGMI is the only one open to them.

As one CGMI leader complained to me, Indonesian students are not politically conscious, and CGMI must work to arouse political consciousness "not openly or directly but by stealth." Members are brought into such activities as protests against the visit of a Dutch aircraft carrier to West Irian in May 1960, peace weeks and peace campaigns made more attractive by lectures and films, and demands for the rejection of Peace Corps volunteers. Some few students have been won to Communist sympathies through CGMI, but the sparseness of their ranks is shown by the difficulties experienced in finding younger students to take over the leadership from those who should have left university years ago. In general, whenever members find that CGMI is Communist-led, most of them leave. Non-Communist student leaders generally estimated in 1960 that no more than 5 or 10 per cent of CGMI members realized that it was controlled by PKI.

Over the past few years the importance of all student organizations has declined due to a decrease in student interest in politics, the growth in importance and social activity of elected student councils in each university,[43] and an increasing concern with study. As study groups gained in importance for the student organizations, CGMI suffered a decrease in its attractiveness partly because it did not realize until after the other organizations the keen interest in such groups, and partly because there were very few Communist university teachers, and so few who could render expert assistance to the students in CGMI's groups.

The question still remains: why have PKI and CGMI failed to attract more than a handful of Indonesian students to the Communist cause? A partial answer might be found in the social origins of the students, and in the general political situation especially since 1956. The great majority of Indonesian university students still come from the social levels above the workers and poor and medium peasants.[44] They come from families which normally would support PNI, Masjumi, or the Socialist Party. Many come from families of government officials with a tradition of nonparticipation in political affairs as a safeguard for future positions and promotion. That some of the children of the middle class and aristocracy have not become Communists is surprising, but the Indonesian middle class and aristocracy have been remarkably free from the occasional reformist or radical devoted to the welfare of the "lower orders" and willing to risk their own future welfare and status for that cause.

The second factor, the general political situation since about 1956, was commented upon by all leaders of student organizations who were interviewed in 1959 and 1960. All claimed that during the previous four years or so a decline had occurred in the originally low political interest of students. This can partly be explained by the fact that the generation which fought in the revolution, and which would be expected to show a greater interest in politics, had largely passed through the universities by 1956 and had been replaced by young students concerned primarily with their studies—and with the jobs and status those studies would provide. The general discrediting of political parties by 1957 has also tended to reduce the students' interest in party politics. Furthermore, very few job opportunities for graduates are to be found outside the government—ministries, services, armed forces, nationalized enterprises, and so on. Because Sukarno and the army, which have become the dominant political forces since 1956, look with a jaundiced eye on the political parties, and because the political future of Indonesia is so uncertain, students have been discouraged from openly engaging in political activity because it could jeopardize their future careers.

3. COMMUNIST SCOUTS AND YOUNG PIONEERS

For the age group below high-school age, PKI established both scout and young pioneer organizations. A Communist-led scout association was already active in 1954. It remained small, its membership was not published, and early in 1961 it was absorbed, by presidential order, in a single, nationwide scout association under Sukarno as chief scout. Perhaps because of the lack of success of the scout association, Aidit in 1959 suggested the formation of a young pioneer organization which took the name Fadjar Harapan (Dawn of Hope).[45]

Despite its clear PKI origin, the Fadjar Harapan constitution declared that the organization was open to all children from six to thirteen years of age, and was "not associated with any political party." [46] Activities were to include sports and play, training in farming and handicrafts, study groups to assist with homework, visits to museums and historical sites, and encouragement to read "about the people's heroes and about the creative mind of the people." Party and Pemuda Rakjat cadres were instructed to study the experiences of pioneer organizations abroad and to adapt them to local conditions.

In the initial stages Fadjar Harapan was to be organized on a local basis with no central leadership. By May 1960 there were 1,000 members in Djakarta and groups were already being formed in the other large towns.[47] Through Fadjar Harapan the Aidit leadership presumably hoped to build a mass organization that would not only attract parents whose children could use the organization's facilities, but also prepare children for entry first into Pemuda Rakjat and IPPI, and then into PKI and its adult mass organizations. The enforced absorption of Fadjar Harapan in 1961 into the government's newly formed national scout association ungraciously prevented the Communist leaders from exploiting a new field of activity.

XVII

WOMEN

The attempt to organize women and to produce women cadres and activists has required patience and special methods. The poorer Indonesian women have even less experience than their menfolk in organizations, they are generally illiterate, and they are traditionally meek, especially in mixed company. But the Aidit leadership has considered the work of attracting and organizing women to be important because not only do women comprise half the electorate, they also play an important role in the economy. A high percentage of workers in industry are women, and women participate in agricultural work as peasants and as laborers on estates. In order to attract and organize women, especially those of the poorer classes, the Indonesian Communists have used the Party itself, the women's mass organization, Gerwani, the SOBSI unions, and BTI. Considerable success has been achieved in drawing women into the Party and the mass organizations, and in the last few years women have begun to occupy cadre and activist positions.

1. THE WORK OF THE PARTY

Mention has already been made of the instruction issued by the central leadership in January 1955 to increase the number of women members and to organize their activities in special women's groups, of the attention paid to the creation of women cadres, and of the increase in female membership of PKI to 100,000 in September 1957 and 258,000 in September 1959. But what has PKI offered women? What has it done to attract them directly?

The PKI election manifesto, endorsed in March 1954, claimed that "for women, to vote PKI means emancipation and the guarantee of equal rights." [1] An article in *Harian Rakjat* just before the Constituent Assembly elections of December 1955, explained at some length what was meant by equal rights.[2] PKI would guarantee equal rights in four fields: in marriage there would be equal freedom for both sexes in choosing a partner, equal rights in divorce and inheritance, joint discussion by mother and father about matters affecting their children, and joint ownership of the children; in the economic sphere, women would participate in the productive process as equals of men; in labor there would be no discrimination against women, and equal pay for equal work would be enforced; and in agriculture, women would have the same share as men when the land was divided. Also appealing particularly to the interests of women have been the frequently repeated Communist demands for the distribution of food and textiles at low prices, the provision of adequate education facilities for all children, and so on.

The methods used by PKI actually to attract women differ according to the social position of the women. An article by one of the leading women Communists, Setiati Surasto, described the methods used among the three broad social groups: the working-class and peasant women, the middle group, and the higher group.[3] Party membership can most easily be extended, she wrote, among working-class and peasant women. They face many difficulties in their lives and can feel personally the leadership and support of the Party in overcoming them. But because in general they are illiterate, have many children, and face an insecure life in terms of both income and marriage, it is difficult to get the poorer women together for meetings, especially meetings that are not very close to their homes. Therefore they are approached by assistance in times of need, and by small meetings of women who live close together. Later, this can be followed by efforts to press their everyday demands and to draw political conclusions from them. And so, gradually, they are prepared for participation in ordinary Party meetings and courses.

The middle group includes traders, middle peasants, middle government employees, students, and their wives—"longer time will be needed in order to attract them." They fear to be connected with the Party, Setiati wrote, because they might thereby lose their social position, or because they have been subjected to reactionary propaganda. PKI assists them in facing their everyday problems, for example by giving explanations of their rights and of such matters as tax and pension regulations.

Few women in Indonesia are prominent intellectuals or high government officials, but in its dealings with the higher groups of women, PKI attempts to win indirect influence over their husbands. Women in this group, Setiati warned, "require special attention." She recognized that they cannot easily be drawn into the Party, and that to try to do so openly would produce the reverse result. "They are afraid of the word Communist" and afraid to lose their own and their husband's positions. The most the Party can do is to invite them at every opportunity to functions as honored guests, and to explain the Party's position scientifically and openly. In this way PKI hopes to win their sympathy.

If they are already convinced [that the PKI position is correct] they will assist and support us. And if they are already convinced, then they can give moral and material support to our struggle, although in general they will not wish to give it openly. We must understand this and not hope for more than they can give.

Setiati emphasized that the middle and higher groups could give financial assistance to the Party, and she called for the regular collection of subscriptions and "support" which would cement their relations with the Party as well as give them a feeling of participation in the Party's struggle.

PKI held its First National Women's Conference from May 26 to 30, 1958. The problems of increasing the number of women members were discussed.[4] Aidit pointed out that "The greatest hindrance to Party work among the working women is the still dominant belief that the present bad conditions are predestined and cannot be changed." [5] Therefore, he said, the Party must work ceaselessly to convince them that the bad situation is man-made, and that through organization a better situation can be created. Sudisman called on the Party to give greater attention to the basic economic problems faced by women.[6] And Suharti listed some of the methods that had proved successful in attracting new women members: talks, preferably given by women cadres, on the rights of women and children and on the Party's stand for equality in marriage; *andjangsono* groups;[7] assistance to households in times of misfortune (death or sickness) or when busy (births, etc.); explaining the Party's stern attitude toward members who break the Communist moral code; and actions to defend the everyday interest of the women masses.[8] An obvious way of increasing women membership has been to persuade male members to bring their wives to meetings, and so gradually raise their political consciousness to the level at which they ask to join the Party.

By its own direct efforts PKI has brought many women into its ranks —but it is impossible to estimate what proportion has been attracted directly, and what through the activities of the mass organizations. At the time of the PKI Seventh National Congress in April 1962, the Aidit leadership was still dissatisfied with the Party's work to attract women members.[9] Although the number of women members was increasing, their percentage was declining. In the future, Aidit declared, "This situation must be remedied; more working women must be drawn into our Party."

2. GERWANI

The Communist-led mass organization for women made its humble entry on June 4, 1950, when Gerwis was founded as the merger of six local women's organizations scattered across Java. Total membership was only 500.[10]

In the first eighteen months of its existence Gerwis made little progress because membership was restricted to "fully politically conscious women."[11] The leadership, which was derived 99 per cent from the bourgeoisie,[12] issued pious demands for improved conditions for poor women,[13] but despite plans for work among the masses[14] made no real efforts to go down and organize them. Activities were concentrated on supporting PKI's political struggle. The result was that several Gerwis leaders were among those imprisoned in the August 1951 mass arrests, and that by December 1951, when the First National Congress was held, membership had risen only to 6,000.[15]

The First Congress concluded, "after criticism and self-criticism," that in the past too much attention had been given to outside actions and not enough to strengthening Gerwis, to internal actions "that directly concern the interests of women in their everyday life."[16] Some leaders and cadres were criticized for their "sectarian manner" of work, others for creating hostility to Gerwis by their unsubtle methods of work, especially in facing non-Gerwis people. The congress also, however, still concerned itself with political matters of little interest to the mass of women, such as West Irian, the cancellation of the Round Table Conference agreement, and a free foreign policy. It was decided, too, to join the International Federation of Democratic Women.

Despite the criticism and self-criticism indulged in at the December 1951 congress, the Gerwis leaders were slow to direct their attention to winning mass support by the study and exploitation of the everyday problems and interests of the women masses. The root of their unwillingness is probably found in their social origins. The Gerwis leaders were almost entirely middle class, and the Indonesian middle class in general has shown itself loath to go among the "lower orders" and organize them. In June 1953 claimed membership was only 40,000,[17] but the beginnings of work among the masses were indicated by a report in February 1953 on the work of Gerwis in East Java.[18] Among the 7,016 members in East Java at that time, Gerwis was running 8 kindergartens, 52 anti-illiteracy courses, 29 courses in handicrafts, mutual assistance in 54 places, and cadre courses in 17.

The Gerwis Second Congress was held in March 1954. Membership had reached 80,000, the number of branches 203.[19] Three foreign delegates attended, including Monica Felton from the International Federation of Democratic Women, and they sat as honorary members of the congress presidium. Umi Sardjono, the new chairman, announced at the close of the congress that Gerwis had thrown away its "sectarian characteristics," and to symbolize the end of sectarianism the name Gerwis was replaced by Gerwani. Consequently a new constitution was drawn up which opened Gerwani to all Indonesian women, 16 years old and over, "irrespective of political, religious and ethnic affiliation," who accepted the Gerwani constitution and program.[20]

The Second Congress decided to increase membership to two and one-half millions by the time of the next congress, but although this target was later criticized as "not objective," [21] a rapid increase in membership was achieved. Membership was claimed to be 400,000 just before the September 1955 general elections, and 500,000 at the time of the Constituent Assembly elections in December 1955.[22] In June 1956, when membership was reported to be 565,147, Gerwani had, in Java, branches in all *kabupatens* and large towns, an organization at the *ketjamatan* level in 40 per cent of the *ketjamatans*, and about 5,000 subbranches at the urban neighborhood and village level; outside Java there were branches or preparations for them in all of Sumatra, in West and South Kalimantan, and in North and South Sulawesi, while lower levels of the organization were already established in West Nusatenggara and Maluku.[23] At the time of the Third Gerwani Congress in December 1957, there were 671,342 members.[24]

In the period between the second and third congresses, Gerwani engaged in political as well as social and economic activities. During the 1955 general elections, 23,000 Gerwani members in Java alone worked in the election committees formed by the government to ensure the smooth execution of the elections; and 23 members ran on the PKI list, and 1 for the small nationalist party PRI. Five members were elected to parliament on the PKI ticket to the Constituent Assembly. In the 1957 local elections, 59 members were elected to local councils,[25] almost all from the PKI lists. Strong support was given to the peace movement, especially in collecting signatures for the Vienna Peace Appeal, and Gerwani's support was given to whatever PKI's political stand happened to be at the moment.[26]

Education on an appreciable scale was begun within Gerwani after the Second Congress. For ordinary members, an anti-illiteracy campaign was started in 1955 and within a year it was claimed that 30 per cent of members could read, though not all of them could yet write.[27] Courses for cadres concentrated on problems of organization and administration, but toward the end of 1957 an attempt was made to systematize cadre education with schools and courses at all levels of the organization and with uniform mimeographed guides for four basic subjects: the history of the national movement, the history of the national and international women's movement, problems of Gerwani organization and development, and instruction on the International Federation of Democratic Women, on the rights of women and children, and on peace.[28] From October 1950 until late 1952 Gerwis had published its own periodical. At the beginning of 1955, Gerwani started a new periodical *Wanita Indonesia (Indonesian Woman)*, but after irregular appearances it ceased publication in the middle of 1956. To replace it, *Berita Gerwani (Gerwani News)* was published, a single sheet devoted exclusively to news of the organization and designed to assist cadres in their work. Early in 1960 it had a circulation of only 2,000.[29]

Between the Second and Third Congresses, Gerwani, from the center to the regions, took an active part in actions to defend the rights of women and children, "which is the fundamental task of a women's organization." [30] In this field Gerwani launched a campaign during the 1955 elections to press its demand for a democratic marriage law, urged through members of parliament that the legal cost of reunion of separated partners should be removed while that of separation should be made greater, participated in committees set up experimentally in some areas by the Ministry of Religious Affairs to solve marriage disputes, demanded heavy penalties in cases of rape and abduction, and, in the subbranches, carried out many small actions of benefit to its members.[31] In defense of the interests of peasant and working-class women, Gerwani assisted BTI and the SOBSI trade-unions. Other social-economic activities included the creation of some training courses for midwives, and the establishment of 179 kindergartens and 3 elementary schools.

By the time of the Third Congress, held from December 22 to 27, 1957, Gerwani claimed 671,342 members, distributed geographically as follows: 613,262 in Java; 59,740 in Sumatra; 2,680 in Sulawesi; 2,260 in Nusatenggara; 1,900 in Maluku; and 1,500 in Kalimantan.[32] Within Java there were branches in every *kabupaten* and city, an organization at the *ketjamatan* level in 75 per cent of all *ketjamatans,* and subbranches in approximately 40 per cent of all villages. Some subbranches had been organized in places of work, but they were disbanded when the SOBSI unions established special women's departments.

From December 1957 to December 1960 Gerwani put into operation a three-year plan by which it was hoped finally to create a system of cadre education. Many cadre courses were held at the various levels, but their number and extent have not been divulged. At the beginning of 1960 the number of full-time cadres was still very low: three at the center, and an average of less than one for each of the branches (in December 1957 there were 183 branches). A considerable amount of part-time labor was available, however, from the women cadres in PKI and other Communist-led mass organizations, and from Gerwani members of parliament and the local representative councils.

The national council's report to the Third Congress in December 1957 criticized what it considered to be a continued overemphasis on political matters which were of little or no interest to the mass of Indonesian women:

Experience until now proves that actions concerning political questions are not balanced by social-economic actions, so that their importance is less directly felt by the women masses.

...this means not that political action is unimportant, but that we must further increase the number of actions concerning the rights of women and children as well as social-economic actions, actions that directly concern the life of the women masses, for example the question of *kampong* improvements, the problem of water, the problem of rice, etc.[33]

The national council's report to the congress declared that "in order to extend membership, every action must be based on the direct interests of the mass of women, discussed with the women themselves, and carried out as well as supported by them." A double guiding principle was laid down for any action: that its purpose should be reasonable so that it received wide sympathy and support from the community, and that it should be made at the right time and with realized limits.

The Third Congress endorsed a comprehensive 27-point program of demands which embraced problems ranging from marriage laws, work laws, and equal rights, to compulsory education, adequate medical provisions, and price controls on essential commodities.[34] With this program Gerwani hoped to appeal to all sections of Indonesian women from working-class and peasant women to the literate middle classes.

At the beginning of 1960, when Gerwani membership was claimed to be about 700,000, which indicated a considerable slowing down in the rate of growth after December 1957, Gerwani was engaged in the following practical work designed to attract and hold its mass membership: [35]

1. A popular activity was the *arisan* whereby all members of a group contributed a certain sum each week and each member in turn received the whole sum.

2. Mutual assistance was organized at times of need, such as death, birth, marriage, illness, and pregnancy.

3. Small-scale credit groups were organized.

4. There were 326 kindergartens and 3 elementary schools. Training courses were being held for kindergarten teachers. A few of the kindergartens were well equipped and had trained teachers, but the majority were still makeshift.[36]

5. In the middle of 1959 the national council decided that each branch should have at least five or six persons competent to manage a coöperative. Courses for coöperative cadres were begun in which officials of the government's Coöperative Service were asked to teach. By early 1960 a few consumer coöperatives had already been created.

6. Anti-illiteracy courses were still the main activity in Central and East Java. Some branches held courses for the general public, sometimes alone and sometimes in coöperation with government agencies.[37]

7. Women were assisted in their marriage problems. Gerwani cadres participated in the semiofficial bodies for the solution of marital disputes, and even occasionally defended members in court in divorce cases.

8. Handicrafts were taught: in the villages, the making of baskets and mats; in the towns, cushions and clothes; and everywhere, cooking.

9. Gerwani led popular campaigns to demand such as a decrease in the price of essential commodities, rice, textiles, sugar, and cooking oil.

10. Some cultural activities were organized, including choirs and drama groups, but these were not yet widespread.

11. Gerwani gave assistance to the other Communist-led mass organizations and to PKI in their efforts to obtain improvements for the different sections of society.

12. Gerwani joined with other women's organizations in celebrat-

ing Kartini [38] Day (April 21) and Mother's Day (December 22), and in the larger cities held its own celebrations for International Women's Day.

The basic members' groups met at least once a month and sometimes as often as once a week.

Membership of Gerwani increased rapidly again from the beginning of 1960. From 700,000 it reached 1,120,594 in December 1961, and 1.5 million in January 1963.[39] This increase may have resulted from the more intense concern with the problems of peasant women indicated by the special Gerwani seminar held in January 1961.[40] As of October 1961, when membership was .9 million, Gerwani had offices in all provinces, in 225 *kabupatens* and municipalities, and in 70 per cent of all *ketjamatans,* and subbranches in 40 per cent of all villages.[41]

It seems that the main attraction of Gerwani for the mass of urban and rural members is Gerwani's social work, the organization of *arisan* groups, small-scale credit groups, mutual assistance, literacy courses, kindergartens, and assistance in the solution of marriage problems. Little direct political education is given to the ordinary members, but Gerwani endeavors to teach them that bad conditions can be changed by organization, and that PKI is the only political party which defends their interests. Gerwani's political importance to PKI lies in its ability to awaken the mass of women to political problems, to mobilize voters, to add support to PKI's political line, to aid the other mass organizations, and to provide a source and training ground for female Party members and cadres.

3. THE WORK OF SOBSI AND ITS TRADE-UNIONS

This section deals not with the work of the Communist-led trade-unions for their members in general, but with the special attention given to women members.

Although the number of women workers is high in Indonesia,[42] SOBSI and its member unions did not give special attention to them until the beginning of 1956, just one year after PKI began to examine the means of attracting and organizing a far larger number of women. On February 25, 1956, the national council of SOBSI passed a resolution concerning women workers and including the following decisions:

1. to demand equal rights for men and women in the same work, including payment of allowances and of the minimum wage;

2. to demand the intensive implementation of work law number 1, 1951, with special attention to the rights of women workers;

3. to oppose discrimination against women effected by some reactionary officials in government offices, enterprises, and services;

4. to fight for special rights for women with regard to pregnancy,
confinement, and work conditions.[43]

The resolution also decided on the formation within the trade-unions
of special women's groups which could discuss the special demands
of women workers and organize an effective fight for their implementation under the leadership of the respective trade-unions.

To indicate its willingness to have women share in the work of the
organization, the national council in February 1956 increased the
number of its women members from one to five. By September 1957,
there were 49 women cadres in the central and regional leadership committees of SOBSI and its member unions, and "The number of women
cadres who lead or participate in leading the basic organizations has
greatly increased." [44] In that month the SOBSI national conference
decided that trade-unions with many women members should form
women's departments, that the work of forming special women's
groups in work places should be completed by the end of 1958, that
cadres should be appointed within SOBSI regional and branch committees to take care of women's affairs, and that women workers should
be promoted within the leadership bodies.[45]

During 1956 and 1957 some of the member unions held special conferences devoted to the problems of women workers; in 1957 some
SOBSI branches were already organizing special cadre courses for
women; and in February 1958 SOBSI held a national seminar on
women workers, the agenda dealing with methods of organizing women
workers, the special socioeconomic problems facing women workers,
and women's rights.[46] The national council secretariat in March 1958
reversed its decision to organize special women's groups, but the special
interests of women workers were promoted by the trade-unions' special
departments and cadres for women's affairs, and by occasional all-
female meetings.[47]

By the end of 1958 few women had yet entered the central leadership
of the SOBSI unions: there were four women out of 39 members of
the central council of the estate workers' union whose membership was
45 per cent female, 9 out of 29 in the cigarette workers' union whose
membership was 65 per cent female, and 3 out of 21 in the textile
workers' union whose membership was also 65 per cent female.[48] But
women were "rapidly" occupying places in the leadership of the basic
organizations. Few statistics have been made available since then of
the increase in women cadres within SOBSI and its member unions; [49]
but although they and the figures for the end of 1958 show a low pro-

portion of women cadres compared with women members, they also indicate considerable success for SOBSI and its unions in developing organizational interest and ability among the women members in a country where, at least among the poorer classes, women have no experience of how to run organizations, especially mixed organizations. The continuing concern of the SOBSI leaders in the problems and role of women workers was shown in the discussions of a national seminar on women workers organized in May 1961.[50]

In short, because women workers constitute a considerable percentage of workers in certain fields of labor, large numbers have been attracted into the SOBSI unions on the basis of their general interests as workers. From February 1956, however, the SOBSI leaders made efforts specifically to attract women workers and to strengthen their ties with the unions through appeals to their specific interests as women workers and through the creation of women activists and cadres. The slow but noteworthy increase in women trade-union cadres gives some indication of the success of these efforts.

4. THE WORK OF BTI

An article entitled "Extending Membership Among Peasant Women," published in *Harian Rakjat* on June 15, 1955, showed how the PKI-led peasant organization BTI has worked to make the peasant women politically aware and then to recruit them as members of BTI or Gerwani.[51] The author, Kartinah, acknowledged that peasant women were backward, shy, and humble, and that they could not be attracted into an organization by merely inviting them to join. Patience was required if they were to be attracted, and, wherever possible, the help of a husband, father, or neighbor was enlisted. The men were expected to explain the purpose of BTI, to take their womenfolk to meetings, and to ensure that they were present at discussions of the situation in their own village.

In this way, Kartinah claimed, the women learned that other women faced the same problems, "and that their suffering is not different." Soon they reached the point of wanting to join with their menfolk in the peasants' struggle, and they learned the importance of organization in solving their problems. Then BTI or Gerwani drew them into its organization. Special care was taken to give them a sense of responsibility and participation by at first asking them to perform easy tasks, such as preparing food for meetings, rendering assistance to others in times of need, and other social work. Lessons were also given to eradicate illiteracy and to teach health matters, sewing, and so on. In short, Kartinah wrote, the peasant women "must be given a little responsibility in the organization because by being given responsibility, even though a little, they feel proud that they can assist the work of the organization and they feel that their energy is not wasted."

Kartinah's article illustrates three characteristics of PKI's work to organize the masses: first, the care and patience employed in raising the consciousness of the masses and in bringing them into an organization; second, the way in which one Communist organization assists the work of the others—in this case BTI helps in the establishment or growth of Gerwani, and Gerwani then assists BTI in the struggle to improve the peasants' conditions; and, third, the article, appearing as it did in the PKI newspaper, clearly envisages the work of the mass organizations as leading eventually to membership in the Party.

XVIII

ETHNIC GROUPS AND
MINORITIES; VETERANS

1. ETHNIC GROUPS AND MINORITIES

The Indonesian people is composed of many ethnic groups. More than 35 discrete groups each contain more than 100,000 members, and there are large numbers of smaller groups.[1] So far there has not developed among the smaller ethnic groups any strong separatist feeling as a reaction against the real or supposed domination of the Javanese, by far the largest group. The national language, Indonesian, is closely related to Malay, but not to Javanese. And if the capital, Djakarta, is located in Java, non-Javanese share the most important positions of power: President—Prime Minister—Supreme Commander Sukarno is part Balinese as well as part Javanese; First Deputy Prime Minister Djuanda is Sundanese; Nasution, Minister of Defense and Chief of the Armed Forces, is a Moslem Batak; the naval chief is Sundanese. The leaders of the main political parties are drawn from a wide range of ethnic groups; Aidit is himself a Sumatran.

It is true, though, that those living outside Java do bear complaints and resentments against "Java" or "Djakarta," meaning the central government. They are often bitter at the waste and corruption at the center, the endless red tape, the lack of interest in the affairs of the outer islands, the artificial foreign-exchange rate that robs them of most of the value of their export crops, and the subsidy of Java from the earnings of their exports. Such discontent has been a prime cause of the acts of insubordination that have occurred in the outer islands, from merely ignoring central government instructions, to large-scale smuggling, to the establishment of local councils in defiance of the central government's apparatus, to open rebellion and the formation of separate but not separatist states. The most militant demands for broad regional autonomy have occurred among the Atjehnese and Minangkabau of Sumatra and the Minahasans of North Sulawesi. Djakarta has paid lip service, but no more, to the goal of regional autonomy.

The ethnic minorities, or, in Indonesian official terminology "the non-native Indonesian citizens," consist of Chinese, Arabs, and Eurasians. Arabs and Eurasians are relatively few in number, but the racial Chinese of Indonesian citizenship amount to about two millions. The ethnic minorities, and especially the Chinese, have suffered considerable discrimination, particularly in the economic sphere where the government has legislated and officials have acted against them.[2]

PKI AND THE ETHNIC GROUPS

None of the ethnic groups in Indonesia has developed a militant ethnic consciousness, nor has the Aidit leadership dared try to develop and exploit such a consciousness. In Indonesia, unlike in India, the growth and very existence of the Party has been at least partly dependent upon an alliance with political forces within the central government—and by coincidence these allies, PNI and Sukarno, are associated with Java and the Javanese; the peoples of the outer islands, by and large, have been associated politically with the two parties strongly opposed to PKI, namely Masjumi and, to a lesser extent, PSI. Also, it is the ethnic Javanese who have provided the readiest and the overwhelming majority of support for PKI and its mass organizations. PKI has therefore trodden warily on the "national question," not wishing to become too closely identified with "Java," but at the same time afraid of alienating its own core support and its chief allies.

During the first years after January 1951, the Aidit leadership was too engrossed in reëstablishing and strengthening the Party and its mass organizations in Java to devote more than passing attention to the non-Javanese areas. Interest in the outer regions was first aroused by the 1955 elections, in which PKI sought to gather the highest possible number of votes, and was then increased after 1956 when the Party leaders were forced to consider seriously the nonparliamentary means that would be necessary in order to win power. A Communist victory even in Java would be difficult without broad support among the Sundanese in West Java, while a victory in Java might be reversed if the outer islands remained in the hands of non-Communists.

In their efforts to attract and organize the members of the various ethnic groups, the PKI leaders have not created specific ethnic group organizations, but have used the ordinary machinery of the Party and its mass organizations. At the same time, the leaders have taken pains to declare their support for the interests of the regions, for the broadest autonomy for the ethnic groups. The PKI Central Committee admitted in October 1953 that the Party "has not yet given much attention to the problem of the ethnic groups in our country." [3] The remedy for this deficiency was begun in March 1954 when the Fifth National Congress endorsed a program calling for the election of democratic regional governments with wide autonomy, and for the right of each ethnic group to use its own language in schools and in court.[4] During the 1955 election campaign, PKI declared:

The Indonesian Republic is a unitary state with many ethnic groups. This means that Indonesia must have a central government that is obeyed by all regions and ethnic groups, but at the same time there must be the broadest autonomy for every ethnic group (provisionally this is possible along the ordinary administrative divisions) for organizing finances, economy, communications, culture and policy special to its area. All ethnic groups, whether large or small, are equal, fraternal, and of mutual assistance, and therefore they may not oppress one another and none may receive special treatment.[5]

It is noteworthy that of the 39 persons elected to parliament on the PKI ticket in September 1955, at least 15 were not ethnic Javanese despite the heavy concentration of PKI votes in the Javanese areas.

In 1956, 1957, and 1958 the problem of the ethnic groups was thrown into prominence by the formation of regional councils in protest against the central government in North, Central, and South Sumatra, and in East Indonesia, and by the formation of the PRRI-Permesta rebel government in February 1958. Both the councils and the rebel government appealed to regional and ethnic loyalties, stressing the alleged unconcern of the government in Djakarta for the problems of the regions and peoples outside Java.

The PKI leaders were strongly opposed to the anti-Communist dissident leaders but were concerned not to appear as opposed to the interests of the regions. They were quick to point out that despite the slogans of "broad autonomy for the regions" and "development of the regions," the councils by their illegal seizure of power hindered the development of democratic regional government, and by their corruption and smuggling accelerated the bankruptcy of the state and hampered efforts to improve the economy of the regions.[6] In order to restate its own concern for broad, democratic, regional autonomy, PKI issued three booklets in April 1958, two months after the outbreak of the rebellion, which declared the Party's support for the formation of seventeen first-level autonomous regions outside Java, and elaborated on its 1955 statement of PKI's goal of regional and ethnic group autonomy.[7]

That PKI successfully avoided being characterized as "Djakartan" or Javanese or opposed to regional interests, is indicated by the Communist and other reports of rapid Party expansion in the outer islands after 1956.[8] Both Lukman and Aidit told the delegates to the PKI Sixth Congress in September 1959 of the great importance of work among the ethnic groups. Aidit called on the Party to improve this work by promoting the culture of the different groups, by promoting and defending broad, democratic, regional autonomy as a step toward ethnic group autonomy, and especially by developing work among the peasants who constituted a majority within the ethnic groups.[9] He told the Central Committee plenary meeting of February 1963 that "the composition of the [Party] membership must be improved from the point of view of ethnic groups and citizens of foreign descent." [10]

PKI AND THE ETHNIC MINORITIES

The PKI program for the ethnic minorities has been simple: equal rights for all citizens, and the prevention of narrow nationalism among the "native" Indonesians at the same time as preventing a feeling of superiority among the minorities.[11]

PKI's earnestness in defense of the ethnic minorities was shown by the Party's campaign in late 1959 and early 1960 against the government's action to evict aliens trading in the rural areas. Because of the muddle of Indonesia's citizenship regulations, many Chinese and some of the few Arabs are no longer sure which nationality they hold. Therefore the eviction of alien rural traders affected many of confused nationality, and profoundly disturbed all members of the ethnic minorities as a possible step toward further discrimination against themselves. Whatever PKI's motives in opposing the eviction measure and thereby arousing the wrath of many political and army leaders, its opposition appeared laudable in the eyes of the minorities, especially the Chinese. When, early in 1963, the Chinese became a target of race riots in several parts of Java, PKI was quick in its condemnation. The Central Committee denounced Indonesian reactionaries for inflaming an anti-Chinese spirit, for setting native Indonesians against citizens of foreign descent.[12] The government and people were asked to give special attention to the existing "symptoms and practices of racial discrimination," and the Central Committee asserted forcefully that "racialism must be fought to the death."

Because the Chinese are viewed with envy and suspicion by many Indonesians, it would be undiplomatic for PKI itself to organize them in any numbers. Therefore, although a few Chinese are in PKI, a separate and officially sovereign association has been formed for them: Baperki.[13]

Baperki (Badan Permusjawaratan Kewarganegaraan Indonesia, Indonesian Citizenship Consultative Council) was founded on March 13, 1954, by Siauw Giok Tjhan, a close associate of PKI,[14] purportedly to unify the different peoples of Indonesia into one people, and to undertake social and educational work especially among the minorities. In fact, Baperki has been an organization of Indonesian citizens of Chinese descent, with a small number of native Indonesians, mostly Communists, also as members.

Baperki's activities have included the building and maintenance of schools and the foundation of a university, but they have been concerned primarily with assisting the Chinese minority to circumvent and combat all official and unofficial discrimination. Membership is not large, perhaps forty or sixty thousand in the whole country. In the September 1955 parliamentary elections Baperki put forward candidates who won 178,887 votes.

If rumor has any basis in truth, Baperki is most useful to PKI as an agent for collecting from the wealthy Chinese businessmen large sums that are channeled into PKI's needy coffers. There would be infinitely greater risk of public detection of this source of Communist funds if it was tapped directly by PKI, rather than by a Chinese organization for ostensibly social purposes.

2. VETERANS OF THE REVOLUTION

Although relatively little actual fighting took place during the revolution against the Dutch, there are approximately 800,000 Indonesian "veterans," that is, persons who in the period from August 17, 1945, to December 27, 1949, joined an official army unit or a recognized armed group in defense of the Republic.[15] The veterans were a major target for PKI organization because they had a higher level of political consciousness than most of the population, because they were, in general, dissatisfied with the fruits of victory, and because they knew how to use weapons. After the transfer of sovereignty in December 1949, hundreds of national and local veterans' organizations were formed, of which the Communist-led Perbepsi became the largest.

Perbepsi was formed on December 30, 1951, by the fusion of 149 national and local groups.[16] In October 1954, it claimed 194 branches and 205,740 members,[17] and in December 1957 it claimed 300,000 members (at which time PKI claimed it had 265,000).[18] The chairman, Supardi, was elected to parliament in 1955 as a "nonparty" member of the PKI ticket.

Perbepsi's three chief social and economic demands were:

1. government acceptance of the principle of preference for veterans;

2. a government policy of settling veterans on land made available by the redistribution of foreign estate holdings and the nonextension of large land leases;

3. provision of vocational training for veterans, and the rehabilitation and employment of those disabled.

The greatest value of Perbepsi for PKI was that it constituted a paramilitary organization that would be available in the event of a major political crisis. Training courses in military matters were given to members, and Perbepsi formations could be seen "marching and drilling to the beat of drums." [19] During the second half of 1953 and during 1954, Perbepsi attempted to persuade and maneuver the government into arming its members within the framework of its proposal of a people's militia to fight the Darul Islam rebels, and, when this was rejected, to maintain security during the elections. The government was unmoved.

At the beginning of July 1957 the PKI Central Committee heard a report on Party work among veterans [20] which stated that if the veterans "are well organized and well led this will greatly assist in changing the balance of power so that the situation moves to the left." But the end of Perbepsi was already at hand. From December 26, 1956, to January 2, 1957, an all-Indonesia Veterans' Congress had been held on the initiative of Nasution, then army chief of staff. The 2,300 delegates had agreed "by acclamation" to form the Indonesian Veterans' Legion which would absorb all existing veterans' organizations.[21] The individual organizations successfully dug their heels in for a while, but by August 1959 army pressure had forced their dissolution and the merger of their membership into the army-controlled Veterans' Legion.

That PKI considers the fusion of all veterans' organizations to be harmful was indicated by the ardent opposition of the Party, Pemuda Rakjat, and SOBSI to later attempts by the army and certain government ministers to form all-embracing youth and trade-union organizations.

XIX

MOBILIZING ELECTORAL SUPPORT

1. PKI'S ELECTION CAMPAIGNS

Once they had decided, within the framework of the national united front policy, to exploit the possibilities for political action offered by the parliamentary regime, the PKI leaders were committed to take part in elections. All-Indonesia elections were held in September 1955 for parliament, and in December 1955 for the Constituent Assembly. Local elections for the provincial, *kabupaten*, and city councils were held throughout Java from June to November 1957, and later in South Sumatra, Riau, and Kalimantan. In both the national and the local elections, PKI applied its organizational and propaganda resources with great effect, especially in Java but also in the outer islands.

It is possible to envisage PKI's tremendous activity in the election campaigns as having reference to three interdependent factors: the general power situation, the extension of Communist support and organization, and the improvement of the Party organization.

The more votes PKI obtained in 1955, the more seats it would procure in parliament and the Constituent Assembly. Politics were still revolving largely around parliament, and an increase in Party representation there could be expected to increase the Party's bargaining position in national politics. Increased parliamentary strength also could be expected to increase the Party's chance of gaining entry into a coalition cabinet. Because the Constituent Assembly was to draw up the future constitution of the country, it was important for the Party to have major representation there as well. By 1957 the power and authority of the parties in general had declined, but it was possibly even more important for PKI to demonstrate its own broad support. The two major power centers in the country were now Sukarno and the army. Sukarno needed PKI in order to help maintain his primary political position, just as PKI needed him in order to keep the army leaders, who included many anti-Communists, from that position. The stronger the support PKI could demonstrate, the surer the Party was of maintaining the alliance with Sukarno and of strengthening his hand vis-à-vis the army. And if Sukarno had declared after the 1955 elections that a party with six million voters (that is, PKI) should not be excluded from the government, would not his case be strengthened by a large increase in Communist votes in 1957?

The election campaigns provided the Party with a government-sanctioned opportunity to intensify and extend propaganda and organizational activity, especially in new areas. During the period of the campaigns, local traditional and conservative authorities could not criticize political activity as divisive, and Party work was extended into areas hitherto closed to it. Furthermore, popular interest in politics was heightened during the campaigns—not only because of the work of the political parties, but also because the Ministry of Information made a great effort to inform the electorate of the reasons for and the methods of voting. The PKI leaders took advantage of this increased interest to present a basic outline of the commendable goals of the Party. Once interest in and sympathy for PKI had been aroused, the Communists moved quickly to recruit the new sympathizers for either the Party or the mass organizations. That is, the electoral support gained during the election campaigns was envisaged as the basis for a rapid expansion of the Communist organizations.

The elections were used to strengthen the Party organization in three ways. First, the campaigns were used to train Party cadres, activists, and members. The Party's election materials were studied intensively at all levels of the organization, and the entire membership received training in the dissemination of Party propaganda and the mobilization of people outside the Party. Second, it is possible that the Aidit leadership, anticipating Communist control of the government in the foreseeable future, was eager to have the largest possible number of ranking cadres enter parliament and the local councils in order to overcome the Party's deficiency in experienced administrators, in persons familiar with matters of government. Third, the election results provided the Party leaders with an objective basis on which to assess the efficiency of the Party organization, the social and geographic areas of Party support, and, from these, the essential fields of Party work. Previously, the leaders had to rely for such assessments on the subjective reports of local cadres.

Both in 1955 and 1957 PKI was competing mainly for the votes of the non-*santris*.[1] Within the non-*santri* electorate, PKI began the election campaigns with a large nucleus of potential voters formed by the membership of the mass organizations, while its efforts to rally electoral support beyond the frontiers of the Party and mass organizations were facilitated by the popular image of the Party that had been built so carefully since 1951, by the politically unsophisticated and uncommitted nature of most of the *abangan* electorate, and by the current political situation.

If PKI had been heard of previously by the mass of the *abangans*, it was most probably as a responsible party, opposed to terrorism, and eager to defend and promote the interests of the people. In their efforts to attract voters, the Party leaders usually did not have to break down existing political loyalties first, while their attempt to make the Party appear attractive was not constantly sabotaged by attacks from other political forces. At the times of the campaigns for both the 1955 and the 1957 elections, PKI was in alliance with PNI, the only other major party active among the *abangans*, and neither party attacked the other.[2] That is, the *abangan* electorate was presented with little anti-Communist propaganda. The attacks made on PKI by the more fanatical wing of the Moslem Masjumi in fact only served to increase *abangan* sympathy for the Communists.

The Aidit leadership early oriented its organization to act as an election machine. For the 1955 elections, Party election committees were formed by mid-May 1954 at every level of the organization down to the *ketjamatan* while at that time committees were already being formed in the villages.[3] PKI's campaign for the 1957 elections was under way by February 1957.[4] Large numbers of full-time election workers were employed by the Party, and the mass organizations were also drawn on extensively for assistance. At least SOBSI, BTI, Pemuda Rakjat, and Gerwani assisted in propaganda work and mobilized people to attend Party meetings and to vote. LEKRA artists designed banners and posters, and helped to provide the popular entertainment that served to attract large crowds to election meetings.

The large funds available to PKI were used not only to gear the organization for election work but also to exploit a wide variety of techniques for winning the attention and support of the populace.[5]

Endorsed by the Fifth National Congress in March 1954, the PKI election manifesto for the September 1955 parliamentary elections was designed to indicate the Party's concern for the welfare of the nation as a whole and of the different sections of "the people." By November 1954, already over one quarter of a million copies of the manifesto had been printed in Indonesian, Javanese, Sundanese, Batak, and Indonesian in the Arabic script.[6] For the local elections, the Central Committee ordered the Party organization in each electoral district to prepare its own election program.[7] Thus the electors were presented with programs designed specifically for their own local situation, programs that analyzed the problems facing each locality and that presented plans for their solution.

As the election campaigns were developed, urban and rural areas were plastered with the hammer-and-sickle, posters were displayed with popular slogans of political and economic content, mass meetings were organized, pamphlets and brochures printed for mass sale and distribution, slogan banners were hung across roads and alleys, kites were flown painted with the Party symbol, and huge billboards were raised in prominent locations.

An important feature of PKI's election campaigns was the use of popular traditional forms of entertainment to attract crowds and put across political propaganda.[8] "People's festivals" were organized in towns and villages, and occasionally lasted several nights.[9] The festivals consisted of songs, Indonesian boxing, folk opera, and dancing, but they began with a short political speech, while the actual entertainment was given a political slant. Another method of election campaigning that PKI used far more than any other party was social welfare work: cleaning *kampongs*, the construction and repair of bridges, public lavatories, public bathing places, and irrigation channels, and assistance at such times as births, marriages, and funerals.

PKI also endeavored to canvass every potential Communist voter during the election campaigns. An article in *Boletin PKI Djawa Timur* (*East Java PKI Bulletin*) showed how and why canvassing was done.[10] In order to attract and "control" voters, the article explained, the Party first visited every voter to remind them to register and to tell them how. In this way, "they know and feel for themselves that there is somebody assisting them." Once registration was completed, the Party kept close contact with the voters in order to answer any queries that might arise. By this close personal contact the "voters concerned remain nurtured and controlled properly." Because the PKI machine was much more extensive and efficient than those of other parties, PKI was far more thorough in personal canvassing than its competitors. The effect of personal contacts on the underprivileged Indonesian masses with no traditional political orientation, must have been much greater than the effect of canvassing among the majority of voters in Western countries who are politically committed and who are used to being wooed by different political parties.

2. THE ELECTION RESULTS

PKI won fourth place in the September 1955 elections, receiving 6,176,914 (or 16.4 per cent) of the total votes.[11] Ahead of PKI were PNI with 8,434,653 votes, Masjumi with 7,903,886 votes, and Nahdatul Ulama with 6,955,141. The fifth-largest party, PSII, trailed far behind the big four, receiving 1,091,160 votes.

PKI received 5,477,707 votes (or 88.7 per cent) in Java, 435,775 (or 7.05 per cent) in North and South Sumatra (the former an area of estate agriculture and Javanese immigration, the latter an area of oil extraction and Javanese immigration), and only 263,432 in the rest of Indonesia. PKI received less than 10 per cent of the votes cast in each of nine of the fifteen electoral districts: Central Sumatra, the three districts of Kalimantan, the two districts of Sulawesi, the two districts of Nusatenggara, and Maluku.

Within Java, Communist support was most heavily concentrated in a rough quadrilateral within the line Gunung Kidul–Semarang–Madiun–Patjitan. Within this area, PKI received over 50 per cent of the total votes in the towns of Semarang and Surakarta, and in four *kabupatens*. In eight of the other eleven *kabupatens* and municipalities within the quadrilateral, PKI received between 40 and 50 per cent of the total votes. Outside this area, PKI received between 40 and 50 per cent of the total votes only in the city of Surabaja and in the *kabupatens* of Blitar and Tjilatjap. Communist support was particularly weak in the whole of West Java, in a belt of Central Java running south from Tegal and Pekalongan, and in the eastern part of East Java, including Madura. PKI received less than 10 per cent of the total votes in 28 of the 80 *kabupatens* in Java: 13 in West Java, 7 in Central Java, and 8 in East Java.

A notable feature of the election results in Java was the similar intensity of Communist support in the urban and rural areas. With two exceptions, Communist support was only fractionally higher in the municipalities than in the surrounding or adjacent rural areas. The two exceptions were Surabaja, where PKI received 41.8 per cent of the votes in the town compared with only 29.6 per cent in the *kabupaten*; and Pekalongan, where PKI received a lower percentage of the votes in the town than in the *kabupaten*.

TABLE 3
PKI Votes, 1955 and 1957/1958

	1955 a. votes	1955 b. % of total	1957/1958 a. votes	1957/1958 b. % of total
Djakarta Raja	96,363	12.6	137,305	19.4
West Java	755,634	10.8	1,297,889	18.2
Central Java*	2,326,108	25.8	3,126,448	32.8
East Java	2,299,602	23.3	2,952,555	29.3
Total Java	5,477,707	20.6	7,514,197	27.4
South Sumatra	176,900	12.1	228,965	15.7
Kalimantan	42,543	3.0	71,076	5.1

*Central Java includes the Special Territory of Jogjakarta.

In the 1957 local elections in Java, PKI received 7,514,197 votes.[12] This represented an increase of 2,036,490, or 37.2 per cent, compared with the September 1955 elections. The increase took place in all of the one hundrd municipalities and *kabupatens*. Regionally, the comparison between the 1955 and 1957 votes is shown in table 3.

Four reasons would seem to explain the rapid and comprehensive increase. First, the Party and its mass organizations had expanded between 1955 and the middle of 1957. Second, the leaders of the other political parties did not consider the local elections to be worthy of the intensive effort made for the 1955 elections, and the campaign work of the other parties declined relative to PKI's. Third, the PKI leaders endeavored to exploit the increasing public sympathy of President Sukarno for the Party, to portray the Party and Sukarno as a radical nationalist team in order to attract the support of the broad masses who still considered him to be the living symbol of active Indonesian nationalism. Fourth, PNI, as the major competitor for the *abangan* votes, had not followed up its electoral success of 1955 with organizational work. By the time of the 1957 elections both the prestige and the morale of PNI had declined appreciably.

A comparison of the voting patterns of 1957 and 1955 (see table 4, page 224) indicates that the sociocultural division between *santris* and *abangans* is important in explaining the political behavior of the Javanese. It appears that the *santri* electorate of the Moslem parties proved remarkably resistant to Communist advances, in marked contrast to the ready disintegration of PNI's *abangan* electorate.[13] Table 4 indicates that, in general, the PNI vote declined sharply, the Moslem vote remained stable, while the PKI vote increased rapidly. If the 1957 votes are compared with the votes in the December 1955 Constituent Assem-

TABLE 4
COMPARISON OF 1957 VOTES WITH 1955 VOTES

	PKI	PNI	Moslem*	Total votes
Djakarta Raja	+ 40,942	− 27,076	− 62,131	− 58,417
West Java	+ 542,255	−134,528	+ 22,678	+155,453
Central Java	+ 800,340	−335,944	+108,022	+524,650
East Java	+ 652,953	−191,128	−156,490	+202,646
Total Java	+2,036,490	−688,676	− 87,921	+824,332

*This comprises the votes received by Masjumi, NU, and PSII.

bly elections, the contrast is even more marked: a PKI increase in Java of 2,024,894 votes, a PNI decrease of 985,747, and a Moslem increase of 51,296. In short, it appears that PKI increased its votes among the non-*santri* population, and that because PNI was the only other large party with support among the non-*santris,* a large PKI increase involved a sharp fall in PNI's electoral support. An analysis of the 1955 and 1957 election results in the hundred municipalities and *kabupatens* seems to confirm this conclusion.

When the 1957 elections were held, PKI was able to capture a large segment of the former PNI electoral support. Whereas the Communist leaders had followed up electoral successes in 1955 with organization work to convert electoral support into organized support (in the Party or in the mass organizations), the PNI leaders did not do so. That is, PNI did little to shape its 1955 electoral support into a conscious and organized body, and many of its former supporters readily transferred their votes to PKI, whose organized presence was felt, and whose organizations were usually the only ones to defend the interests of the different sections of the community. PKI's gains at the expense of PNI were facilitated also by the belief among the leaders of PNI, as among the leaders of all parties except PKI, that the local elections were unworthy of the effort made for the 1955 elections to parliament and the Constituent Assembly. But perhaps of greater importance in explaining the large decrease in PNI votes was the demoralization taking place within PNI's ranks. In 1955, according to the claim of PNI leaders, the government officials, village *lurahs*, and schoolteachers had been instrumental in mobilizing the large PNI vote. By the middle of 1957, the future of parliamentary democracy was in grave doubt, the prestige of the political parties had fallen sharply, PNI no longer seemed able to maintain its former leading role in the government, and as PNI's hold on the government declined, so did its ability to dispense patronage. The result was that many of those who had worked

TABLE 5
PKI's ELECTORAL POSITION BY ELECTORAL DISTRICTS: 1957

	PKI 1st	2nd	3rd	4th	Less than fourth	Total
Djakarta Raja	—	1	—	—	—	1
West Java	5	5	7	4	2	23
Central Java	20	5	12	2	—	39
East Java	19	6	7	1	4	37
Total Java	44	17	26	7	6	100

hard to mobilize votes for PNI in 1955 either worked less hard or not at all in 1957.

The only Communist gains that seemed to have been made at the expense of the Moslem parties were small, except in a few of the heavily Moslem areas.[14] The details of the 1955 and 1957 election results indicate that both PKI and PNI were able to make a little headway at the expense of the Moslem parties in a small number of the heavily Moslem areas. In other Moslem areas, in contrast, the Moslem vote increased more than PKI's—as in the *kabupatens* of Pekalongan and Demak. In short, there are indications that where the *santris* are in an overwhelming majority the non-*santri* parties can gain a few votes from the Moslem parties, but where the *santris* are faced with a significant number of non-*santris*, their cohesiveness is such that the non-*santri* parties can make little headway among them.

The increase in Communist votes in Java occurred at a fairly similar rate in urban and rural areas. In terms of regions, the most rapid increase was in West Java (71.8 per cent), followed by Djakarta Raja (42.5 per cent), Central Java (34.4 per cent), and East Java (28.4 per cent). PKI received over 50 per cent of the votes cast in eleven of the eighty *kabupatens*,[15] and in six of the twenty municipalities. Between 40 and 50 per cent of the total votes was received in eight *kabupatens* and in four towns. Not only did PKI emerge as the largest party in Java as a whole, but it was the largest party in 44 of the one hundred local council districts in Java, and the second largest in 17 of them (see table 5).

The maps showing the geographical distribution of PKI, PNI, and the Moslem parties' electoral support in 1957[16] indicate the limits of Communist electoral support at that time and suggest the possibilities for later Communist advance. If the *abangan-santri* thesis does hold in terms of political behavior, as is indicated by the comparison of the 1957 and the 1955 election results, the *santri* population could be expected to form an effective block to large Communist gains in the near

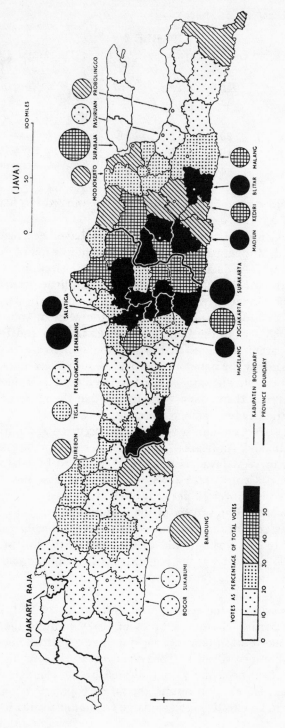

MAP 1. PKI votes, 1957.

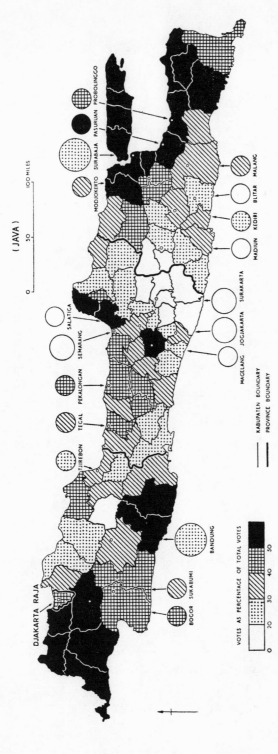

MAP 2.   Combined votes of the Moslem parties, 1957.

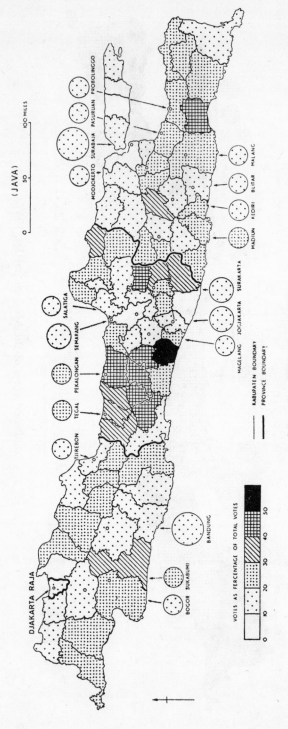

MAP 3. PNI votes, 1957.

future in areas of West Java, along the north coast of Central Java, and in parts of East Java, especially in Madura and adjacent parts of the mainland.[17] That is, PKI could not expect to make a rapid advance among the 38.0 per cent of the Javanese electorate that voted Moslem in 1957. On the other hand, PKI could expect to make considerable inroads among the 6,275,919 PNI voters—who were fairly evenly distributed throughout Java, and who were in higher proportions in the rural areas. Since the 1957 elections, PNI has not increased significantly its organizational activity among the mass of either the urban or the rural population, so that it can be assumed that the network of the Party and its mass organizations, which continued to expand after 1957, has already drawn in many of those who voted for PNI in 1957. That Communist gains were not limited to Java is shown by the rapid increase in Communist votes in South Sumatra and the four provinces of Kalimantan.

Part five

THE NATIONAL UNITED FRONT
AND THE OTHER
POLITICAL FORCES

XX

PKI's POLITICAL BEHAVIOR UNDER
THE NATIONAL UNITED FRONT

The Aidit leadership concluded that without the tolerance and alliance of the non-Communists it would be impossible to gain time for the growth of the Party and its mass organizations, to isolate and destroy the anti-Communist forces, and eventually to win power. Mention has already been made of how, in order to win mass support as well as the tolerance and sympathy of the non-Communist political forces, the Party built an image of itself as patriotic, sympathetic to religion, militantly democratic, strongly opposed to the use of force in the pursuit of political objectives, and self-effacing and responsible in seeking the national good.[1] But PKI had also to alter its behavior towards the non-Communist political forces.

The PKI leaders have frequently repeated sentiments around the theme expressed by Aidit at the end of 1954: "PKI's political attitude towards a person or a party at a given time depends on the political attitude of the person or party at that time. In determining its policy, PKI is not motivated by feelings of grievance or revenge."[2] In other words, PKI would treat as enemies only those who were openly anti-Communist.

Aidit took every occasion to stress that care should be taken not to antagonize unnecessarily what he called the middle force, those elements which were ostensibly non-Communist and anti-imperialist. In

1956 he admitted that contradictions, that is, differences of interest, existed and would arise between the progressive and the middle forces, especially between the workers and the national capitalists and between PKI and the parties of the national bourgeoisie.[3] "But it would be wrong for these contradictions to be sharpened." He said they "must and can be solved by means of discussion, by means of mutual concessions, and in a mutually beneficial manner. In this way the contradictions between the progressive force and the middle force can be prevented from harming national unity, and from benefiting the reactionary force." Aidit promised that PKI would not take steps which could harm other democratic parties—provided those parties did not attempt to harm national unity, that is, provided they did not attack PKI. Furthermore, PKI would always show restraint toward the other parties:

The Communists must be skilled at restraining themselves in criticizing the statements and actions of people from democratic parties. Statements or actions that may hurt our feelings but are not important need not be criticized. The Communists only criticize statements or actions that promote disunity, divide the strength of the masses and show vacillation in carrying out the anti-imperialist and anti-feudal policy. It is also important that the manner of criticism must truly concern the problem and not give vent to passions and feelings.

The PKI leaders have also recognized that under the national united front policy PKI and its mass organizations must support the "reasonable interests" of the national bourgeoisie.[4] PKI and SOBSI, for example, have been loud in their demands for government protection of national industrialists and businessmen in their struggle against foreign competition. Aidit's concern to help the non-Communists led him to tell the PKI Central Committee in December 1960 that "It is also our duty to look after non-Party cadres and cadres of the other democratic parties . . . , to assist them with complete sincerity."[5]

Having established the importance of restrained and friendly behavior towards the non-Communist political forces, the Aidit leadership was faced with the problem of how to avoid "tailism," avoid merely following the non-Communists. How could PKI be restrained and friendly and yet at the same time foster the growth among the non-Communists of those left-wing elements and sentiments most sympathetic to PKI and most eager to eradicate the remnants of imperialism and crush the internal reactionaries? The answer was expressed by Lukman in a course guide for use in the Party central school and province-level schools.[6]

Lukman pointed out that in view of the "vacillating and two-faced" nature of the national bourgeoisie with respect to the revolution (that is, it wished to oppose imperialism but at the same time feared the continuation of the revolution because it would bring victory to the working class), PKI must avoid two major errors in its dealing with the national bourgeoisie. The Party must avoid right opportunism, that is, concentrating on the need for unity without waging a struggle against the undesirable characteristics of the middle group; and left opportunism, that is, concentrating on fighting such undesirable characteristics without giving sufficient attention to the question of unity. Lukman reminded Party cadres that incorrect criticism, as in the first seven months of 1948, could alienate the national bourgeoisie and even drive it to act against the Party.

He then showed how the correct implementation of the principle "unite and fight," encourage and criticize, could foster, or help foster, the desirable elements in the national bourgeoisie, in the non-Communist political forces:

Besides being skilled at correctly criticizing the vacillations and errors of the policies of the national bourgeoisie, we must also be able correctly to encourage and popularize the progressive attitudes and measures of the national bourgeoisie. By correct criticism of the vacillations and errors of the national bourgeoisie, and by encouragement and praise of what is good of that class, every statement of the working class and its party will have a convincing force; in other words, the working class and its party will hold the initiative. In implementing this method, a problem that is always important to remember is the changing situation: when, and about what, must criticism be emphasized and when, and about what, must encouragement be emphasized.[7]

This was the way, he concluded, to foster the progressive elements within the national bourgeoisie, to encourage those in the center to move left, and to isolate the stubborn. In other words, this was the way in which PKI could avoid "tailism" and could draw the national bourgeoisie leftward while at the same time being moderate and friendly.

XXI

THE PERIOD OF PARLIAMENTARY
DEMOCRACY, 1952–JULY 1959

1. THE APPROACH TO PNI

During 1951 Aidit and his colleagues observed and analyzed political developments in Indonesia. They concluded that they required alliance with important political forces if the Party and its mass organizations were to expand rapidly, and if the Party was ever to regain admittance to the government. Between the two main parties, PNI and Masjumi, the choice of potential ally fell on PNI. That party had demonstrated that it was basically non-Communist, not anti-Communist, that it contained strongly anti-Western leaders, and that it was willing to coöperate with PKI in its own struggle to achieve a dominant role in the government.

The Sukiman coalition cabinet resigned on February 23, 1952, when all parties condemned a Mutual Security Aid (MSA) agreement signed without cabinet approval by Foreign Minister Subardjo (Masjumi). PKI now made an active bid to win the confidence of PNI and to intensify the differences between PNI and Masjumi. On February 25, 1952, the PKI Central Committee called for a "progressive and anti-fascist cabinet" that would include PNI, PSI, members of the Political Parties' Consultative Council, and "other groups who agree with the program of the progressive, anti-fascist cabinet." [1] Acceptable to all but Masjumi, the proposed cabinet program envisaged rejection of MSA aid, the return of West Irian, the release of all arrested in August 1951, the guarantee of full freedoms, direct and free general elections, and the eradication of the Darul Islam Moslem rebels. Furthermore, PKI called for the rejection of Masjumi participation in the next cabinet because of Masjumi's close connections with the Darul Islam, and because one of its ministers had signed the MSA agreement. In short, PKI offered PNI the possibility of forming a cabinet without Masjumi.

On March 1, 1952, Sukarno appointed Prawoto Mangkusasmito of Masjumi and Sidik Djojosukarto of PNI as formateurs. PKI, alarmed lest another Masjumi-PNI coalition government would be formed with Masjumi predominance, expressed its disquiet at the "lack of resolution" being shown by "several nationalist leaders" in defense of PNI's stand for the cancellation of the Japanese Peace Treaty, the MSA agreement and the Round Table Conference agreement, for the eradication of the Darul Islam rebels, and for strong measures to effect the return of West Irian.[2]

When Prawoto and Sidik failed to reach agreement, Sukarno appointed PNI's Wilopo as formateur. PKI gave him a guarded welcome and offered support if he chose a truly progressive and anti-fascist cabinet.[3] Once Wilopo's cabinet was installed, the Aidit leadership expressed its disappointment at the inclusion of Masjumi, but, in line with the new and evolving concept of the national united front, for the first time declared the Party's willingness to support a cabinet that did not include "progressive" ministers:

. . . apart from the question of whether or not PKI sits in the cabinet, PKI is ready, with honesty, to give its support to the Wilopo cabinet provided that the cabinet follows an entirely new political course. PKI will support the Wilopo cabinet provided that the government has courage and acts to abandon the old political course, that is, the war policy and the anti-national, fascist policy, and follows a new political course, a national policy founded on democracy and peace . . . PKI wishes that the Wilopo cabinet, following a new political course, will have a long life.[4]

For the first time PKI offered support to other political parties without asking the price of participation in government. In other words, PKI offered its coöperation and alliance to those parties and groups which were not anti-Communist and which were most opposed to "imperialism." In return it asked only that they should implement part of their anti-imperialist policy, and that they should permit PKI and its mass organizations freedom from repression. Such easy terms for Communist support strongly attracted many nationalists who themselves wished "to complete the revolution" by eliminating imperialist power, who were becoming increasingly antagonistic toward and fearful of Masjumi, and who placed a high premium on "office."

During the period of the Wilopo cabinet, which was installed on April 3, 1952, and which resigned on June 3, 1953, four major political developments occurred that were of significance to PKI:[5] the further widening of the breach between Masjumi and the Nationalists; an increasing willingness on the part of a growing number of Nationalists to coöperate with PKI; increased antagonism between Hatta, Masjumi, and PSI on the one hand and PKI on the other; and the breakaway from Masjumi of the Nahdatul Ulama.

It became evident to PNI that its coöperation with Masjumi and PSI was often injurious to its own interests.[6] For example, changes in the structure and size of the army which were envisaged by the pro-PSI minister of defense would have reduced the influence of the PNI supporters in both the officer corps and the ranks. The cabinet also moved toward the organization of early general elections which PNI feared because it was generally believed that as Masjumi had the best grass-roots organization the Moslem party would win a majority of votes. Furthermore, due to an adverse balance of trade, the cabinet, which included a PSI member as minister of finance, initiated budget, credit, and import policies which burdened primarily the social groups most closely associated with PNI, that is, the civil servants and the new group of Indonesian importers and exporters.

Thus a large and increasing number of Nationalists came to view coöperation with Masjumi as harmful to their own and their party's interests. At the same time, the religious issue was of great importance in generating antagonism towards and fear of Masjumi. In general the Nationalist leaders were oriented toward traditional Javanese culture and disliked and feared the militant Islam of many Masjumi leaders. For many Nationalist leaders, an Islamic state was the greatest threat to what they liked of Indonesia, to what they wanted for Indonesia, and to their own positions. In the first four months of 1953 a bitter feud broke out between some of the more radical Masjumi members and Nationalist leaders over the issue of an Islamic state. Hypocritical Moslems were roundly denounced, and hot rejoinders flew back and forth. Feith concludes that the radicalism exhibited by some of the Masjumi leaders "heightened the fears of the P.N.I.—and of President Soekarno—of Masjumi strength." [7] This fear made PKI's task of winning the Nationalists' friendship much easier.

As the general elections drew nearer, the Nationalists looked for allies who could help them to postpone the elections as long as possible and to consolidate PNI's hold on government officials, whose influence in the elections could be, and eventually was, decisive. PKI's offer of support with minimal conditions gained in attractiveness. Feith considers that in 1952 the Sidik Djojosukarto faction in PNI decided on a more thorough exploration of the possibilities of coöperation with PKI, and that some of the chief PNI leaders were perhaps already working towards a PNI-led cabinet excluding Masjumi[8]—a development PKI had propounded since the fall of the Natsir cabinet in March 1951. In Feith's opinion: ". . . it is clear that a section of the P.N.I. leadership was henceforth prepared to assist in a strengthening of the P.K.I.'s position, and in particular to help the party regain nationalist respectability."

For such Nationalists, PKI's low-price offer seemed to show that PKI was weak and of no immediate threat, whereas Masjumi was a direct and powerful threat. "To strengthen the P.K.I. and weaken the Masjumi was demanded by the very mechanics of the P.N.I.'s power position." Sukarno's support of PNI also gave the Nationalists confidence that they could hold their own against even a considerably stronger PKI. As a result, many Nationalists increased their coöperation with PKI until toward the end of the Wilopo cabinet a major section of PNI was working in close alliance with PKI in order to bring down the government.

During the period of the Wilopo cabinet hostility increased between PKI and Hatta and Masjumi, and strong antipathy developed between PKI and PSI. Hatta and Masjumi attacked PKI as the tool of the new imperialism. The closer PKI moved to PNI, the more virulent became the exchange of abuse, with Hatta and Masjumi anxious to warn the Nationalists of the dangers inherent in any alliance with the Communists, and PKI endeavoring to denigrate the anti-Communists on its own account and in order to please its new-found Nationalist friends. In March 1953, Masjumi leader Sukiman issued a much-publicized appeal that Indonesia, like India, should adopt a firmly anti-Communist policy in internal affairs.

PKI's attitude to PSI varied before the formation of the Wilopo cabinet. The PSI leaders were not liked because they had, early in 1948, split away from the Socialist Party which later fused with PKI; and because they were aware of Communist tactics and not hesitant to explain them to other non-Communists. On the other hand, during the Sukiman cabinet PSI had been a staunch opponent of the August 1951 arrests, and had opposed signing the Japanese Peace Treaty in September 1951. As late as February 1952, PKI sent warm greetings to the PSI congress.[9] Then, on May 25, 1952, Aidit attacked PSI for creating its own trade-unions, for ridiculing the peace movement, and for

refusing to join PKI-led national unity actions.[10] This was the end of
PKI's vacillations, and the Party later explained PSI's policy during
the Sukiman cabinet in terms of a conflict within the imperialist camp:
PSI being a tool of the British, whereas Sukiman was a tool of Washington.[11]

The violence of PKI's attacks on PSI by the end of 1952 are partly
explained by three factors. First, the period of the Wilopo cabinet
witnessed the growth of ties between Masjumi and PSI. Second, PSI
had much support in the army and on October 17, 1952, connived in
an attempted *coup d'état* that would have led to some form of dictatorship, and probably an anti-Communist dictatorship because many
of the higher and pro-PSI army officers had become strongly anti-Communist as a result of the Madiun rebellion. Third, as PNI and Sukarno
considered PSI an enemy, PKI attempted to curry more favor with
them by attacking PSI.

A major political development during the Wilopo cabinet was the
breakaway of Nahdatul Ulama from Masjumi in August 1952.[12] In one
blow Masjumi lost almost fifty per cent of its popular support, and a
new, large Moslem party was established that did not adhere to Masjumi's political line. The NU leaders consisted mostly of politically
inexperienced religious leaders, and as the party's prospects brightened
came to include a smattering of opportunists who joined for personal
profit. Unlike Masjumi, NU was to show itself ready to coöperate with
the Nationalists and Communists when coöperation could serve personal or party interests. In fact, NU was to show itself more ready to
work with the Nationalists and Communists than with the Masjumi
leaders toward whom the break left much bitterness.

The appearance of NU altered considerably the political picture.
Not only was Masjumi weakened, but the Nationalists were encouraged
to form a government without Masjumi. Neither PNI nor Sukarno
dared form a government that completely excluded the Moslems, but
now the amenable NU could be brought into the cabinet and Masjumi
could be excluded. Such an arrangement could not be labeled anti-
Islam.

On June 19, 1952, Sakirman told parliament that PKI would support the new Wilopo cabinet while retaining the right to criticize
sharply any measures "conflicting with democratic rights, national interests, and the interests of the people." [13] Some Party members were
bewildered by the new tactic of conditional support for a government
without Communist representatives, but as early as mid-July the Cen-

tral Committee explained that the advantages of the tactic were already being felt: "a rather broad opportunity" had been opened to PKI and "other people's organizations" to work openly, not in semisecrecy as formerly, and the leadership of PKI and its mass organizations had been able to emerge from hiding.[14]

At the same time as they gave the government their support, the PKI leaders sought to bring together PKI and PNI. At first collaboration was on small matters. For example, PKI and PNI were among the 62 parties and organizations which formed a joint committee to celebrate National Awakening Day on May 20, 1952. The committee issued a statement containing a condemnation of colonialism, an agreement on the need for democracy in all fields, and demands for security (meaning the eradication of the Darul Islam rebels), the return of West Irian, and the cancellation of "all agreements with other states that harm the people and the state." [15] It was significant that neither Masjumi nor PSI signed the statement. Other early forms of PKI-PNI collaboration included parallel statements by leaders of both parties urging strong action against the Darul Islam rebels, vigilance in face of foreign subversive activities, and determined retaliation against Dutch insults.[16]

On July 28, 1952, a debate began in parliament that was to lead to an attempted coup, and to much closer relations between PKI and PNI. The immediate reasons for the debate were the suspension by Colonel Nasution, the army chief of staff, of an insubordinate officer, and the plans drawn up by the Ministry of Defense and the armed forces' leadership for the demobilization of 80,000 troops. The demobilization would have reduced especially those groups with little or no formal education, which by and large consisted of those with the closest personal and political ties with Sukarno and PNI. The Nationalists and Communists quickly turned the debate into an attempt to remove from the Ministry of Defense and armed forces those persons who were pro-PSI or were believed to be so.

PKI's participation in the debate had two purposes: to stay close to PNI; and to weaken PSI's position in the Ministry of Defense and the army—but without causing a cabinet crisis. The balance of forces was still such that a crisis might have resulted in a new Sukiman-type government. The Communists first attempted to bring together the major government parties behind proposals that would have opened the possibility of personnel changes in the Ministry of Defense and the armed forces.[17] But after Sukarno intervened to pressure hesitant PNI leaders to be more resolute against PSI, PKI swung fully behind the

Nationalists. PNI, NU, and PSII representatives sponsored a motion calling for a commission to report on the possibility of improving the defense leadership. This was passed on October 16 by 91 votes to 54, PNI, PKI, NU, and PSII voting for, Masjumi, PSI and the Protestant and Roman Catholic parties voting against. For the moment it appeared that PNI and PKI had succeeded in their objective. And then, on October 17, a section of the army attempted a coup.

The coup failed partly because the army was divided and partly because Sukarno refused to be intimidated. When the coup had failed, lower officers removed pro-coup commanders in East Java, East Indonesia, and North Sumatra. PNI and PKI worked closely in demanding the removal of all who had been implicated in the coup attempt, and subsequently many persons were removed. Colonel Nasution was removed as army chief of staff on December 5, 1952, the pro-PSI minister of defense resigned on January 1, 1953, the PSI secretary-general of the Ministry of Defense was replaced on March 31, 1953, and, finally, the pro-PSI armed forces chief of staff was eliminated when his post was abolished on November 4, 1953. The advantage PNI and pro-PNI officers gained by the removal of those implicated in the coup further estranged Masjumi from the Nationalists.

One of the principal demands of the October 17 group had been the dissolution of the appointed parliament and the holding of general elections. PKI strenuously opposed the dissolution of parliament because action at the parliamentary level was providing it with the opportunity to establish coöperation with the Nationalists and certain Moslem groups, and because the Party feared that the dissolution of parliament at that time could lead to a dictatorship. The Nationalists feared a dictatorship and also elections in the near future—and PKI was quite willing to help stave off elections in order to win PNI's favor.

Hundreds of petitions poured in, mainly from joint local action committees, evidently sponsored by PNI and PKI, calling for parliament to continue.[18] The electoral bill was presented to parliament in February 1953. By the 27th some two hundred amendments had been proposed, and the debate showed signs of dragging on indefinitely. PKI also seemed to be employing delaying tactics for PNI's advantage and proposed, for example, that a census be held before the elections, which would have delayed them for at least two years. Due to strong public pressure against further delays and due to the taunts of Masjumi leaders that the Nationalists were afraid of elections, PNI, and therefore PKI, changed tactics. The bill was rushed through by April 1, 1953. The Nationalists presumed that if the government was weak and a cabinet crisis possible, then the bill could be passed but its implementation delayed by other means.

In the first part of April 1953 a motion was introduced in parliament, with PNI support, calling for the opening of an embassy in Moscow before the end of the year. Masjumi was strongly opposed to the motion, but when it was passed by 82 votes to 43 on April 9, Masjumi declared that it would resign from the cabinet only when the embassy was established. The main forces in PNI were now eager to bring down the government and they used a Communist motion as the means.

On March 16, 1953, five peasant squatters were shot and killed by police in Tandjung Morawa, near Medan, while resisting eviction from estate lands. The PNI in North Sumatra was eager to exploit the shooting in order to embarrass and, if possible, remove the Masjumi governor of the province. In mid-May the pro-Communist leader of the peasant organization SAKTI introduced a motion of no confidence in the minister of the interior, Masjumi's Mohamad Rum, who was blamed for the shooting. This was soon modified, probably to win support from PNI, but Rum declared that he still considered the motion to be one of confidence. As late as May 23 PNI's official attitude to the motion was still unknown, but the North Sumatran section of the party threatened to secede unless the motion was supported. PNI then made a last offer to abstain from voting in return for Masjumi approval of PNI's candidate for minister of information—an offer that was rejected. Finally, the Wilopo cabinet resigned on June 3, before a vote could be taken on the motion.

A majority of the PNI leaders had at last decided that the cabinet could be replaced by one more advantageous to themselves. That they were prepared to seek PKI's coöperation in the subsequent cabinet crisis was shown by the statements in March and April by the PNI second deputy chairman and chairman that the party was non-Communist, not anti-Communist, and that it was prepared to coöperate "with all political tendencies in the community." [19] PKI was willing to bring down the cabinet because it was fairly certain that the balance of power in Indonesia was far more in the progressives' favor than when the cabinet was formed, so that there was little fear that a more right-wing government would be formed.

PKI's first proposal after the fall of the cabinet was that a PNI member be made the formateur and that both Masjumi and PSI be excluded from the next cabinet.[20] At the same time, PKI called for a united front cabinet, including PKI.[21] From June 15 to June 21, formateurs from PNI and Masjumi unsuccessfully tried to reach agreement on a new coalition cabinet. When they failed, PKI at once repeated its demand that a PNI member be made the sole formateur, but, significantly, PKI now dropped its request for Communist representation in the future cabinet.[22] On June 23, after the appointment on the previous day of PNI's Mukarto Notowidigdo as formateur, PKI called for PNI to resist courageously any attempted intimidation by Masjumi and PSI, repeated its demand for a government without Masjumi and PSI, and charged that the United States has already earmarked four hundred million rupiahs for use by Masjumi and the other reactionary parties in the forthcoming elections.[23] A week later, Aidit wrote an almost hysterical article describing the horrors a Masjumi government would unleash.[24]

When Mukarto failed to form a cabinet, PKI declared that it was now proved that any attempt to establish a PNI-Masjumi coalition would fail. Again PKI proposed a PNI member as formateur, but Sukarno appointed to this role Burhanudin Harahap of Masjumi. This led PKI to new heights in its attacks on Masjumi and PSI. While Mukarto had been formateur, 26 parties and organizations, including PKI, PNI, PSII, and the Communist mass organizations, had established in Jogjakarta an action committee to fight for a cabinet excluding Masjumi and PSI. When the Masjumi formateur was appointed, PNI moved much closer to PKI and joint demonstrations were held throughout the country to demand a PNI-led cabinet and the eradication of the Darul Islam rebels.

The increase in the strength of PNI and its allies compared with Masjumi that had occurred during the Wilopo cabinet, and PNI's ability to use PKI support without giving any obvious concessions, emboldened PNI to demand of Masjumi a distribution of cabinet seats that the latter found unacceptable. On July 18 Harahap returned his mandate, and on the 20th Sukarno appointed as formateur Wongsonegoro of the minor nationalist party PIR. Joint demonstrations and delegations continued, PKI expressed its support for Wongsonegoro in his efforts to form a new cabinet, negotiations lengthened, and it became clear that PNI was prepared to take the major role in a coalition cabinet that would exclude Masjumi and PSI. The PNI leaders at last risked a complete break with Masjumi and a leftward shift of alliances. But the risk seemed slight and the gain immense. No one really believed that PKI would be able, in the foreseeable future, to challenge the government, while PNI control of the government apparatus would bring personal and party enrichment as well as the means to face general elections with some confidence.

On July 30, 1953, the new cabinet was announced. The prime minister was Ali Sastroamidjojo, of PNI, and the other members of the cabinet included three from PNI, three from NU, two from PSII, and eleven who were from other minor parties or were non-party. PKI hailed the cabinet as "a glorious victory of democracy over fascism." [25]

The Aidit leadership could look back with satisfaction over the period of the Wilopo cabinet. Conditional support of the cabinet had helped reëstablish the Party's respectability, and it had been repaid by freedom from government repression. At the time the Sukiman cabinet had fallen, the PKI leaders were either in prison or in hiding, and total Party membership was about 8,000. But during the Wilopo cabinet all those arrested in August 1951 were released, all Party and mass organization leaders came back into the open, and the expansion of the Party was begun. By the time the Wilopo cabinet fell, Party membership was over 130,000. In short, the "progressive force" had consolidated itself and begun a rapid expansion.

What of the "middle force," the national bourgeoisie? Aidit, speaking to the PKI Fifth Congress in March 1954, declared that the correct Party tactic towards the Wilopo cabinet had improved and widened the road for unity with the national bourgeoisie, a unity broken since 1948 when the national bourgeoisie had sided with the compradores at the time of the Madiun rebellion.[26] In other words, PKI had successfully exploited the growing PNI opposition to Masjumi policies and PNI fear of the fanatical Moslems. PKI had exacerbated policy differences between PNI and Masjumi into antagonisms by strengthening PNI's hand to the point where PNI was increasingly unwilling to compromise with Masjumi. And PKI had suggested that PNI interests would best be served by a PNI-led cabinet excluding Masjumi and PSI, finally making such a cabinet possible and attractive by offering PKI support at no greater price than friendship and tolerance.

At the same time as the growth of the progressive force and the attraction of the middle force leftward, the "reactionary force" had been further isolated from the middle force and had been considerably weakened. The PSI position in the army and the Ministry of Defense had been almost annihilated. Masjumi and PSI had been further separated from PNI, and even excluded from office—a fact which in itself increased their antagonism toward PNI, the more so as PKI support for PNI was in part responsible for their exclusion. Masjumi itself had split, and the friendliness shown by PNI and PKI toward NU encouraged a further widening of the rift. Finally, a blow had been struck against the imperialists because the new Ali cabinet was led by a PNI committed to the reduction of imperialist economic and political power, and to a "free and active" foreign policy.

2. ALLIANCE WITH PNI

After the formation of the Ali cabinet, many of the prominent PNI leaders came to acknowledge openly and to justify their coöperation with PKI. For example, PNI Chairman Sidik Djojosukarto readily admitted at the beginning of October 1953 that he had recently sent an instruction to all party branches which read: "Establish close relations with the PKI and coöperate closely with the NU. I am confident you will carry out this task tactfully." [27] Sidik claimed that the instruction followed logically from the "close coöperation with both parties" in parliament as a result of NU's participation in and PKI's support for the cabinet. On May 19, 1954, the West Java PNI leader Gatot Mangkupradja even proposed a common front between the Nationalists and Communists in the coming elections in order to defeat "the opposite side." [28] The alliance with PKI was advantageous not only because it helped maintain PNI in and Masjumi out of the government. It also meant that PKI withheld criticism of the worsening economic situation and corruption, and that PKI turned its fire of vicious denunciation against the party PNI considered to be its most dangerous rival.

The advantages to PKI of its alliance with PNI were obvious: freedom from government repression, regained respectability, and the separation of the non-Communists from the anti-Communists. But the Aidit leadership had to take care that support for the government in general did not conceal PKI's own identity as a revolutionary party. This problem became more acute when the Ali cabinet demonstrated corruption and economic ineptitude. The solution was a combination of support and criticism: defense of the government against reactionary attacks, which helped promote alliance with the Nationalist and non-Masjumi Moslem participants in the government; but enough criticism for the Party to maintain itself as the nucleus of social protest, and to make quite clear to members and the public in general that although the current government may be better than previous reactionary ones, only a people's democratic government could solve the major social-economic and political problems facing the country. This combination of support and criticism for bourgeois governments has been maintained down to the present, except for the brief period of the Masjumi-led cabinet from August 12, 1955, to March 3, 1956.

Sakirman, speaking in parliament on September 7, 1953, set the tone for PKI's attacks on the opposition's criticism of the government when he denounced Masjumi and PSI for mouthing old utterances of Van Mook (the last Dutch lieutenant-governor of the East Indies), Hitler, and the United States Information Service.[29] Toward the end of September, when rebels declared Atjeh to be a part of the Darul Islam, PKI launched a suitable attack on the "colonial-militarist-feudal-fascist elements in Atjeh" and offered full support to crush them.[30] On December 31, 1953, Aidit listed seven important and desirable actions taken by the cabinet in the brief period since it took office,[31] and then told the Party congress in March 1954 that the government was not really to blame for economic conditions because it had to bear the results of the disasterous economic and financial policies of the Hatta, Natsir and Sukiman governments as well as of the PSI Finance Minister in the Wilopo cabinet.[32]

At the same time as defending and complimenting the government, however, PKI presented the government with the demands to be met during 1954,[33] and the Party congress of March 1954 put forward twelve demands to be met by the government if it wished to continue to receive Communist support.[34] The PKI leaders did not expect the government to take the demands too seriously because, firstly, the government was not capable of implementing them fully, and secondly, if it could have implemented them the economic situation would have been improved and real or potential discontent reduced. The demands were for popular consumption, to show that the Party had the interests of the people at heart, and to show that the government was incapable of solving the major problems facing the country.

During February 1954, Masjumi made a show of strength in Djakarta that was countered by joint PKI-PNI action. Masjumi announced that it would hold a demonstration on the 13th to demand a change in the recently appointed Djakarta Raja election commission, which included only one Masjumi member. Nine political parties, including PKI, PNI, NU, PSII, and Perti, and eight mass organizations immediately issued a statement declaring Masjumi's intention to be the removal of PNI's mayor and the creation of an all-Masjumi election commission.[35] On the 13th Masjumi held a rally attended by 30,000. One week later, 27 parties and mass organizations combined to hold a giant rally, addressed by speakers from PKI, PNI, NU, and Perti, and attended by 250,000. The rally adopted a resolution which rejected Masjumi's demand and called for alterations in the Masjumi-dominated city council.[36] Masjumi in turn replied with a rally of half a million people on the following day, and used it to attack what were considered insults to Islam made by Nationalist leaders. An army captain was killed during the second Masjumi rally, which led PKI to emit loud cries of horror and to request that the government ban all Masjumi demonstrations.[37] The anti-Masjumi parties could not compete with Masjumi's crowd-raising, but on April 12 a joint delegation, including PKI and PNI representatives, visited the minister of internal affairs to discuss the matter of changing the composition of the Djakarta city council.[38] The government obliged by increasing the number of council members from 25 to 60 on June 18, thus giving large representation to the non-Masjumi groups.

At some time around the beginning of June 1954, a Committee for Coöperation between Parties and Organizations in Djakarta was established, probably on the basis of the joint anti-Masjumi actions. It contained a broad range of parties and mass organizations, including all government parties plus PKI, but excluding Masjumi and PSI.[39] The committee was active in demanding stern measures against the Dutch, the unilateral abrogation of the Indonesia-Netherlands Union, and the immediate creation of a province of West Irian.[40] Boyd Compton reported that local party chiefs in other cities were forced by their Djakarta headquarters to establish similar committees, but that in at least Surabaja the local committee soon disappeared amidst disputes between members.[41] Informal coöperation continued where the formal committees disappeared, and took the form of joint manifestos, statements, and a few mass meetings.

Meanwhile the campaign for the 1955 general elections was under way. In its election manifesto, endorsed in the March 1954 congress, PKI early demonstrated its self-effacing friendliness towards the parties of the "middle force" by calling on the electors "to vote for PKI and the other democratic parties," and not merely for PKI.[42] On May 18, 1954, Aidit urged all democratic parties who were convinced of the need to defeat Masjumi-PSI in the general elections either to pool their surplus votes or to agree not to attack one another during the campaign.[43] No vote-pooling was arranged between PKI and any other major party, but by an unspoken agreement none of the government parties or PKI engaged in mutual recrimination during the campaign. Their combined fire was aimed especially at Masjumi, and even NU joined in the attack on its fellow Moslem party.

In October 1954 the Ali cabinet was threatened by dissension within its own ranks. On October 17 the minor nationalist party PIR called for the resignation of the cabinet, and PIR split into an opposition faction led by what PKI was already calling "the Tadjuddin Noor clique," and a progovernment faction led by Deputy Prime Minister

Wongsonegoro. In the resultant cabinet reshuffle, the minor Moslem party Perti entered the government. Sukarno worked hard to drum up support for the government, persuaded the wavering PSII leaders to keep in line, and attacked the government's opponents as traitors.

PKI reacted by denouncing the PIR anti-government group as "fully supported by the Dutch and American imperialists, the Kuomintang and their accomplices," by assuring the government of the Party's support, and by threatening that if the government fell PKI would demand participation in the next cabinet.[44] When Masjumi introduced a motion of no confidence in the government's policy to liberate West Irian, Aidit in parliament declared that if a Masjumi-PSI cabinet were to replace that of Ali, then the general elections would be held according to procedures applied by Bao Dai, Syngman Rhee, Zahedi, and Mohammed Ali.[45] Aidit's words were no mere rhetoric as far as PKI was concerned. The memory was still fresh of the August 1951 arrests and of Sukiman's proposal for a stern anti-Communist policy, while the Anti-Communist Front, sponsored by a wing of Masjumi, was currently leading a strenuous campaign against PKI.

Fortunately for both PNI and PKI, the Masjumi motion was defeated on December 14 by 115 votes to 92 with 6 abstentions. After the split in PIR, total government support in parliament was only 119 votes, including 17 PKI, 2 each of SOBSI and BTI, and 9 Progressives, including several fellow travelers; the opposition held 101 votes; and the Murba party, with 4 votes, remained neutral.[46] Thus, from October 1954 the Ali cabinet was directly dependent on Communist votes. This did not give PKI a special lever because PNI was fully aware that PKI needed the cabinet in order to prevent a possible Masjumi-led, anti-Communist alternative; but it did demonstrate to PNI the benefits of coöperation with the Communists.

As the PNI leaders found it increasingly necessary to appeal to anti-Dutch feeling as a means of winning support and diverting attention from their obvious failures in the economic field, joint West Irian action committees were established throughout Indonesia. These included PNI, PKI, and other political parties and mass organizations, though usually excluding Masjumi and PSI. The first major action by one of the committees was in Djakarta where a mass demonstration of over half a million people was organized on December 5, 1954. The speakers included two Communists.[47]

At the beginning of May 1955, PKI and SOBSI proved of service to the government by breaking a strike of the PSI-led KBSI trade-union federation. The strike began in Djakarta on May 7 as a protest against deteriorating economic conditions. PKI and SOBSI leaders denounced the strike as "reactionary, anti-worker," and as "a sabotage effort." They claimed it was part of the imperialist plot to overthrow the Republic.[48] SOBSI used its members as strikebreakers, and the strike collapsed.

The end of the Ali cabinet was approaching, not because of opposition within parliament but because of unrest within the army leadership at the government's "interference" in army affairs. In brief, many high army officers were becoming increasingly concerned at the application of the political spoils system to the army. Opposition crystallized especially against Minister of Defense Iwa Kusumasumantri, a close friend of both Sukarno and the Communists. When the army chief of staff resigned, Iwa did not consult the army but appointed a Colonel Bambang Utojo as the new chief. Bambang Utojo was considered a partisan of PNI and Sukarno, and the other officers did not believe him to be professionally qualified for the highest post in the army. PKI welcomed the appointment under the headline "Tactics of the '17th Octoberists' Again Defeated," [49] and the Party was particularly relieved because the acting chief of staff, Colonel Zulkifli Lubis, was an adamant anti-Communist.

The central army leadership boycotted the installation of Bambang Utojo on June 27, 1955, and refused to recognize his appointment. Iwa summoned Lubis to his office, Lubis refused to go. Iwa dismissed him, Lubis refused to accept dismissal, and the army regional commanders backed Lubis despite strong pressure from Sukarno to accept Utojo. In the midst of the events PKI proposed disciplinary measures against the insubordinate officers, and called on the people to give "the greatest possible assistance" to the government "in order to remove the danger of military dictatorship, the danger of fascism." [50] Party members and sympathizers were mobilized to state their conviction of the sagacity of the government's appointment of Bambang Utojo as army chief of staff.[51]

On July 18 Sukarno left on a pilgrimage to Mecca, and one of the cabinet's chief props was removed. It became clear that the army leaders would reject any compromise with the cabinet, including the resignation of Iwa who had departed for Mecca with the president. First the minor nationalist party Parindra and then NU decided that the cabinet should resign—which it did on July 24.

The first Ali cabinet had stayed in power for two years, a record for Indonesia. The benefits PKI reaped from its apparently selfless support for the cabinet in general and PNI in particular were considerable.

First, the government had permitted PKI and its mass organizations to work with a minimum of government restrictions and obstruction. It was during the period of the Ali cabinet that the Aidit leadership developed what was the largest nongovernmental organization in Indonesia: PKI grew from about 130,000 members to almost one million; SOBSI consolidated its organization; the Communist-led peasant organizations fused, and their claimed membership increased from about 400,000 to about 3.5 millions; Pemuda Rakjat's claimed membership rose from less than 70,000 to about 500,000; and Gerwani claimed that its membership rose from about 45,000 to about 400,000.

Second, the advantages of coöperation between Nationalists and Communists were demonstrated to an important section of PNI, and also to Sukarno. Third, coöperation with the Nationalists permitted PKI to regain its nationalist respectability, to promenade alongside prominent nationalists in campaigns demanding militant action against Dutch imperialism. Fourth, an unstated agreement was reached between PKI and the government parties not to attack one another during the election campaign—which made the Communists' task of winning mass support much easier.

Fifth, Communist support of the Ali cabinet permitted the cabinet to remain in office for many months longer than it would otherwise have done, and each month of the PNI-led cabinet which excluded Masjumi increased the rift between those two parties. This was especially so when the cabinet depended directly upon PKI votes. Sixth, Communist support permitted the cabinet to remain in office longer, and so allowed PNI to consolidate its hold over the civil service, particularly over the rural administrative service, with which it was to emerge as the largest single party in the September and December 1955 general elections. This meant that the future parliamentary balance would be tipped away from Masjumi. Seventh, PKI support of the government gave the Party full freedom to attack the anti-Communists, especially Masjumi and PSI, with little fear of government action against the attacks.[52] On the other hand, the government in September 1953 banned demonstrations by anti-Communists to celebrate the outbreak of the Madiun rebellion.

The PSI leader Sjahrir has suggested that the Communists supported the Ali cabinet "because they believed it would lead the country into a blind alley more quickly than any other."[53] Certainly the period of the Ali cabinet was marked by extensive corruption, inflation, and general decline in standards of living. But what might be called the economic incapacity of the groups in the Ali cabinet was merely a fortunate coincidence for PKI, who chose to support them primarily because they were less hostile to PKI and more hostile to Western colonialism than were Masjumi and PSI.

NU had taken its place on the political scene by joining the Ali cabinet. The Aidit leadership extended a warm hand of friendship because the NU leaders were prepared to take opposite sides to Masjumi and showed their willingness to coöperate with any political group as long as they felt coöperation could benefit themselves, their party or their Islamic principles.

As soon as the Ali cabinet resigned, PKI proposed that instead of a completely new cabinet there should be a reshuffled Ali cabinet entrusted with carrying out the elections and opening new discussions with the army leadership.[54] Vice-President Hatta, acting in Sukarno's absence, appointed three formateurs on August 1, 1955: Wilopo, Sukiman, and Assaat, the last an independent politician closely linked with Masjumi and PSI. They failed to reach agreement, and on August 3, Hatta appointed Burhanudin Harahap of Masjumi as formateur. PKI thereupon mobilized the Party and its mass organizations to flood the head of state with petitions and telegrams demanding the preservation of parliamentary democracy and the rejection of a Masjumi-led government. On August 7, Aidit proposed an all-party cabinet, though one not led by Masjumi, that could settle the dispute with the army and carry out "truly free and honest elections." [55]

However, Harahap succeeded in forming a cabinet, which was installed on August 12, 1955, and included members of NU, PSII, PSI, and four smaller parties as well as Masjumi. PNI and PKI moved into the opposition.

Aidit declared that Masjumi and PSI "collaborate with the federalists, the hirelings of the Dutch imperialists," and that this reactionary combination "threatens the democracy and unity of the Indonesian Republic. At the bidding of the Dutch imperialists, these parties are inciting the Darul Islam and other terrorist gangs to anti-democratic activities." [56] But Aidit was wary of offending those parties other than Masjumi and PSI which were in the government. He explained that merit could be discerned among "certain ministers of the cabinet who belong to the parties that formerly belonged to the Ali Sastroamidjojo government and that show good will."

In keeping with its policy of selective attacks on the government, PKI criticized the Harahap cabinet for its financial and economic policy, its defense policy and its foreign policy—because the ministers in charge of those policies were members of Masjumi, PSI, or the Roman Catholic Party. Especially the question of rising prices, not a new phenomenon in Indonesia, was used throughout the life of the cabinet to win broad support and to embarrass the government.

When the new cabinet began to take active steps to bring to trial the beneficiaries of the most blatant examples of corruption under the previous cabinet, PKI displayed the value of its friendship to the Nationalists. PKI attacked instead of praised the anticorruption drive. Sakirman, speaking in parliament, declared that "To combat corruption in a dishonest way is to create greater corruption." [57] He defended Djody Gondokusumo, the PRN minister of justice in the Ali cabinet, the first prominent person brought to account, for his courage in fighting the "Kuomintang plot" and reactionary elements in his ministry. *Harian Rakjat*, in an editorial, commented that the anticorruption slogan could be used as a first step toward fascist power, as witness the Dimitrov case in Hitler's Germany.[58] Such defense of the notoriously corrupt must have raised doubts among the less politically sophisticated Party members, but Aidit reminded them that "In pursuing the unity policy we must not do anything strange or deformed in the eyes of those who should unite with us." [59] In other words, unity was paramount, and, if necessary, even corruption must be excused.

Two issues tied PKI and PNI closer together: the question of negotiations with the Dutch, and, more importantly, the question of forcing the government to resign once the provisional results of the September 1955 parliamentary elections were known.

In December the government opened negotiations with the Netherlands in order to settle peacefully the return of West Irian, the abrogation of the Indonesia-Netherlands Union, and a change in the terms of the Round Table Conference agreement. NU and then PSII objected to the negotiations, and on January 18, 1956, PSII withdrew from the government. PNI, PKI and PSII demonstrated their joint, militant opposition to imperialism in general and Dutch imperialism in particular by organizing a giant anticolonial rally in Djakarta on January 15, 1956. The speakers at the rally were Ali Sastroamidjojo, Aidit, and a PSII leader. The rally also called for a caretaker government to replace the Harahap cabinet.

The provisional results of the September 1955 parliamentary elections were known by the first week in October 1955. Aidit called for the formation of a national coalition government that would be led by PNI and NU, would also include PKI, Masjumi, PSII, the Protestant Party "as well as other parties and groups," and would pursue the "anti-colonial policy" of the Ali cabinet.[60] On November 14, PNI, PKI and some smaller groups began a boycott of parliament. Next day, however, the government succeeded in receiving seventeen votes more than the necessary quorum, and on the 17th the government parties voted to advance the date of the parliamentary recess from December 10 to November 21. The government continued in office, though PKI pointed out that only 83 of the government's votes were valid as the rest came from groups and individuals who had received no popular support in the elections.[61]

When PNI showed no readiness to consider PKI for inclusion in the next cabinet,[62] PKI changed its proposals. On November 30, 1955, Aidit stated that because Masjumi had rejected the idea of an all-party cabinet, PKI now proposed a cabinet of PNI, NU, PSII, and Perti with Communist support but not participation.[63] PKI would give, he said, "real and critical" support for such a cabinet if its program was acceptable.

Early in 1956, throughout the country joint PNI-PKI meetings were held and joint delegations formed to demand a transitional cabinet whose composition was more in line with the election results. On February 16, PNI, NU, PSII, and Perti tabled in parliament a joint motion of no confidence in the government, and on the 27th PNI and NU issued an ultimatum to Masjumi that unless the cabinet resigned by March 2, then both parties would refuse to consider future coöperation with Masjumi. When the official announcement was made, on March 1, of the distribution of seats according to the September 1955 elections, 68 members of parliament resigned—including those from PNI, PKI, NU, and PSII. Two days later the cabinet returned its mandate.

The general elections had not led to a simplification in the number of parties, and after the new distribution of parliamentary seats the two largest parties combined still could not command a majority.[64] Multiparty coalition government was still necessary, a situation to PKI's advantage.

The PKI leaders expressed their relief at the fall of the "reactionary" Harahap cabinet, and again proposed an improved version of the Ali cabinet in which neither PKI nor Masjumi would participate.[65] "But if Masjumi must sit in it, then so also must PKI in order to counterbalance Masjumi policy." The PNI leaders, however, were reportedly under pressure from NU, whose representation in parliament had increased from 8 to 45, and presumably afraid that Masjumi and NU together with such as the Protestant and Roman Catholic parties,

IPKI, and several smaller groups, might form a cabinet to the exclusion of themselves. They consequently negotiated with Masjumi for a broad coalition cabinet.

Ali Sastroamidjojo as formateur presented his proposed cabinet to Sukarno for ratification on March 16. The President delayed ratification for four days because, according to *Harian Rakjat*, he was dissatisfied with the composition and wanted to have included either Professor Purbodiningrat, a well-known fellow traveler, or Sadjarwo, who for many years was a member of the BTI leadership—which Masjumi refused.[66] The PKI Politbureau on March 18 welcomed Ali as formateur and the cabinet program he presented, but criticized the proposed inclusion of Masjumi and the weak attitude taken by PNI and NU toward Masjumi.[67] The Politbureau approved Sukarno's hesitation over ratifying the proposed cabinet, and called on "the democratic parties" to improve its composition. Feith reports that PKI tried to have Purbodiningrat, Sadjarwo or the pro-Communist Hanafi included in the cabinet.[68] This sounds plausible as none of the three was openly a PKI member, and would therefore not raise violent objections from the non-Masjumi parties, while any of the three might have served as a listening post in the cabinet.

Ali's second cabinet was finally installed, unaltered, on March 24, 1956. It consisted of five PNI members, including Prime Minister Ali also in charge of the Ministry of Defense, five Masjumi members, five NU, two Protestant Party, two PSII, two Roman Catholic Party, one IPKI, one Perti, and one nonparty. PKI could do no more than offer critical support, for opposition might have meant forfeiting the goodwill of PNI in particular. It also might have given Masjumi the opportunity to persuade the rest of the cabinet to pursue an anti-Communist policy.

3. THE APPROACH TO SUKARNO

The second Ali cabinet, which was to return its mandate on March 14, 1957, proved to be a turning point in Indonesian politics. Four major political developments occurred that forced the Aidit leadership to seek a basic alliance with Sukarno rather than with PNI.

The first development was the drastic decline in the prestige of the parliamentary system and of political parties in general. When the second Ali cabinet took office, the political parties were still the most important and decisive political forces. Many deficiencies were recognized in the actual practice of parliamentary democracy—for example, widespread corruption and the spoils system, the failure to promote economic development, and frequent cabinet changes due to disputes between and within the many parties—but hopes had been pinned on the general elections as a means of somehow removing them. Then, after the new cabinet was installed, and the new parliament two days later, nothing seemed to have changed. There were still the squabbling parties, the same old faces in the cabinet, the same economic gloom. As a result, there developed among the politically conscious Indonesians a widespread feeling that the parliamentary system—"free fight liberalism" as Sukarno was to call it—had failed and must be replaced. The political parties did little to defend the parliamentary system.

The second major political development was closely related to the first. As the political parties virtually surrendered their authority and admitted their inability to solve Indonesia's economic and political problems, two extraparliamentary political forces rose to fill the power vacuum: Sukarno and the army. By the time the Ali cabinet resigned, these two political forces dwarfed the parties.

The third development was the removal from the central government of the last representatives of what PKI calls the reactionary force, which included Hatta, Masjumi, and PSI. After Sukarno had made it plain that he no longer wanted Hatta as vice-president, Hatta resigned at midnight on November 30, 1956. Masjumi withdrew from the cabinet on January 9, 1957. With the removal from the central government of Hatta and Masjumi, who by and large represented much of the population outside Java, and the implacable opposition of Sukarno (and therefore PNI) and PKI to their return, important segments of the population of the outer islands came to feel increasingly that the government in Djakarta in no way represented their interests. This feeling was one of the factors which led many of the leaders of the outer islands to reject, with varying degrees of politeness, the authority of the central government.

The fourth development, also closely related to the others, was a political realignment by Sukarno. Until the September 1955 elections, Sukarno had identified himself closely with the party he had helped establish, PNI. Then, toward the end of 1955, Sukarno sought the friendship of PKI, and this alliance with the Communists was firmly cemented by early 1957. Two basic factors explain why Sukarno wanted this alliance: his struggle to achieve and maintain a dominant political position, and his wish "to complete the revolution."

In 1956 the hegemony of the political parties was drawing to a close and it became clear that a new arrangement of political power was in the offing. Sukarno wished to become the dominant political force in the country, and needed allies to help counterbalance the other emerging power, the army. He viewed the army with suspicion because many of its officers were eager to establish either an army-led governmen or an army-backed government in which his political opponents, Hatta and Masjumi, would probably have played a major role. PNI, despite rare floutings of his wishes, was his reliable ally: it was dependent upon him for its mass support and for his assistance in political maneuvers. But his own popularity and political skill combined with PNI support were still insufficient to counter the army, Masjumi, and other political opponents. Therefore Sukarno sought the alliance of PKI, not only the largest but the best organized party (by mid-1957, PKI claimed over one million members, and more than seven million members in its network of mass organizations). PKI organization could be used to demonstrate to the army Sukarno's apparent great popularity, his legitimate position as father and leader of the revolution, by mobilizing enormous crowds for his meetings, by deluging the country with his slogans. Communist support would be of importance in parliament and the Constituent Assembly. With PKI on his side, Sukarno could feel fairly certain that the central army leadership dare not attempt to oust him for fear of civil war. And he could force concessions from the army by threatening to bring PKI into the cabinet or other governmental positions. At the same time, Sukarno reportedly believed that if the PKI leaders became truculent he could remove their mass support with one speech, as he believes he did in September 1948.

Apart from seeking PKI's alliance for purely power reasons, Sukarno probably viewed PKI as the only party able and willing to assist him toward his major policy goal, "the completion of the revolution." What he means by this is nebulous, but it includes maintaining the people in a state of nationalist fervor through mass actions toward the elimination of all imperialist and neoimperialist (that is, Western) political, economic, and cultural power in Indonesia. PNI had proved to be corrupt, fundamentally conservative, and clearly incompetent. NU, a party of conservative religious leaders, was of little use in implementing Sukarno's revolutionary task. Only PKI, combining a vociferous anticolonialism with size and efficient organization could be of much assistance.

The changing political situation created serious tactical problems for the Aidit leadership. As will be seen, PKI worked hard to assist the second Ali cabinet and thus to save parliamentary democracy or at least stave off its demise. But when it was clear that the regime would be drastically overhauled, PKI was forced to adapt its basic national united front policy to the special circumstances of a political situation in which the role of parliament would be greatly reduced, and in which the chief power centers would be the army on the one hand and Sukarno on the other. The old parliamentary alliance might still serve a useful purpose, but a new alliance obviously had to be established with either the army or Sukarno in order to safeguard the existence of the Party. Within the army there arose loud voices advocating the abolition of all parties, and many prominent officers, both in the central command and in the regions, were outspokenly anti-Communist. Therefore the PKI leaders, in private reluctantly, but in public eagerly, accepted Sukarno's proffered hand.

The *rapprochement* between PKI and Sukarno was the result of developments over several years.

Strong attacks on Sukarno had continued during the first months after the Aidit leadership gained control of PKI. Then, as the new form of the national united front was formulated and implemented, the attacks on him were halted when it was realized that he was a popular nationalist symbol and that he was opposed to Masjumi and PSI, the most ardent anti-Communist parties. Alimin, at a ceremony on May 25, 1952, to celebrate the founding of PKI, even led cheers for Stalin, Mao Tse-tung, Kim Il Sung and . . . Sukarno.[69]

In his August 17 speech in 1952, Sukarno, much to PKI's delight, pointed out that the transfer of sovereignty was neither complete nor unconditional, and that the fight against imperialism in Indonesia was as yet unfinished. At the time of the October 17, 1952, attempted coup by a section of the army leadership, Sukarno proved his opposition to military dictatorship and was instrumental in the removal of PSI members and sympathizers from important posts in the army and the Ministry of Defense. But, with the memory still fresh in their minds of Sukarno's alliance with the anti-Communists at the time of the Madiun rebellion and during the Sukiman cabinet, the PKI leaders still could not regard him as a true political ally. In November 1952 he was categorized with the old group of intellectuals who had "ceased to be progressive the moment they themselves occupied places of leadership in society," who defended the status quo and were afraid of the revolutionary forces, and "who, in general, can at the most be neutralized, especially in revolutionary times." [70]

During the first Ali cabinet, however, Sukarno's actions opened the possibility that he might become an important ally for PKI. It was partly due to Sukarno's intervention that Masjumi and PSI were excluded from the cabinet, and he did his utmost to defend the cabinet, even accusing its opponents of being foreign agents. On August 17, 1953, he outspokenly attacked the Darul Islam as an enemy of the state and people, which the government had previously been afraid to do. And from December 1954 he began to advocate national unity specifically embracing the Communists. In that month he proposed a congress to include all parties and tendencies in order to create the power with which to liberate West Irian. The formation of the congress was left to the parties. Masjumi, PSI, and the two Christian parties refused to coöperate from the beginning, and PNI withdrew in about July 1955, after which the congress organization fell under Communist control. Although the congress never came to anything important, the very idea was most attractive to the PKI leaders as such a congress would bring the parties together, increase nationalist, anti-Dutch agitation, and strengthen the identification of PKI with Sukarno's charisma.

Sukarno's actions during the Burhanudin Harahap cabinet further increased PKI's readiness for and decreased its fear of alliance with him. He made his opposition to the cabinet quite clear, intervened in a dispute among airforce officers in order to save the pro-Communist airforce chief, and prior to the Constituent Assembly elections toured the country speaking on West Irian and Pantjasila. More than this, he expressed his belief that it was ". . . illogical that the Indonesian Communist Party, whose ideology and ideals are supported by six million people, should be excluded from the government." [71] On January 15, 1956, he told the mass rally against colonialism that had been addressed by Ali, Aidit, and PSII's Arudji Kartawinata:

Now facing me is the Triple-A: Ali-Arudji-Aidit. . . . The present Triple-A is an anti-imperialist Triple-A, an anti-colonial Triple-A, a Triple-A defending the people's rights. This makes me happy, this is why my heart is alight to receive the present Triple-A.

This Triple-A represents three groupings. As has just been said by Mr. Dipa Nusantara Aidit, your giant meeting is indisputable proof that there can be Moslem-Nationalist-Communist unity.

For 37 years I have worked for unity. Therefore I am happy to see unity now created. . . . How can I, who have worked for unity for 37 years, how can I say, "Heh, Indonesian people, unite, unite, but twenty per cent, sixteen millions, that is, the Communists, are not included . . ."? Can we create unity while bunging twenty per cent, sixteen millions, the Communists, down a mouse-hole? [72]

Then, at the time of the formation of the second Ali cabinet, Sukarno, as has been seen, is said to have delayed endorsement of the cabinet while he unsuccessfully attempted to have several fellow travelers included in it.

The ground was therefore prepared for the shift in PKI's basic alliance from PNI to Sukarno. The ideal situation for PKI would have been the continuation of parliamentary democracy and the paramount role of the parties, but also an alliance with Sukarno. When this was impossible because of the changed political situation, the PKI leaders threw in their lot with the president.

The second Ali cabinet was soon faced with grave insubordination from prominent army officers. The first major affront to the government occurred on August 13, 1956, when Foreign Minister Ruslan Abdulgani of PNI was arrested by the West Java military commander on charges of corruption. In November, Colonel Zulkifli Lubis of the central army command planned an unsuccessful coup. And on December 20 the first of the regional councils in defiance of Djakarta's authority was set up when former members of the long-demobilized Banteng Division, led by Lieutenant Colonel Achmad Husein, took over the government of Central Sumatra. Two days later, Colonel Simbolon, the army commander in North Sumatra, announced that he had taken over the government in his region and that he refused to recognize the Ali government. The central government acted quickly and successfully against Simbolon, replacing him by his second-in-command who effected a countercoup on December 27. This did not deter other regional commanders. On March 2, 1957, Lieutenant Colonel Sumual took over the government of East Indonesia; and, after some months of rumblings, the military commander of South Sumatra did likewise in his area on March 9.

PKI's fear of the army was justified by the arrest of members of the Party and its mass organizations by the councils established by the dissident army commanders. PKI was therefore the first party militantly to oppose the regional councils. On December 23, 1956, the PKI Politbureau issued a statement denouncing Husein's action as "anti-democratic" and Simbolon's as "rebellion." [73] The Politbureau blamed Masjumi and PSI for the creation of the councils and for Lubis' attempted coup, and declared that the action of regional commanders "divides and stabs the Indonesian Republic from within; in this way they directly benefit the Dutch and American imperialists." Finally, the Politbureau called on the people to assist the government and armed forces in settling the two Sumatran affairs.

At the same time as the acts of insubordination by the regional army commanders, the government coalition was falling apart. On December 26, 1956, the small party IPKI, which had close ties with many high army officers, withdrew from the government; on December 30, the Protestant Party called for the dissolution of the cabinet; and on January 9, 1957, Masjumi withdrew into the opposition.[74] Many leaders of the army as well as Masjumi and many smaller parties sought a solution to the crisis in a fresh period of coöperation between Sukarno and Hatta, and there was much talk of making Hatta prime minister. This prospect was a grim one for PKI which at once claimed that the withdrawal of Masjumi actually strengthened the government.[75] On January 11, 1957, Aidit expressed PKI's continued support for the government and declared that the Party would not ask for cabinet posts.[76] On February 7, a PKI member told parliament that the resignation of the cabinet would mean capitulation before the "military coup plot." [77] Across the country PNI, PKI and the Communist mass organizations held meetings in support of the government.

At this point Sukarno announced his concept for solving Indonesia's political troubles, and PKI turned to the president as the only political force capable of preventing the emergence of either military dictatorship or a right-wing anti-Communist government headed by Hatta. After the combined opposition of all political parties except Murba to his suggestion of October 28, 1956 to "dream away the existence of so many parties," Sukarno on February 21, 1957, announced his long-awaited concept. It contained two main points: a "mutual-coöperation" cabinet that would reflect the parties' representation in parliament and would thus eliminate opposition; and a National Council that would include representatives from all important functional groups in society, would advise the cabinet in its work, and would be headed by himself. In answer to the question why Communists should be included, he replied that a party that had won six million votes could not be ignored, and that "everybody is needed in the work towards national progress." [78] The concept was Sukarno's first step toward Guided Democracy.

The PKI leaders gave Sukarno's concept a joyous welcome[79] because it was a rebuff to proposals for an army-led or Hatta-led cabinet, and because it promised early Communist participation in the cabinet, something that the alliance with PNI had notably failed to produce. For Sukarno's benefit, and perhaps as justification to ordinary members of the Party's new alliance with a highly dubious "democrat," the Politbureau claimed that:

the Western system of democracy carried out in Indonesia up to the present has been harmful to the development of the revolutionary and democratic movement,

that the Western system had proved unable to solve the fundamental problems in society, and that it had been used by "the foreign imperialists and their puppets within the country" to play off one group against another.[80] The Politbureau claimed that the concept in no way disturbed the party system or the parliamentary system, and that it permitted the development of democracy. It must already have been evident, however, that the future of political democracy was severely limited.

While Masjumi expressed opposition to the concept, and succeeded in persuading NU, PSII, PIR, and the Roman Catholic Party to issue a joint statement rejecting it, and while PNI hesitated over its choice of a policy, the PKI leaders launched into feverish activity to arouse mass support for Sukarno's proposal. An Action Committee of Support for Bung Karno's Concept was immediately established in Djakarta with Communist Suharto Rebo as chairman. Demonstrations and rallies were organized throughout the country to express support for the concept. The largest meeting was organized in Djakarta only three days after the official announcement of the concept, when a million people were gathered together.

The government finally resigned on March 14, having been unable to cope with the regional acts of insubordination and having lost the support of many of the original member parties. Sukarno placed the whole country under a state of war and siege which gave great powers to the army commanders in their capacity as war administrators. Sukarno attacked those who wished to exclude PKI from a coalition government, commenting "They want me to ride a horse, but insist that they must first chop off one foot of the horse. I cannot and will not ride a three-footed horse." [81] SOBSI, probably made brave by expressed or presumed support from Sukarno, led a 24-hour strike in South Sumatra on March 18 to demand the restoration of civil government there.[82] On the following day the SOBSI leaders told PNI formateur Suwirjo that if a cabinet were formed including Masjumi but not PKI, "SOBSI will not hesitate and is always in readiness to lead a total strike action all over Indonesia." [83]

PKI wanted Suwirjo to succeed because the alternatives, ranging from Hatta to Sukarno as formateur, were much less attractive. Aidit therefore told Suwirjo that PKI accepted his proposed program, that PKI would support a cabinet based on PNI and NU, and that PKI would demand a mutual-coöperation cabinet only if Masjumi was brought into the next cabinet.[84] The PKI leaders knew that the army and NU were strongly opposed to Communist participation in the cabinet, and so they again deferred PKI's claim in order to encourage NU to accept another cabinet that excluded both PKI and Masjumi. But NU was adamant in its insistence on including Masjumi, and Suwirjo returned his mandate on April 2. Two days later Sukarno appointed himself, "citizen Sukarno," as formateur of an "emergency extra-parliamentary business cabinet." Masjumi at once condemned Sukarno's action as illegal, but PKI called on "the entire people and armed forces to give the fullest assistance to our President-Supreme Commander." [85] On April 7, the Politbureau declared Sukarno's action to be fully legal, but also raised the slogan "prevent all abuses of the state of war and siege." [86]

The new cabinet, the Djuanda cabinet, was installed on April 9. It included four PNI members, four NU, two Masjumi, one each from PSII, IPKI, SKI, Murba, and the Protestant Party, and eight nonparty persons. Masjumi rejected the cabinet outright as unconstitutional and expelled its two members who had joined the cabinet; NU refused to identify itself with the cabinet, but permitted its members to participate as individuals. Significantly, Sukarno did not choose any of the PNI leaders as ministers, and the 23 cabinet members were almost all political nonentities who owed their position to the president and who would be amenable to Sukarno's commands.

Within the new cabinet, PKI could count five "progressives" who were considered at least quite friendly toward the Party: PSII Minister of Information Sudibjo, ex-BTI Minister of Agriculture Sadjarwo, Murba Minister of Education and Culture Prijono, Minister for Veterans' Affairs Chairul Saleh, and Hanafi, Minister for the Mobilization of the National Strength for Reconstruction.

4. ALLIANCE WITH SUKARNO CEMENTED

The period of the Djuanda cabinet, from April 9, 1957, to July 6, 1959, marked the transition from parliamentary democracy to the formal assumption of power by Sukarno. In April 1957, however, Sukarno still preferred to rule indirectly. Once he had formed the cabinet he stepped back into the guise of constitutional president. Prime Minister Djuanda declared that although he led an "extra-parliamentary business cabinet" he felt he was responsible to parliament.

One of the first major acts of the Djuanda cabinet heartened PKI and indicated that Sukarno might truly be aiming at a mutual-coöperation cabinet and not just talking about one in order to win Communist support. On July 12, 1957, the National Council was installed as an adviser to the cabinet. Its forty-five members represented what Sukarno calls "functional groups," [87] and included nine persons who either were Communist or known to be sympathetic to PKI. The newspaper *Indonesia Raja* reported that the president's original list of members had been mostly "leftists," but that it had been modified by the cabinet.[88]

In April 1957, Aidit explained that the Djuanda cabinet was not the 100 per cent implementation of Sukarno's concept, but that "it is a phase which, according to the hard facts of the situation, must be traversed before 100 per cent implementation." [89] While supporting the cabinet, PKI raised as its major slogan, "Implement Bung Karno's Concept 100 Per Cent!" Efforts were made to identify the Party as closely as possible with the president. Communist policies, programs, and requests came to be justified by suitable quotations from Sukarno's speeches and writings of thirty years. This close identification served several purposes at the time. It strengthened Sukarno's friendship with PKI, and it made it very difficult for PKI's opponents to attack the Party without appearing to attack the president. Furthermore, it permitted PKI to exploit his tremendous personal appeal in order to win votes in the local elections held from June to November 1957 in Java, and then in some of the outer regions.

PKI's identification with Sukarno played some part in enabling the Party to emerge as the largest party in the local elections. In Java, the Communist vote was increased from 5,477,707 in September 1955 to 7,514,197. PKI was now the largest party in Central Java, and the second largest in the other regions of Java.[90] It appeared that at least some of the Communist gains were made at the expense of PNI.

The Communist gains caused much resentment among the other political parties. As soon as the results of the first, the Djakarta Raja, elections were known, a *Harian Rakjat* editorial stated in reply to charges that PKI-PNI-NU coöperation was benefiting only PKI:

PKI does not like it if coöperation benefits only the other side, but neither does PKI like it if coöperation benefits only its own side. This is the elementary principle of coöperation: the principle of equal status and mutual benefit.[91]

Aidit advised PNI and NU that they had lost votes because they had not been resolute enough in adhering to the path of democracy and unity with the people, nor in attacking the reactionaries.[92] He said that the results showed "a shift to the left of the Indonesian people," and that only parties that realized this and also swung left would gain the people's confidence.

Some of the regional leaders of PNI in particular were angered by PKI's electoral gains. First the Central Java section of the party and then the East Java, North Sumatra and West Java sections instructed their branches to cease coöperation with PKI.[93] Worse still for PKI, on August 10, 1957, the PNI secretary-general declared PNI's readiness to coöperate with Masjumi and NU "in the interest of the defense of democratic principles," [94] and although PNI-Masjumi coöperation did not materialize on a national level, the PNI regional councils in West and Central Java and North Sumatra expressed their desire for such coöperation.[95] PNI national and local leaders attacked PKI as a Soviet tool, while the PNI newspaper on November 14 declared that PKI was trying to create a "second Yenan" in East Sumatra as a prelude to an armed take-over of all Indonesia.[96] NU leaders also said harsh things about PKI.[97]

In the developing situation, in which the regional army-led councils were taking stern anti-Communist measures at the same time as apparently strengthening their position vis-à-vis the central government, and in which important elements in PNI and NU were becoming ever more critical of PKI and were seemingly moving toward a *rapprochement* with Masjumi, the PKI leaders could only maintain their support of the government and endeavor to move even closer to Sukarno.

Lavish praise of Sukarno became a regular feature of PKI statements and speeches, and is widely believed to have made a favorable impression on the flattery-loving president. In August 1957, when Sukarno launched a "New Life Movement," a vaguely defined movement to renovate the life of the Indonesian people, the PKI Central Committee at once ordered all Party leaders in the regions to assist in its implementation.[98] On August 19, Aidit was among the presidential party which did a little but much publicized work in cleaning one of Djakarta's markets. On October 20, Aidit declared PKI's acceptance of the Pantjasila unchanged as the basis of the state.[99] As Sukarno created the Pantjasila and was currently striving to win its acceptance by the Constituent Assembly, PKI's own espousal of it unchanged, despite objections to the first *sila,* the belief in God the Almighty, was a gesture of friendship toward the president.

Apart from praising Sukarno and giving support to his ideas and to the government he had appointed, the PKI leaders also increased their attacks on the common enemies, the army-led regional councils, Masjumi, and PSI. The increasingly derogatory attacks on the councils was illustrated by a booklet, written by the Communist leader in West Sumatra.[100] The "fascism of the 'Banteng Council–PSI' " was attacked for its "little warlord government," its protection of Dutch capital, and its efforts to bring down both Sukarno and the cabinet. PKI opposition to the councils was not limited to words. A 24-hour general strike was launched by SOBSI against the Garuda Council in South Sumatra on March 18, 1957, and on August 21, PKI organized a giant rally in Bukit Tinggi, the capital of West Sumatra, in protest against the Banteng Council. These were the only nonverbal actions taken by political parties against the councils, and afforded evidence for Sukarno that PKI would stand bravely at his side in his dispute with the councils.

Communist attacks on Masjumi and PSI continued, especially for their alleged complicity in the creation of the regional councils. In November 1957, both *Harian Rakjat* and another Communist newspaper in Djakarta, *Bintang Timur,* published a report from China which had originated in the Indian periodical *Blitz* and which linked Masjumi and PSI with "the American plot to overthrow the Sukarno regime." [101] The report also claimed that Masjumi had requested Taiwan to furnish more assistance to the Darul Islam rebels.

It should be noted that at the same time as it gave support to the Djuanda cabinet, PKI also made sufficient criticisms of the government in order still to present itself to its members and society at large as a critical and revolutionary party. SOBSI strongly criticized a regulation of August 24, 1957, which banned all strikes in "vital" industries, enterprises, and offices.[102] On August 27, parliament voted 94 to 81 against a government draft state of emergency law and for amendments proposed by PKI.[103] A popular campaign was waged to urge the government to implement SOBSI and BTI proposals for the distribution of rice at low prices, and in October *Harian Rakjat* called on the government to end the ban by local and regional army commanders on the shipment of rice from their areas.[104] Toward the end of the year, Communist representatives in parliament criticized the government's budget for its low allocations for such as the Ministry of Education and Culture, thus implying that expenditure on the armed forces was too high.[105] Such criticism was, however, kept very much in check so that it would neither alienate the government or its supporters, nor provoke repression by pro-government local army commanders.

Toward the end of 1957 an anti-Dutch campaign spread across Indonesia in preparation for the United Nations' discussion of the West Irian question at the end of November. In the second week of November, Sukarno went so far as to warn that if the United Nations did not back Indonesia's claim for West Irian, then Indonesia might use methods that "would startle the world" in order to win the territory. On November 18, Sukarno and several political leaders, including Aidit, addressed a Liberate West Irian rally in Djakarta. The rally endorsed a resolution which demanded that should the United Nations fail to uphold Indonesia's claim, then the government should nationalize the vital enterprises owned by the Dutch and accelerate the participation of Indonesians in the management of all Dutch enterprises.[106] When the United Nations failed to give the necessary two-thirds vote in favor of the Indonesian claim, the government ordered a general strike against all Dutch enterprises for December 2. Local boycotts against Dutch companies and nationals had already begun in different parts of Indonesia. On December 3, workers began taking over Dutch concerns. The initial actions apparently were taken by members of KBKI, PNI's trade-union federation, but SOBSI quickly joined in with enthusiasm.

The extent to which PKI was responsible for the course of events which led to the take-over of all Dutch enterprises is difficult to ascertain. Certainly the Communists were happy to encourage or foment anti-Dutch feelings, and Communist mass organizations had called for stern measures and boycotts, while PKI gave its support to the government's threat to take "the other road" to liberate West Irian. On October 21, however, the *Harian Rakjat* editorial, while it agreed that "clear measures must be begun" against Dutch capital, pointed out that Indonesia was in no position to confiscate at one stroke all Dutch capital in the country.[107] On November 4, the Central Committee issued a statement by Aidit which also spoke vaguely of "taking action in proportion to the Dutch stubborn and insolent attitude," but put forward no concrete proposals for action. It would appear that Sukarno was one if not *the* prime mover in the campaign to seize all Dutch enterprises,[108] and that PKI gladly followed him, though always careful never to get one step ahead in case that would bring retribution.

Hearsay has it that many members of the cabinet, and probably including Djuanda, were opposed to such drastic action against the Dutch partly because they feared the economic disruption that was expected to ensue. But once the take-over had taken place they were presented with a *fait accompli* that they had to support. The first government reaction to the workers' take-over was to declare all Dutch enterprises to be under government management. The PKI leaders, probably afraid that the workers' action might frighten the national bourgeoisie and the army into an alliance with Masjumi, called on the workers in the seized enterprises to avoid "adventurist" acts, to maintain firm work discipline, to assist the new management "with all their energy," and to help prevent sabotage.[109] On December 13, Nasution, as army chief of staff, ordered the military to take over and supervise directly in the name of the Republic all Dutch enterprises—a measure that PKI welcomed as "good." [110] PKI also suggested that "In order to prevent sabotage, to increase production and to raise quality it would be very wise" for the government to introduce worker participation in the management councils of the enterprises.[111] This the army refused to countenance.

Criticism of the take-over, which came from Hatta and Masjumi, mostly condemned the lack of preparation which was resulting in economic chaos. PKI, in order to demonstrate its support for the government and to pursue its basic policy of isolating the reactionaries, denounced all opponents of the government as traitors.[112] Abulhajat, a "non-party" member of parliament elected on the PKI list, introduced a motion of confidence in the sagacity of the government's efforts to free West Irian. The motion was carried on February 28, 1958, by 95 votes to 20, with PNI, NU, and PKI voting for, Masjumi and PSI against, and IPKI and the Protestant and Roman Catholic parties abstaining.[113] Meanwhile the PRRI-Permesta rebellion had broken out.

An assassination attempt against Sukarno on November 30, 1957, marked the end of efforts at *rapprochement* between Sukarno and his Djuanda cabinet on the one hand and the dissident regional councils on the other. Sukarno left on a forty-day "rest tour" of the world on January 6, 1958. While he was away the Banteng Council on February 10 presented the central government with a five-day ultimatum either to withdraw the mandate of the Djuanda cabinet and designate Hatta and the Sultan of Jogjakarta as formateurs, or to see the establishment of a separate state in Central Sumatra. Next day the cabinet rejected the ultimatum and dishonorably discharged the leading army officers who had drawn up the ultimatum. The rebel government was announced on February 15, and was soon joined by the Permesta rebel council in North Sulawesi. Later, the PRRI established loose liaison with the Daud Beureueh Moslem rebels in Atjeh, the Darul Islam in West Java, and the Kahar Muzakar Moslem rebels in South Sulawesi. It must be noted that the new government was not separatist, but sought to become the government of all Indonesia.

Sukarno returned to Indonesia on February 16. He apparently was the chief voice demanding stern measures against the rebels, although army chief Nasution reportedly was also eager to quell the insubordination of regional army officers. Aidit, on the 17th, called for immediate and firm action against the "corrupt and treacherous 'revolutionary government'" and against those who supported it.[114] The rebel government was outspokenly and actively anti-Communist. To delay action against it would have made possible the consolidation of its as yet untested strength. A compromise would have produced only a result to PKI's disadvantage. Aidit's call was therefore loudly echoed by the Party and its mass organizations. As the rebels were closely associated with Masjumi and PSI, and were more sympathetic to Hatta than to Sukarno, both PNI and NU also demanded the speedy elimination of the PRRI.

The central government acted with uncharacteristic speed. Large

numbers of troops landed in East Sumatra on March 7, and on the
west coast of Sumatra on April 17. The rebel forces were quickly
pushed into the jungle where they continued to exist as guerrilla bands
for over three years. PKI not only gave verbal support to the central
government, but also claimed that in Central Sumatra members of
the Party and of Pemuda Rakjat took to the hills and actively fought
the rebels.[115] Widespread reports indicate that the Communists served
as sources of intelligence for the advancing government troops and
were of assistance in helping reëstablish an administration in the
cleared areas. Persons from North Sulawesi also reported that Communists from Tondano organized guerrilla units to harass the Permesta
rebels there. Communist support to the government forces can have
been of only peripheral importance, but it did demonstrate PKI's support for the Djakarta regime. It also resulted in the government forces
tolerating organizational activities by PKI and its mass organizations
in the cleared areas at a time when all political activity was theoretically banned there.[116]

In the heat of the first weeks of the rebellion, PKI was unwilling
to make criticisms of the government. The Central Committee, in its
meeting from March 31 to April 3, 1958, blamed the rising price of
rice on the rebels, Kuomintang agents, commission agents, and landlords—but not on the government.[117] When a cabinet reshuffle occurred
in June 1958, Aidit pledged even stronger support.[118] Once the danger
of the rebellion was past, however, PKI resumed its policy of support
plus criticism. Individual government measures that received criticism
included the alien tax act, of July 1958, which imposed a severe head
tax on all aliens, which in effect meant on the Chinese; the foreign
investments act, of September, which if implemented would have established conditions for the regulated inflow of foreign private capital;
the 1959 budget; and a decree of May 1959 which stated that licences
for foreign-owned, that is, Chinese-owned, shops in all villages and
subdistrict capitals would be withdrawn by the end of 1959.

The economic situation gave the Party the greatest opportunity for
criticism of the government that would be of broad popular appeal.
The take-over of Dutch enterprises had caused considerable economic
disruption, and then the rebellion caused even more. Enormous quantities of new money were printed to finance the antirebel operations.
Inflation rocketed. From the beginning of September 1958, SOBSI
waged a campaign to prevent increases in the price of rice. At the end
of October, Lukman warned the government that unless it wished to
face great opposition inside and outside parliament, then it should
withdraw its proposals to further increase the official price of rice.[119]

The government did withdraw them on November 5. When the SOBSI national council met from December 22 to 28, 1958, it pointed to the confused nature of the general economic situation and of state finances, and to the marked deterioration in the workers' living standards.[120] Instead of blaming only the rebels, the imperialists, and the corrupt, the council attributed the situation in part to the government's inadequate economic and financial policies.

The Aidit leadership was presumably forced to criticize the government or else risk losing the support of its cadres and the populace in general who were directly suffering the deteriorating economic conditions. As formerly and in the future, however, PKI had to tread warily lest its criticisms became so harsh as to alienate the ruling groups and drive them toward the anti-Communists.

The rapid removal of the PRRI-Permesta as a threat to the central government greatly strengthened the position of both Sukarno and the central army leadership, and enabled the former to move further toward Guided Democracy, the latter toward greater participation in government. Parliamentary democracy suffered in the middle and was finally eliminated.

PKI was weak relative to Sukarno, the army, and the non-Communists in general. The Aidit leadership therefore was prevented from effecting any major change in the course of political events. At the same time the Communist leaders decided on a delicate tactical line which would on the one hand try to influence the course of events as far away as possible from dictatorship, and on the other seek to retain Sukarno's now all-important protective arm and to provide the army with no just cause for severe repression. In practice, this line consisted fundamentally of rear-guard action in defense of parliamentary democracy and the party system, hearty promotion of Sukarno's main policy decisions (though at the same time working to influence their actual implementation along lines desirable to the Party), avoidance of "adventurist" action that might frighten or offend the ruling groups, and the reiteration of strong opposition to dictatorship, both personal and military.

The major political force which was most intolerant of the political parties and of the parliamentary system was the army. Army participation in extramilitary affairs had been greatly increased under the state of war and siege decree of March 14, 1957, by which the army commanders had become war administrators. Then, beginning in June 1957, the army established coöperation committees between the army and the functional groups, such as youth, workers, peasants, and women, which contained all existing mass organizations in their respective fields and were designed primarily so that the army could keep watch and some control over the functional groups. When the Dutch enterprises had been seized, army officers entered their management, and on February 10, 1958, an army-led National Front for the Liberation of West Irian was established to channel all activities in the campaign. It looked possible at first that the Front might become a powerful organization under army control, but, reportedly due to Sukarno's opposition, it failed to become significant. As of May Day 1958, the army brought the May Day trade-union rallies under control, banning parades and scrutinizing the texts of speeches. It was also suspected by the Communists that the army was behind the August 24, 1957, ban on strikes in "vital" enterprises and offices, and also the postponement, announced on September 22, 1958, of the 1959 general elections.

The PKI leaders naturally viewed with alarm the growing army participation in nonmilitary affairs, especially as the army was, by and large, anti-Communist, and as there were rumors that many important officers wanted a military dictatorship. Therefore, at the same time as hailing the eternal unity of the army-people *dwitunggal* (two-in-one), PKI waged an intensive campaign among Party members to warn against the fascist danger presented by the army, and publicly opposed army "interference" in nonmilitary affairs. The first outspoken opposition to army interference was made by both PKI and SOBSI in November 1958.

Aidit, speaking to the Central Committee on November 19, 1958, said that the people were willing to give certain powers to the armed forces so long as those powers were not misused, but he complained of "the interference by certain officers in economic, financial and governmental policy matters." [121] "In brief, the growing interference of certain officers in economic and financial matters can lead to demoralization, can give birth to warlords, and is a threat to the purity of the patriotic armed forces of the Republic." Aidit also attacked the army's use of the state of war and siege to restrict democratic liberties by such measures as the prohibition of political meetings and the prohibition of strikes.

During December 1958, the extension of the state of war and siege for another year was accepted unanimously by parliament, probably because opposition would have been futile and might have antagonized the army into increased pressure for an end to parliamentary activities. Shortly afterward, at the beginning of 1959, PKI reportedly struck a blow which threatened to remove Nasution from his post as army chief. The Party leaked the news of massive army illegal trade dealings through Tandjung Priok, the port of Djakarta.[122] Nasution should have taken the blame, but it was placed on officers around him who were moved to other posts. If this report is correct, it would mean that PKI greatly antagonized the army leadership but at the same time earned the thanks of Sukarno who was attempting to reduce the power and prestige of the central army command.

Communist opposition to the army became more courageous during the first months of 1959, and one suspects that the courage derived from Sukarno's connivance. On January 31, Lukman stated the Party's opposition to the appointment to parliament of unelected representatives of the armed forces,[123] while in May Aidit declared: "There has never yet been, nor will there ever be, anything to prove that a military dictatorship can save the people and further advance world developments." If a military dictatorship were established, Aidit warned, then the Indonesian Communists would fight it.[124]

The PKI fear of and shadow boxing with the army forced the Party to a greater reliance on Sukarno as its protector against the military. The essential nature of the alliance in turn compelled PKI to support Sukarno's moves toward Guided Democracy, while at the same time pleading for the maintenance of the party system and for the greatest possible authority for parliament.

In a statement issued on October 24, 1958, Aidit attempted to show that support of Guided Democracy was "the most revolutionary policy." [125] He acknowledged that liberal democracy had failed to solve Indonesia's major problems and was associated with corruption and bureaucracy. As an alternative, PKI accepted Guided Democracy on the understanding that it was opposed to both dictatorship and liberalism. He then defined the antiliberal aspects of Guided Democracy in the political field as the 100 per cent implementation of Sukarno's concept, that is, the creation of a cabinet based on proportional representation; and in the economic field as building the state sector of the economy to a dominant position. Aidit claimed that only Sukarno should be the guide in Guided Democracy, and "not as a dictator, but as a democrat who resolutely observes the party system and the rights of parliament." Sukarno would require special rights in order to guide, but Aidit insisted that this was "The only way to defeat military or individual dictatorship on the one hand, and to defeat liberalism on the other," the only way to implement Sukarno's concept.

Sukarno's precise definition of Guided Democracy had not been revealed, and here Aidit was attempting to formulate a definition for the president and then to use the Party and its mass organizations to popularize it. Aidit's definition involved relinquishing a little of democracy in order not to antagonize Sukarno or strengthen the hand of those demanding the complete abolition of the party and parliamentary system. In short, an attempt at a tactical retreat to a position chosen by the Party. But the retreat was to continue. At the end of December 1958 and in January 1959, the PKI leaders were vocal in their defense of parliament. They praised it for the record amount of work done in 1958, spoke of "the great prestige of parliament," and declared that "Only fascists and foul thieves do not respect a parliament chosen by the people." [126] On January 11, 1959, however, when Sukarno bluntly asked for PKI's opinion of his proposal for the inclusion of appointed functional groups in parliament, Aidit was forced to declare the Party's support "in principle." [127]

On February 19, 1959, the cabinet reached important decisions on the implementation of Guided Democracy. The cabinet decided: first, to ask the Constituent Assembly to restore the 1945 constitution;[128] second, to introduce an act to simplify the party system; third, that functional groups would be included as every second candidate in all electoral lists, with the armed forces receiving 35 appointed representatives; and fourth, that a National Front would be established to assist the president. Five days later the PKI Politbureau announced its support for a return to the 1945 constitution.[129]

Sakirman, writing in 1960, gave the official PKI version, and one with a ring of truth, of why the Party decided to support the return to the 1945 constitution.[130] He explained that at the time that the cabinet decided to urge the restoration of the 1945 constitution, PKI had little choice but to agree. The Constituent Assembly had been meeting for two years but had made little headway toward a new constitution because the Pantjasila and Moslem blocs were unable to compromise. At the same time, certain groups outside the assembly were putting forward the demand for the complete dissolution of political parties. In such a situation, according to Sakirman, PKI was faced with three possibilities: to unite with the anti-Pantjasila bloc, led by Masjumi, and so permit the assembly to continue, with the possibility of completing its work by compromises harmful to the people's struggle; to take a passive attitude, or reject Sukarno's appeal for the restoration of the 1945 constitution, which would have meant in effect uniting with the anti-Pantjasila forces, continuing the assembly meetings, or supporting the continuation of the 1950 constitution; or to unite with "the democratic groups" led by Sukarno by accepting his appeal unconditionally but at the same time fighting outside the assembly for conditions to prevent the misuse of the 1945 constitution by "reactionary groups."

Sakirman explained that for PKI the third possibility was the best,

bearing in mind the national united front policy of isolating the reactionaries. To agree with the reactionaries to continue the Constituent
Assembly was not possible either politically or psychologically. To
agree to the continuation of the 1950 constitution, Sakirman claimed,
would have strengthened the hand of the "fascist elements" who wished
to dissolve the parties. Therefore in order to isolate further the reactionary group and to strengthen the unity of the democratic group,
PKI took quick and concrete steps to overcome the critical situation
by urging the restoration of the 1945 constitution.

On April 22, 1959, Sukarno asked the Constituent Assembly to
approve the restoration of the 1945 constitution. Masjumi succeeded
in rallying the other Moslem parties, NU, PSII, and Perti, to present
a solid front, so that when three votes were taken in the assembly on
May 30 and June 1 on a proposal to restore the original constitution,
the proposal failed to obtain the necessary two-thirds majority. In the
last session of the assembly, Aidit proposed the dissolution of the
assembly on the grounds that it had failed to draft a new constitution
and was no longer representative of the balance of forces in society.[131]
He also pointed out that there were now two ways of legalizing the
1945 constitution. Either a new Constituent Assembly could be elected,
which was the democratic and constitutional way, or the president
could decree the restoration of the old constitution, a course that PKI
could accept because the constitution had the support of a majority
in the assembly.

On June 4, 1959, the central war administrator placed a temporary
ban on all political activities. Aidit at once instructed all Party members to observe the ban, "the purpose of which is none other than to
prevent unnecessary contradictions from arising among the ranks of
the people." [132] He called on members to intensify their education, and
to "ponder deeply over the steps that we have taken up to the present
and . . . give serious thought to the future steps so as to further
strengthen national unity." Sukarno returned from a two-month world
tour on June 29, and on July 5 decreed the restoration of the 1945
constitution. The Djuanda cabinet resigned on the following day, and
Sukarno was left to form his own presidential cabinet which, under the
terms of the 1945 constitution, would not be responsible to parliament.

XXII

PKI AND GUIDED
DEMOCRACY, JULY 1959—JULY 1963

Sukarno announced his new cabinet on July 12, 1959. The civilian ministers were either nonparty persons or party members who could not be expected to go against the president's wishes. Prominent party leaders were conspicuously absent. The armed forces were represented by eleven ministers. PKI could count five ministers who might act as listening posts for the Party: Minister of Agrarian Affairs Sadjarwo, Yamin, minister in charge of social-cultural affairs, Minister of Education and Culture Prijono, and Sudibjo and Sudjono, the two ministers entrusted with "mobilizing the people's energy."

In the rapid turbulence of events that occurred in the next four years, Guided Democracy became a reality. And the Aidit leadership was compelled to adjust to the radically altered political environment. The following pages discuss four main questions: What *is* Guided Democracy? What is the nature of the PKI-Sukarno alliance? What have been PKI relations with the other political forces under Guided Democracy? Finally, what has been the effect of Guided Democracy on PKI?

1. THE MEANING OF GUIDED DEMOCRACY

Guided democracy is the system by which power is maintained by the present central ruling group in Indonesia. The group consists of two main forces, President Sukarno and the central army leadership; a small number of close civilian collaborators unassociated with any particular party, such as First Deputy Prime Minister Djuanda; and several persons associated with political parties but acting largely independently of them as advisors and practitioners for the more eminent members of the ruling elite. Foreign Minister Subandrio and Information Minister Ruslan Abdulgani are in this last category. The predominant role is played by Sukarno and the highest army officers. Their association in the exercise and maintenance of power has been marked by both close coöperation and covert competition. Coöperation has taken the form of joint protection of the position of the ruling group. Competition has concerned attempts to weaken the influence of the other, without at any time risking a break in the basic collaboration. Sukarno, on the one hand, has successfully safeguarded the continued existence of those political parties which are prepared to render him public support. The army, on the other hand, has sought to curtail PKI severely and to render support to the more moderate members of the elite who at times are in opposition to one or more of Sukarno's radical policies. But both Sukarno and the army leadership have been eager to remove from the political parties any ability, even right, to control major policy decisions. Both have also been eager to ensure that PKI is unable to develop any independent bases of power from which it could successfully challenge the ruling group.

The "guidance" aspect of Guided Democracy has been forcefully demonstrated. Under the terms of the 1945 constitution, Sukarno, as president, holds wide and only vaguely defined powers. The cabinet is chosen by him and is responsible to him, not to parliament. Step by step, the constitutional powers of the president have been used (or abused) to concentrate power in the hands of the new ruling group. On March 5, 1960, Sukarno dissolved the elected parliament after it had dared to criticize the government's budget. An appointed parliament was announced in June of that year. Half the members of the new parliament are from "reliable" political parties, half from "functional groups," including 35 members of the armed forces. General elections were promised for before the end of 1962, security conditions permitting, but they are still relegated to an uncertain future. To make quite clear that elected party representatives could not expect a dominant role even in a future parliament, the government in mid-1962 proposed an election law that would have provided for a parliament one-third elected, two-thirds appointed. When all political parties protested vigorously, the government agreed to establish an election law committee that included party representatives, among them Aidit. But even the future role of parties in the legislative process was now severely threatened. The appointive system was extended in 1960 beyond parliament to the regional, district, and municipal councils, and to the chief functionaries of the administrative divisions. PKI received satisfactory representation in the appointed parliament. Aidit claimed that including Communists in the functional groups, PKI had 50 members, or just under 20 per cent of the total. NU leaders estimated Communist representation to be between 65 and 70.[1]

During 1960 the government tightened its control of newspapers and journals. The army officers, as war administrators under the state of war and siege, had already exercised their power to invoke frequent suspensions against publications that contained news or opinions they did not like. Then, on February 15, 1960, a decree announced that henceforth the government would withhold newsprint from any publication whose contents failed to develop public opinion and/or national culture along the lines laid down in Sukarno's Independence Day speech of August 17, 1959. On October 12, 1960, publishers were told that their newspapers and journals must support and defend the principles of the August 17, 1959, speech, assist in the abolition of liberalism, imperialism, and separatism, promote an independent foreign policy and avoid being instruments of the Cold War, and promote the Indonesian personality. On October 31, the government revoked the licenses of several Djakarta newspapers, including the pro-Communist *Pantjawarta*, formerly *Sin Po*. On the same day the licenses were indefinitely suspended of all seven journals published by the PKI Central Committee, and of the journals of most Communist-led mass organizations. In November 1962, the pro-Communist Surabaja newspaper *Djawa Timur* was closed. *Harian Rakjat* was saved from extinction only by Sukarno's protection, but its contents were carefully toned down so as to give no offense to any of the inner core of the ruling group.

Not surprisingly, political parties were themselves brought under government scrutiny. On January 12, 1960, Sukarno issued a law entitled "Conditions and Simplification of the Party System." Four stipulations of this law were of grave concern to PKI:

1. political parties must accept and defend the 1945 constitution and the Pantjasila, and must use peaceful and democratic methods to attain their political goals;

2. political parties may receive assistance from abroad only with the consent of the government;

3. the president may order an investigation into the administration, finances, and wealth of any party;

4. the president may dissolve any party whose program is aimed at

undermining the principles and objectives of state policy, or which has not officially condemned the actions of any member of the party who has acted in support of a rebellion.

Sukarno used the law to ban all but ten political parties. The ten that survived, including PKI, agreed to render Sukarno full support, and adapted their constitutions to include acceptance of the Pantjasila and of peaceful means to achieve their goals. Masjumi and PSI were banned in August 1960. Later in 1960 each party was required to present the government with a list of their branches, and details on each of its members. Such a requirement was a severe blow to PKI, but the Party complied to the new order on February 4, 1961. Several regional army commanders exercised their state of war and siege powers to suspend all activities by PKI and its mass organizations. Such suspensions were in force in South Sumatra/Djambi and South Sulawesi from August 1960 to December 1960, and in South Kalimantan from August 1960 to August 1961.

In short, "guidance" has meant control by the ruling group over parliament, the regional and local councils, the press, and even, to a certain degree, of the political parties themselves. Guidance has also meant that the government will permit no militant political or economic actions of which it does not approve. The Communists have been made fully aware of this. In July 1961 PKI reported that 72 of its members were in prison in West Java;[2] they were rumored to have attempted to win control of several villages. In August 1961, Njono told the SOBSI national council that approximately 900 SOBSI cadres, activists, and ordinary members were under arrest, mostly in North Sumatra where they had attempted to take-over Belgian estates within the framework of Indonesian protest at developments in the Congo.[3] "Tens of cadres," he said, had been arrested or thrown in prison for defending the workers' interests.[4] On July 4, 1961, members of the SOBSI tobacco workers' union seized a Belgian cigarette factory in Malang, also within the framework of the protests against developments in the Congo. Again the government acted quickly and severely, although it too was committed to an anti-Belgian policy. The factory was restored to its owners; SOBSI cadres were arrested, and subsequently sentenced to prison terms; some workers were dismissed; and later claims by the workers for improved wages and work conditions were rejected.[5] Strikes have been banned in all "vital" enterprises—which has been interpreted by the authorities as a blanket ban. Pemuda Rakjat members were arrested in 1962 for an unauthorized demonstration outside the Japanese embassy in Djakarta. And most of the Communist mass organizations were treated severely as a result of a peasant incident in a Kediri village in November 1961. Several squatters were shot while resisting eviction from government estate lands. The authorities replied with the arrest and imprisonment of several cadres, including the BTI chairmen for East Java. All BTI, Pemuda Rakjat, Gerwani, and Sarbupri activities were suspended for ten months in the entire residency of Kediri. The speed and ease of governmental repression in all cases of unauthorized militancy was a warning to the Communists to walk only on the peaceful road to socialism.

Guidance, or the elimination of "free-fight liberalism," is, however, only a part of Guided Democracy. The other is consultation by the ruling group with those organized forces in society that are willing to accept the group's over-all guidance. Consultation is effected through a broad range of appointed assemblies and councils which include the leaders of all remaining political parties as well as the leaders of functional groups. The most prominent of these assemblies and councils are the parliament, the Provisional People's Consultative Assembly, the Supreme Advisory Council, the National Planning Council, and the regional, district, and municipal councils. The government also created the National Front. In January 1962 all political parties and most mass organizations were enrolled. By August 1962 over 200 political parties, mass organizations, and functional groups were reported to have joined, with a total membership of 33 millions. Communists were given important representation in all of its committees, from the center to the villages. The five-point program of the National Front was announced by Sukarno on February 13, 1963: to consolidate past victories, including the return of West Irian and the maintenance of security; to help increase production; to continue the struggle against imperialism and neocolonialism; to effect political indoctrination; and to carry out a "re-tooling" of the state apparatus.[6] The government has also sought to involve political parties and mass organizations in overcoming the country's economic difficulties by creating several semirepresentational councils with specific tasks: councils in government estate, manufacturing, and trading enterprises to increase productivity, and councils to supervise agricultural productivity, the distribution of rice, and the collection of rice from the peasants at regulated prices. Both "enterprise councils" and agricultural councils were being formed actively during the latter half of 1962 and in 1963.

Certainly the government does not tolerate fundamental criticism from the members of the assemblies, councils, and the National Front. But these bodies, most of them the creations of Guided Democracy, serve several functions. They are used as rewards for political coöperation and as a facade of "democratic legitimacy" for the regime. Some of them involve the political parties and mass organizations, including the Communist ones, in the actual implementation of government policies. And they serve as consultative bodies, as formalized links between the ruling group and most of the organized elements in Indonesian society. They provide the government with information on the areas and strengths of popular (or at least elite and subelite) discontent and wishes, and they do allow the representatives of important sectors of society a certain expression of opinion, a means of pressing for governmental action in some, if restricted, fields.

What are the goals of Guided Democracy, other than the maintenance of power in the hands of the rulers? Sukarno is a man of action rather than a long-term planner. He seeks "to complete the Revolution." The ultimate goal is a "free and prosperous" nation, with its own identity, and organized under "Guided Democracy," "Guided Economy," and "Socialism-à-la Indonesia." He has afforded no detailed description of the future utopia, but the short-term goals along the road were contained in the three-point program he gave his new cabinet in July 1959: food and clothing for the people; internal security; and a struggle against imperialism and neocolonialism, in particular the restoration of West Irian to Indonesia. Many doubted in July 1959 that the government would achieve all or any of these goals within the three years stipulated by Sukarno. Given Sukarno's personality and the military nature of the other major component of the ruling coalition, it was to be expected that the government would give priority to the second and third points of its program.

Internal security came to Indonesia suddenly. In the second half of 1961, the government's promise of generous treatment persuaded most rebel leaders to surrender. All important PRRI-Permesta rebels still in Indonesia "returned to the fold of the Republic" with their followers, as did Kahar Muzakar in South Sulawesi. Many rebel army leaders and troops were reincorporated into the national army; others were settled with their families on land grants in Sumatra. Early in 1962 the army mounted a campaign against the Darul Islam in West Java and adjacent areas of Central Java. The capture of the Darul Islam leader, Kartosuwirjo, in June 1962 ended the bloody rebellion that had lasted since 1948. Thus, by a combination of military action and generous surrender terms, the Sukarno government brought internal security to virtually all areas of Indonesia for the first time since 1945.[7]

With the solution of the internal security problem, the government could direct its full attention to the liberation of West Irian. For several years after 1949 the Indonesian government used diplomatic means to win West Irian. They met with no success. Then Indonesia applied economic pressure, culminating in the seizure of all Dutch property in December 1957. Still the Dutch refused to move. The Sukarno government then determined to face the Netherlands with armed might. When the Western countries understandably balked at providing the modern aircraft, ships, and army equipment required to attack a NATO ally, the Indonesian government turned to the Soviet Union. A loan of $450 million for arms purchases was obtained in January 1961, and later increased to about $1,000 million. Early in 1962 several million Indonesian "volunteers to liberate West Irian" were registered by the government, and several thousands received military training. By the middle of 1962, according to Indonesian official sources, 1,400 guerrillas had been landed in Irian[8] and the possibility grew of a military conflict of some magnitude. At this point the United States intervened more actively to seek a face-saving formula whereby the territory could be transferred to Indonesia. The Netherlands, unwilling to reopen war with Indonesia, and now deserted by her main ally, signed an agreement with Indonesia in August. There would be an interim period of United Nations administration starting October 1, 1962. On May 1, 1963, Indonesian sovereignty was recognized over West Irian.

The Sukarno government, therefore, established internal security and also successfully concluded the thirteen years of struggle for West Irian. But these victories were gained at the expense of the economy. According to official statements, the West Irian campaign had come to absorb 75 per cent of all government expenditure. Meanwhile factories worked at only 25 per cent of capacity for want of imported raw materials; production of staple and export crops either stagnated or declined; and inflation accelerated.[9] According to official statistics, consumer prices rose 35 per cent during 1960, not an unusual rate for Indonesia; but from January 1961 to February 1963, the price index of nineteen consumer goods in Djakarta rose 600 per cent. Many private and government enterprises gave substantial wage increases, and many workers were protected from starvation by the distribution of rice free or at low prices. But wage increases trailed far behind prices, while from January 1961 into 1963, government officials and workers received no increase at all. The result was severe hardship among many sections of the population, especially in the cities. Hardship was rendered more onerous by the importation of expensive automobiles and other luxuries for the members or close associates of the ruling elite.

Finally, mention must be made of Sukarno's goal of Nasakom, that is, Nasionalis-Agama-Komunis (Nationalist-Religious-Communist) unity. By Nasakom he means that nationalist, religious, and Communist leaders and organizations should be included in the consultative process of Guided Democracy, and in the implementation of many of the government's policies. He means, too, that these three elements in society should work together harmoniously, and desist from mutual recriminations. The purpose of Nasakom is basically to obtain acquiescence to the government and its policies, although Sukarno may also be sincere in his repeated claim that he wishes Nasakom in order to end or severely dampen the conflicts and antagonisms that rent Indonesia after the withdrawal of the Dutch at the end of 1949. PNI and NU have had direct representation in the Sukarno cabinet from its inception, but special treatment was necessary for PKI. Most government leaders, probably including Sukarno, are averse to giving PKI control of ministries, for fear of how the Party could exploit such a position. To avoid this danger, and yet at the same time publicly bind PKI to government policies and afford PKI a consultative role at the highest government levels, Sukarno has used several devices. We have seen that he granted PKI significant representation in the appointed parliament, in the leadership of the National Front, and in the many appointed assemblies and advisory councils. He has gone further. On March 9, 1962, Aidit and Lukman were appointed as ministers—not in control of ministries, but to render advice, when requested by Sukarno, on economic and international affairs. On January 18, 1963, Sukarno installed a Council of Assistants to the Revolutionary Leadership, with Aidit among its thirteen members. Six days later, the Supreme Advisory Council established an eleven-man committee, including Aidit and two other Communists, to formulate proposals for Sukarno on economic stabilization. Significantly, the positions given PKI close to the center of government are without power. The government seeks to utilize Communist brains and to identify the Party with that field in which it has been least successful and least popular, namely, economic affairs.

2. THE NATURE OF THE PKI-SUKARNO ALLIANCE

In the three years from about mid-1956, when parliamentary democracy collapsed and extraparliamentary forces moved into the center of the political stage, PKI was still too weak, relative to the other political forces, to make a bid for power. The Aidit leadership had mass support, but it was not militant. Because the more politically conscious and influential sections of Indonesian society had proved, and continued to prove, resistant to the Party's blandishments, the Aidit leadership had been forced to seek support among the masses, the workers, peasants, and poorer sections of the "petty bourgeoisie," who were still by and large outside the political process. In order to win mass support it was necessary to present an image of PKI that would be both attractive to the poorer, generally passive, elements of society, and acceptable to significant sections of the non-Communist political forces who controlled the means of repression and who could have made Communist organizational work extremely difficult if not impossible. This image was one of PKI as fervently patriotic, sympathetic to religion, peaceful in pursuit of its goals, painstakingly solicitous of the small problems consciously felt by its potential supporters, moderate in demands, and self-effacing in the friendliness shown toward most other Indonesian political forces. With this image, plus organizational tenacity and skill, PKI became the largest, most efficient, most disciplined party in Indonesia. In the period of parliamentary democracy, for which, essentially, the national united front had been conceived, the Aidit leadership used its mass following to good effect. The breach between PNI and Masjumi had been widened to an unbridgeable gap, PKI won significant representation in the elected and multiparty parliament, PKI worked in close coöperation with PNI and even some Moslem parties, and the future held the prospect of greatly increased parliamentary representation and a coalition cabinet including Communists in control of ministries. But this hopeful situation had been swept away. President Sukarno and the army took over the dominant political roles, and sought to curb, or harness, the power of the parties. Worse still, many army officers wished to abolish all parties, or at least PKI. PKI, large but unmilitant after years of the national united front policy, was forced to seek an accommodation with Sukarno. Certainly the Party could have survived severe government repression, but it would have survived only as a mere underground shadow of its former self. And the Aidit leadership was always conscious of what had happened to many of its colleagues in the "White terror" that followed the abortive Madiun rebellion. They must also have been fearful of the effect that a sudden break in the national united front policy would have had on the unity of Party cadres.

In the period of Guided Democracy, the main purpose of the Sukarno alliance for PKI has been the maintenance of Sukarno as the dominant force in or behind the government. Dependent upon PKI support, he was expected to protect the Party from repression by the army—both the central army command and the regional commanders—and he could exert his influence to prevent PNI and NU from attacking the

Party. The Aidit leadership was proved correct in both expectations. Sukarno prevented the army from banning or severely repressing PKI and its mass organizations. Among his more public interventions on the behalf of PKI, Sukarno insisted against army opposition that the PKI Sixth National Congress be permitted to convene—and he himself delivered a friendly speech to the congress; he frustrated army-inspired attempts in 1960 and 1961 to obtain the fusion of SOBSI and Pemuda Rakjat into tame, all-embracing organizations, as had occurred with the veterans' Perbepsi; and he insisted on the revocation of bans on PKI and its mass organizations imposed in August 1960 by army commanders in South Sumatra/Djambi, South Kalimantan, and South Sulawesi. At the same time, the leaders of the other surviving political parties were required to affirm their belief that only Nasakom unity could solve the problems confronting Indonesia.

There were other advantages which the Aidit leadership could hope for from the alliance with Sukarno. First, it was expected that the Party could exploit Sukarno's popularity, especially in Java, by close identification with him. Dangers, of course, attended such utilization of his popularity. If the identification became rooted and he were then to become unpopular, the Party would suffer likewise (and it is to be noted that Sukarno is not so popular in several regions, particularly outside Java). Another danger in close identification was that if Sukarno was built up or maintained in the eyes of many Party members as the great leader and father of the revolution, then he might gain a corresponding degree of control over Party members. This would reduce the Party leaders' control over their own supporters. A second advantage PKI sought in its alliance with Sukarno was leverage to exert pressure for the preservation of the widest democratic freedoms— that is, to retain a significant role for political parties in the shaping of government policies, to permit the expansion of PKI and its ancillary organizations, and to permit PKI to train its members to an increasing "class consciousness" or militancy. As we have seen, Sukarno, with the full agreement of the army leaders, relegated the political parties to a controlled consultative role; but parties and parliament were not dissolved, and their leaders were even given a significant role in the highest advisory councils. And if the government steadfastly repressed any signs of independent militancy by the Communists, at least the Communist organizations continued to function, albeit under government scrutiny. Seminars, conferences, and congresses were held regularly, and the education system was greatly developed. Furthermore, between July 1959 and April 1963, PKI claimed to have increased its membership from 1.5 million to over 2.0 millions, the four major Communist mass organizations from 7.8 to 12.0 millions.

A third possible advantage from the alliance was that with Sukarno in a dominant position, the government would emphasize fervent nationalism to the neglect and detriment of economic stability or development. The government did concentrate on West Irian and then, in the early months of 1963, on confrontation with Malaya over the proposed Malaysian Federation. But the direct benefit to PKI was limited. Anticolonial agitation was closely channeled through government or government-sponsored bodies. The economy deteriorated, but the government's means of repression prevented any growth of overt militancy among the general population. To attack the government for economic conditions would have been condemned as treason against the West Irian campaign and, anyway, would have brought down severe repression. It even appeared, in 1962 and early 1963, that the Aidit leadership was genuinely concerned to help alleviate economic suffering. It was feared, perhaps, that forces to the political right of Sukarno, and even Sukarno himself, might turn to Western governmental and private sources of capital and technical skill as a way out of the economic morass.

Finally, the Aidit leadership hoped that the alliance would bring Communist participation in the cabinet—which has been Sukarno's declared goal since the end of 1955. In March 1962, Aidit and Lukman were made special ministers without portfolio. This they viewed as an unwanted embarrassment rather than the political lever they had expected. At the end of 1962 PKI renewed with vigor the campaign for a truly Nasakom cabinet in which the parties would have representation proportionate to their popular support. As of mid-1963, however, no Communist held charge of a government ministry.

Sukarno has understood and exploited the major dilemma faced by the PKI leaders. He knows that they can either earn his protection by rendering him support in his competitive collaboration with the army; or they can break the alliance, which would very probably alienate much of the existing Communist support, divide the cadres, and bring about a strongly anti-Communist government. In brief, the alliance was and is vital for PKI to continue in anything like its present form; for Sukarno the alliance, especially after July 1959, was only a secondary matter. Without the support of PKI, Sukarno almost certainly would have remained president. Ouster by the army leadership was improbable due to the personal and professional rivalries within the army (often encouraged by Sukarno's intrigues), and to the support he received from PNI, NU, and the bulk of government officials. And as time passed after July 1959, it appears that the army leaders came to recognize fully the advantages of continued collaboration with Sukarno (and he shared with them the privileges and exercise of power), as well as the needless risks of open defiance of him. After all, the army leaders are mostly young men, while Sukarno is not immortal. Fully comprehending this basic situation, Sukarno has continued his alliance with PKI. At the same time he has implemented, with the willing assistance of the army, a policy of domestication of all parties, of which the most unwilling has been PKI.[10]

3. PKI ACTIVITIES UNDER GUIDED DEMOCRACY

On July 13, 1959, Aidit announced that PKI would do everything possible to ensure the implementation of the cabinet's three-point program.[11] The Party's attitude, he declared, would be basically the same as that taken toward the preceding Djuanda cabinet: unreserved support for measures of benefit to the people, criticism of "wavering" measures, and strong criticism of ministerial action harmful to the people.

In the period of Guided Democracy the Aidit leadership has had limited maneuverability. The basic principle of unity with the "middle forces" has been maintained.[12] As Aidit told the PKI Central Committee in December 1961: "Above all else, national unity!" He reminded the committee that:

in carrying out our national struggle we must hold firmly to the basic principle: place the interests of class and of the Party below the national interest, that is, place the national interest above the interests of class and of the Party.[13]

In other words, the Aidit leadership sought to preserve the image of the Party developed since 1951, to keep close to the important political forces of the center (now Sukarno and his allies), and yet at the same time work within the available narrow limits to pull political development in a direction more beneficial, or less harmful, to PKI.

Due to the vital nature of the alliance with Sukarno, the Party reserved fulsome praise for the president. Aidit went so far as to demonstrate that it was quite compatible with Marxism for a nonproletarian such as Sukarno to become the leader of a socialist Indonesia.[14] After all, neither Marx nor Engels was a worker! For both flattery and protective reasons, PKI came to construct its demands, requests, and criticisms within a framework of Sukarno quotations, aptly chosen from speeches and writings of more than thirty years. And if the Party criticized certain cabinet ministers, it was careful not to implicate

Sukarno, but to portray him as the glorious leader ill-served by un-worthy aides.

In the four years following the installation of the Sukarno cabinet in July 1959, PKI's activities as they directly affected other political forces may be analyzed in three categories: the defense of democratic liberties; support for many government policies; and criticism of cer-tain ministers and their actions.

PKI's hardest battle during the period of the Sukarno cabinet has been a continuous one for the preservation of political freedom. It was fundamentally a losing battle because the Party was too weak to withstand the combined pressure of Sukarno and the army who worked together to domesticate the parties. The first of the overt measures to restrict the sphere of party activities arrived at the end of July 1959. All higher government officials were given until August 31 to resign from political parties. PKI protested ineffectually.[15] At the beginning of September 1959, the government announced that henceforth the heads of provinces, *kabupatens*, and towns would be appointed, not elected as formerly, and that they and the members of their executive councils would have to resign from party membership. This new measure raised a storm of protest from all political parties. The government then agreed to review the system after a trial year—and then quietly forgot to. The guidance aspect of Guided Democracy was taking shape. At this point, the PKI congress in September 1959 courageously endorsed the following statements:

. . . the people of Indonesia not only love democracy, but under the alert leadership of the Party the people actively defend democracy.

For the progressive development of Indonesia, PKI will continue to fight against the danger of military dictatorship or individual dictatorship, and at the same time to defend and extend democracy. But in case a military or individual dictatorship cannot be prevented, . . . the duty of every Communist will be to fight it with all his strength.[16]

Despite the words of courage, primarily intended to boost the morale of the congress delegates, the retreat continued. Neither PKI nor any other political party had sufficient weapons with which effectively to counter the combined will of the new ruling group.

In the last months of 1959, PKI made clear what it considered to be the important role of parliament under the 1945 constitution,[17] and, made bolder by PNI support, asserted, during the parliamentary de-bates of December 1959 through February 1960, parliament's right to control the budget.[18] Sukarno thereupon demonstrated his power by dissolving parliament on March 5, 1960. Two days later, Aidit sent a telegram to Sukarno expressing extreme regret at the action which, he wrote, "seriously endangers democratic life in our country." [19] Aidit proposed that either a new parliament be elected or a temporary parliament be nominated in conformity with the balance of forces among the people. PKI's *Review of Indonesia* commented that the guided part of Guided Democracy had already been elaborated; "it now remains for the 'democracy' aspect of it to be established." [20] In order not to alienate the parties too far, Sukarno invited the chairmen of PKI, PNI, and NU to his palace in Bali to discuss the composition of a new parliament. On March 29, 1960, the appointed parliament was announced. Of the 261 members, 131 were from functional groups, including 35 representatives of the armed forces, and 130 were from the political parties, including 30 from PKI.[21] Masjumi and PSI were excluded. General elections for a new parliament were promised for before the end of 1962, security conditions permitting.

Aidit announced PKI's reluctant acceptance of the new parliament, commenting that an appointed one was better than none at all.[22] That the appointed parliament would have only minor power was demonstrated by the government announcement on April 20 that the 1960 budget was in operation by decree. When 1962 arrived, the year promised for fresh general elections, the government announced its regret that they would have to be postponed until after West Irian was in Indonesian hands. Aidit accepted the postponement as "realistic and wise." [23] But PKI did not acquiesce as quietly as the other remaining political parties to the increasing infringement of democratic freedoms and the role of political parties. In June 1960, the Party expressed opposition to an extension of the appointive system from parliament to the provincial, *kabupaten*, and city councils.[24] When its opposition proved futile, the Party and the mass organization raised cries of protest because Communist representation in the appointed councils was often greatly reduced.[25] Sukarno early in 1961 agreed to a review of the appointed councils, and PKI was given larger, though still reduced, representation.[26] If PKI accepted the postponement of general elections, it expressed its opinion that "Only the group with crimes against the people can fear general elections." [27] And for those who might be contemplating the imposition of one "ism" on Indonesia, Aidit warned that "Only the fascists and those who thirst for civil war can think of allowing only one 'ism' for the Indonesian people." [28] In a more poetic vein, and with echoes of Mao Tse-tung, Aidit declared:

For me, our party life must be like a garden of flowers. In a garden of flowers are many kinds of flowers, but each flower contributes to the beauty of the garden. . . . Various kinds of flowers of many colors become a bouquet that is pleasing to the eye.[29]

An objective of constant attack by the Communists was the state of war and siege, first introduced in March 1957 when the second Ali Sastroamidjojo government fell. Army commanders at the center and in the regions used their powers to circumscribe the activities not only of PKI but also of its mass organizations. Public meetings and demonstrations required approval, and their speeches and agendas were scrutinized. Newspapers and journals were banned or suspended at will. After April 1, 1959, closed meetings were permitted on the sole condition that the authorities be informed in advance of the intention to hold one—zones of military operations excepted. In practice, however, many, if not all, war administrators under the state of war and siege retained the power to prohibit closed meetings, or to send along a representative to those that were held. The government finally announced in October 1962 that the state of war and siege regulations would be withdrawn by May 1, 1963. A seventeen-man committee, including Aidit, was appointed to formulate proposals as to how the regulations should be ended.

Aidit warned, in February 1963, that the bureaucratic capitalists and other reactionaries were seeking ways to retain the state of war and siege regulations despite their formal abolition. Speaking pointedly for the benefit of the army officers, he stated that as of May 1, 1963, the political leadership of the revolution must truly lead those with rifles.[30]

In short, the Aidit leadership was forced to accept severe restrictions on the role and freedom of political parties. But at the same time PKI fought a more courageous verbal battle than any other remaining party for the broadest possible democratic freedoms, for a significant role for political parties. It is difficult to determine what effect was achieved by Communist speeches, delegations, petitions, and telegrams. It is certain, however, that political parties survived primarily because they were needed by President Sukarno in the context of his competitive collaboration with the army leadership.

The Aidit leadership rendered support to the Sukarno cabinet in the implementation of its three-point program, which was, in order of governmental action: internal security; anti-imperialism, with emphasis on the "return of West Irian to the Republic"; and food and clothing for the people. At the same time, PKI attempted to influence implementation along lines more desirable to itself.

In the realm of internal security, the Communists were largely bystanders. Personal reports indicate that Communists acted in an intelligence capacity, supplying to the army what information they could on the disposition of rebel bands. The PRRI-Permesta rebellion ended, however, as a result of government offers of lenient treatment. Somewhat belatedly, PKI expressed its grave concern at the leniency afforded the former rebels, including the incorporation of rebel units into the national army. One of the lessons to be learned from the murder of President Kassim of Iraq by former rebels who had been pardoned, was that "one may not give mercy to counterrevolutionary groups and rebels." [31] The Darul Islam rebels were virtually liquidated by unaided military action in the first six months of 1962. To underplay the role of the army in establishing internal security and in forcing the Dutch to relinquish West Irian, PKI always hailed the victories as the result of the glorious people-army *dwitunggal*, two-in-one, the people being given precedence.

PKI has been an eager assistant of the Sukarno government's war on imperialism and neocolonialism. On a lesser scale, for example, the Party gave vociferous support to the government's statements in defense of Lumumba in the Congo, the Tibetan people against the reactionary Dalai Lama, and the Omanis against their British oppressors. At the time of the Fourth Asian Games, held in Djakarta in August and September 1962, PKI at first opposed the inclusion of teams from Israel and Taiwan as "agents of imperialism." When the government decided on exclusion, Indonesia was suspended from the Olympic Games Committee. PKI warmly praised Sukarno's subsequent defiant threat to organize a Games of the New Emerging Forces of the World, to be attended by nations of Asia, Africa, Latin America, and the Soviet bloc. The above were only side issues in the government's struggle against imperialism. The major objective was control of West Irian. In January 1961, Indonesia began to purchase massive supplies of military equipment from the Soviet Union for this purpose. On December 19, 1961, Sukarno ordered the Indonesian people to prepare for general mobilization. This was a flamboyant gesture as the 300,000-man army was amply numerous to quell the small Dutch garrison in Irian. Aidit at once declared his Party's full support for militant action. At the same time, the Communists sought to achieve something they had failed to win in the past: the military training of the civilian population.[32] Pemuda Rakjat, BTI, and the SOBSI trade-unions undertook a rapid registration of their members for military training. Requests poured in for the opening of training camps. The government, however, was not so foolish as to train the Communist masses. Ultimately only a few thousand army-selected volunteers were taught how to use arms. The Communists, undeterred, asked the government to confiscate all the Dutch assets seized in December 1957—which officially had been nationalized, the question of compensation pending a solution of the West Irian dispute. The government was unmoved, and the Dutch relinquished control of the territory on October 1, 1962.

Once West Irian was removed from Dutch hands there existed the possibility that the Indonesian government might now resolutely tackle the disastrous economic situation. Then the Malaysia crisis loomed. Aidit had condemned Malaysia as a creation of British neocolonialism as early as January 1962.[33] In September 1962, Foreign Minister Subandrio first expressed official Indonesian hostility to the proposed Malaysia. The hostility blossomed into a "confrontation": Indonesian warships patrolled the Malayan coast, aircraft flew along the borders. A government-sponsored committee was formed, with Communist participation, to arouse the Indonesian people to the grave neocolonialist danger threatening them. When an anti-Malaysia revolt broke out in Brunei and Sarawak early in December 1962, the Indonesian government gave limited support—at least to the extent of allowing the rebels to use Indonesian territory as a base for operations. The PKI leaders were jubilant, because the Malayan government was both anti-Communist and allied with the Western nations. Starting in December 1962, SOBSI trade-unions threatened boycott action against British ships, airlines, and companies operating in Indonesia.[34] On May 16, 1963, a one-week boycott started against BOAC, followed by a threatened withdrawal of SOBSI members from the Shell Oil Company.[35] Communist organizations raised the question of confiscating British capital. Then, suddenly, at the end of May the Malayan prime minister flew to visit Sukarno, amicable talks were held, and from June 7 to 11 the foreign ministers of Indonesia, Malaya, and the Philippines not only discussed Malaysia in a conciliatory manner, but even agreed to work toward close and formalized relations among their three countries, especially in the field of defense. In other words, the Indonesian government had performed, without warning, an apparent *volte-face* and was accepting close coöperation with two "agents of imperialism"! The PKI leaders were confused.

While the government pursued its primary goals of internal security and the incorporation of West Irian, the economic situation deteriorated rapidly. Production declined in almost all fields except oil, of which 90 per cent was produced by foreign companies. Foreign exchange was used for military equipment, to the detriment of consumer goods and industrial raw materials. Inflation accelerated to an unprecedented rate. The government had failed in the third point of its program, food and clothing for the people. Apart from criticism of ministerial incapacity in the economic field, which will be treated below, the PKI leaders sought to divert government actions into channels favorable to the Party. During 1962, it appears, too, that the Communists became genuinely alarmed at the economic chaos to the extent of providing genuine and concrete assistance to the government.

When all Dutch enterprises passed into government hands in December 1957, SOBSI had declared that their efficient management required worker representation. This was quietly ignored. Once Guided Democracy was under way, dedicated to a guided economy and popular participation in economic activities, SOBSI revived its proposal. In September 1960, Njono requested the formation of workers' councils in all state productive and trading enterprises, their function to be one of rendering advice "on all matters." [36] His request was taken up as a general demand by all major Communist organizations. Such councils would, of course, allow SOBSI cadres legally to infiltrate the economic apparatus, and would provide the Communist unions with added leverage for improving the wages and working conditions of their members. On October 12, 1961, the government issued the rules governing the creation of "enterprise councils" in government enterprises. The new councils were to include a majority of worker and peasant representatives; their one task was to increase production. A year later, some 160 councils were already in operation. But it appeared that once again the government had outwitted the Communists. Trade-union and peasant representatives sat in advisory councils; their knowledge and brains were used, and they were thus identified, to a certain extent, with management, without gaining any control over management—a development somewhat similar to the inclusion of leading Communists on top-level government advisory councils. In an attempt to exploit the situation despite the undesirable aspects, SOBSI unions early in 1963 began to train cadres especially for work in the enterprise councils. During 1962 the government also created widely representative councils, long demanded by the Communists, to assist in such matters as the collection of rice at low prices determined by the government, the supervision of the often corrupted distribution of basic food and clothing items, and raising agricultural productivity.

During 1962 it appears that the Aidit leadership became gravely concerned over the economic situation. In February 1962 the PKI Politbureau announced its belief that Indonesia could at the same time win West Irian and overcome economic difficulties.[37] This may have merely been a way of explaining Communist criticism of the government's economic incapacity. On the other hand, it may have reflected a fear that the people would react against the fervent nationalist causes, long and loudly exposed by PKI, that were causing such hardship. Aidit's statement to the Central Committee on February 10, 1963, was, however, unequivocal. He declared that unless the economic difficulties were overcome, then "the middle group" could easily swallow the neocolonialist concepts put forward by the reactionaries, namely, foreign investment and an economic stabilization plan conceived and implemented with Western aid.[38] Unless the economic difficulties were overcome, then the middle group might do "the same as the reactionaries." That is, Aidit was afraid that the ruling group would turn to the West for aid in solving the grave economic problems. Were this to happen, the position of PKI would be in grave jeopardy. To prevent it happening, the Communists were already giving concrete assistance in the economic sphere, apart from the assistance required from the members of appointed advisory councils.

At the beginning of February 1962, PKI launched the "1001 movement" to promote "1001 ways to increase food production." [39] Special committees were formed, with the assistance of the Communist mass organizations, down to the local level. Sometimes working in conjunction with government services, sometimes alone, the Communists endeavored to show townspeople how to grow fruit trees and vegetables; peasants were shown how to increase their productivity by such means as making compost, more intensive use of dry-season crops, and mutual coöperation in improving irrigation. Any success in the movement, would, of course, increase the people's trust in the Party. But far more was needed in order to demonstrate to the government that Indonesia could solve its economic problems without resort to massive foreign aid. During 1962, BTI participated in a government-sponsored conference to discuss agricultural productivity; in January 1963 it organized its own productivity seminar. In August 1962 the Communist transport workers' union participated in a national conference to discuss means of overcoming transportation problems; in October Sarbupri held its own conference to discuss estate production; and in March 1963 the Communist miners' union held a conference to find means of overcoming the continuous decline in mining output. Each seminar and conference was treated very seriously, lengthy reports prepared, and detailed proposals published. The repeated theme was that Indonesia with only secondary foreign aid, preferably from the socialist countries, could overcome its economic problems.

While expressing fundamental support for the Sukarno government, the Aidit leadership has criticized, often strongly, both cabinet ministers and many government officials. To do so was necessary if the

Party was to retain its role as the nucleus for social and economic discontent, and to demonstrate to cadres that the leaders were militant and courageous. To do so was possible because Sukarno allowed limited criticism as part of the price paid for the Communist alliance. Sukarno himself was never implicated in criticism; in turn, he never came to the public defense of any of his ministers under attack. Two main themes have been interwoven in Communist criticism of government action and inaction: the incapacity and at times counterrevolutionary activities of certain ministers and government officials; and the need for a genuinely representative cabinet in order to fulfill the government's program and overcome the major difficulties facing the nation.

As early as August 6, 1959, Aidit expressed disappointment at the composition of the cabinet, suspicion at the inclusion of so many military personnel, and his determination to work for Communist inclusion in the cabinet.[40] Communist participation in the government, he said, "is just as certain as the fact that the Indonesian people will wake up tomorrow to see the sun rising in the east, and to see it setting in the west in the evening." In September, SOBSI warned of "secret counterrevolutionary passengers" in the cabinet.[41] The first major attack on the government was launched in December 1959 and January 1960 when the Party and its mass organizations led a massive campaign to protest the government's economic measures, and to demand a 25 per cent increase in wages with a 50 per cent cut in the price of essential commodities. Delegations, petitions, letters, and telegrams flooded in— until Nasution ordered strict measures against demonstrations held under the cloak of economic grievances.

In the midst of the agitation against the government's economic measures, Lukman on January 10, 1960, declared that the people had lost its hope and trust in the cabinet's ability.[42] Sukarno was requested to replace the deficient ministers. The request for an alteration in the composition of the cabinet was continued until Sukarno left the country for another world tour on April 1.[43] The moment Sukarno left, PKI at once dropped the request, and denounced efforts toward a cabinet reshuffle as aimed at creating new tensions.[44] It was feared that without Sukarno a reshuffle might mean a swing to the right. Once he returned, the request was resumed.

A strong attack was made on many cabinet ministers on July 8, 1960, when the PKI Politbureau issued a document entitled "An Evaluation of the Kerdja Cabinet After One Year in Office." [45] According to the Politbureau, "a year is long enough to know which of the president's assistants or ministers are capable and which of them are not, or do not wish to carry out in all earnestness the three-point program of the Kerdja cabinet." It then went on to attack "the inability of the Minister of Trade, Arifin Harahap"; Minister of Labor Ahem Erningpradja, who "does not defend the interests of the workers"; Yamin, for "harboring dangerous illusions about the imperialists"; Foreign Minister Subandrio for pursuing a foreign policy that "is more one of needing imperialism than of opposing it," and for exacerbating Indonesian-Chinese relations; Minister of Internal Affairs Ipik Gandamana, for issuing anti-democratic regulations; and Minister of Information Maladi, for his toleration of the reactionary Democratic League. As for the army, the Politbureau claimed that "it is not such a difficult thing" to smash the rebels, "so long as a serious attempt is made to do so," so long as the security forces ceased "also waging a fight against the people and the Communists." However: "In contrast with some of his minister assistants . . . we see the effort made by President Sukarno to pave the way for the implementation of the program of his cabinet." The Politbureau ended with a plea for changes in the composition of the cabinet. For a while after July 8, though, criticism was toned down. Distribution of the July 8 statement was declared illegal, Sakirman was temporarily arrested, and the five full members of the Politbureau were "investigated." Only in April 1961 were they told that the incident would be "frozen," that is, no further action would be taken against them as long as they and other members of the PKI Central Committee refrained from similar action.

During 1961 and 1962 consumer goods, including rice, became increasingly scarce and expensive. The government was forced to make drastic increases in the price of rice and other goods; railway, gas, and electricity charges were raised as much as 300 per cent. As wages lagged behind prices, often far behind, PKI and its mass organizations issued demands, almost always ineffective, for increased wages and reduced prices. A fresh climax of criticism was reached at the Central Committee meeting in February 1963.[46] Aidit told the Central Committee that although the Kerdja cabinet was already three and a half years old, it had fulfilled only a part of its program in the fields of security and anti-imperialism, while food and clothing for the people was "entirely not yet carried out." The president's assistants in the financial field "have failed"; there was mismanagement in the economic-financial sphere, while rumors mounted of "deviations in the handling of the state's wealth"; and taxation policy was designed to take from the poor and give to the "bureaucratic capitalists or the newly rich." State enterprises were hamstrung by mismanagement. Production was falling due to corruption, large-scale smuggling, and waste, which could only be described as sabotage. Official statistics were often worthless. Indonesia was still dependent for its foreign exchange on the crises-ridden capitalist market. In the sphere of foreign relations there existed a grave dualism between the anti-imperialist lines laid down by President Sukarno, and the officials in the state apparatus who sought aid from West Germany and Japan, invited the United States Peace Corps, proposed an American-model economic stabilization plan, and dragged their heels over ambassadorial-level relations with North Korea, Cuba, and East Germany.

Aidit was careful, as usual, to portray Sukarno as a leader betrayed by unworthy assistants, and also to frame his criticisms by constant reference to statements by the president. The only way out of the present undesirable situation, said Aidit, was to bring political authority into line with the economic and political aspirations of the true revolutionaries. In short, Indonesia needed a "mutual coöperation cabinet based on proportional representation"—as Sukarno had demanded in his speeches of February 21, 1957, and August 17, 1959, and as had been confirmed by the Provisional People's Consultative Assembly, the supreme authority of the state under the 1945 constitution. But PKI was seeking more than merely meaningful entry into the cabinet. The Communists had already taken up Sukarno's call for a revolutionary "retooling" of the entire state apparatus, and for a purge of "Communist-phobia." A Politbureau statement of October 12, 1962, had demanded, of course in line with Sukarno's own wishes, the "concrete and systematic eradication" of all Communist-phobia, worker-phobia, and people-phobia "both in the civilian and military spheres." [47] The present Committee for the Retooling the State Apparatus itself needed retooling to include political parties and mass organizations.

"Retooling" and "A Nasakom Cabinet" were made the slogans of a massive campaign instituted in October 1962 and carried into 1963. Petitions and telegrams bombarded the government, polite delegations hounded officials. Local branches of the National Front, the Youth Front, the Women's Front and the non-Communist political parties were cajoled and harassed into acquiescence, with the reminder that to be opposed would be to betray the goals expressed by President Sukarno. By February 1963 PNI, the nationalist party Partindo, the minor Moslem party Perti, and many local leaders of NU and PSII had publicly affirmed their belief that only a Nasakom cabinet could achieve solutions to Indonesia's problems. But as of the middle of 1963 the government was still unmoved by this display of popular support for the goals propounded by its president/prime minister/supreme commander. The government was also unmoved by the Communist threat that "To reject a mutual coöperation cabinet . . . is to reject the peaceful road" to socialism.[48]

For all their efforts, the Communists were unable to achieve much effect on government policy or the implementation of policy. After outlining current PKI activities to the Seventh National Congress in April 1962, Aidit admitted: "However, all the Communists' efforts as mentioned above are of limited scope because every proposal can be rejected or neglected by the government and every action can be disapproved, prohibited and obstructed by the authorities."[49] And if Aidit and Lukman were brought into the extended cabinet in March 1962, Aidit readily acknowledged that they had "no power whatsoever."[50]

4. THE EFFECT OF GUIDED DEMOCRACY ON PKI

It would be astonishing if in any Communist Party the size of PKI there was no opposition to, or at least questioning of, a policy that acquiesced, albeit with muffled protest, in the institution of the semi-authoritarian Guided Democracy guided by persons with little visible concern for the welfare of the masses. A scrutiny of Party speeches and documents indicates that in the early months of the Sukarno cabinet there were considerable doubts among Party members as to the correctness of a policy of support for the government. Those doubts were apparently removed.

Sakirman, writing in May 1960, admitted that there was concern within the Party at the support given for the return to the 1945 constitution and for the establishment of Guided Democracy.[51] Some comrades were asking whether Guided Democracy was not in fact "a semi-fascist political and economic system more criminal than liberal democracy." Others were concerned that the Party, by identifying with the Sukarno government, would be blamed by the people for the continuing economic deterioration. In reply, Sakirman said that since the failure of the Constituent Assembly to produce a new constitution, the Party "has tried hard to decide on a correct and true political attitude" on the basis of a Leninist analysis of the Party's past and present experience. The situation "is difficult," he admitted, especially as the middle group held state power, possibly a unique situation never before faced by a Communist Party. But the Party already had the correct strategy and main tactics of the Indonesian revolution. Where the Party was not yet in complete agreement was "concerning problems of day-to-day tactics or short-term political tactics." He repeated the official Party view that the contradictions between the ruling groups and the democratic forces outside the cabinet were not basic, but were contradictions within the people. In order to reassure the doubtful, he declared that the Party's general line, especially since the restoration of the 1945 constitution, "has given beneficial results and gives a perspective that will make the internal and external reactionaries tremble."

In December 1961 Aidit implied that some Party committees were not implementing Central Committee instructions as they should.[52] At the same time, Jusuf Adjitorop spoke of the need to "combat more intensively the symptoms of sectarianism in the Party's relations with the non-Party intellectuals, and at the same time prevent various sectarian manifestations in the Party." [53] Four months later, however, Aidit informed the Seventh National Congress that ideological education had greatly strengthened Party discipline and unity.[54] He asserted that "the national front policy is more deeply understood by the Party's cadres." Further:

The increased ideological strength of the Party can also be seen in the increasingly strong unity in the Party with the reduction in the contradictions within Party committees that have their source in different views on policy. Once each policy line and tactic is decided upon and explained by the Central Committee, it is immediately understood by Party cadres at the center and in the regions.

Aidit claimed in February 1963:

We can say that the Party is consolidated in the political, ideological and organizational spheres because this certainly is a fact. There is unanimity of thought in our Party on both internal and external policy and on its attitude to the International Communist Movement.[55]

Anti-Communist rumors for some years have pictured a widening rift within the Aidit leadership. On the one side is Aidit, a "Moscow" man, eager to pursue the peaceful national united front policy as it was developed late in 1951 and early in 1952; on the other is Lukman, a "Peking" man, prepared to explore the possibilities of militant confrontation with the national bourgeoisie, including Sukarno. It must be stated that so far there has been no concrete evidence to support these rumors. Certainly there must be intensive discussion within the Politbureau on internal policy and tactics, and on the differences within the Communist world movement that flared into prominence in the later months of 1961. But it appears that the Party leadership is in basic agreement on both internal and external policy. The reasons are readily understood.

The present national united front strategy cannot be discarded. This is a truth with which the PKI leaders must live, at least for the present. Any semblance of militancy or hostility toward the "bourgeoisie" as a whole or toward the ruling group could bring down the most disastrous governmental repression. Therefore, while the leadership may differ over particular tactics, it is necessarily united in terms of basic internal strategy. During the period of parliamentary democracy the leaders were united because the national united front strategy was bringing the Party rapidly and visibly closer to the center of power. Under Guided Democracy, the leadership is united because any marked deviation from the strategy could spell the destruction of the Party and of its leaders. While Aidit is away from Djakarta or Indonesia on Party or governmental work, the Communist line proceeds unchanged. The "militant" Lukman, it should be noted, is the author of the course guide for the Party's national- and province-level political schools which strongly reminds cadres that "Incorrect criticism can help force the national bourgeoisie to take reactionary measures." To drive home his point, he reminds the cadres that incorrect criticism of the national bourgeoisie in the first months of 1948 helped pave the way to Madiun.[56] And it was Lukman who, at the Central Committee meeting of February 1963, delivered the lengthy report reaffirming the need for the Communists to win the national businessmen and industrialists to the Party's side.[57]

Because there is unanimity within the PKI leadership on internal strategy, as well as apparently harmonious personal relations between the leaders, there is no higher cadre who wishes to use the China-Russia dispute as a means of ousting or demoting rivals. PKI has taken a consistent line since the dispute was aired unequivocally in the Soviet attack on the Albanian Workers' Party in October 1961.[58] Aidit, who led the PKI delegation to the Twenty-second Congress of the Communist Party of the Soviet Union, refused to join in the attacks on the Albanian leaders. Since then, PKI has repeated on many occasions the right and the need for every Communist Party to determine its own strategy and tactics free from external interference. The achievements of the Albanian government have been prominently displayed in *Harian Rakjat,* and Albanian Communist leaders invited to address PKI cadres. PKI has also called for a halt in public attacks made by any Communist Party against another—and has published the Chinese

Communist Party's statements to that effect. On the other hand, PKI acknowledges the CPSU's right to evaluate Stalin's role in the Soviet Union, and gives support for the fundamental Soviet propositions that there are peaceful roads by which Communist parties may win power, and that war is not inevitable against the capitalist powers. This centrist position seems to satisfy not only the higher cadres but also the lower cadres, whose knowledge of external affairs is largely limited, anyway, to what they are told by the Politbureau. In short, as of the middle of 1963 there is no concrete evidence to suggest that either internal or external political developments since July 1959 have caused any appreciable rent in the characteristic solidarity of PKI.

The most important question in a discussion of PKI in the era of Guided Democracy is a simple one: have the Indonesian Communists moved any closer to the assumption of power? The answer is not only complicated but tentative.

There is ample evidence to support the repeated contention of PKI leaders that the progressive force is growing stronger, while the reactionaries, though still strong, grow weaker, and the middle force gives indications of a move to the left. Since July 1959 the Party has grown to over 2 million members, the Communist mass organizations to about 12.5 millions. Both the Party and its mass organizations have expanded and have intensified their educational systems, with the result that cadres are more united with the leadership in an understanding of "the tasks of the national united front." The reactionaries have suffered the defeat of the PRRI-Permesta and the Darul Islam rebels. Their parties, Masjumi and PSI, have been banned. While a section of the middle force has moved rightward to become exploitative bureaucratic capitalists, in league with the reactionaries, an important section has moved to the left. The government has strenuously opposed the Dutch in West Irian, and has denounced Western imperialism and neocolonialism in other parts of the world. The government has given the Communists significant representation in the appointed parliament, the Provisional People's Consultative Assembly, other high advisory councils, the National Front, and in the more recent enterprise councils and distribution councils. Furthermore, Sukarno constantly preaches the need for a Nasakom cabinet, and the leaders of most remaining political parties have declared their support for such a cabinet. Two Communists already sit, though powerlessly, in the extended cabinet.

Despite the above evidence, Aidit is fully aware "there is no class which voluntarily wishes to share its power with another class . . . the national bourgeoisie, unless compelled, does not wish to share power with the proletariat." [59] Has Guided Democracy enabled the Party to build any greater power with which to compel the "national bourgeoisie" to share or relinquish control of the state?

The Aidit leadership conceived its national united front policy within a multiparty parliamentary democracy. Extraparliamentary political forces were of relatively secondary importance: President Sukarno somewhat ineffectually pulling strings from behind the scenes, and the army deeply divided in terms of personal, regional, and political loyalties and in terms of professional origin.[60] Ever conscious of the bloody failure of the Madiun rebellion, Aidit and his colleagues designed a strategy that could bring PKI to power by peaceful means or by the minimum exercise of force. As the social and political elite remained impervious to Communist infiltration, the Aidit leadership turned to the slow and painstaking task of attracting and disciplining the support of the urban and rural masses. In order to win mass support, and at the same time retain the tolerance of the government for Communist organizational activity, Indonesian Communism took on a particular character. The essentials of this character were, and are, self-abnegation, friendliness toward any but a very restricted number of "class enemies," sympathy toward religion, detailed solicitude for the problems of the poor, fervent patriotism, and peacefulness in the pursuit of goals. Mass organization and mass membership were achieved. With them the Party won notable successes under parliamentary democracy. Then the parliamentary system crumbled, and from the ruins emerged Guided Democracy. The national united front policy was maintained because there was no feasible alternative. To openly oppose the extraparliamentary forces would have produced severe repression and the loss of most of the Party's mass following.

Now that the parliamentary road to power has been firmly blocked, what other roads remain open? Theoretically there are several roads: rebellion or the threat, stated or implied, of rebellion; infiltration; and acclamation. The Sukarno government has acted to close these roads too.

A Communist rebellion is out of the question in the foreseeable future. The character of the Communist mass support won under the national united front policy is such that few Indonesian Communists would support insurrection against the authorities. The few who might come forward would be readily decimated by the modernized armed forces and police acting in conjunction with the anti-Communists and the large body of present non-Communists who would be expected to become anti-Communist in such a situation. The very few who might survive would be without friendly frontiers in their rear to afford supplies and refuge. Rebellion might be a long-term goal if the mass membership, or a significant part of it, could be trained to militancy. For the generally passive Indonesian masses, militancy would best be developed by experience in acts of militancy of an increasing scope. In this respect, the authorities have barred strikes and deal severely with the few outbursts of independent militant action by either workers or peasants—even when that militancy is effected in the praiseworthy name of anti-imperialism. Militancy might also be achieved, more slowly, through education. The authorities closely censor the press, and ensure that political education keeps within narrow, approved bounds.

Meanwhile, PKI may be experiencing a process of declining revolutionary morale among some cadres. There are two facets to this process, one more obvious, the other more complex. The more obvious aspect is the inevitable discouragement among those cadres who come to believe that the Party is getting no nearer to the center of power. To avoid this happening, the Aidit leadership constantly claims that the progressive force gains strength daily. The other aspect of the decline in revolutionary morale is the *embourgeoisement* of cadres. It seems possible that a number of cadres are finding sufficient satisfaction of their material and status ambitions that they have lost or are losing the will to overthrow the existing order. Sukarno has given PKI and its mass organizations large representation in the many appointed advisory councils; at another level, the Party and its mass organizations provide cadres with positions of status and security within the Communist subcommunity. It is possible that some cadres come to feel their present positions to be a fully acceptable substitute for power—especially as the forceful pursuit of power may well lead to the grave.

PKI might win power by infiltration, but this is highly unlikely. With Communists in the armed forces, the upper echelons of the bureaucracy, or the inner cabinet, the Party might be able to achieve a position from which it could, backed by the mass organizations, seize power bloodlessly, or nearly so. The ruling group, however, has been aware of this possibility. No Communist has been given charge of a ministry or any governmental position of actual power. The higher levels of the bureaucracy remain resistant to Communist courting. The army, in the last seven years, has been greatly unified and modernized under the leadership of Nasution. In short, the verbal espousal of

Nasakom unity and coöperation has not been transformed into a Nasakom sharing of governmental power.[61]

Finally, PKI might win power by acclamation. Such a possibility has never loomed large in Indonesia, and has grown no larger during the period of the Sukarno cabinet. Certainly inflation continues at a hectic pace, and there are often grave shortages of basic consumer goods. But the situation is very different from that in Weimar Germany or the last years of Kuomintang China. In the economic field, the Indonesian government manages to ensure a minimum of basic goods and occasional luxuries to the politically important people—the armed forces, the public servants, the leading politicians, and the white-collar groups in general—while in the villages the appearance of a truly impoverished rural proletariat is impeded by the tendency to share available wealth not too unequally among all villagers. The administrative apparatus in the towns and countryside is unimpaired and, with the final collapse of the PRRI-Permesta and Darul Islam rebellions, government control now reaches to all parts of Indonesia for the first time since independence. Of greatest importance, the non-Communist ruling group is now more firmly entrenched in power, and more cohesive, than it was in 1959. And the ruling group is certain of its own ability to govern. The economic deterioration can be readily explained as the regrettable price paid for the successful struggles to establish internal security and gain West Irian. At the same time, PKI, unlike the Chinese Communist Party in the years before 1949, does not stand as a strong alternative ruling group with a distinctive program. The Party submits to the indignities of government control, and the obstacles to its victory (for example, the army, the Moslems, and the outer islands) are so great as to suggest that even if victory could be achieved it would be at the expense of a protracted civil war. Furthermore, the close identification of PKI with many of the government's policies, from anti-imperialism and land reform to Nasakom unity and socialism, does not suggest that the Party has a clearly distinctive program capable of solving the country's main problems. In other words, neither the present ruling group, nor the large "middle force" outside the government, has given any indication of turning to PKI as the only force capable of governing well.

As of the middle of 1963, Aidit and his colleagues must have been both apprehensive and hopeful. Apprehensive that the governing group might turn to the right and crush or further obstruct the Communist organizations. Hopeful because they were convinced of the inevitability of a Communist victory. Early in 1952 they had taken the major decision to build mass support—which by definition, in the Indonesian context, meant nonmilitant support. Their chief concern in mid-1963, as in the entire period after the demise of parliamentary democracy, was to protect, expand, and steel their mass support so that it could be used, whenever the right moment arrived, as the springboard to state power. Still young, and having amply demonstrated their patience over the preceding twelve years, they were prepared to work for many more years before the right moment arrived. Meanwhile, however, the fate of Indonesia would be determined largely by the action or inaction of the non-Communists.

Notes

Notes

I. THE SOCIOECONOMIC SITUATION IN JAVA

1 "Census of the Republic of Indonesia of the Year 1961," Consulate General of Indonesia, New York, mimeographed (New York, 1962). The population includes an estimated 700,000 in West Irian, but excludes members of the armed forces and their families living in military barracks. These latter could number about one million persons.

2 All statistics for Java also include the island of Madura, which is administratively part of East Java.

3 "The Population of Indonesia," Indonesian Participants in the December 1955 United Nations Seminar on Population in Asia and the Far East, *Ekonomi dan Keuangan Indonesia* (Feb., 1956), pp. 94-95.

4 *Atlas Van Tropisch Nederland* (Batavia, 1938), map 18a.

5 "The Population of Indonesia," p. 91.

6 *News and Views Indonesia*, Indonesian Embassy, Canberra, Australia, IV (Aug. 17, 1959), 14. Another official estimate is that in 1958 peasant agriculture occupied 63.3 per cent of the total land area of Java (*Statistical Pocketbook of Indonesia, 1960*, Central Bureau of Statistics [Djakarta, 1960], p. 48).

7 An official commission estimated in 1937 that only about 300,000 hectares of land were still available for cultivation in Java, that is, enough to absorb the population increase for 3½ years (Karl J. Pelzer, *Pioneer Settlement in the Asiatic Tropics* [New York, 1945], p. 162 n. 9). In 1960 the Indonesian Ministry of Agrarian Affairs calculated that 181,934 hectares of "neglected" land were available for food production in Java ("Tanah-Tanah Terlantar" ["Neglected Lands"], Departemen Agraria [Department of Agrarian Affairs], mimeographed [Djakarta, 1960]).

8 From 1951 to 1959 inclusive, only 231,474 migrants left Java to settle in the outer islands (*Statistical Pocketbook, 1960*, p. 16).

9 See Sie Kwat Soen, "The Use of Fertilizers in Indonesia," *Ekonomi dan Keuangan Indonesia* (Sept., 1954), pp. 603-614. Soen estimated, for example, that up to 1 million hectares of irrigated rice land in Indonesia were phosphate deficient and would need up to 100,000 tons annually of double superphosphate; in fact, only 5,000 tons were being used for rice cultivation, compared with 400,000 tons in India and 2,200,000 tons in Japan.

10 "Daftar Rata-Rata Luas Tanah Sawah Tiap-Tiap Pemilik Sawah dalam Propinsi, Tahun 1957" ["List of Landholding Averages of Owners of *Sawah* by Province, 1957"], Departemen Agraria, mimeographed (Djakarta, n.d.); "Daftar Rata-Rata Luas Tanah Darat Tiap-Tiap Pemilik Darat dalam Propinsi, Tahun 1957" ["List of Landholding Averages of Owners of Unirrigated Farm Land by Province, 1957"], Departemen Agraria, mimeographed (Djakarta, n.d.). As an estimated 50 per cent of peasants are landless, in 1957 only 0.28 hectare of *sawah* was available for each peasant and his dependents.

11 If the detailed figures of *sawah* and unirrigated landholdings and landowners, given in table 1, are added up, they do not equal these general figures. The ministry's reports do not explain the discrepancy.

12 No details were given for the residency of Kediri, which contains five *kabupatens*.

13 *Himpunan Keputusan Kongres / Konperensi Organisasi-Organisasi Tani Massa* [*Compilation of the Decisions of Congresses and Conferences of Peasant Mass Organizations*], Kementerian Agraria [Ministry of Agrarian Affairs] (Djakarta, 1951), p. 25; PKI, "Masaalah Tani di Indonesia" ["The Peasant Question in Indonesia"], *BM* (June 15–July 1, 1951), p. 304.

14 *HR*, Aug. 16, Nov. 25, 1954.

15 *Statistical Pocketbook, 1960*, p. 62. Of the estate lands in Java, 371,300 hectares were under crops (*ibid.*, p. 63).

16 *Report to the Government of Indonesia on Social Security*, International Labour Office (Geneva, 1958), p. 15.

17 *Commercial Crops of Estates, 1957*, Biro Pusat Statistik [Central Bureau of Statistics] (Djakarta, n.d.), p. 18.

18 *Statistical Pocketbook, 1960*, p. 78.

19 The following paragraphs are concerned with the villages of the ethnic Javanese who number about 40 millions and inhabit Central Java, areas along the north coast of West Java, and most of East Java. It is the ethnic Javanese who have provided PKI with the majority of its supporters and members. The only recent work on the Sundanese village of West Java is Andrea Wilcox Palmer, "The Sundanese Village," in G. William Skinner, ed., *Local, Ethnic, and National Loyalties in Village Indonesia: A Symposium* (New Haven, 1959), pp. 42-51. No recent research has been made on the Madurese villages of Madura and the adjacent areas of Java. For a brief description of village forms in the different regions of Java, see B. ter Haar, *Adat Law in Indonesia* (New York, 1948), pp. 71-73.

20 For a fairly full list of nonagricultural persons to be found in the Javanese village, see PKI, "Program Perubahan Tanah dan Tuntutan kaum Tani" ["Program of Land Change and Peasants' Demands"], *BM* (Dec., 1951), pp. 13-15.

21 Donald R. Fagg, "Authority and Social Structure: A Study in Javanese Bureaucracy" (Ph.D. dissertation, Harvard University, 1958), p. 136.

22 W. Hollinger, quoted in Clifford Geertz, *The Social Context of Economic Change: An Indonesian Case Study* (Cambridge, Mass., 1956), p. 14. As almost all village-right land is *sawah*, then, if Hollinger's figure is correct, up to 50 per cent of all *sawah* is

still ultimately owned by the village. Geertz found that 24 per cent of *sawah* in the subdistrict he studied was still village-right land; *ibid.*

23 Compton reports that generally about half the households in the villages of Modjokerto *kabupaten* of East Java possessed a share of village land; Boyd R. Compton, *Modjokerto I*, Institute of Current World Affairs Report (New York, 1956), p. 7.

24 Hollinger estimates that 27.5 per cent of all village-right land is used by the village officials (quoted in Geertz, *op. cit.*, p. 14 n. 8).

25 *Ibid.*, p. 14. Geertz found that even in the most suburban village he studied, only about 10 per cent of *sawah* was held by persons outside the village. It should be noted in contrast, however, that Indonesian government officials found in November, 1959, that 34 per cent of 20,488 owners of *sawah* in Indramaju district, West Java, were absentee landowners ("Laporan Penjelidikan Landreform didaerah Kawedanaan Indramaju" ["Report of Land Reform Investigation in Indramaju District"], Dewan Pertimbangan Agung [Supreme Advisory Council], mimeographed [Djakarta, 1960], pp. 3, 5). An investigation of the district of Batang (in Pekalongan *kabupaten*), which includes 3 *ketjamatans* and 67 villages, found that "There are some villages in which almost all the land (*sawah*) is owned by persons outside the village"—but only three such villages were actually named (Dewan Pertimbangan Agung, "Kesimpulan Hasil Penjelidikan di Kawedanan Batang" ["Conclusions of the Results of the Investigation in Batang District"], mimeographed [Djakarta, 1960], pp. 1-2). It should be noted, however, that the Pekalongan areas has the heaviest concentration of large landholdings, and therefore probably of absentee landownership, in Central Java.

26 PKI, "Laporan Mengenai Pekerdjaan Partai dikalangan kaum Tani" ["Report Concerning Party Work among the Peasants"], *BM* (April-May, 1959), p. 134. On November 20, 1959, parliament passed an act providing for a minimum share of 50 per cent of the crop for the tenant. This new law is now being slowly implemented.

27 Robert Ravenelle Jay, "Santri and Abangan: Religious Schism in Rural Central Java" (Ph.D. dissertation, Harvard University, 1957), p. 52. Jay also wrote (*ibid.*, p. 58) that "the coercive power of close neighbor and kin bonds, together with the shortage of land, permit only the tougher, more aggressive independent landholding households to resist demands for some kind of sharecrop concessions."

28 Ann Ruth Willner, "Social Change in Javanese Town-Village Life," *Economic Development and Cultural Change*, VI (April, 1958), 233.

29 Clifford Geertz, *The Development of the Javanese Economy: A Socio-Cultural Approach* (Cambridge, Mass., 1956), p. 47.

30 See Asmu, "Masaalah Landreform" ["The Question of Land Reform"], *BM* (Jan,. 1960), p. 24.

31 Justus Maria van der Kroef, "Indonesia: Economic Dualism," *Current History*, XXV (Nov., 1953), 293. Only ethnic Indonesians are allowed to own agricultural land in Indonesia.

32 Jay, *op. cit.*, p. 52.

33 Professor A. G. Pringgodigdo, president of Airlangga University, told me that during the Japanese occupation, while he was a *wedana* in the Banjumas region, the Japanese issued a regulation forbidding loans of more than twelve months duration. The peasants, however, would not report many of their longer-term debts to the *wedana* because they felt that they had the duty to pay them. When Pringgodigdo told the peasants that the interest rates were extortionate, they replied that when they were in need the Chinese moneylender was always ready to help with goods or

money. He told me that the peasants thought of the moneylenders as a help rather than an enemy. If this attitude is as widespread as my impression would indicate, it helps explain why PKI apparently lost no popular support because of its attempt in 1959 to reverse the government's decision to evict all foreigners from the villages. It should be noted that in Java there were no reports of the villagers molesting the Chinese who were being evicted. For a less idyllic picture of the "debt-serfdom" of the Javanese peasants, see D. H. Burger, *Structural Changes in Javanese Society: The Village Sphere* (Ithaca, 1957), p. 12.

34 Geertz, *Social Context of Economic Change*, p. 15.

35 Jay, *op. cit.*, pp. 58-60.

36 *Ibid.*, pp. 60, 65.

37 Paul M. Kattenburg, *A Central Javanese Village in 1950* (Ithaca, 1951), pp. 13-14.

38 For a brief description of the social effects of the campaigns for the 1955 elections, see Herbert Feith, *The Indonesian Elections of 1955* (Ithaca, 1957), *passim*.

39 For a brief description of the discontented, more ambitious, younger generation in the village, see Boyd R. Compton, *Village Notebook II. What to Believe In?* Institute of Current World Affairs Report (New York, 1955), pp. 8-13; also his *Modjokerto I*, pp. 14-17.

40 Apparently the position of *lurah* is still usually retained within one or two families in each village, but there is increasing competition between members of the large families, the competitors often seeking the aid of a political party.

41 Herbert Feith, "Indonesia," in George McTurnan Kahin, ed., *Governments and Politics of Southeast Asia* (Ithaca, 1959), p. 209. See also Fagg, *op. cit.*, esp. pp. 232, 420-421, 439, 460; and Selosoemardjan, "Social Changes in Jogjakarta" (Ph.D. dissertation, Cornell University, 1959), pp. 178-186.

42 Fagg, *op. cit.*, p. 378; see also pp. 105-106.

43 Clifford Geertz, "The Javanese Village," in Skinner, *op. cit.*, p. 35.

44 Robert Ravenelle Jay, "Local Government in Rural Central Java," *Far Eastern Quarterly*, XV (Feb., 1956), 215.

45 Geertz, "Javanese Village," p. 35.

46 Hurustiati Subandrio, "Javanese Peasant Life: Villages in East Java" (dissertation for Postgraduate Diploma, London University, 1951), p. 26.

47 This division is described at greatest length by Geertz in *Development of the Javanese Economy*, p. 93 *et seq.*; *The Religion of Java* (Glencoe, Illinois, 1960); *Social Context of Economic Change*, esp. pp. 84-147; and "Religious Belief and Economic Behavior in a Central Javanese Town: Some Preliminary Considerations," *Economic Development and Cultural Change*, IV (Jan., 1956), 138-158. See also Boyd R. Compton, *Village Notebook V*, Institute of Current World Affairs Report (New York, 1956); Fagg, *op. cit.*, esp. pp. 115-118; Jay, "Santri and Abangan"; and Munawir Sjadzali, "Indonesia's Muslim Parties and their Political Concepts" (M.A. thesis, Georgetown University, 1959), pp. 46-49. The information and analyses in these sources are remarkably uniform and were largely verified by myself in conversations with many Javanese.

48 Geertz, *Social Context of Economic Change*, p. 141.

49 Jay, "Santri and Abangan," p. 232.

50 See below, pp 223-225, 229.

51 See map 2, p. 227.

52 The main causes of rapid growth in urban population include the population pressure in the rural areas; insecurity in the rural areas during the revolution and,

in West Java, since the revolution; the growth of the governmental bureaucracy since 1945; and the world-felt glamour of city life.

53 Gerald S. Maryanov, *Decentralization in Indonesia as a Political Problem* (Ithaca, 1958), p. 50.

54 It must be noted that in Indonesia considerable prestige is still attached to achievements in formal education, while the same applies, especially in Java, to aristocratic origin.

55 Geertz, *Social Context of Economic Change*, p. 149 n. 118. The government's National Planning Bureau claimed that at the end of 1953 there were 370,389 employees of the central government and 229,332 employees (excluding village officials) of provincial, municipal, and *kabupaten* councils, with the status of government personnel *(Statistical Pocketbook, 1960*, p. 236).

56 A. M. de Neuman, *Industrial Development in Indonesia* (Cambridge, England, 1955), pp. 20-21; Peter H. W. Sitsen, *Industrial Development of the Netherlands Indies* (New York, 1942), p. 5. A lower estimate is that in 1939 up to 600,000 workers were engaged in small-scale, nonmechanized industry (Jan O. M. Broek, *Economic Development of the Netherlands Indies* [New York, 1942], pp. 81-82).

57 *Report to the Government of Indonesia*, pp. 16-18. More than three-quarters of the companies circularized answered, and the report adds that by implication it was the smaller companies that did not. It should be noted that the industrial undertakings are not concentrated in any one part of Java. Of about 400,000 workers in medium and large undertakings in Java, approximately 146,000 were in West Java, 151,000 in Central Java, and 103,000 in East Java.

58 For details of the percentage of women workers in certain industries, see n. 42, p. 347.

59 W. F. Wertheim, *Effects of Western Civilization on Indonesian Society* (New York, 1950), p. 46. For information on the development of towns in Indonesia, and living conditions of the Indonesian urban population before World War II, see W. F. Wertheim, ed., *The Indonesian Town* (The Hague and Bandung, 1958).

60 Kementerian Perburuhan, *Laporan Kementerian Perburuhan, April 1957–April 1959* [Ministry of Labor Report, April 1957–April 1959] (Djakarta, 1959), pp. 25-28; and *Laporan Kementerian Perburuhan, April-Djuni 1958* (Djakarta, 1958), pp. 8-9.

61 The supply of currency is a rough indicator of inflation. It has risen from 240.0 million rupiahs in March, 1938, to 3,328.1 millions at the end of 1951, 7,473.7 millions at the end of 1954, 14,091.4 millions at the end of 1957, 33,514 millions at the end of 1959, and 64,491 millions at the end of 1961 *(Statistical Pocketbook, 1960*, p. 183; *HR*, April 10, 1962).

62 Benjamin Higgins, *Indonesia's Economic Stabilization and Development* (New York, 1957), p. xv.

63 *ITUN*, March, 1960, p. 4.

64 Indonesia does not have adequate statistics of industrial production, but such figures as imports of industrial raw materials, provided in the annual reports of the Bank Indonesia, indicate general slow growth in production since 1950 with a recession starting in 1958 as a result of the confiscation of Dutch enterprises in December 1957 and the outbreak of civil war in February 1958. But only the imports of malt, paper, cloves, and bar iron were higher in 1958 than in 1940.

65 Estimates of the number of unemployed in Indonesia range widely from 15 millions by PKI leader Njoto towards the end of 1954 (quoted in Justus Maria van der Kroef, "Indonesia's Economic Difficulties," *Far Eastern Survey*, XXIV [Feb., 1955],

21), to 1,736,000 by the Ministry of Labor in 1958 (Bank Indonesia, *Report for the Year 1958-1959* [Djakarta, 1959], p. 234). Njoto's figure must have included the partly employed or the "not fully employed," and if so his figure seems reasonable. The Indonesian National Planning Bureau ("Indonesia's Economic Developments, 1953," *Ekonomi dan Keuangan Indonesia* [July, 1954], p. 436) in 1954 estimated that 30 to 40 per cent of the Indonesian labor force, and more in Java, was underemployed.

II. THE INDONESIAN COMMUNIST PARTY, 1920-1951

1 For the history of PKI up to the failure of the Communist revolts of 1926 and 1927, see D. N. Aidit, *Sedjarah Gerakan Buruh Indonesia* [*History of the Indonesian Labor Movement*] (Djakarta, 1952); Harry J. Benda, "The Communist Rebellions of 1926-1927 in Indonesia," *Pacific Historical Review*, XXIV (1955), 139-152; Harry J. Benda and Ruth T. McVey, eds., *The Communist Uprisings of 1926-1927 in Indonesia: Key Documents* (Ithaca, 1960); J. Th. Petrus Blumberger, *Le Communisme aux Indes Neerlandaises* (Paris, 1929); G. S. Bousquet, *A French View of the Netherlands Indies* (London, 1940), pp. 24-27; Arnold C. Brackman, *Indonesian Communism: A History* (New York, 1963), pp. 3-21; George McTurnan Kahin, *Nationalism and Revolution in Indonesia* (Ithaca, 1952), pp. 74-87; "Official Report, Dated January 1927, of the Government of the Dutch East Indies on the Communist Disturbances of November 1926," in *Annaire de Documentation Coloniale Comparee, 1927*, I (Brussels, 1928), 181-200; PKI, *40 Tahun PKI* [*PKI 40 Years*] (Djakarta, 1960), pp. 7-30; PKI, *Pemberontakan Nasional Pertama di Indonesia (1926)* [*The First National Rebellion in Indonesia, 1926*] (Djakarta, 1961); B. Schrieke, "The Causes and Effects of Communism on the West Coast of Sumatra," in his *Indonesian Sociological Studies: Selected Writings*, Part I (The Hague and Bandung, 1955), pp. 83-166; Sudijono Djojoprajitno, *PKI-SIBAR Contra Tan Malaka* (Djakarta, 1962 [?]); Jeanne S. Mintz, "Marxism in Indonesia," in Frank N. Trager, ed., *Marxism in Southeast Asia* (Stanford, 1959), pp. 177-187; Robert Van Niel, *The Emergence of the Modern Indonesian Elite* (The Hague and Bandung, 1960), p. 154 *et seq.*; and Alexandre Von Arx, *L'Evolution Politique en Indonesie de 1900 a 1942* (Fribourg, Switzerland, 1949), pp. 185-208.

2 For the official PKI story of Communist underground activities during these twenty years, see PKI, *40 Tahun PKI*, pp. 31-43.

3 For the history of PKI from its reëstablishment in 1945 to the outbreak of the Madiun rebellion in September, 1948, see Brackman, *op. cit.*, pp. 44-93; Hartono, "The Indonesian Communist Movement, 1945-1948: Its Development and Relations with the Soviet Union" (M.A. thesis, Columbia University, 1959); Kahin, *op. cit.*, p. 158 *et seq.*, Ruth T. McVey, *The Soviet View of the Indonesian Revolution* (Ithaca, 1957); pp. 9-70; PKI, *40 Tahun PKI*, pp. 44-57; and PKI, *Lahirnja Partai Komunis Indonesia dan Perkembangannja* [*The Birth and Growth of the Indonesian Communist Party*] (Djakarta, 1951), pp. 15-23.

4 PKI, *Lahirnja*, p. 17.

5 PKI, *Djalan Baru untuk Republik Indonesia* [*New Road for the Indonesian Republic*] (7th ed.; Djakarta, 1953).

6 The best account of the Madiun rebellion and the events leading up to it is Kahin, *op. cit.*, pp. 259-303. Also good is Hartono, *op. cit.*, pp. 84-96. For the more important PKI accounts of the rebellion, see n. 2, p. 329.

7 PKI, *Lahirnja*, p. 23. The personal observation of those who helped put down the rebellion confirms that many thousands were arrested.

8 Much of the information on the period December, 1948, to January, 1951, was provided in statements made to the author by Djaetun.

9 This was confirmed by Djaetun and Darsono (a veteran Communist who returned to Indonesia in 1950 after many years of exile, during which he had broken with the Communists) in conversations with the author. The Aidit leadership later made Tan Ling Djie the scapegoat for the "errors" committed in this period.

10 Alimin, *Riwajat Hidupku* [*The Story of My Life*] (Djakarta, 1954), p. 44.

11 *Sin Po*, July 25, 1950.

12 *Ibid.*, Nov. 18, 1949.

13 For brief biographies of Aidit, see D. N. Aidit, *Menempuh Djalan Rakjat* [*Along the People's Road*] (4th ed.; Djakarta, 1954), pp. 3-4, and *BM* (Sept.-Oct., 1953), pp. 479-80.

14 For brief biographies of Lukman, see *BM* (Sept.-Oct., 1953), pp. 481-482, and *HR*, Sept. 7, 1955.

15 PKI, *40 Tahun PKI*, p. 66. For brief biographies of Njoto, see *BM* (Sept.-Oct., 1953), pp. 483-484, and *HR*, Sept. 7, 1955.

16 Editorial, "Memasuki Tahun 1951" ["Entering 1951"], *BM* (Jan. 1-15, 1951), p. 4.

17 *Loc. cit.*

18 *Sin Po*, Oct. 19, 1950.

19 *BM* (Jan. 1-15, 1951), p. 26.

20 *Loc. cit.*

21 The full text of the December 2, 1950, statement is given in *Sin Po*, Dec. 6, 1950.

22 *Ibid.*, Dec. 11, 1950.

23 *BM* (Jan. 1-15, 1951), p. 22.

24 D. N. Aidit, "Madju Terus untuk Sukses-Sukses jang Lebih Besar" ["Continue To Advance for Greater Successes"] in his *Pilihan Tulisan* [*Selected Works*], I (Djakarta, 1959), 202.

25 *Ibid.*, p. 203.

26 *BM* (Jan. 1-15, 1951), p. 50.

27 For brief biographies of Sudisman, see Parlaungan, *Hasil Rakjat Memilih Tokoh-Tokoh Parlemen* [*The Results of the People's Election of Members of Parliament*] (Djakarta, 1956), pp. 295-296, and *HR*, Sept. 7, 1955.

28 PKI, *Putusan-Putusan Sidang Pleno Central Comite Partai Komunis Indonesia* [*Decisions of the PKI Central Committee Plenum Meeting*] (Djakarta, 1953), p. 4.

III. PROLOGUE

1 For political developments in Indonesia up to September, 1950, see George McTurnan Kahin, *Nationalism and Revolution in Indonesia* (Ithaca, 1952). A thorough analysis of political developments from December, 1949, to March, 1957 is Herbert Feith, *The Decline of Constitutional Democracy in Indonesia* (Ithaca, 1962).

2 *RI* (March, 1957), p. 3.

3 As PKI explanations of the differences between the Indonesian and Chinese situations, see, for example, a speech by Sakirman on October 2, 1950, given in

Risalah Perundingan 1950/1951 [*Indonesian Parliamentary Debates 1950/1951*], III 1142-1143; interview with D. N. Aidit, quoted in A. Doak Barnett, *Echoes of Mao Tse-tung in Djakarta,* American Universities Field Staff Report (New York, 1955), pp. 7-11; D. N. Aidit, *Djalan ke Demokrasi Rakjat bagi Indonesia* [*The Indonesian Road to People's Democracy*] (Djakarta, 1955), p. 37; and D. N. Aidit, *The Birth and Growth of the Communist Party of Indonesia* (Djakarta, 1958), p. 27.

4 D. N. Aidit, "Revolusi Oktober dan Rakjat-Rakjat Timur" ["The October Revolution and the Peoples of the East"], *BM* (Oct.-Nov., 1957), p. 383.

5 The lack of interest shown by Moscow in PKI until after the period in which the national united front was defined is indicated by the Cominform journal, the number of foreign Communist delegates to PKI congresses, and the number of PKI delegations invited abroad.

From the end of 1948 until August, 1954, the Cominform journal *For a Lasting Peace, For a People's Democracy!* made little mention of Indonesia, and none whatsoever during 1952, the year in which PKI began to implement its form of the national united front. From August 1954 until 1956, when the journal was discontinued, articles on PKI appeared regularly—written by Aidit, not by Russian "experts." In March 1954 only one foreign Communist attended the PKI Fifth Congress, compared with seven who went to the Sixth Congress in September 1959. And from July 1950, when Aidit and Lukman returned from abroad, until the beginning of 1956, only two PKI delegations visited the Soviet bloc, and none before December 1952. In contrast, between January 1956 and January 1960, thirteen PKI delegations visited the Soviet bloc. Perhaps in order to provide the foreign parties with material on PKI's policy and tactics, in mid-1954 the Indonesian Communists began to publish a monthly periodical in English devoted to the work of the Party and its mass organizations in the Indonesian situation.

IV. A SEMICOLONIAL, SEMIFEUDAL COUNTRY

1 For the Communist roots of the Aidit leadership's theory, see Justus Maria van der Kroef, "Lenin, Mao and Aidit," in Walter Laqueur and Leopold Labedz, eds., *Polycentrism: The New Factor in International Communism* (New York, 1962), pp. 197-218.

2 See, for example, PKI, *Konstitusi PKI* (Djakarta, 1951), p. 11.

3 The results of the Round Table Conference, as accepted by the Indonesian and Dutch delegations on November 2, 1949, are to be found in *Round Table Conference Results* (The Hague, n.d.), pp. 7-78.

4 D. N. Aidit, *Menudju Indonesia Baru* [*Toward a New Indonesia*] (2d ed.; Djakarta, 1955), pp. 27-31.

5 *Ibid.,* p. 29.

6 PKI, "Program Perubahan Tanah dan Tuntutan kaum Tani" ["Program of Land Change and Peasants' Demands"], *BM* (Dec., 1951), p. 8.

7 D. N. Aidit, "Haridepan Gerakan Tani Indonesia" ["The Future of the Indonesian Peasant Movement"], *BM* (July, 1953), pp. 332-340.

8 PKI, *Program PKI* (Djakarta, 1954), pp. 5-10.

9 *Ibid.,* pp. 7-8.

10 D. N. Aidit, *Masjarakat Indonesia dan Revolusi Indonesia* (Djakarta, 1957),

pp. 39-44. This booklet was published in English as *Indonesian Society and the Indonesian Revolution*. I have used the English version.

[11] *Ibid.*, pp. 39-40.

[12] *Ibid.*, pp. 40-41.

[13] In 1952 the White Engineering Corporation of New York undertook an investigation of foreign capital in Indonesia. Its report to the Indonesian government showed that 70 per cent of the $2,100 million of foreign investments was Dutch. The general findings of the report are quoted in *RI* (March, 1957), p. 29. Much of the remaining non-Dutch capital was invested in the oil industry (Caltex, Stanvac, and Shell) and in estates. But the seizure of Dutch enterprises brought into government hands most foreign banks, interisland shipping, most estates, and the bulk of the export-import trade.

[14] PKI, *Bahan-Bahan untuk Kongres Nasional ke-VI Partai Komunis Indonesia* [*Materials for PKI's Sixth National Congress*] (Djakarta, 1958), pp. 8-9.

[15] D. N. Aidit, *Untuk Demokrasi dan Kabinet Gotong Rojong* [*For Democracy and a Mutual Coöperation Cabinet*] (Djakarta, 1959), pp. 36-37.

[16] M. H. Lukman, *Tentang Konstitusi PKI* [*Concerning PKI's Constitution*] (Djakarta, 1959), pp. 17-18.

[17] Aidit claimed in 1958 that 41 per cent of Indonesia's exports went to the United States, 35 per cent to Western Europe, 16 per cent to African and Asian countries excluding China, 4 per cent to Australia, and only 4 per cent to the Soviet bloc (D. N. Aidit, "Economic Difficulties and the Communist Party's Proposals," *World Marxist Review* [Sept., 1958], p. 71.)

[18] Lukman, *op. cit.*, pp. 17-18.

V. THE BASIC TARGETS OF THE INDONESIAN REVOLUTION

[1] PKI, *Konstitusi PKI* (Djakarta, 1951), p. 12.

[2] PKI, *Program PKI* (Djakarta, 1954), p. 10.

[3] D. N. Aidit, "Fly High the Banners of 'Land to the Peasants' and Fight for One Victory after the Other," *RI*, Supplement (June-July, 1959), p. 12.

VI. THE DRIVING FORCES OF THE REVOLUTION

[1] D. N. Aidit, *Indonesian Society and the Indonesian Revolution* (Djakarta, 1957), p. 61.

[2] Aidit's figures appear to be exaggerated. In a booklet entitled *Masaalah Front Persatuan Buruh* [*The Question of the Workers' United Front*] (Djakarta, 1959), p. 14, the leaders of the Communist trade-union federation, SOBSI, stated that "the Indonesian workers constitute only 10 per cent of the total Indonesian population, while the peasants constitute not less than 70 per cent. The remaining 20 per cent of the population is comprised of other groups, such as students, small urban industrialists, national industrialists and intellectuals." The SOBSI leaders also stated that "most of the workers consist of casual laborers, both in government work, such as forestry, autonomous areas, estates, and general works, and in private

enterprise, such as in sugar enterprises, oil companies, fishing, agriculture, and so on."

3 Aidit, *op. cit.,* p. 62.

4 PKI, *Bahan-Bahan untuk Kongres Nasional ke-VI Partai Komunis Indonesia* [*Materials for PKI's Sixth National Congress*] (Djakarta, 1958), p. 13.

5 Aidit, *op cit.,* p. 62. See also PKI, *Mengapa Front Nasional* [*Why the National Front*] (Djakarta, 1957), pp. 8-10.

6 Aidit, *op. cit.,* pp. 62-63.

7 *Ibid.,* p. 62.

8 *Ibid.,* p. 61.

9 See, for example, PKI, *Program PKI* (Djakarta, 1954), p. 8, and PKI, *Bahan-Bahan,* p. 15.

10 PKI, *Mengapa Front Nasional,* p. 7.

11 PKI, "Program Perubahan Tanah," *BM* (Dec., 1951), p. 24.

12 D. N. Aidit, "Haridepan Gerakan Tani Indonesia" ["The Future of the Indonesian Peasant Movement"], *BM* (July, 1953), p. 340.

13 PKI, "Program Perubahan Tanah," pp. 15-22.

14 Aidit, *Indonesian Society,* pp. 60-61.

15 *Ibid.,* p. 59.

16 See Mao Tse-tung, "The Chinese Revolution and the Chinese Communist Party," in *Selected Works* (London, 1954), III, 90-92.

17 PKI, *Konstitusi PKI* (Djakarta, 1951), p. 11.

18 Alfred G. Meyer, in *Leninism* (Cambridge, Mass., 1957), p. 115n, writes: "An ideological study surveying the uses of the term [petty bourgeoisie] would . . . constitute a virtual history of Marxist social theory. Such a study would reveal the flexibility of this concept, which has been used as a label for any group not fitting into the simple bipolar schemes Marxism seeks to apply."

19 From my own sampling of Communist cadres, however, it would seem that they were drawn mainly from a group that has been ignored by the Aidit leadership in its sociopolitical analysis: the white-collar workers in government and private employment, including teaching.

20 The terms anti-Communist and non-Communist as used in this study require explanation. To be anti-Communist is to be openly anti-Communist, verbally or otherwise. To be non-Communist is to be neither openly pro-Communist nor openly anti-Communist. A non-Communist may be, in sentiments or in theory, anti-Communist, but for some reason (often political expediency) unwilling to express his anti-Communism. It should be noted that many Indonesians, and especially those associated with PNI and Sukarno, consider openly expressed anti-Communism to be in some way reactionary, pro-Western, and therefore proimperialist, a contravention of Indonesia's independent position in the Cold War. This belief inhibits the open expression of hostility to Communism among a large section of the Indonesian political elite. It should also be noted that, of course, anyone may shift from being non-Communist to anti-Communist, and vice versa. One of the constant concerns of the Aidit leadership has been to remove or prevent any grounds for the politically important non-Communists becoming anti-Communist.

21 Aidit, *Indonesian Society,* pp. 50-51.

22 D. N. Aidit, *Djalan ke Demokrasi Rakjat bagi Indonesia* [*The Indonesian Road to People's Democracy*] (Djakarta, 1955), p. 53.

23 Aidit, *Indonesian Society,* p. 57.

24 Aidit, *Djalan ke Demokrasi Rakjat*, p. 53.

25 Aidit, *Indonesian Society*, p. 58.

26 D. N. Aidit, "For National Unity," *World Marxist Review* (Feb., 1960), p. 21.

27 Aidit's speech to the CPSU Twenty-second Congress, *HR*, Oct., 27, 1961.

28 Aidit, *Indonesian Society*, p. 57.

29 D. N. Aidit, "Djadikan PKI Pemimpin Tani jang Sedjati ["Make PKI the True Leader of the Peasants"], *HR*, July 18, 1961.

30 Aidit, *Indonesian Society*, p. 64.

VII. THE NATIONAL UNITED FRONT

1 PKI, *Program PKI* (Djakarta, 1954), pp. 21-22. This statement was repeated in the PKI program endorsed by the September, 1959, congress (Njoto, *Tentang Program PKI* [*Concerning PKI's Program*] [Djakarta, 1959], p. 52).

2 D. N. Aidit, *Perkuat Persatuan Nasional dan Persatuan Komunis!* [*Strengthen National Unity and Communist Unity!*] (Djakarta, 1961), p. 24.

3 Herbert Feith, "Indonesian Politics, 1949-1957: The Decline of Representative Government" (Ph.D. dissertation, Cornell University, 1961), p. 227.

4 *Sin Po*, Sept. 12, 1950.

5 Both Sukarno and Hatta are nonparty. However, Sukarno has been closely associated with PNI, whose antecedent he helped to establish in 1927, while Hatta leaned toward Masjumi and the democratic socialist PSI.

6 *Sin Po*, Oct. 27, 1950.

7 This sentence is, of course, a broad generalization and ignores the many differences of opinion in all parties. It does, however, hold for the attitudes of the dominant groups in Masjumi and PNI.

8 Editorial, "Seluruh Rakjat Anti-KMB" ["The Whole People against the RTC"], *BM* (Feb. 1, 1951), p. 56.

9 *Sin Po*, March 21, 1951.

10 *Ibid.*, March 22, 1951.

11 *Loc. cit.*

12 These documents are given in *BM* (March 15–April 1, 1951), pp. 168-171.

13 Editorial in *ibid.*, pp. 161-164.

14 M. H. Lukman, "Mewudjudkan Front Nasional" ["To Realize the National Front"], *ibid.*, p. 172.

15 *Sin Po*, May 12, 1951.

16 Under the 1950 Indonesian constitution, when a cabinet resigned the president appointed one or more cabinet formateurs to form the next cabinet. The formateurs were not necessarily party leaders or even members of political parties, and they did not necessarily sit in the subsequent cabinet.

17 *Sin Po*, April 11, 1951.

18 See the speeches made in parliament by Sakirman on May 31, June 11, and June 15, 1951, given in *Risalah Perundingan 1951* [*Indonesian Parliamentary Debates*], X, 4242-4254; XI, 4760-4772, 5116-5117.

19 *Sin Po*, May 24, 1951.

20 D. N. Aidit, *Perdjuangan dan Adjaran-Adjaran Karl Marx* [*The Struggle and the Teachings of Karl Marx*] (Djakarta, 1950), p. 5; Njoto, "Pemalsuan Marxisme" ["Falsification of Marxism"], *BM* (Jan. 1-15, 1951), p. 17.

318   *Notes*

21 "Keterangan CC PKI tentang Peristiwa Madiun" ["PKI Central Committee Statement on the Madiun Affair"], *Sin Po*, Feb. 10, 1951; Mirajadi, "Tiga Tahun Provokasi Madiun" ["Three Years since the Madiun Provocation"], *BM* (Aug.-Sept., 1951), pp. 40, 45-46, 48.

22 *Sin Po*, July 7, 1951.

23 *HR*, Aug. 7, 1951.

24 PKI, *40 Tahun PKI* [*PKI 40 Years*] (Djakarta, 1960), p. 69.

25 *HR*, Aug. 25, 1951; Alamputra, "Mengatasi Kelemahan-Kelemahan" ["Overcoming Weaknesses"], *BM* (Aug.-Sept., 1951), p. 22.

26 Sobromalisi, "Tentang Perebutan Kekuasaan" ["Concerning Seizure of Power"], *BM* (Aug.-Sept. 1951), pp. 12-15; Alamputra, *op. cit.*, pp. 20-21.

27 Iman, "Razzia Agustus: Satu Bagian dari Rentjana Pengeluasan Perang Amerika" ["The August Arrests: A Part of the American Warmongering Plan"], *BM* (Aug.-Sept., 1951), p. 9.

28 *HR*, Aug. 24, 1951.

29 *HR*, Dec. 19, 1951.

30 *Risalah Perundingan 1951*, XIV, 7415.

31 PKI, *Djalan Baru untuk Republik Indonesia* [*New Road for the Indonesian Republic*] (7th ed.; Djakarta, 1953), pp. 31-33.

32 M. H. Lukman, *Tentang Front Persatuan Nasional* [*Concerning the National United Front*] (Djakarta, 1960), p. 54; see also p. 55.

33 See, for example, the appeals made in parliament by Communist representative Hutomo Supardan on October 2, 1950, and by his colleague Peris Pardede on October 9, 1950 (*Risalah Perundingan 1950/1951*, III, 1187; IV, 1678). See also M. H. Lukman, "Menudju Front Persatuan" ["Toward the United Front"], *BM* (Feb. 1, 1951), pp. 57-59.

34 D. N. Aidit, *Indonesian Society and the Indonesian Revolution* (Djakarta, 1957), p. 51.

35 *HR*, Aug. 16, 1951.

36 *PKI-B* (April 26, 1952), p. 9.

37 PKI, *Program PKI*, pp. 19-20; Njoto, *Tentang Program PKI*, p. 51.

38 In PKI usage, the term cadre is applied to an active Party worker with fairly important responsibilities within the Party. The implication is that a cadre has received relatively thorough political education.

39 Sakirman, "Apa Arti Sokongan PKI kepada UUD 1945 dan Demokrasi Terpimpin" ["The Meaning of PKI's Support for the 1945 Constitution and Guided Democracy"], Part I, *BM* (May-June 1960), pp. 213-214.

40 D. N. Aidit, "Bersatu untuk Menjelesaikan Tuntutan Revolusi Agustus 1945" ["Unite To Complete the Demands of the August 1945 Revolution"], *HR*, Aug. 1, 1956.

41 Also see below, pp. 125-126, 234.

42 This quotation is from Aidit's report to the PKI Central Committee plenum held at the end of December, 1960 (D. N. Aidit, "Madju Terus Mengempur Imperialisme dan Feodalisme!" ["Continue To Advance To Destroy Imperialism and Feudalism!"], *HR*, Jan. 2, 1961).

43 This quotation is from Anwar Sanusi's speech to the PKI Central Committee plenum held at the end of December, 1960 (*HR*, Jan. 18, 1961).

44 *PKI-B* (March 7, 1952), pp. 3-6; PKI, *40 Tahun PKI*, p. 72.

45 Aidit, "Bersatu."

VIII. THE PARTY LEADERSHIP

1 PKI, *Putusan-Putusan Sidang Pleno Central Comite Partai Komunis Indonesia* [*Decisions of the PKI Central Committee Plenum Meeting*] (Djakarta, 1953), p. 4.

2 "Resolusi Terhadap Kawan Tan Ling Djie" ["Resolution Concerning Comrade Tan Ling Djie"], *ibid.*, pp. 4-5.

3 *PKI-B* (July 25, 1953), p. 109.

4 PKI, *op. cit.*, p. 4.

5 For brief biographies of Sakirman, see Parlaungan, *Hasil Rakjat Memilih Tokoh-Tokoh Parlemen* [*The Results of the People's Election of Members of Parliament*] (Djakarta, 1956), pp. 286-287; *HR*, Sept. 7, 1955.

6 D. N. Aidit, "Some Results of the Fifth National Congress of the Indonesian Communist Party," *FALP*, Oct. 15, 1954, p. 3.

7 *TI*, March 18, 1954.

8 *HR*, July 4, 1956.

9 *HR*, March 22, 1954.

10 *HR*, Aug. 9, 1955.

11 *HR*, Aug. 6, 1956.

12 The number of PKI representatives in parliament increased from 19 before to 32 after the September, 1955, elections; PKI had 60 members elected to the Constituent Assembly in the December, 1955, elections; and PKI representation in the regional and local councils of Java increased from a negligible number to 624 in 1956, when the councils were formed on the basis of the 1955 parliamentary elections, and to 973 in the latter half of 1957 after local elections had been held.

13 D. N. Aidit, "Fase Baru dan Penjesuaian Organisasi Dengan Situasi" ["A New Phase and Bringing the Organization into Line with the Situation"], *BM* (March-April, 1958), pp. 144-149; "Putusan-Putusan Sidang Pleno ke-VI Central Comite PKI" ["Decisions of the Sixth Plenary Session of the PKI Central Committee"], *ibid.*, p. 153.

14 PKI, *Dokumen-Dokumen Kongres Nasional ke-VI PKI* [*Documents of PKI's Sixth National Congress*], I (Djakarta, 1960), 218-220.

15 *PKI dan Perwakilan* (Dec., 1956), p. 201. In 1958 they were reported to be only ordinary members of the group's nine-man leadership committee (*ibid.*, [Fourth Quarter, 1958], p. 29).

16 *HR*, Feb. 13, 1963.

IX. THE EXPANSION AND EDUCATION OF PARTY MEMBERSHIP

1 This figure is deduced from Aidit's statement (D. N. Aidit, "Ideological Work in the Communist Party of Indonesia," *World Marxist Review* [July, 1959], p. 24) that there were 7,910 full and candidate members at the beginning of 1952, and from the undoubted growth of the Party during 1951. There is doubt, however, as to the accuracy of Aidit's figures. At another time he stated that PKI membership had reached "the teens of thousands" (belasan ribu) by August, 1951 (D. N. Aidit, "Menudju Persatuan Nasional dengan Semangat Revolusi Agustus" ["Toward National Unity with the Spirit of the August Revolution"], *PKI-B* [Aug., 1954], p. 102).

On the other hand, this apparent discrepancy could be explained if the government's mass arrest of Communists in August, 1951, had caused many members to break temporarily their contact with the Party through fear of further government action.

2 *Sin Po*, Sept. 26, 1950.

3 *BM* (Nov. 1, 1950), pp. 186-187.

4 See *BM* (March 1, 1951), pp. 156-158, for the details of the reorganization of the Party in Sumatra.

5 D. N. Aidit, "Garis-Garis Pokok Perdjuangan Ideologi Didalam PKI" ["The Fundamental Lines of the Ideological Struggle in PKI"] *BM* (May 15-June 1, 1951), p. 265. Kalimantan is the Indonesian name for Borneo, Sulawesi is the name for Celebes, and Nusatenggara is the name given to the Lesser Sundas stretching from Bali in the west to the Indonesian part of Timor in the east.

6 D. N. Aidit, *The Birth and Growth of the Communist Party of Indonesia* (Djakarta, 1958), p. 38. George McTurnan Kahin, "Indonesian Politics and Nationalism," in William L. Holland, ed., *Asian Nationalism and the West* (New York, 1953), p. 189, states that in August, 1951, 15,000 persons were arrested, of whom many were Communists. I can see no reason, however, why Aidit should have understated the magnitude of the arrests.

7 D. N. Aidit, "Membolsewikkan PKI" ["Bolshevizing PKI"], *BM* (March 1, 1951), pp. 129-134.

8 PKI, *Konstitusi PKI* (Djakarta, 1951), p. 18.

9 Aidit, "Garis-Garis," p. 266.

10 *BM* (March 1, 1951), pp. 132, 156.

11 *PKI-B* (March 7, 1952), pp. 6-7.

12 PKI, *Konstitusi;* PKI, *Lahirnja Partai Komunis Indonesia dan Perkembangannja* [*The Birth and Growth of the Communist Party of Indonesia*] (Djakarta, 1951).

13 Joseph Stalin, *Masaalah Tani* [*The Peasant Question*] (Djakarta, 1951).

14 D. N. Aidit, *Lenin dan Indonesia* [*Lenin and Indonesia*] (Djakarta, 1960), pp. 31-32.

15 *BM* (April 15-May 1, 1951), p. 253.

16 *HR*, April 8, 1952.

17 D. N. Aidit, *Djalan ke Demokrasi Rakjat bagi Indonesia* [*The Indonesian Road to People's Democracy*] (Djakarta, 1955), p. 45.

18 Because Party work among the peasants was still little developed, the small Communist-led and Communist-influenced peasant organizations could not have been expected to give the Party significant support at the time of the August arrests. But most of the cadres and almost all the members of SOBSI also responded with indifference to the arrest of the PKI and SOBSI leaders.

19 D. N. Aidit, "Madju Terus untuk Sukses-Sukses jang Lebih Besar" ["Continue To Advance for Greater Successes"], in *Pilihan Tulisan* [*Selected Works*], I (Djakarta, 1959), 203. See also Aidit, *Djalan ke Demokrasi*, p. 46, and PKI, *40 Tahun PKI* [*PKI 40 Years*] (Djakarta, 1960), p. 72.

20 *PKI-B* (March 7, 1952), pp. 3-6.

21 Sudisman, "Peladjaran Fundamentil Selama 32 Tahun Berdirinja PKI" ["The Fundamental Lesson of 32 Years of PKI"], *PKI-B* (May 20, 1952), p. 12.

22 PKI, *Bahan-Bahan untuk Kongres Nasional ke-VI Partai Komunis Indonesia* [*Materials for PKI's Sixth National Congress*] (Djakarta, 1958), p. 54.

23 *PKI-B* (May, 1953), pp. 78-81.

24 A fraction is a group of Communists operating in a non-Party organization such as parliament, a trade-union, and a peasant association.

25 Herbert Feith states (*The Indonesian Elections of 1955* [Ithaca, 1957], p. 29) that before 1953 PKI had established itself in villages in many plantation and mining areas and in some other areas, but that PKI political activity was largely confined to the towns.

26 Boyd R. Compton, *Indonesian Communism: The Ranks Swell*, American Universities' Field Staff Report (New York, 1954), p. 8.

27 Aidit, *Djalan ke Demokrasi*, p. 47.

28 *HR*, Oct. 23, 1953.

29 M. H. Lukman, "Tentang Agitasi dan Propaganda Partai" ["Concerning Party Agitation and Propaganda"], *BM* (Sept., 1952), pp. 62-63.

30 Aidit, *Djalan ke Demokrasi*, p. 60.

31 Sudisman, "J. V. Stalin, Pentjipta dan Organisator Partai Komunis" ["J. V. Stalin, Communist Party Creator and Organizer"], *BM* (March, 1953), p. 111.

32 *Ibid.,* p. 110. The Indonesian works were the PKI constitution and agrarian program; *Djalan Baru untuk Republik Indonesia* [*New Road for the Indonesian Republic*]; *Kewadjiban Front Persatuan Buruh* [*The Duty of the Workers' United Front*]; *Lahirnja;* and D. N. Aidit, *Menempuh Djalan Rakjat* [*Along the People's Road*]. The Chinese works were Mao Tse-tung, *New Democracy and People's Democratic Dictatorship;* Liu Shao-chi, *The Mass Line* and *Nationalism and Internationalism;* and Kian Ling, *The Method of Thought, Work, Criticism and Self-Criticism.* Joseph Stalin, *The National Question* and *Dialectical and Historical Materialism*, and Leontiev, *Introduction to Marxist Political Economy*, were the Russian works.

33 *PKI-B* (May, 1953), pp. 78-81.

34 *HR*, Oct. 31, 1953; Feb. 25, 1954.

35 In October, 1960, the government withdrew the publication permits of most political journals. Among them were all the journals issued by the PKI Central Committee, and most of the journals issued by the national councils of the Communist mass organizations.

36 *PKI-B* (May, 1953), p. 79.

37 *Ibid.*, p. 80.

38 *PKI-B* (Oct. 10, 1952).

39 The evidence consists of the notices appearing in *Harian Rakjat* of the literature available in the Party's bookshops.

40 Compton, *op. cit.*, p. 6.

41 *PKI-B* (Feb. 10, 1953), pp. 18-19.

42 D. N. Aidit, "Kongres Nasional ke-V Partai Komunis Indonesia" ["PKI's Fifth National Congress"], in *Pilihan Tulisan*, I, 280; *FALP*, Jan. 22, 1954, p. 6.

43 Aidit, *Pilihan Tulisan*, I, 281.

44 "Resolusi Terhadap Kawan Tan Ling Djie," ["Resolution Concerning Comrade Tan Ling Djie"] in PKI, *Putusan-Putusan Sidang Pleno Central Comite Partai Komunis Indonesia* [*Decisions of PKI Central Committee Plenum*] (Djakarta, 1953), pp. 4-5.

45 "Referat Tentang Tan Ling Djie-isme" ["Report on Tan Ling Djie-ism"], *HR*, March 19, 1954.

46 *Loc. cit.*

47 PKI, *40 Tahun PKI*, p. 77.

48 D. N. Aidit, "Some Results," *FALP*, Oct. 15, 1954, p. 3. A candidate member is one who has not yet completed the period of candidacy (of from six months to

five years, depending on the candidate member's social and political background) which is demanded of all prospective Party members. A candidate member has the duties and rights of a full member, except that he may not vote in Party meetings, nor may he be elected to Party offices. The period of candidacy is used "to give basic Party education to the candidate member and also ensure supervision by Party organizations of his political quality" (PKI Djawa Tengah, *Konstitusi Partai Komunis Indonesia* [Semarang, 1955], pp. 31-34; PKI, *AD-ART (Konstitusi) PKI [PKI's Constitution]* [Djakarta, 1962], pp. 39-42).

49 D. N. Aidit, "Perkuat Persatuan Nasional dan Perkuat Partai!" ["Strengthen National Unity and Strengthen the Party!"], in *Pilihan Tulisan,* I, 297.

50 *FALP,* Nov. 19, 1954, p. 2; *BM* (Feb.-March, 1956), p. 112.

51 Feith, *op. cit.,* p. 24.

52 D. N. Aidit, *Untuk Kemenangan Front Nasional dalam Pemilihan Umum [For the Victory of the National Front in the General Elections]* (Djakarta, 1955), p. 25.

53 D. N. Aidit, "Haridepan Gerakan Tani Indonesia" ["The Future of the Indonesian Peasant Movement"], *BM* (July, 1953), pp. 332-340.

54 A. van Marle, "The First Indonesian Parliamentary Elections," *Indonesie,* IX (1956), 262.

55 D. N. Aidit, *Untuk Persatuan jang Lebih Luas dari Semua Kekuatan Nasional di Indonesia [For the Broader Unity of all National Forces in Indonesia]* (Djakarta, 1955), pp. 31-32.

56 See, for example, Aidit, *Untuk Kemenangan,* pp. 27-28; D. N. Aidit, *Pertahankan Republik Proklamasi 1945! [Defend the 1945 Proclamation Republic!]* (Djakarta, 1955), pp. 28-29; and M. H. Lukman, "Tugas Partai Sesudah Pemilihan Umum" ["The Party's Task after the General Elections"], *BM* (Nov.-Dec. 1955), pp. 379-381.

57 Njoto, "Masaalah Pendidikan didalam Partai" ["The Question of Education in the Party"], in D. N. Aidit, *Bersatu untuk Menjelesaikan Tuntutan-Tuntutan Revolusi Agustus 1945 [Unite To Complete the Demands of the August 1945 Revolution]* (Djakarta, 1956), p. 64.

58 Lukman, "Tugas Partai," p. 380.

59 Njoto, "Masaalah Pendidikan," pp. 64-75.

60 *HR,* Feb. 25, 1954; Jan. 26, 1955; Jan. 21, 1956.

61 *HR,* Jan. 21, 1956.

62 *HR,* March 23, 1956.

63 *BM* (Jan. 1955), inside front cover; Njoto, "10 Tahun Bintang Merah" ["10 Years of Bintang Merah"], *BM* (Nov.-Dec.; 1955), p. 371.

64 *HR,* Nov. 4, 1954. In 1955 the PKI Central Java province committee published the Party constitution, including the Party's general program, in Javanese. Perhaps other province committees published it in other regional languages.

65 *HR,* Dec. 31, 1955.

66 PKI, *Konstitusi PKI* (3d ed.; Djakarta, 1954), pp. 56-57.

67 D. N. Aidit, "Mengaktifkan Grup Partai" ["To Activate the Party Group"], in *Pilihan Tulisan,* I, 361-366.

68 M. H. Lukman, "Bagaimana Mentjiptakan Kader Wanita" ["How To Form Women Cadres"], *KP,* Jan. 1, 1955, pp. 5-6.

69 D. N. Aidit "Fase Baru," *BM* (March-April, 1958), pp. 149-152; "Ideological Work," pp. 24-25; *Untuk Demokrasi dan Kabinet Gotong Rojong [For Democracy and a Mutual Coöperation Cabinet]* (Djakarta, 1959), pp. 131-133; and "Ubah Imbangan Kekuatan untuk Melaksanakan Konsepsi Presiden Soekarno 100%!"

[("Change the Balance of Power in Order To Implement President Sukarno's Concept 100%!"], *HR,* July 5, 1957; also Amir Anwar Sanusi, "Results of the First Three-Year Plan," mimeographed translation (Djakarta, 1959) pp. 2-5; and PKI, *Bahan-Bahan,* pp. 55-56; *Resolusi tentang Laporan Umum CC PKI kepada Kongres Nasional ke-VI* [*Resolution Concerning the PKI Central Committee's General Report to the Sixth National Congress*] (Djakarta, 1959), pp. 69-70, 77-80; *PKI 10 Tahun,* pp. 88-90.

70 Aidit, "Ideological Work," p. 24.

71 PKI, *Bahan-Bahan,* p. 53.

72 PKI, *Resolusi tentang Laporan Umum,* p. 66.

73 D. N. Aidit, "The Sixth National Congress of the Communist Party of Indonesia," *RI* (Nov.-Dec., 1959), p. 45.

74 *Loc. cit.*

75 Suharti Suwarto, "Mendjelang Konferensi Nasional Wanita Komunis" ["Awaiting the National Conference of Communist Women"], *BM* (Sept., 1957), p. 343.

76 Setiati Surasto, "Memperluas Keanggotaan Partai dikalangan Wanita" ["To Extend Party Membership among Women"], *KP* (Feb., 1957), pp. 19-21; Suharti Suwarto, "Mendjelang," p. 342; Ibrahim, "Sedikit Pengalaman tentang Menjelenggarakan KPS Wanita" ["Some Experience in Organizing a Section-Level Women's Political Course"], *KP* (Dec., 1958), pp. 242-244.

77 Suharti Suwarto, "Mendjelang," pp. 343-344.

78 For the main documents of the conference, see *BM* (June, 1958), pp. 241-285.

79 PKI, *Bahan-Bahan,* p. 54; Anwar Sanusi, *op. cit.,* p. 3.

80 Anwar Sanusi, *op. cit.,* p. 3. This report contains most of the published statistics on the results of the plan.

81 Parjono, "Tjara Mempersiapkan Peluasan Anggota untuk Memperkuat Partai" ["The Method of Preparing the Extension of Membership in Order To Strengthen the Party"], *KP* (May, 1958), pp. 56-59.

82 Under the provisions of the April 1951, March, 1954, September, 1959, and April, 1962, Party constitutions, anyone wishing to enter PKI has to spend from six months to five years as a candidate, depending on his social origin and previous political activity. Even after the period of candidacy his promotion to full membership requires sponsorship by long-standing Party members and the endorsement of higher committees.

83 This evidence is discussed below in the section dealing with Communist funds in Indonesia, pp. 111-112.

84 PKI, *Resolusi tentang Laporan Umum,* p. 79.

85 Aidit, "Ubah Imbangan Kekuatan."

86 *Loc. cit.*

87 Aidit, "Ideological Work," pp. 24-25.

88 Ibrahim, *op. cit.,* pp. 242-244.

86 Wahjoedi, "Pengalaman Mengadjar dalam Sekolah Politik" ["Experience in Teaching in Political Schools"], *KP* (Dec., 1958), p. 241.

90 *Ibid.,* pp. 240-241.

91 Achmad Sjafii, "Pengalaman Sekolah Politik" ["Experience with a Political School"], *KP* (Aug., 1958), pp. 148-149.

92 Simat, "Sekolah Politik dan Pengaruhnja" ["Political Schools and Their Influence"], *KP* (June, 1958), p. 81.

93 Aidit, "Ubah Imbangan Kekuatan."

94 Anwar Sanusi, *op. cit.,* p. 4.

95 Aidit, "The Sixth National Congress," p. 45.

96 For the main documents of the Party conference on work among women, see *BM* (June, 1958), pp. 241-285.

97 For the main documents of the seminar on economics, see *Ekonomi dan Masjarakat*, nos. 2-3 (1959).

98 For the main documents of the Party conference on work among peasants and fishermen, see *BM* (April-May, 1959), pp. 121-222.

99 B. O. Hutapea, "Some Lessons from the First National Peasants Conference of the CPI," *RI* (Aug., 1959), p. 33.

100 "Laporan Mengenai Pekerdjaan Partai dikalangan kaum Tani" ["Report on Party Work among the Peasants"], *BM* (April-May, 1959), p. 138.

101 Siswojo, "Beladjar-Sendiri" ["Self-Study"], *KP* (Nov., 1956), pp. 21-23; Jono, "Beladjar Sendiri," *KP* (May, 1958), pp. 65-67.

102 Anwar Sanusi, *op. cit.*, p. 4.

103 Rewang, "Memperbaiki Gerakan Mempeladjari Putusan-Putusan CC dikalangan Anggauta dan Tjalon-Anggauta" ["To Improve the Movement among Members and Candidate Members To Study Central Committee Decisions"], *KP* (May, 1958), pp. 60-62.

104 *HR*, Feb. 4, 1957.

105 *HR*, Dec. 31, 1960.

106 Njoto, "Soal Pendidikan dan kaum Inteligensia" ["The Problem of Education and the Intellectuals"], *HR*, July 5, 1957.

107 *HR*, Jan. 3, 1959.

108 Aidit, *Pilihan Tulisan*, I, II, (Djakarta, 1959, 1960).

109 N., "Buku-Buku Teori dalam Bahasa-Bahasa Daerah ["Books of Theory in Regional Languages"], *BM* (Jan.-Feb., 1957), p. 76.

110 In 1960 the price per copy of the PKI periodicals in Indonesian was about 3.50 rupiahs for *Bintang Merah*, one rupiah for *Kehidupan Partai*, six rupiahs for *PKI dan Perwakilan*, four rupiahs for *Mimbar Komunis*, seven rupiahs for *Ilmu Marxis*, and eight rupiahs for *Ekonomi dan Masjarakat*. The daily wage for an urban or estate worker was about 10 to 20 rupiahs; for an agricultural laborer, 7.50 to 15.

111 See, for example, Kisman, "Sedikit Pengalaman Mengusahakan Perpustakaan" ["Some Experience in Organizing a Library"], *KP* (Dec., 1958), pp. 245-247.

112 Wahjoedi, *op. cit.*, pp. 240-241.

113 *HR*, Sept. 24, 1958.

114 *HR*, Sept. 22, 1958.

115 *HR*, Nov. 3, 1958.

116 *HR*, Jan. 20, 1959.

117 *HR*, Sept. 22, 1958.

118 Aidit, "Ideological Work," p. 25.

119 Most of the following information on UNRA was obtained from Siswojo, "Intensify the Anti-Imperialist Struggle on the Ideological Front," *RI* (Sept.-Oct., 1959), p. 32; *HR*, Sept. 28, 1959; and especially from interviews with H. Porkas, the national secretary of UNRA, Djaetun, the president of UNRA in Jogjakarta, and Sujitno, a member of the secretariat of the Surabaja UNRA.

120 In 1960 the entrance fee was 50 rupiahs; the monthly fee for each course was 20 to 30 rupiahs.

121 The editor of a Surabaja newspaper told me of the example of the local newspaper *Trompet Masjarakat* which was led by a non-Communist but which fre-

Notes

325

quently carried pro-Communist material because its journalists were Communists.

122 *RI* (Sept.-Oct., 1959), p. 33.

123 *RI* (Feb., 1959), p. 6.

124 Aidit, "The Sixth National Congress," p. 40.

125 M. H. Lukman, *Tentang Konstitusi PKI* [*Concerning PKI's Constitution*] (Djakarta, 1959), pp. 54-55; Njoto, *Tentang Program PKI* [*Concerning PKI's Program*] (Djakarta, 1959), pp. 8-9.

126 D. N. Aidit, "Building the Organization Is Important, but Building Ideology Is Even More Important," *RI*, Supplement (June-July, 1959).

127 PKI, *Bahan-Bahan*, pp. 68-69.

128 Aidit, *Untuk Demokrasi*, pp. 156-157.

129 D. N. Aidit, "For National Unity," *World Marxist Review* (Feb., 1960), p. 26.

130 The question of solidarity within PKI during the period of the Aidit leadership is discussed below, pp. 101-106.

131 Djokosudjono, "Sukseskan Gerakan Achiran dan Siapkan Diri Melaksanakan Plan 4 Tahun Partai" ["Make the Concluding Movement a Success and Prepare Oneself To Implement the Party's 4-Year Plan"], *HR*, Feb. 27, 1963.

132 D. N. Aidit, *Untuk Demokrasi, Persatuan dan Mobilisasi* [*For Democracy, Unity, and Mobilization*] (Djakarta, 1962), p. 81.

133 Djokosudjono, *op. cit.*

134 In March, 1961, circulation of *Harian Rakjat* was 60,000. The goal was then to reach 100,000 by the end of January 1962. On June 1, 1961, however, the government reduced newsprint to all newspapers with the excuse that there was insufficient foreign exchange for more. *Harian Rakjat* was cut back to 44,000 where it stayed until at least mid-1963.

135 *HR*, July 27, 1962.

136 In the Sixth Congress, Lukman had issued a directive: "In attracting new members, orientation to the working class in the towns and villages is important in order to safeguard the composition of the Party membership so that the percentage of the proletarian element in the Party, although it does not constitute a majority, at least remains proportionate to elements from classes other than the working class." In order to increase the percentage of working-class full members, Lukman called on all Party committees to devote special attention to the provision of elementary political education for working-class candidate members so that they could become full members as soon as the minimum period of candidacy was completed (Lukman, *Tentang Konstitusi PKI*, p. 37).

137 The results of the national education seminar are given in PKI, *Untuk Pendidikan Nasional, Kerakjatan dan Ilmiah!* [*For National, Popular, and Scientific Education!*] (Djakarta, 1962).

138 For the main speeches and the conclusions of the conference, see *HR*, July 18, 20, 21, 24, 25, 1961; also PKI, *Konfernas Tani Ke-II PKI* [*PKI Second Peasants' Conference*] (Djakarta, 1962).

139 The main documents of the Seventh Congress have been published: Aidit, *Untuk Demokrasi Persatuan dan Mobilisasi*; M. H. Lukman, *Tentang Konstitusi PKI Dan Penpres No. 7/1959* [*Concerning the PKI Constitution and Presidential Decision No. 7, 1959*] (Djakarta, 1962); PKI, *Resolusi-Resolusi Kongres Nasional ke-VII (Luarbiasa) Partai Komunis Indonesia* [*Resolutions of the PKI Seventh (Extraordinary) National Congress*] (Djakarta, 1962); and PKI, *Program Partai Komunis Indonesia* (Djakarta, 1962).

140 D. N. Aidit, *Berani, Berani, Sekali Lagi Berani!* [*Courageous, Courageous, and*

Again Courageous!] (Djakarta, 1963), pp. 67-70; Djokosudjono, *op. cit.*

141 Aidit, *Berani*, p. 67.

142 It also means that the collection of information on PKI is made more difficult because there are no important ex-Communists from the post-1950 period.

143 D. N. Aidit, *Madju Terus Menggempur Imperialisme dan Feodalisme! [Con-
tinue To Advance To Destroy Imperialism and Feudalism!]* (Djakarta, 1961), p. 25.

144 There is the danger for the Party leaders, however, that the more they give
political education to their cadres, and the more Communist literature they make
available in Indonesian, the more they increase the possibility that a politically
self-assured body of cadres might be created from which they could be attacked on
Marxist-Leninist grounds. Such a danger would loom large if national or international imperatives forced an alteration in the Party's present over-all strategy, or
if a split occurred within the Aidit leadership.

145 Thirty-nine persons were elected to parliament on the PKI ticket in September 1955; 60 were elected to the Constituent Assembly in December 1955. After
the September 1955 elections, PKI was allocated 624 seats in the provincial and
local councils in Java alone, and in the 1957 local elections increased them to 973.
Since 1956 PKI and/or its mass organizations have received a number of seats in
the National Council, the Supreme Advisory Council, and the National Planning
Council. Between 55 and 75 members of the new, appointed parliament, installed in
June 1960, owe their positions to membership in PKI or its mass organizations,
as do about 100 to 150 members of the new Provisional People's Consultative
Assembly.

146 From the little the PKI leaders have published concerning opposition within
the Party to their policies or instructions, it is clear that many of the lower committees give formal agreement to policies and then quietly shelve those they do
not like. For example, some committees which opposed the concept of a mass
party "forgot" to implement the first membership drive, while some have continued to be slow in promoting candidate members to full membership. Many
committees which were unable to see the value of women members did not openly
question or oppose the directive to increase women membership; they quietly
ignored it. Still other committees have ignored but not openly questioned directives
to collect membership dues or to forward stipulated percentages of those collected
to the higher committees.

147 Alimin's statement is given in full in *HR*, July 4, 1956.

148 Aidit, *Bersatu untuk Menjelesaikan*, pp. 97-98; *HR*, Aug. 9, 1956.

149 Alimin, *Peladjaran Karl Marx [The Teachings of Karl Marx]* (Djakarta, 1958);
Alimin, *Perdjuangan Klas Karl Marx [The Class Struggle of Karl Marx]* (Djakarta, 1959).

150 In April, 1963, Aidit officially thanked President Sukarno for having provided
Alimin with a government house. The obstreperous veteran was apparently returned once more to the Party's good graces (*HR*, April 6, 1963).

151 PKI, *40 Tahun PKI*, pp. 31-51.

152 Herbert Feith, "Indonesian Politics, 1949-1957; The Decline of Representative Government" (Ph.D. dissertation, Cornell University, 1961), p. 327; Kahin,
op. cit., p. 140.

153 MMC stands for Merbabu-Merapi Complex. Merbabu and Merapi are two
adjacent volcanoes in Central Java.

154 George McTurnan Kahin, "Indonesia," in Kahin, ed., *Major Governments*

of Asia (Ithaca, 1958), p. 557 n. 25. The anti-Communist newspaper *Pedoman* on January 14, 1955, also mentioned rumors that the MMC area was being used to train military cadres.

155 Mao Tse-tung's "Strategic Problems of China's Revolutionary War" was serialized in *Bintang Merah* and also published in booklet form; Vo Nguyen Giap's *What is the Liberation Army?* was published in booklet form. These two works were made available in Indonesian at a time when very few foreign Communist materials had been translated. However, as the military phase of the revolution had just been completed, there was still considerable interest in materials on guerrilla warfare. Furthermore, as the preface to Mao's work in booklet form indicates, the young PKI leaders may have expected that Indonesia would have to take up arms again in order to rid herself of the semicolonial status imposed by the Round Table Conference agreement.

156 See, for example, *Ichtisar Gerakan Tani* [*Survey of the Peasant Movement*] (April, 1951), pp. 2-3, and *HR*, Nov. 19, 1954.

157 PKI, "Praktek Gangster Amerika" ["American Gangster Practices"], *BM* (May 15-June 1, 1951), pp. 276-277.

158 "Masaalah Tani di Indonesia" ["The Peasant Question in Indonesia"], *BM* (June 15-July 1, 1951), p. 304.

159 For a description of this effort at image building, see below, pp. 121-127.

160 *Keng Po*, Jan. 13, 1955; *Pedoman*, Jan. 14, 1955.

161 *Geledek*, May 31, 1959.

162 *Nasional*, April 11, 1960.

163 *Bupati* is the title given to the civil servant in charge of a *kabupaten; pamong pradja* is the name given to the members of the rural administrative civil service.

X. COMMUNIST FUNDS IN INDONESIA

1 PKI, *Konstitusi PKI* (Djakarta, 1951), pp. 53-54.

2 M. H. Lukman, *Tentang Konstitusi PKI* (Djakarta, 1959), p. 90.

3 Amir Anwar Sanusi, "Sedikit tentang Penarikan Iuran dan Penjetorannja" ["Something on the Collection and Forwarding of Membership Dues"], *KP* (Oct. 1956), pp. 8-12.

4 Isk, "Mendjadikan Soal Keuangan Masaalah bagi Seluruh Partai" ["Make the Problem of Finances a Matter for the Whole Party"], *KP* (Nov., 1956), pp. 24-27.

5 For example, D. N. Aidit, "Ubah Imbangan Kekuatan," *HR*, July 5, 1957; D. N. Aidit, "Untuk Melantjarkan Pemasukan Uang Iuran" ["To Speed Up the Entry of Membership Dues"], *KP* (May, 1958), p. 67; and D. N. Aidit, *Untuk Demokrasi dan Kabinet Gotong Rojong* (Djakarta, 1959), p. 85.

6 Anwar Sanusi, *op. cit.*, pp. 11-12.

7 Aidit, "Untuk Melantjarkan Pemasukan," p. 67.

8 Concerning SOBSI, see SOBSI, *Mengatasi Keuangan dalam Serikat-Buruh* [*Overcoming the Problem of Finances in the Trade Unions*], (Djakarta, 1956); and Moh. Munir, *Pedoman Penjelesaian Plan Organisasi 1958* [*Survey of the Implementation of the 1958 Plan of Organization*] (Djakarta, 1959), p. 29. On BTI, see Djadi, "Sekali Lagi tentang Keuangan" ["Once Again about Finances"], *ST* (May, 1957), pp. 6, 15. For information on Gerwani, see Gerwani, *Meluaskan Aksi-Aksi untuk Memperkuat*

Tuntutan Hak-Hak Wanita-Anak-Anak dan Perdamaian [*Extending Actions To Strengthen the Demand for the Rights of Women and Children and for Peace*] (Djakarta, 1956), p. 34; and Gerwani, *Lebih Giat Meluaskan Gerakan untuk Terlaksananja Piagam Hak-Hak Wanita Indonesia* [*More Active in Extending the Movement for the Implementation of the Charter of Indonesian Women's Rights*] (Djakarta, 1958), pp. 78-79.

[9] PKI, *op. cit.*, p. 53.

[10] Lukman, *op. cit.*, p. 90.

[11] *HR*, Nov. 17, 1953.

[12] *HR*, Dec. 14, 1953. The new building was opened on August 19, 1954.

[13] *RI* (Sept.-Oct., 1959), p. 33.

[14] Ruslan, "Peranan Anggota/Tjalon-Anggota dalam Gerakan Dana Pemilihan DPRD" ["The Role of Members and Candidate Members in Financing the Local Elections"], *KP* (April, 1957), pp. 59-61.

[15] "Pengumpulkan Fonds Pemilihan Umum" ["Collect General Election Funds"], *KP* (March, 1955), p. 38; S. Ridwan, "Pekan Sokongan Sukarela" ["A Week of Voluntary Support"], *KP* (May 1, 1955), p. 72; Ruslan, *op. cit.*, p. 61.

[16] Aidit, "Ubah Imbangan Kekuatan."

[17] Hartojo, "Luaskan Aksi-Aksi kaum Tani untuk Mengembangkan Kekuatan Progresif" ["Extend Peasant Actions in Order To Develop the Progressive Force"], *ST* (Oct., 1957), p. 11.

[18] Jusuf Adjitorop, "Kongres jang didukung Rakjat" ["A Congress Supported by the People"], *BM* (Sept.-Oct., 1959), pp. 370-371.

[19] The produce collected consisted of over 5 tons of rice, 10 quintals of sugar, 5 quintals of coffee, 30 kilograms of tea, 234 kilograms of salted fish, over 1,000 coconuts, 10 quintals of cassava, more than one ton of vegetables, and 20,000 cigarettes.

[20] The surplus congress funds which went toward the construction of the house of culture may have been included in the 4 million rupiahs that were claimed to have been collected for the house.

[21] *HR*, May 9, 1962.

[22] Editorial, *ST* (March, 1957), p. 1.

[23] Mimeographed circular, Aug., 1960.

[24] See n. 145 on p. 326 for the number of Communists in parliament, the People's Consultative Assembly, the Constituent Assembly, and the local representative councils. The number in the Supreme Advisory Council and the National Planning Council is low.

[25] PKI, *Konstitusi PKI* (3d ed.; Djakarta, 1954), p. 64; Lukman, *op. cit.*, p. 90; PKI, *AD-ART (Konstitusi) PKI* (Djakarta, 1962), p. 92.

[26] Amir Anwar Sanusi, "The Results of the First Three-Year Plan," mimeographed (Djakarta, 1959), p. 3.

[27] *HR*, June 4, 1957.

[28] Compton, writing from East Java in April, 1956, repeated reports that branch chairmen of PKI were receiving 1,000 rupiahs per month, activists in any field a basic salary of 500 rupiahs (Boyd R. Compton, *Red Surabaja*, Institute of Current World Affairs Report [New York, 1956], pp. 6, 8). He commented: "It appears that no other Indonesian party can afford to pay out so much to its important lower-level workers."

[29] The extent of formal cadre training in PKI has been mentioned above; that in the Communist-led mass organizations is given below in the sections on the various organizations.

30 *BB*, Jan. 9, 1957, p. 5. By September, 1957, however, the campaign had brought in only 388,722 rupiahs (SOBSI, *Dokumen-Dokumen Konferensi Nasional (1957)* [Djakarta, 1958], p. 97).

31 Information from conversation with a member of the SOBSI headquarters staff.

32 Information from interviews with members of the East Java SOBSI headquarters.

33 The students taking part in schools are lodged together in hostels so that they can more easily participate in study and discussion groups and undertake self-study.

34 The cost of publication was greatly reduced when, in October 1960, the government withdrew the publication permits of all PKI Central Committee journals and most journals of the Communist-led mass organizations.

35 *PKI-B* (March 7, 1952), pp. 6-7; (Feb. 10, 1953), p. 19.

36 *Damai*, I (April, 1953), 16.

37 SOBSI, *Mengatasi Keuangan*, p. 18.

38 *BB*, March 13, 1957, p. 4.

39 Gerwani, *Lebih Giat*, p. 77.

40 Editorial, *ST* (March, 1957), p. 1; Adjitorop, *op. cit.*, p. 371; *HR*, May 9, 1962.

41 Herbert Feith, *The Indonesian Elections of 1955* (Ithaca, 1962), pp. 27-28.

42 Robert S. Elegant, *The Dragon's Seed* (New York, 1959), p. 247.

43 George McTurnan Kahin, "Indonesia," in Kahin, ed., *Major Governments of Asia* (Ithaca, 1958), p. 559.

44 Feith, *op. cit.*, p. 27.

45 A. Doak Barnett, *A Choice of Nationality: Overseas Chinese in Indonesia*, American Universities' Field Staff Report (New York, 1955), p. 26.

46 Herbert Feith, *The Wilopo Cabinet, 1952-1953: A Turning Point in Post-Revolutionary Indonesia* (Ithaca, 1958), pp. 37-38.

XI. THE CULTIVATION OF GENERAL APPEALS

1 *Sin Po*, Sept. 26, 1950.

2 For the major pronouncements of the Aidit leadership on the Madiun rebellion, see "Keterangan CC PKI tentang Peristiwa Madiun" ["PKI Central Committee Statement on the Madiun Affair"], *Sin Po*, Feb. 10, 1951; Mirajadi, "Tiga Tahun Provokasi Madiun" ["Three Years since the Madiun Provocation"], *BM* (Aug.-Sept., 1951), pp. 39-52; PKI, *Buku Putih tentang Peristiwa Madiun* [*White Book on the Madiun Affair*] (Djakarta, 1953); D. N. Aidit, *Aidit Menggugat Peristiwa Madiun* [*Aidit Accuses the Madiun Affair*] (Djakarta, 1955); D. N. Aidit, *Konfrontasi Peristiwa Madiun (1948); Peristiwa Sumatera (1956)* [*Confrontation with the Madiun Affair (1948); The Sumatran Affair (1956)*] (Djakarta, 1957); PKI, *PKI 40 Tahun* [*PKI 40 Years*] (Djakarta, 1960), pp. 56-58.

3 D. N. Aidit, *Menempuh Djalan Rakjat* [*Along the People's Road*] (4th ed.; Djakarta, 1954), p. 32.

4 Pantjasila was revealed by Sukarno on June 1, 1945, as the five basic principles of Indonesian nationalism: nationalism, internationalism, representative government, prosperity, and belief in God the Almighty. PKI adopted the Pantjasila *in toto* in October, 1959.

5 See, for example, Aidit's claim, made during the campaign for the Constituent Assembly elections of December 1955, that "PKI in the Constituent Assembly will

staunchly defend all elements of the Proclamation Republic that bind the greater part of the people. These elements, among others, are: the national flag Merah-Putih, the national anthem Indonesia Raja, the Indonesian language as the language of unity . . . and the Republic's motto 'Unity in Diversity' " (D. N. Aidit, *Pertahankan Republik Proklamasi 1945!* [*Defend the 1945 Proclamation Republic!*] [Djakarta, 1955], p. 32).

6 Herbert Feith, *The Wilopo Cabinet, 1952-1953: A Turning Point in Post-Revolutionary Indonesia* (Ithaca, 1958), pp. 86-87.

7 D. N. Aidit, *Djalan ke Demokrasi Rakjat bagi Indonesia* [*The Indonesian Road to People's Democracy*] (Djakarta, 1955), p. 38.

8 D. N. Aidit, *Untuk Demokrasi dan Kabinet Gotong Rojong* [*For Democracy and a Mutual Coöperation Cabinet*] (Djakarta, 1959), pp. 13, 12. Only after the Dutch agreed in August, 1962, to transfer West Irian to Indonesia, did the Aidit leadership declare that "the number one enemy of the Indonesian people and the most dangerous enemy at the present time is U.S. imperialism" (D. N. Aidit, *Berani, Berani, Sekali Lagi Berani!* [*Courageous, Courageous, and Again Courageous!*] [Djakarta, 1963] p. 28).

9 *Sin Po*, May 12, 1951. PKI has received help from both the USSR and China in its efforts to dispel Moslem fears about persecution of religion under communism. Many delegations consisting of or including Indonesian Moslems have been invited to both countries. Their impressions have been almost always favorable and have been widely broadcast by PKI. For an example of how well the Indonesian Moslem delegations are treated, see V. Jefremov, *Delegasi Ulama Indonesia di Sovjet Uni* [*An Indonesian Ulama Delegation in the Soviet Union*] (Djakarta, 1957). Both the Soviet Union and China publish periodicals in Indonesian which occasionally contain articles purporting to portray the free life of Islam under communism.

10 *PKI-B* (Aug., 25, 1953), p. 138.

11 D. N. Aidit, *Untuk Kemenangan Front Nasional dalam Pemilihan Umum* [*For the Victory of the National Front in the General Elections*] (Djakarta, 1955,) p. 23.

12 Amar Hanafiah, "Pengalaman Tjara Menarik Simpati Kiaji-Kiaji" ["Experience in Methods of Winning the Sympathy of Kiajis"], *KP* (May-Aug., 1957), pp. 69-72.

13 That the Aidit leadership is even willing to claim that work for the Party is the implementation of God's law is exemplified by the following quotation from a speech made by a Communist *kiaji*, in reply to one made by a Masjumi member, in the Constituent Assembly: "To the honorable Mr. H. Moh. Thaha, from my own *kampong* in Solo, I express my thanks for his urging me to return to Islam. But Mr. H. Moh. Thaha himself knows that I have never left Islam. And if the honorable gentleman urges me to return to Islam, in the meaning of to carry out God's law in political practice, then according to my own experience of 33 years in the Indonesian Communist Party (PKI), that is the only place to practice the law of God in its political meaning, and not anywhere else. When the honorable gentleman truly wishes to carry out God's law and to devote himself wholeheartedly to good works, then let him do it with me within the Indonesian Communist Party (PKI)" (from the speech of K. H. Achmad Dasuki Siradj, in *Tentang Dasar Negara Republik Indonesia* [*Concerning the Basis of the State of the Republic of Indonesia*], II [Djakarta, n.d.], 336).

14 *HR*, Dec. 9, 1955.

15 M. H. Lukman, *Tentang Konstitusi PKI* [*Concerning PKI's Constitution*] (Djakarta, 1959), pp. 25-26.

16 Reported by D. N. Aidit in *Perkuat Persatuan Nasional dan Persatuan Komu-*

nis! [Strengthen National Unity and Communist Unity!] (Djakarta, 1961), p. 26.

17 Herbert Feith, *The Indonesian Elections of 1955* (Ithaca, 1957), p. 15.

18 This statement requires slight modification. On March 9, 1962, Aidit and Lukman were appointed as advisory ministers without portfolio. They were not brought into the inner core of the cabinet.

19 PKI, "Construct a National Economy without New Foreign Investments," *RI* (March, 1957), pp. 28-33.

20 Runturambi's speech in the conference has been published in booklet form as Runturambi, *Politik Pembangunan Sekarang [Development Policy Now]* (Djakarta, 1957). Aidit's speech has been published as D. N. Aidit, "Let Us Carry Out Planned Construction of Our Country," *RI* (Dec., 1957), pp. 27-30.

21 Sobromalisi, "Tentang Perebutan Kekuasaan" ["Concerning Seizure of Power"], *BM* (Aug.-Sept., 1951), pp. 10-15.

22 For example, when, after the 1956 Soviet Communist Party congress, the PKI Central Committee considered the question of whether or not Indonesia could peacefully make the transition to a people's democracy, it concluded, echoing the 1951 article, that "it is a possiblity, and one which we must strive with all our strength to make reality. Thus, if it depends on the Communists, the best way, the ideal way, for transition to the system of people's democratic power . . . is the way of peace, the parliamentary way. Thus, if it depends on the Communists, the road of peace will be chosen because the Communists certainly are not murderers" (quoted in D. N. Aidit, "Revolusi Oktober dan Rakjat-Rakjat Timur" ["The October Revolution and the Peoples of the East"], *BM* [Oct.-Nov., 1957], p. 381).

23 There are a few exceptions to this generalization, but very few.

24 From the speech of S. Utarjo on October 29, 1951, *Risalah Perundingan 1951 [Indonesian Parliamentary Debates, 1951]*, XV, 7324.

25 D. N. Aidit, *Menudju Indonesia Baru [Toward a New Indonesia]* (2d ed.; Djakarta, 1955), p. 44.

26 *HR*, Oct. 18, 1952.

27 For a discussion of PKI's struggle against the restrictions on democracy after April, 1957, see below, p. 220 *et seq.*

XII. APPEALS TO SPECIFIC SECTIONS OF SOCIETY

1 M. H. Lukman, "Partai dan Organisasi Massa" ["The Party and Mass Organizations"], *BM* (Feb. 15, 1951), pp. 104-105, 119.

2 PKI, *Konstitusi Partai Komunis Indonesia* (Djakarta, 1951), p. 21. This obligation, worded slightly differently, has been incorporated in succeeding Party constitutions. The constitutions of the mass organizations contain a similar obligation for their members, with, of course, "the Party" being replaced by the name of the particular organization.

XIII. THE WORKERS

1 *RI* (May, 1958), p. 5.

2 Interview with Asrarudin.

3 *Sin Po,* Nov. 21, 1950.

4 Although Njono did not officially ask to join PKI until December, 1954, he has been a close associate of the Aidit leadership and might even be considered a member of it. He was elected to parliament as a Communist representative in September, 1955, and in September, 1959, was elected to the PKI Central Committee and, more important, as one of the two candidate members of the Politbureau. In February, 1963, he became one of the seven full members of the Politbureau.

5 George McTurnan Kahin, "Indonesian Politics and Nationalism," in William L. Holland, ed., *Asian Nationalism and the West* (New York, 1953), p. 138.

6 John Wolfard, "Strengthening the Indonesian Trade Union Movement," *World Trade Union Movement* (May 1-15, 1953), p. 17.

7 Boyd R. Compton, *Indonesian Communism: The Ranks Swell,* American Universities' Field Staff Report (New York, 1954), p. 8.

8 *Ibid.,* p. 7.

9 SOBSI, *Sedjarah Gerakan Buruh Indonesia* [*History of the Indonesian Labor Movement*] (Djakarta, 1958), pp. 86-87.

10 Lebaran, or Idul Fitri, is the Moslem holiday and feast at the end of the Ramadan fast. In Indonesia the workers expect to receive a bonus for Lebaran equal to one month's pay.

11 *HR,* Nov. 27, 1951; Nov. 26, 1953.

12 *HR,* Jan. 11, 1955; SOBSI, *Dokumen-Dokumen Konferensi Nasional SOBSI (1957)* (Djakarta, 1958), p. 93.

13 SOBSI, *Dokumen-Dokumen,* p. 93.

14 SOBSI, "Forward for the Consistent Realization of the Political Manifesto," mimeographed (Djakarta, 1960), p. 1.

15 *HR,* May 3, 1963.

16 It is even difficult in Indonesia to define what a trade-union member is. Very few "members" pay any dues, and it has been often commented that SOBSI has become so popular among workers because it receives funds from elsewhere and can afford *not* to collect dues. Furthermore, many workers obtain employment only seasonally. A SOBSI member must therefore be defined as someone who considers himself a member; he may pay dues or not, but he would take any problem to the SOBSI activist for solution, would attend some meetings organized by SOBSI, and would in general participate in labor action led by SOBSI.

17 Harry Goldberg, *Gerakan Buruh di Indonesia* [*The Labor Movement in Indonesia*] (Djakarta, 1952), p. 19.

18 Iskandar Tedjasukmana, *The Political Character of the Indonesian Trade Union Movement* (Ithaca, 1958), pp. 25, 28.

19 J. Henry Richardson, "Indonesian Labor Relations in Their Political Setting," *Industrial and Labor Relations Review,* XII (Oct., 1958), 65-66.

20 SOBSI, *Konstitusi SOBSI* (Djakarta, 1955), pp. 27-28.

21 *Ibid.,* pp. 28-29.

22 *Ibid.,* p. 35.

23 *BB,* Dec. 5, 1956, p. 3.

24 SOBSI, *Dokumen-Dokumen,* pp. 96-97.

25 *BB,* Dec. 5, 1956, p. 3; interview with a member of the SOBSI national headquarters.

26 *ITUN* (Dec., 1958), pp. 8-9; Moh. Munir, *Pedoman Penjelesaian Plan Organisasi 1958* [*Survey of the Implementation of the 1958 Plan of Organization*] (Djakarta, 1959), pp. 27-28.

27 Interview with a member of the SOBSI national headquarters.

28 Leaders of SOBSI in East Java told me, for example, that the regional council in their province had organized seven shifts of its school between the beginning of 1959 and May, 1960, each shift meeting every day for a month, and each attended by about thirty cadres. At the *kabupaten* level courses were held regularly, lasting for from fifteen days, if full-time attendance could be achieved, to one and a half months.

29 Njono, *Untuk Mempertahankan dan Memperluas Hak-Hak kaum Buruh* [*To Defend and Extend the Workers' Rights*] (Djakarta, 1959), p. 69.

30 The zeal of the SOBSI leaders in training their cadres to utilize all opportunities to assist the workers and at the same time increase Communist influence was again demonstrated early in 1963. During 1962 and 1963 the government began to create "enterprise councils" to advise in the management of government estates, factories, and trading offices. By April, 1963, SOBSI had opened special schools to train teachers who would in turn train SOBSI representatives in the purposes and broader possibilities of the councils (*HR*, April 10, 1963). Cadres by that time were also beginning to receive education in business economics.

31 Tedjasukmana, *op. cit.*, p. 71.

32 In 1954 a small, semimonthly *Buletin SOBSI* had been issued, reaching a total circulation of 10,000 in May, 1955; in March, 1956, it was replaced by the larger *Bendera Buruh.*

33 Njono, *op. cit.*, p. 68.

34 *ITUN* (March, 1960), p. 7. According to information given by a member of the SOBSI national headquarters early in 1960, this figure is exaggerated and should have been 7,000 to 8,000. The *ITUN* figure could be true and yet deliberately misleading: while *Harian Rakjat* was temporarily banned for two weeks in December, 1959, the copies printed of *Bendera Buruh* probably were greatly increased.

35 The complete plan, including sections dealing with education and with women members, was published as SOBSI, *Plan Organisasi 1958* (Djakarta, 1957).

36 The results of the 1958 plan were given in Munir, *op. cit.*

37 Kastari, "Sekali Lagi Masalah Klompok" ["Once More the Question of Groups"], *BB*, Feb. 25, 1960, p. 2.

38 Editorial, "SOBSI 12 Tahun" ["SOBSI 12 Years"], *BB*, Nov. 20, 1958, p. 1.

39 Njono, *Tentang Aksi, Kader dan Demokrasi* [*Concerning Action, Cadres, and Democracy*] (Djakarta, 1961), p. 12.

40 Njono, *Dorong Madju Demokrasi dan Produksi serta Landjutkan Perdjuangan Pembebasan Irian Barat* [*Urge the Progress of Democracy and Production and Further the Struggle To Liberate West Irian*] (Djakarta, 1962), pp. 28-29.

41 Njono, "Menjerah Berarti Kalah dan Susah, Berdjuang Berarti Menang dan Senang" ["To Surrender Means Defeat and Sorrow, To Fight Means Victory and Content"], *HR*, May 3, 1963.

42 Interview with a member of the SOBSI national headquarters.

43 Interview with SOBSI leaders in East Java. The total of 510,000 members included 130,000 seasonal workers.

44 Interview with leaders of SOBSI in Jogjakarta.

45 Munir, *op. cit.*, pp. 21-22.

46 SOBSI, "Forward for the Consistent Realization," p. 1.

47 Tedjasukmana, *op. cit.*, p. 80.

48 *BB*, Oct. 10, 1956, p. 3; Oct. 24, 1956, p. 3. These figures correlate closely with Goldberg's estimate (*op. cit.*, p. 19) in 1952 that Sarbupri membership was 350,000

or a little more. Between May, 1962, and March, 1963, Sarbupri at different times claimed 500,000, 1 million, and 1.5 million members. The most frequent claim was 500,000.

49 *BB*, March 13, 1957, p. 3; Tedjasukmana, *op. cit.*, p. 31. The same figure was given in September, 1962 (*HR*, Sept. 21, 1962).

50 *HR*, Jan. 11, 1962.

51 *HR*, March 19, April 1, 1963.

52 PKI, *Resolusi tentang Laporan Umum CC PKI Kepada Kongres Nasional ke-VI [Resolution on the PKI Central Committee's General Report to the Sixth National Congress]* (Djakarta, 1959), p. 90.

53 *HR*, March 26, 1962.

54 *HR*, Dec. 21, 1962.

55 *HR*, April 1, 1963.

56 *HR*, July 20, 1951; March 22, 1963; Thahib, "The Indonesian Oil Workers Form a Single Union," *World Trade Union Movement* (Feb. 1-15, 1952), p. 34.

57 Tedjasukmana, *op. cit.*, p. 32; *HR*, Nov. 19, 1962; March 30, 1963.

58 *BB*, July 15, 1959, p. 2; SOBSI, "Forward for the Consistent Realization," p. 1. I am not sure if these figures include employees and officials of the autonomous districts and municipalities.

59 *HR*, Nov. 9, 1962.

60 *BB*, April 30, 1958, p. 6; *HR*, June 2, 1961.

61 *HR*, July 9, 1960.

62 *BB*, Sept. 30, 1957, p. 1.

63 The term SOBSI here includes also its member unions because general policy comes from PKI and is implemented throughout the SOBSI organization and unions.

64 PKI, *Kewadjiban Front Persatuan Buruh [The Duty of the Workers' United Front]* (Djakarta, 1952).

65 *Ibid.*, p. 19.

66 *Ibid.*, p. 23.

67 *Ibid.*, pp. 23-24.

68 B. O. Hutapea, "Menjambut Tahun 1953" ["Welcoming 1953"], *BM* (Dec., 1952), p. 163.

69 A. M. Adinda, "Menjambut Lahirnja Konstitusi Baru SOBSI" ["Welcoming SOBSI's New Constitution"], *Zaman Baru*, Oct. 15, 1952, p. 3.

70 *Zaman Baru*, Aug. 30, 1952, p. 1.

71 B. O. Hutapea, "Sikap SOBSI Terhadap 'Modal Nasional' " ["SOBSI's Attitude toward 'National Capital' "], *Zaman Baru*, Sept. 30, 1952, pp. 11-13, 16.

72 SOBSI, *Konstitusi SOBSI*, p. 20.

73 *BB*, Nov. 29, 1957, p. 1.

74 *Ibid.*, p. 4.

75 SOBSI ineffectually claimed such immunity at the end of August, 1960, when three regional army commanders placed temporary bans on the activities of PKI and associated organizations.

76 SOBSI, *Dokumen-Dokumen*, p. 25.

77 *RI*, Jan., 1959, p. 33.

78 Sugiri, "The Great Horizons Open to Indonesian Trade Unions," *World Trade Union Movement* (Aug.-Sept., 1958), p. 42.

79 The speech of the SOBSI representative in the conference has been published in booklet form as Runturambi, *Politik Pembangunan Sekarang [Development Policy Now]* (Djakarta, 1957).

80 Njono, *Tegakkan Pandji-Pandji Persatuan* [*Uphold the Banners of Unity*] (Djakarta, 1956), p. 9.

81 SOBSI, *Program SOBSI Mengenai Perbaikan Ekonomi guna Perbaikan Upah dan Djaminan Sosial kaum Buruh* [*SOBSI's Program for Improving the Economy in Order To Improve the Workers' Wages and Social Security*] (Djakarta, 1955), pp. 12-13.

82 Editorial, "Mendjelang Kongres ke-VI Partai" ["Preparing for the Party's Sixth Congress"], *KP* (Nov., 1958), p. 222.

83 D. N. Aidit, *Untuk Demokrasi dan Kabinet Gotong Rojong* [*For Democracy and a Mutual Coöperation Cabinet*] (Djakarta, 1959), p. 169. Also see Njono's statement to the SOBSI national council in August, 1961 (Njono, *Tentang Aksi*, pp. 51-52).

84 SOBSI, *Masaalah Front Persatuan Buruh* [*The Question of the Workers' United Front*] (Djakarta, 1959), p. 32.

85 The Natsir government's regulation is given in Kementerian Perburuhan [Ministry of Labor], *Peraturan Perburuhan dan Peraturan Administrasi Perburuhan* [*Labor Regulations and Labor Administration Regulations*] (Djakarta, 1953), pp. 435-440.

86 The September, 1951, emergency law is given in Kementerian Perburuhan, *Himpunan Peraturan-Peraturan Perburuhan (1945-1955)* [*Collection of Labor Regulations (1945-1955)*] (Djakarta, 1955), pp. 41-49.

87 Interview with Surjanatakusuma, secretary of the Central Labor Disputes Arbitration and Conciliation Committee since its founding in 1951.

88 The programs of demands endorsed by the January, 1955, congress were not quite so full. They are given in SOBSI, *Program SOBSI*, pp. 13-27.

89 *BB*, May 15, 1960, pp. 2-4.

90 *BB*, April 28, 1960, pp. 2-4.

91 For the background to this strike, the Sarbupri demands, and the favorable government attitude to the strikers, see Kementerian Perburuhan, "Dokumentasi Pemogokan Sarbupri sampai 28-8-1950" ["Documentation of the Sarbupri Strike up to 28-8-1950"], mimeographed (Jogjakarta, 1950).

92 Kahin, *op. cit.*, p. 159 n. 19.

93 Wolfard, *op. cit.*, p. 20.

94 Hutomo, "Indonesian Plantation Workers Want Higher Wages," *World Trade Union Movement* (Oct. 16-31, 1953), p. 30; Bank Indonesia, *Report for the Year 1953-1954* (Djakarta, 1954), p. 143.

95 Njono, *Tegakkan*, pp. 8-9; *RI* (April, 1957), pp. 29-30.

96 Njono, "Some Problems of the Indonesian Workers," *ITUN* (May, 1957), p. 4.

97 Ngadiman Suseno, "Successes in the Beginning of the Year," *ITUN* (Feb.-April, 1959), p. 9; *HR*, Dec. 18, 19, 1958.

98 *ITUN* (Jan., 1959), pp. 7-8.

99 Ngadiman, "Apa 'Ketjil Hasil' Itu?" ["What Is 'Small but Successful'?"], *BB*, Dec. 20, 1957, p. 3.

100 This general conclusion was reached largely through interviews with officials of the Ministry of Labor, and especially with officials of the Labor Disputes Arbitration and Conciliation Service.

101 PKI, *Kewadjiban*, pp. 17-18.

102 SOBSI, *Sedjarah*, p. 95; *BB*, July 15, 1959, p. 2. SOBSI claimed that of the workers represented in the "meeting" in July, 1959, 60 per cent belonged to SOBSI unions. In May, 1962, the "meeting" was reported to include fifty-eight trade-unions

with 1,435,434 members. *HR*, May 18, 1962.

103 SOBSI, *Sedjarah*, p. 95; *HR*, Jan. 7, 1960.

104 *HR*, Dec. 3, 1959; interview with Iskander Wahono, secretary-general of KBKI, the PNI trade-union federation.

105 SOBSI, *Dokumen-Dokumen*, p. 18.

106 *HR*, March 30, 31, 1953.

107 SOBSI celebrated May Day alone in Djakarta in 1963. No reason was given for this break in a ten-year tradition.

108 *World Trade-Union Movement* (July 16-31, 1953), pp. 9-10. On their return, the SOBSI and non-Communist GBSI delegates issued a joint statement full of praise for the Chinese government, and concluding with the call to all Indonesian trade-unionists "to take more positive action to form a workers' united front. With their united strength the Indonesian workers can certainly take the road of China, free themselves from the shackles of imperialism and build up their homeland."

109 Forty-four Indonesian trade-unionists were invited, for example, to attend May Day celebrations in 1957: twenty to China, eleven to the Soviet Union, eight to North Korea, three to North Vietnam, and two to East Germany. Of the forty-four, only sixteen were from SOBSI, while eighteen were from other trade-union federations, three from nonfederated unions, one from the Communist-led village officials' association, and six from unidentified unions (*BB*, April 24, 1957, p. 6).

110 The only post-1950 example of militant action by SOBSI against another trade-union perhaps gives some evidence that SOBSI would have benefited from more aggressive action. In May, 1955, SOBSI used its members to break a strike by the PSI-led KBSI, and SOBSI leaders claimed later that the collapse of the strike and the "unmasking" of the KBSI leaders caused many members of KBSI unions to leave them and join SOBSI.

111 *Buletin SOBSI* (June 20, 1955), pp. 1-2.

112 *Buletin SOBSI* (Aug. 20, 1955), p. 8.

113 *ITUN* (March, 1957), p. 6.

114 The story of trade-union developments in part of this period is given in outline in Sandra Nitidihardjo, "Gerakan Buruh Indonesia" ["The Indonesian Labor Movement"], mimeographed (Djakarta, 1956), pp. 79-97; Tedjasukmana, *op. cit.*, pp. 25-130; also in the Ministry of Labor's periodical *Tindjauan Masa'alah Perburuhan* [*Survey of the Labor Question*]. I also received much assistance from officials of the Ministry of Labor, and especially from cadres of the various trade-union federations.

115 Interview with Iskander Wahono, secretary-general of KBKI.

116 *Tindjauan Masa'alah Perburuhan* (May, 1958), p. 8.

117 Interview with A. Z. Abidin, secretary-general of KBSI.

118 Interview with Agus Sudono, first secretary of SBII. Active membership was far smaller, as it was in all other trade-unions.

119 See, for example, Njoto, "Menjerah Berarti," *HR*, May 3, 1963.

120 Richardson, *op. cit.*, p. 65.

121 *ITUN* (Feb., 1960), p. 2; Tedjasukmana, *op. cit.*, p. 39.

122 For example, the monopoly of Sarbupri has been broken by the rise of the KBSI affiliate Perbupri, Sarbupri-SOBRI, Sarbupri-Coerdian, the KBKI's estate workers' union, SBII, Sarbumusi of the NU, and regional unions; the monopoly of SBKA among railway workers has been broken by the KBSI affiliate PBKA, which in 1960 was dominant in West Java, and by the small, PNI-led KBKA; Perbum now has perhaps only 50 to 60 per cent of all oil workers; and the SOBSI post,

telegraph, and telephone union now contains only a minority of workers in that field.

123 See above, p. 311, n. 65, for estimates of the number of unemployed and underemployed. The number of nonorganized workers has been estimated by Njono at 3 million, and by Tedjasukmana at about 2 million (Njono, "Beberapa Peladjaran dari Kongres Nasional ke-II SOBSI" ["Some Lessons from SOBSI's Second National Congress"], *BM* [Jan., 1955], p. 8; Tedjasukmana, *op. cit.*, p. 25). Tedjasukmana's estimate specifically excluded workers in "very small undertakings" who "usually do not form associations."

124 These are representative quotations from conversations with me.

125 In 1935 there were 111 trade-unions with 72,675 members, and in 1939, 75 unions with 109,547 members (Peter H. W. Sitsen, *Industrial Development of the Netherlands Indies* [New York, 1942], pp. 46-47).

126 In 1939 there were only eighteen strikes, of from one to eighteen days, involving a total of 1,628 workers *(ibid.,* p. 47).

127 To illustrate this point: in March, 1960, the SOBSI seamen's and harbor worker's union, which has a virtual monopoly in the ports of Java, tried to stage strikes in Tandjung Priok, Semarang, and Surabaja. A display of force by the army caused the strikes to collapse immediately and the workers to submit without protest to the arrest of the union cadres. And in this example the union was pressing justifiable social-economic demands, not political ones.

128 PKI, *Program PKI* (Djakarta, 1954), pp. 16-17.

129 PKI, *Manifes Pemilihan Umum PKI* [*PKI's General Election Manifesto*] (Djakarta, 1954), p. 19. It should be noted that the verb "memilih" means both "to vote" and "to elect."

130 *Program Secom PKI Kotapradja Surabaja untuk Pemilihan DPRD Kotapradja Surabaja* [*The Program of the Surabaja City PKI Section Committee for the Elections for the Surabaja City Representative Council*] (Surabaja, 1957), pp. 9-10.

131 The danger of fire in the densely packed and inflammable *kampongs* is very great during the dry season, and each year thousands of homes are destroyed.

132 In November, 1959, for example, the PKI Djakarta Raja committee instructed all committees, cadres, and members in its area to form fire brigades in each *kampong* (*HR*, Nov. 5, 1959).

133 Letter from Irene Tinker Walker to the author, October 25, 1960.

134 John D. Legge, *Problems of Regional Autonomy in Contemporary Indonesia* (Ithaca, 1957), p. 23.

135 The best account of the RKKS is given in Boyd R. Compton, *Red Surabaja*, Institute of Current World Affairs Report (New York, 1956), pp. 8-15.

136 *Ibid.,* p. 9.

XIV. THE PEASANTS

1 PKI, *Djalan Baru untuk Republik Indonesia* [*New Road for the Indonesian Republic*] (7th ed.; Djakarta, 1953), p. 10.

2 PKI, *Lahirnja Partai Komunis Indonesia dan Perkembangannja* [*The Birth and Growth of PKI*] (Djakarta, 1951), p. 22.

3 See, for example, "Masaalah Tani di Indonesia" ["The Peasant Question in Indonesia"], *BM* (June 15-July 1, 1951), pp. 303-306; PKI, "Program Perubahan

Tanah dan Tuntutan kaum Tani" ["The Program of Land Change and Peasant Demands"], *BM* (Dec., 1951), pp. 7-22, 32-36.

4 D. N. Aidit, "Haridepan Gerakan Tani Indonesia" ["The Future of the Indonesian Peasant Movement"], *BM* (July, 1953), pp. 332-340.

5 *Ibid.*, p. 339. *Pologoro* is unpaid labor and services performed by the villagers for the village officials; *rodi* is compulsory, unpaid labor for the government. *Setoran paksa*, in this context, is probably the compulsory sale of a certain proportion of the rice harvest to the government, at prices fixed by the government and below the market price.

6 *Ibid.*, p. 335. Aidit made clear to the Party cadres who would be reading his article, however, that peasant private ownership of land would not be the final stage of the agrarian revolution. The peasants' own experience plus "the leadership and education of the Party" would lead to the voluntary abandonment of private for collective agriculture.

7 D. N. Aidit, "Indonesian People in Struggle for Complete Abolition of Colonial Regime," *FALP*, Aug. 27, 1955, p. 5.

8 D. N. Aidit, "Madju Terus Menggempur Imperialisme dan Feodalisme!" ["Continue To Advance To Destroy Imperialism and Feudalism!"], *HR*, Jan. 2, 1961.

9 See above, pp. 40-42.

10 "Laporan Mengenai Pekerdjaan Partai dikalangan kaum Tani" ["Report on Party Work among the Peasants"], *BM* (April-May, 1959), p. 138.

11 Ismail Bakri, "Dengan Berani Terus Melawan Kaum Penghisap Besar di Desa" ["With Courage Continue To Fight the Big Exploiters in the Village"], *HR*, Feb. 19, 1963. For some of the early results of the information-collecting campaign, see *ST* (Jan., 1959), p. 10; and Asmu, "Masaalah Landreform" ["The Question of Land Reform"], *BM* (Jan., 1960), pp. 21-25.

12 PKI, *Bahan-Bahan untuk Kongres Nasional ke-VI Partai Komunis Indonesia* [*Materials for the Sixth PKI National Congress*] (Djakarta, 1958), p. 53; PKI, *Resolusi tentang Laporan Umum CC PKI kepada Kongres Nasional ke-VI* [*Resolution Concerning the PKI Central Committee's General Report to the Sixth National Congress*] (Djakarta, 1959), p. 66.

13 Amir Anwar Sanusi, "The Results of the First Three-Year Plan," mimeographed (Djakarta, 1959), p. 3.

14 The following information was gathered largely from conversations with cadres of PKI and its mass organizations; see also, "Laporan," pp. 135, 144-145.

15 "Laporan," p. 131.

16 *Ibid.*, p. 132.

17 "Laporan Tambahan Mengenai Masaalah Mengembangkan Pekerdjaan Massa kaum Tani" ["Additional Report on the Question of Developing Mass Work among the Peasants"], *HR*, July 10, 1957.

18 "Laporan," *BM* (April-May, 1959), p. 146; B. O. Hutapea, "Some Lessons from the First National Peasants' Conference of the C.P.I.," *RI* (Aug., 1959), pp. 32-33.

19 *Ichtisar Gerakan Tani* [*Survey of the Peasant Movement*] (July-Aug., 1951), p. 15.

20 BTI, *Tentang Agitasi dan Propaganda* [*Concerning Agitation and Propaganda*] (Djakarta, 1954), p. 3.

21 *Sin Po*, Dec. 27, 1951.

22 The difficulties faced by the Communist leaders of SAKTI in bringing about

fusion with BTI are given in Sidik Kertapati, *Untuk Persatuan dan Memperluas Perdjuangan Tani* [*For Unity and Extending the Peasants' Struggle*] (Djakarta, 1955), pp. 24-37.

23 *HR*, Sept. 21, 22, 1953.

24 D. N. Aidit. "Mengatasi Kelemahan Kita" ["Overcoming Our Weaknesses"], in his *Pilihan Tulisan*, I (Djakarta, 1959), 502 n. 14.

25 Sidik Kertapati, *op. cit.*, p. 44.

26 "Laporan," *BM* (April-May, 1959), p. 129.

27 *HR*, April 5, 1955.

28 Sidik Kertapati, *op. cit.*, p. 23.

29 *HR*, July 23, 1956.

30 The report of the executive committee of the national council to the council meeting is given in full in *ST* (March, 1955), pp. 1, 6-7.

31 Asmu, "Beladjar dari Sidang Pleno DPP-BTI ke-III untuk Mengatasi Kelemahan Pekerdjaan Partai dilapangan Perdjuangan Tani" ["Learning from the Third Plenum of the BTI National Council in Order To Overcome Weaknesses in the Party's Work in the Sphere of the Peasants' Struggle"], *BM* (Feb.-March, 1955), p. 61.

32 The list of leaders elected in the congress is given in *ST* (Oct., 1957), p. 3.

33 *ST* (Jan., 1959), pp. 6-7.

34 Hartojo, "Luaskan Aksi-Aksi kaum Tani untuk Mengembangkan Kekuatan Progresif" ["Extend Peasant Actions in Order To Develop the Progressive Force"], *ST* (Oct., 1957), p. 11.

35 *Loc. cit.*

36 "Laporan Umum Sidang DPP Pleno II BTI" ["General Report to the BTI Second National Council Plenum"], *ST*, Supplement (May-June, 1959), pp. 29-30.

37 Among the ethnic Javanese, a family in which a death has occurred is obliged to provide certain ritual feasts for kin and neighbors, and the proper fulfillment of this obligation is considered necessary for the welfare of the entire neighborhood. Neighborhood death associations are organized to assist poor families who could not otherwise fulfill this obligation. In an *arisan* group, all members contribute a certain sum each week, and each member in turn receives the whole sum.

38 "Laporan," *BM* (April-May, 1959), p. 144.

39 *ST* (May, 1957), p. 11.

40 Asmu, "Beladjar," p. 61; Parto, "Memperbaiki Pekerdjaan Partai dikalangan kaum Tani" ["Improving Party Work among the Peasants"], *KP* (Oct., 1958), p. 205; Hutapea, *op. cit.*, p. 32.

41 Hutapea, *op. cit.*, p. 32; "Laporan," *BM* (April-May, 1959), p. 135.

42 The plan was never published in full, but its general outline was obtained from several references in *ST*: "Laporan Umum," *ST*, Supplement (May-June, 1959), pp. 31-33; *ibid.* (July, 1959), pp. 1-2; *ibid.* (Nov., 1959), p. 4; A. Rachman, "Arti Plan 3 Tahun BTI" ["The Meaning of BTI's Three-Year Plan"], *ibid.* (June, 1960), p. 3; *ibid.* (June, 1960), p. 7.

43 *ST* (June, 1960), p. 7.

44 Mimeographed document seen at the BTI East Java office, Surabaja.

45 *HR*, Nov. 16, 1959.

46 *ST* (July, 1960), p. 5.

47 *ST* (Aug.-Oct., 1962), p. 25. This issue is devoted to the Sixth Congress. As the second three-year plan was completed at the end of April 1963, BTI claimed the

following: 7,099,105 members, 21,263 subbranches at the village level, 2,186 organizations at the *ketjamatan* level, 262 *kabupaten*-level organizations, and 21 province and island committees (*HR*, Aug. 26, 1963).

48 See above, pp. 112, 327 n. 8.

49 Much of the following information on PPDI was obtained from an interview with three of PPDI's central leaders.

50 The statement is given in *Djaman Baru*, March 30, 1953, p. 20.

51 In February, 1960, SOBSI reported PPDI's membership to be 200,000 (*ITUN* [Feb., 1960], p. 2). In December, 1962, PPDI claimed 450,000 members (*HR*, Dec. 19, 1962).

52 The long list of general and specific demands adopted by the May, 1951, congress is given in *Djaman Baru*, March 30, 1953, pp. 23-24, and *Ichtisar Gerakan Tani* (July-Aug., 1951), pp. 13-14. An account of PPDI work concerning the more important problems facing village officials is given in Sugijono, "Dengan tanpa pandang bulu P.P.D.I. selalu tampil kedepan untuk Bela Nasib para Pamong Desa" ["Without any Discrimination Whatsoever, PPDI Is Always to the Fore in Defending the Welfare of the Village Officials"], *Suara Pamong Desa* (Nov., 1958-Jan., 1959), pp. 89-98.

53 Kementerian Agraria [Ministry of Agrarian Affairs], "Undang-Undang Darurat no. 8 tahun 1954" ["Emergency Law No. 8, 1954"], mimeographed (Djakarta, 1954).

54 Kementerian Agraria, "Undang-Undang Darurat no. 1 tahun 1956" ["Emergency Law No. 1, 1956"], mimeographed (Djakarta, 1956).

55 See, for example, *HR*, June 16, 1954; *ST* (Feb., 1960), p. 2; *ST* (Aug.-Oct., 1962), pp. 27-28.

56 The PRRI-Permesta rebellion finally disintegrated in the latter half of 1961. The Darul Islam rebellion in West Java largely collapsed after the capture of its leader in June, 1962.

57 See, for example, "Program Perubahan Tanah," *BM* (Dec., 1951), p. 19; "Resolusi tentang Mengikutsertakan Rakjat dalam Membasmi Sisa-Sisa Gerombolan 'PRRI-Permesta' 'DI-TII'" ["Resolution concerning the People's Participation in Eradicating the Remnants of the 'PRRI-Permesta' 'DI-TII' Gangs"], *BM* (April-May, 1959), p. 206.

58 Boyd R. Compton, *Indonesian Communism: The Ranks Swell*, American Universities' Field Staff Report (New York, 1954), p. 9.

59 BTI, *Konstitusi BTI* (Djakarta, 1954), pp. 9-10.

60 "Laporan," *BM* (April-May, 1959), p. 139.

61 Aidit, "Haridepan," pp. 339-340.

62 PKI, *Tuntunan untuk Bekerdja dikalangan kaum Tani* [*Guide for Working among the Peasants*] (Djakarta, 1955), p. 47.

63 "Laporan," *BM* (April-May, 1959), p. 141; D. N. Aidit, *Indonesian Society and the Indonesian Revolution* (Djakarta, 1958), p. 61.

64 PKI, *Tuntunan*, p. 44.

65 Asmu, "Beladjar," pp. 59-60.

66 See above, pp. 37-38, 45, for a discussion of the Aidit leadership's tactical separation of the struggle against imperialism and the struggle against feudalism, and of the leadership's tactical separation of "bandit landlords" from "patriotic landlords."

67 Hutapea, *op. cit.*, pp. 30-31.

68 A leading PNI member of parliament told me in interview that this Communist motion was designed to create unrest if passed and attractive propaganda

if passed or not. He claimed that if the 6:4 motion had become law, the landlords and wealthy peasants who had formerly leased land would have then worked it themselves with laborers in order to receive a higher income than the 40 per cent of yields allowed in the bill proposed by PKI. This would have forced a large number of tenant farmers and sharecroppers to become agricultural laborers.

69 *PKI dan Perwakilan* (Fourth Quarter, 1959-First Quarter, 1960), pp. 137-146.

70 *ST* (Jan., 1960), p. 3. The italics are mine.

71 For information on the *klompoks*, see *ST* (May-June, 1961), p. 7; and PKI, *Konfernas Tani ke-II PKI* [*PKI Second Peasants' Conference*] (Djakarta, 1962), pp. 11-17.

72 D. N. Aidit, "Fly High the Banners of 'Land to the Peasants' and Fight for One Victory after the Other." *RI* Supplement, (June-July, 1959), pp. 13-14.

73 Suta, "Gerakan Koperasi dikalangan kaum Tani" ["The Coöperative Movement among the Peasants"], *ST* (July, 1961), p. 2. See also Bakri, *op. cit.*

74 Department of Information, *Land Reform in Indonesia and Basic Regulations Governing This* (Djakarta, 1961), and "Keputusan Menteri Agraria tentang Penegasan Luas Maksimum Tanah-Pertanian" ["Decision of the Minister of Agrarian Affairs Concerning the Definition of Maximum Agricultural Landholdings"] *Pembangunan Desa* (March-April, 1961), pp. 38-44.

75 Bakri, *op. cit.*

76 PKI, *Konfernas Tani ke-II*, p. 6.

77 *HR*, June 6, Oct. 23, 1962; Jan. 30, 1963.

78 Susilo Prawiroatmodjo, *Tindjauan Singkat Organisasi Tani di Indonesia* [*Brief Survey of Peasant Organizations in Indonesia*] (Djakarta, 1955), pp. 50-54.

XV. THE PETTY BOURGEOISIE

1 See above, pp. 42-43.

2 See above, pp. 157-159.

3 See below, pp. 203-208.

4 See below, pp. 195-198.

5 See below, pp. 188-195.

6 The Sea Fisheries Service, Department of Agriculture, estimated that in 1959 there were 734,500 fishermen in Indonesia. Of these, 215,700 were in Java, 215,100 in Sulawesi, and 141,200 in Sumatra *(Statistical Pocketbook of Indonesia, 1960,* Central Bureau of Statistics [Djakarta, 1960], p. 84).

7 "Penghisapan Feodal terhadap Nelajan" ["Feudal Exploitation of Fishermen"], *HR*, July 20, 1962.

8 "Conclusions on the Question of Fishermen in Indonesia," *RI,* Supplement (June-July, 1959), pp. 9-10.

9 PKI, "Development of Work among Fishermen," mimeographed (Djakarta, 1960), p. 1.

10 PKI, *Konfernas Tani ke-II PKI* [*PKI Second Peasants' Conference*] (Djakarta, 1962), pp. 40-41.

11 PKI, *Konstitusi PKI* (Djakarta, 1951), p. 11; D. N. Aidit, *Indonesian Society and the Indonesian Revolution* (Djakarta, 1958), p. 59.

12 "Bekerdja dalam kalangan Intelektuil" ["Work among the Intellectuals"], *BM* (Oct.-Nov., 1952), pp. 120-123.

13 Aidit, *op. cit.*, p. 59.

[14] PKI, *Resolusi tentang Laporan Umum CC PKI kepada Kongres Nasional ke-VI* [*Resolution Concerning the PKI Central Committee's General Report to the Sixth National Congress*] (Djakarta, 1959), pp. 92-93.

[15] It is noteworthy that of the forty-six full and candidate members of the PKI Central Committee elected in September, 1959, I know of only two who had university degrees.

[16] For a discussion of the reasons, including social origin, which explain why the university students, the future intellectuals, are not attracted to PKI, see below, p. 198.

[17] LEKRA, *Menjambut Kongres Kebudajaan* [*Welcoming the Cultural Congress*] (N.p., 1951), p. 1.

[18] LEKRA, "Laporan Umum Pengurus Pusat LEKRA kepada Kongres Nasional ke-I LEKRA" ["The General Report of the National Council to the First LEKRA Congress"], mimeographed (N.p., 1959), p. 27; LEKRA, "Keputusan-Keputusan Kongres Nasional ke-I LEKRA" ["Decisions of the First LEKRA Congress"], mimeographed (N.p., 1959), p. 1.

[19] *HR*, July 31, 1962.

[20] Interview with Joebaar Ajoeb, LEKRA secretary-general, and Basuki Resobowo, a member of the LEKRA secretariat.

[21] The chairman of the People's Artists (Pelukis-Pelukis Rakjat) ran as a "non-party" candidate on PKI's list in the 1955 elections.

[22] *HR*, May 21, 1963.

[23] *Zaman Baru* is the continuation of the Communist-controlled Surabaja political periodical of the same name which virtually disappeared in 1953, to be revived as a regularly issued, well-produced LEKRA periodical in mid-1956.

[24] This is not to imply that LEKRA members are paid for their work in aid of PKI and its mass organizations. Their labor may be given free.

[25] LEKRA, "Laporan Umum," pp. 15, 26. *Dalangs* are the storytellers in the *wajang* dramas; *ludruk* and *ketoprak* are traditional forms of music-drama; *gamelan* is the name of the Javanese orchestra that accompanies the *wajang* and music-dramas. In line with other Communist organizations, BAKOKSI has initiated an educational program. A one-month school was opened for 200 BAKOKSI cadres and officials on January 14, 1963 (*HR*, Jan. 12, 31, Feb. 16, 1963).

[26] *RI* (Dec., 1957), p. 24.

[27] LEKRA, "Keputusan-Keputusan", p. 2.

[28] LEKRA's inability to persuade its members to adopt socialist realism is illustrated by Sukarno's reaction to the LEKRA art exhibition held at the time of the 1959 congress: "My friends, I have seen an exhibition of paintings by members of LEKRA; I must say that you are very liberal minded. I found so many styles and schools of painting—naturalism, realism, surrealism, impressionism, cubism, futurism, etc. When I asked the artists why there are so many styles, their answers revolved around the individuality of the artist, freedom of the artist, etc." (mimeographed manuscript of the speech [Djakarta, 1959]).

XVI. YOUTH

[1] Interview with Moh. Fatchan and Anwar Nasution, then, respectively, first and second deputy secretary-generals of Pemuda Rakjat, and with Qodar, a member of the Pemuda Rakjat executive council.

2 *Sin Po*, March 22, 1951.

3 *Ibid.*, Nov. 8, 1950; interview with Fatchan, Nasution, and Qodar.

4 In October, 1951, for example, the Pemuda Rakjat leadership ordered all branches to coöperate with other youth organizations in establishing joint committees to celebrate Heroes' Day (*HR*. Oct. 15, 1951). In February, 1952, Pemuda Rakjat joined with several other youth organizations, including PNI's Pemuda Demokrat, in the celebration held in Bandung of the International Day of Youth Solidarity against Colonialism (*HR*, Feb. 22, 1952).

5 *HR*, Nov. 13, 15, 17, 1952; also interview with Fatchan, Nasution, and Qodar.

6 A report in *HR*, Jan. 2, 1952, stated that 150 Pemuda Rakjat members, arrested in August, 1951, were still in prison.

7 Pemuda Rakjat, *Peraturan Dasar Pemuda Rakjat* [*Pemuda Rakjat's Constitution*] (3d ed.; Djakarta, 1954), pp. 14, 41.

8 Pemuda Rakjat, *Rol Pemuda dalam Perdjuangan untuk Kemerdekaan Nasional dan Perdamaian Dunia* [*The Role of Youth in the Struggle for National Independence and World Peace*] (Djakarta, 1955), p. 37.

9 *Ibid.*, pp. 37-38. The figure for Java included the insignificant membership in Nusatenggara because at that time Nusatenggara was included in the area of the East Java regional committee.

10 Asmudji, "Meluaskan Penerbitan Organisasi" ["To Extend Publishing by the Organization"], *Buletin Pemuda Rakjat*, no. 1 (1955), p. 5; *HR*, July 26, 1956.

11 Asmudji, *op. cit.*, p. 6.

12 Pemuda Rakjat, *Menudju Persatuan Pemuda Indonesia jang Luas* [*Toward Broad Unity of Indonesian Youth*] (Djakarta, 1956), p. 45.

13 In January, 1954, a semimonthly *Pemuda Baru* [*New Youth*] was to begin, but was not heard of subsequently; toward the end of 1955 a monthly *Generasi Baru* [*New Generation*] was appearing, although the circulation of it and all Pemuda Rakjat brochures and pamphlets was less than 2,250; and from the end of 1955 the monthly *Buletin Pemuda Rakjat* appeared, though by July, 1956, it had been combined with *Generasi Baru* (*HR*, Dec. 30, 1953; Asmudji, *op. cit.*, p. 5; Pemuda Rakjat, *Menudju*, p. 53).

14 Pemuda Rakjat, *Menudju*, pp. 51-52.

15 *Ibid.*, p. 52.

16 *HR*, July 10, Oct. 23, 1953; July 28, 1955; July 3, Sept. 10, 1957; June 28, 1962.

17 Pemuda Rakjat, "Diktat" ["Outline for Cadre Courses"], mimeographed (Djakarta, n.d.), pp. 33-37.

18 Under the Pemuda Rakjat constitution, there is a committee for each province or province-level area, a commissariat in each *kabupaten* and large town to coördinate the branches and a branch that coördinates the work of several subbranches in which ordinary members participate. Groups further divide ordinary members as a means of implementing the work of the subbranch (Pemuda Rakjat, *Peraturan Dasar Pemuda Rakjat* [5th ed.; Djakarta, 1958], pp. 31-43).

19 Pemuda Rakjat, *Pemuda Pengawal Kemerdekaan Nasional Indonesia* [*Youth, the Guardian of Indonesian National Independence*] (Djakarta, 1957), p. 6.

20 Pemuda Rakjat, "Laporan Umum pada Sidang Dewan Nasional ke-III ["General Report to the Third Meeting of the National Council"], mimeographed (Djakarta, 1958), p. 13.

21 *Ibid.*, pp. 13-19.

22 The report did comment that the national council was still running a school

for preparing cadres from Java for work in the outer islands, and that some commissariats and branches had, on their own initiative, organized schools and courses on politics and theory.

23 There were two reasons for this priority: first, many cadres of PKI and its mass organizations were killed by the rebels; and, second, the central government placed a ban on all political activity in the war zones, so that PKI used its mass organizations to fill the political gap left by the withdrawal of the rebels and the ban on party activities.

24 Interview with Fatchan, Nasution, and Qodar.

25 *HR,* Jan. 12, 1959.

26 Interview with Pemuda Rakjat leaders in East Java and Jogjakarta.

27 Pemuda Rakjat, *Setia Mengabdi Kepentingan-Kepentingan Vital dan Tjita-Tjita Revolusi Agustus 1945 [Loyal in Serving the Vital Interests of Indonesian Youth and the Aspirations of the 1945 Revolution]* (Djakarta, 1962), p. 50.

28 Pemuda Rakjat leaders claim that when the PRRI-Permesta rebellion broke out in 1958, Pemuda Rakjat cadres and activists played an active and at times heroic part in opposing and even openly fighting the rebels.

29 Sukatno, "Untuk Memperluas Diskusi-Diskusi dikalangan Anggota!" ["To Extend Discussions among Members!"], *Buletin Pemuda Rakjat,* no. 1 (1955), p. 3.

30 Pemuda Rakjat, *Menudju,* pp. 63-67.

31 Pemuda Rakjat, *Rol Pemuda,* pp. 50-51.

32 Sukatno told the Fifth Congress in July, 1956, for example, that in the Tjirebon area of West Java Pemuda Rakjat had taken the initiative in demanding that the division of the rice harvest between the landowner and sharecropper be made in the fields, and in refusing to carry the landlords' share free of charge to the rice barns (Pemuda Rakjat, *Menudju,* p. 21).

33 Interview with Fatchan, Nasution, and Qodar.

34 *HR,* Nov. 6, 1959. See also Pemuda Rakjat, *Setia Mengabdi,* pp. 57-59.

35 The 1958 plan of organization and education called on each commissariat to provide uniforms for at least 100 team members.

36 *HR,* Nov. 12, 13, 1958.

37 Much of the information on IPPI was received in conversations with Maruli Silitonga, a non-Communist leader of IPPI for many years.

38 It should be noted, however, that in February, 1963, the Central Java section of IPPI held its first cadre course, attended by 200 students (*HR,* Feb. 5, 1963).

39 Much of the information on CGMI was obtained from interviews with national leaders of CGMI, the PNI student organization GMNI, the Moslem student organization HMI, and the socialist student organization GMS; also from local leaders of these organizations in Jogjakarta and, to a lesser extent, in Surabaja.

40 Banggas, "Memperbaiki Pekerdjaan Partai dikalangan Mahasiswa" ["To Improve Party Work among the Students"], *BM* (Feb., 1958), pp. 57-65.

41 The term "mahasiswa" as used in the titles of the student organizations is roughly translated as "university student" but it also applies to students in post-high-school academies and teachers' colleges.

42 *HR,* Feb. 18, 1963.

43 Early in 1960 the only universities or colleges where a CGMI member was president of the student council were Padang and Malang. CGMI members had held that position in the large Gadjah Mada University in Jogjakarta from 1956 to 1958, but in the latter year the non-Communists had exposed CGMI's Communist orientation, with the result that by the academic year 1959-60 CGMI held only one

of the twenty-seven occupied seats on the student council.

44 For some statistical evidence to support this statement, see Leslie H. Palmier, "Occupational Distribution of Parents of Pupils in Certain Indonesian Educational Institutions," *Indonesie*, X (1957), 320-376, esp. 369.

45 "Experimen jang Berhasil" ["Successful Experiment"], *BM* (Sept.-Oct., 1959), pp. 409-410.

46 Fadjar Harapan, "Constitution of Fadjar Harapan," mimeographed trans. (Djakarta, 1960), pp. 2-3.

47 *HR*, May 17, 1960.

XVII. WOMEN

1 PKI, *Manifes Pemilihan Umum PKI* [*PKI's General Election Manifesto*] (Djakarta, 1954), p. 19.

2 *HR*, Dec. 14, 1955.

3 Setiati Surasto, "Memperluas Keanggotaan Partai dikalangan Wanita" ["Extending Party Membership among Women"], *KP* (Feb., 1957), pp. 19-21.

4 The major documents of the conference are given in *BM* (June, 1958), pp. 241-285.

5 D. N. Aidit, "Wanita Komunis Pedjuang untuk Masjarakat Baru" ["Communist Women, Fighters for a New Society"], *BM* (June, 1958), p. 247.

6 Sudisman, "Dengan Ketabahan jang Besar Mendidik dan Mempromosi Kader-Kader Wanita" ["With Great Resolution Educate and Promote Women Cadres"], *BM* (June, 1958), p. 250.

7 *Andjangsono* groups are small groups of organization members that call on neighbors for friendly visits and chats. They were used by PKI and its mass organizations especially around the times of general elections.

8 Suharti, "Menghidupkan Grup Wanita dan Meluaskan Keanggotaan Partai dikalangan Wanita" ["Activating Women's Groups and Extending Party Membership among Women"], *BM* (June, 1958), p. 256.

9 D. N. Aidit, *Untuk Demokrasi, Persatuan dan Mobilisasi* [*For Democracy, Unity, and Mobilization*] (Djakarta, 1962), pp. 95-97.

10 Gerwani, *Peraturan Dasar Gerwani* [*Gerwani's Constitution*] (Djakarta, 1954), p. 7; Suharti Suwarto, "Indonesian Women Struggle for Peace and Their Rights," *FALP*, March 9, 1956, p. 4.

11 Interview with Mrs. Umi Sardjono, chairman of Gerwani since March, 1954.

12 Umi Sardjono, "Praeadvies tentang Organisasi" ["Report on Organization"], *Wanita Sedar* [*Enlightened Woman*] (Feb. 15, 1951), p. 33. In this report, Umi Sardjono declared that although the workers and peasants, the oppressed, should lead the organization, "facts as they are in Indonesia show that their awareness is still very low. The oppressed workers and peasants are not yet aware that they should take the leadership of the revolution." In such a situation, 99 per cent of the Gerwis leadership were bourgeois, "because they can most quickly accept our theories and teachings for leading the struggle to victory."

13 See, for example, the demands for working women drawn up by the First Gerwis Conference in February, 1951 (*Wanita Sedar* [March 15, 1951], p. 15). The First Gerwis Congress in December, 1951, formulated a plan for a democratic marriage law which would ensure equal rights and obligations for both sexes, protect wives and children in cases of divorce or separation, establish a minimum age for

marriage of 17 for women and 20 for men, and "in principle" guarantee monogamy (*ibid.* [Jan., 1952], p. 6).

14 The First Gerwis Conference in February, 1951, for example, drew up a detailed program for work in the villages (*ibid.* [March 15, 1951], p. 16).

15 *HR*, June 5, 1957.

16 *Wanita Sedar* (Jan., 1952), p. 3.

17 *HR*, June 9, 1953.

18 *Djaman Baru*, Feb. 28. 1953, p. 29.

19 *HR*, March 26, 1954.

20 Gerwani, *op. cit.*, p. 11.

21 The Gerwani leaders claimed in December, 1957, that the target was unrealistic because for more than a year after their Second Congress the whole organization was busy changing its structure in line with the new constitution; because Gerwani did not have the number of cadres required to achieve the target in a society where women are unaccustomed to taking part in organization; and because in deciding on the target figure no attention had been given to the problems posed by "difficult regions," such as insecure, mountainous, and isolated areas, especially outside Java (Gerwani, *Lebih Giat Meluaskan Gerakan untuk Terlaksananja Piagam Hak-Hak Wanita Indonesia* [*More Active in Extending the Movement for the Implementation of the Charter of Indonesian Women's Rights*] [Djakarta, 1958], p. 69).

22 *HR*, June 13, 1955; Jan. 21, 1956.

23 Gerwani, *Meluaskan Aksi-Aksi untuk Memperkuat Tuntutan Hak-Hak Wanita-Anak-Anak dan Perdamaian* [*Extending Actions To Strengthen the Demand for the Rights of Women and Children and for Peace*] (Djakarta, 1956), pp. 26-27.

24 Gerwani, *Lebih Giat*, p. 68.

25 *RI* (Jan., 1958), pp. 27-28.

26 For example, Gerwani expressed support for the first Ali Sastroamidjojo government, opposition to the Burhanudin Harahap government, support for Sukarno's concept of an all-party government, and support for the president in his efforts as cabinet formateur in April, 1957.

27 Gerwani, *Lebih Giat*, p. 73.

28 *Ibid.*, pp. 74-76.

29 Interview with Umi Sardjono.

30 Gerwani, *Lebih Giat*, p. 51.

31 In general the Indonesian woman is very insecure in her marriage because her husband may easily repudiate the marriage. According to the statistics of the Ministry of Religious Affairs, in the years 1954 through 1958 the number of marriage repudiations within the Moslem community was from 50 to 52 per cent of the total number of new marriages plus reconciliations between separated partners (*Statistical Pocketbook of Indonesia, 1960*, Central Bureau of Statistics [Djakarta, 1960], p. 18). This insecurity greatly enhances the appeal of an organization that demands a democratic marriage law, and that aids the wife in her efforts to prevent repudiation by the husband.

32 Gerwani, *Lebih Giat*, pp. 68, 71; source shows 10,000 error in total.

33 *Ibid.*, p. 70.

34 The program of demands is given in full in *ibid.*, pp. 125-127.

35 The following information was obtained in conversations with Umi Sardjono and with Gerwani leaders in East Java and Jogjakarta.

36 In January, 1963, there were 905 kindergartens and 6 elementary schools (*HR*, Jan. 11, 1963).

37 The Gerwani Fourth National Congress was told in December, 1961, that there were 46,785 pupils and 1,016 teachers in Gerwani anti-illiteracy courses *(HR,* Dec. 14, 1961).

38 Kartini is a national heroine; she was one of the first to attempt to give education to girls.

39 *HR,* Dec. 14, 1961; Jan. 11, 1963.

40 For the speeches, documents, and resolutions of this seminar, see Gerwani, *Seminar Nasional Wanita Tani [National Seminar on Peasant Women]* (Djakarta, 1962).

41 *HR,* Oct. 26, 1961.

42 A survey of medium and large manufacturing enterprises in 1955 found that about 35 per cent of the 450,000 workers reported were women *(Report to the Government of Indonesia on Social Security,* International Labour Office [Geneva, 1958], pp. 17-18). Of 1,452,000 workers employed by more than 25,000 officially registered enterprises in 1956, 416,784 were women workers (Njono, "Women Workers of Indonesia," *World Trade Union Movement* [March, 1956], p. 9). According to a PKI estimate given in May, 1958, women comprised 45 per cent of workers in estates, 65 per cent in textile enterprises, 60 per cent in light industry, and 65 per cent in cigarette enterprises, with a large number also in the government ministries and services (Sundari, "Memperbesar Aktivitet Gerakan Wanita untuk Memenangkan Partai dalam Pemilihan Umum Parlemen ke-II" ["Increasing the Activity of the Women's Movement in Order To Bring Victory to the Party in the Second Parliamentary General Elections"], *BM* [June, 1958], p. 263).

43 *BB,* March 17, 1956, p. 3.

44 SOBSI, *Dokumen-Dokumen Konferensi Nasional SOBSI (1957)* (Djakarta, 1958), p. 94.

45 SOBSI, *Plan Organisasi 1958* (Djakarta, 1957), pp. 5-6.

46 *BB,* Oct. 15, 1957, p. 6; Jan. 30, 1958, pp. 1, 3.

47 Moh. Munir, *Pedoman Penjelesaian Plan Organisasi 1958 [Survey of the Implementation of the 1958 Plan of Organization]* (Djakarta, 1959), pp. 15-16.

48 *Ibid.,* p. 17.

49 In August, 1959, the estate workers' union, Sarbupri, claimed that it had 681 women activists in a membership of perhaps 350,000 to 400,000 *(BB,* Aug. 25, 1959, p. 3). In May, 1960, the East Java SOBSI leaders told me that women constituted about 5 per cent of the cadres, but 30 per cent of total membership, in the province.

50 See SOBSI, *Peranan Buruh Wanita dalam Pembangunan [The Role of Women Workers in Development]* (Djakarta, 1961).

51 Kartinah, "Memperluas Keanggotaan dikalangan Wanita Tani" ["Extending Membership among Peasant Women"], *HR,* June 15, 1955.

XVIII. ETHNIC GROUPS AND MINORITIES; VETERANS

1 G. William Skinner, "The Nature of Loyalties in Rural Indonesia," in Skinner, ed., *Local, Ethnic, and National Loyalties in Village Indonesia: A Symposium* (New Haven, 1959), p. 5.

2 For a description of discrimination against the Indonesian citizens of Chinese descent see Donald E. Willmott, *The National Status of the Chinese in Indonesia* (Ithaca, 1956), esp. pp. 51-57, 60-62.

3 PKI, *Putusan-Putusan Sidang Pleno Central Comite Partai Komunis Indonesia* [*Decisions of the PKI Central Committee Plenum Meeting*] (Djakarta, 1953), p. 57.

4 PKI, *Program PKI* (Djakarta, 1954), pp. 13-14.

5 *HR*, Nov. 18, 1955.

6 See, for example, M. H. Lukman, "Kesetiaan PKI pada Politik Front Persatuan dan Pembelaan Kepentingan Rakjat" ["PKI's Loyalty to the United Front Policy and to the Defense of the People's Interests"], in D. N. Aidit *et al.*, *37 Tahun Partai Komunis Indonesia* [*PKI 37 Years*] (Djakarta, 1957), pp. 14-17.

7 The three booklets were issued under the title *Menudju Otonomi Daerah Seluasluasnja* [*Toward the Broadest Regional Autonomy*], I-III (Djakarta, 1958). A. R. Nungtjik was the author of the first, *Autonomy and Its Sphere of Authority*; Peris Pardede wrote the second, *Abolition of the Pamong Pradja System;* and Hutomo Supardan, Harjowisastro, and J. Piry wrote the third, which consisted of essays on "The Budget," "Determining the Boundaries of Autonomous Regions," and "Level-III Autonomy."

8 See above, pp. 86, 99.

9 D. N. Aidit, *Untuk Demokrasi dan Kabinet Gotong Rojong* [*For Democracy and a Mutual Coöperation Cabinet*] (Djakarta, 1959), pp. 175-176; M. H. Lukman, *Tentang Konstitusi PKI* [*Concerning PKI's Constitution*] (Djakarta, 1959), pp. 25-26.

10 D. N. Aidit, *Berani, Berani, Sekali Lagi Berani!* [*Courageous, Courageous, and Again Courageous!*] (Djakarta, 1963), p. 69.

11 See, for example, D. N. Aidit, "Bersatu untuk Menjelesaikan Tuntutan Revolusi Agustus 1945" ["Unite To Complete the Demands of the August 1945 Revolution"], *HR*, Aug. 1, 1956.

12 *HR*, March 22, 1963.

13 Much of the information on Baperki was obtained in interview from a Baperki leader in Surabaja.

14 Siauw Giok Tjhan in January, 1951, had founded the semiweekly newspaper *Suara Rakjat*, which in July, 1951, became the daily *Harian Rakjat*, the official mouthpiece of PKI. He was director and then codirector of *Harian Rakjat* until October 31, 1953.

15 Moh. Munasir, "Veterans' Problems," *Veteran* (Aug., 1959), p. 16; see also pp. 41-42.

16 D. N. Aidit, "Ubah Imbangan Kekuatan untuk Melaksanakan Konsepsi Presiden 100%" ["Change the Balance of Power in Order To Carry Out the President's Concept 100%"], *HR*, July 5, 1957.

17 *TI*, Oct. 21, 1954.

18 *HR*, Dec. 20, 1957; Sudisman, "Semangat Bukit 1211," *BM* (Dec., 1957), p. 512.

19 Boyd R. Compton, *Indonesian Communism: The Ranks Swell*, American Universities' Field Staff Report (New York, 1954), p. 11.

20 "Laporan Tambahan Mengenai Pengalaman Bekerdja dikalangan Bekas Pedjuang (Veteran)" ["Additional Report on Experience in Working among the Veterans"], *BM* (May-July, 1957), pp. 264-267.

21 Munasir, *op. cit.*, p. 16.

XIX. MOBILIZING ELECTORAL SUPPORT

1 The *santris* in general were expected to vote for, and apparently did vote for, the specifically Moslem parties.

2 At the local level some PNI leaders did attack PKI, but their attacks were inhibited further by the widespread belief that to be anti-Communist was to be proimperialist.

3 *HR*, May 19, 1954.

4 *RI* (Feb., 1957), p. 6.

5 An account of the campaigns for the 1955 elections is given in Herbert Feith, *The Indonesian Elections of 1955* (Ithaca, 1957), p. 9 *et seq.*

6 *HR*, Nov. 4, 1954.

7 Examples of province-level programs may be found in *HR*: for East Java on June 13, 1957; for Central Java on June 20, 1957; for West Java on July 1, 1957; and for West Kalimantan on April 29, 1958. As examples of programs for municipalities, see *Program Secom PKI Kotapradja Surabaja untuk Pemilihan DPRD Kotapradja Surabaja [The Program of the Surabaja City PKI Section Committee for the Elections for the Surabaja City Representative Council]* (Surabaja, 1957); and *Manifes Pemilihan Umum PKI untuk DPRD Kotapradja Jogjakarta [PKI General Election Manifesto for the Jogjakarta City Representative Council]* (Jogjakarta, 1957). As an example of a program for a *kabupaten*, see "Program Seksi Comite PKI Sleman untuk Pemilihan Umum DPRD Sleman" ["The Program of the Sleman PKI Section Committee for the Elections for the Sleman Representative Council"], unpublished manuscript, (Sleman, 1957).

8 In April, 1955, the secretary of PKI's Central Java province committee reported that "people's artists" not only had created many kinds of songs and dances propagandizing PKI, but they also had given political content to old songs and dances. The Central Java committee was at that time holding a course for two persons from each of the sixteen section committees to train them as dancing, singing, percussion, and *gamelan* cadres (Siswojo, "Seni untuk Menang dalam Pemilihan Umum" ["Art for Bringing Victory in the General Elections"], *KP*, April 1, 1955, p. 57).

9 For accounts of people's festivals, see Boyd R. Compton, *The Silent Election*, Institute of Current World Affairs Report (New York, 1955), p. 4; also Selosoemardjan, "Social Changes in Jogjakarta" (Ph.D. dissertation, Cornell University, 1959), p. 216. I also received information from members of the Indonesian rural administrative service.

10 Typed translation of Soekarman, "How To Win the General Elections for PKI," which had appeared in *Boletin PKI Djawa Timur* (Sept., 1958).

11 The results of the Constituent Assembly elections of December, 1955, are largely ignored in the following paragraphs because they showed only minor changes compared with the September, 1955, elections. For discussions of the results of the September, 1955, elections, see Feith, *op. cit.*, p. 57 *et seq.*; Justus Maria van der Kroef, "Indonesia's First National Election: A Sociological Analysis," *American Journal of Economics and Sociology*, XVI (April, 1957), 237-249; XVI (July, 1957), 407-420; and A. van Marle, "The First Indonesian Parliamentary Elections," *Indonesie*, IX (1956), 257-264.

12 The results of the 1957-58 local elections were obtained from the Election Bureau of the Ministry of Internal Affairs. For Java, they are the combined totals of votes cast for the *kabupaten* and town councils; for South Sumatra and Kalimantan they are the votes cast for the provincial councils.

13 Professor George Kahin, of Cornell University, has suggested to me that the *santri-abangan* antithesis may be both an oversimplification and politically misleading. He notes that there is as yet no good evidence to indicate, for example, that considerable numbers of *santris* did not vote for PNI, nor that many *abangans* did

not support NU. I concede that far more detailed field research will be required to clarify the nature and political significance of the *santri-abangan* division in Javanese society. I assert, however, that my conversations with Javanese local politicians and government officials, as well as my examination of the *kabupaten* and city election results, afford strong support for the admittedly tentative conclusion that the *santri-abangan* antithesis is of major importance in understanding the political behavior of a significant part of the Javanese population.

14 In three electoral districts, Djakarta Raja, Djember (East Java), and Sumenep (Madura), the total Moslem (that is Masjumi, NU, and PSII) vote fell by 161,782, while the PKI vote increased by 74,869. This is not proof, however, that many former Moslem voters switched to PKI, because in the same three districts the PNI vote fell by 35,974, and the total vote fell by 111,891.

15 In the *kabupaten* of Magetan (East Java), PKI received 49.99 per cent of the votes, but was given a majority of the council seats because it had formed an electoral alliance with Permai, which received 0.72 per cent of the votes.

16 For the 1957 distribution of PKI, PNI, and Moslem (that is, Masjumi, NU, PSII, Perti, and AKUI combined) votes, see the maps on pp. 226-228. AKUI and Perti votes are not included in the figures within the text because I was unable to obtain details as to their votes in the 1955 elections.

17 As of this writing, it is too soon to know what the former supporters of Masjumi will do now that the party is banned. It is not to be expected, however, that many of them will turn to PKI.

XX. PKI's POLITICAL BEHAVIOR UNDER THE NATIONAL UNITED FRONT

1 See above, pp. 121-127.

2 D. N. Aidit, *Tiga Interviu* [*Three Interviews*] (Djakarta, 1954), pp. 13-14.

3 D. N. Aidit, "Bersatu untuk Menjelesaikan Tuntutan Revolusi Agustus 1945" ["Unite To Realize the Demands of the August 1945 Revolution"], *HR*, Aug. 1, 1956.

4 M. H. Lukman, *Tentang Front Persatuan Nasional* [*Concerning the National United Front*] (Djakarta, 1960), p. 39. See also M. H. Lukman, *Adjakan PKI kepada Kaum Pengusaha Nasional* [*PKI Support to the National Businessmen*] (Djakarta, 1963). This latter is a report submitted to the Central Committee plenary session. "Pengusaha" includes industrialists, for whom Lukman urged particular Communist support.

5 D. N. Aidit, *Madju Terus Menggempur Imperialisme dan Feodalisme!* [*Continue To Advance To Destroy Imperialism and Feudalism!*] (Djakarta, 1961), p. 21.

6 Lukman, *Tentang Front*, pp. 36-39.

7 *Ibid.*, p. 38.

XXI. THE PERIOD OF PARLIAMENTARY DEMOCRACY, 1952–July, 1959

1 *HR*, Feb. 25, 26, 1952.

2 *HR*, March 10, 1952.

3 *HR*, March 24, 1952.

4 *HR*, April 23, 1952.

5 The political developments during the period of the Wilopo cabinet are covered by Herbert Feith. *The Wilopo Cabinet, 1952-1953: A Turning Point in Post-Revolutionary Indonesia* (Ithaca, 1958).

6 *Ibid.*, pp. 94-96.

7 *Ibid.*, p. 161.

8 *Ibid.*, p. 97.

9 *PKI-B* (Feb. 15, 1952), p. 2.

10 *HR*, May 27, 1952.

11 Sakirman, "Beberapa Pengalaman Fraksi PKI dalam DPRS RI . . ." ["Some Experiences of the PKI Parliamentary Group . . ."], *BM* (Jan., 1956), p. 12.

12 The reasons for the breakaway are outlined in Feith, *op. cit.*, pp. 44-45, and Munawir Sjadzali, "Indonesia's Muslim Parties and Their Political Concepts" (M.A. thesis, Georgetown University, 1959), pp. 29-30.

13 *HR*, June 20, 1952.

14 "Apa Sebab PKI Memberi Kesempatan Bekerdja pada Kabinet Wilopo" ["Why PKI Gives the Wilopo Cabinet the Opportunity To Work"], *HR*, July 14, 1952.

15 *HR*, May 21, 1952.

16 Feith, *op. cit.*, p. 94.

17 T. Mangunsumbogo, "Fakta dan Dokumen-Dokumen untuk Menjusun Buku 'Indonesia Memasuki Gelanggang Internasional': Periode V: 1950-1954" ["Facts and Documents for Making a Book 'Indonesia Enters the International Arena': Period V: 1950-1954"], Vol. VIB, mimeographed (Djakarta, 1959), pp. 164-165.

18 Herbert Feith, "Towards Elections in Indonesia," *Pacific Affairs*, XXVII (Sept., 1954), 243-244.

19 *TI*, March 13, 1953; Feith, *Wilopo Cabinet*, p. 190 n. 51.

20 *HR*, June 8, 1953.

21 *HR*, June 5, 16, 1953.

22 *HR*, June 22, 1953.

23 *PKI-B* (July 1, 1953), pp. 100-104.

24 D. N. Aidit, "Histeria dikalangan Reaksi" ["Hysteria among the Reactionaries"], in *Pilihan Tulisan [Selected Works]*, I (Djakarta, 1959), 147-149.

25 *PKI-B* (Aug. 15, 1953), p. 124.

26 D. N. Aidit, *Djalan ke Demokrasi Rakjat bagi Indonesia [The Indonesian Road to People's Democracy]* (Djakarta, 1955), pp. 47-48.

27 *TI*, Oct. 9, 1953.

28 *TI*, May 25, 1954; *HR*, May 22, 1954.

29 *HR*, Sept. 8, 1953.

30 *HR*, Sept. 24, 1953.

31 D. N. Aidit, "Perkuat Kedudukan Republik! Tugas Pokok Rakjat Indonesia ditahun Datang" ["Strengthen the Position of the Republic! The Basic Task of the Indonesian People in the Next Year"], *PKI-B* (Dec. 31, 1953), p. 202.

32 Aidit, *Djalan ke Demokrasi*, p. 28.

33 Aidit, "Perkuat Kedudukan," p. 203.

34 PKI, *Program PKI* (Djakarta, 1954), pp. 25-29.

35 *HR*, Feb. 12, 1954.

36 *HR*, Feb. 19, 22, 1954.

37 *PKI-B* (March, 1954), pp. 28-29.

38 *HR*, April 13, 1954.

39 *TI*, June 23, 1954.

40 *TI*, July 5, 1954.

41 Boyd R. Compton, *Indonesian Communism: Friends and Allies,* American Universities' Field Staff Report (New York, 1955), pp. 6-7.

42 PKI, *Manifes Pemilihan Umum PKI [PKI's General Election Manifesto]* (Djakarta, 1954), p. 20.

43 *PKI-B* (May, 1954), p. 55. Under the version of proportional representation as practiced in the 1955 elections, two or more parties, organizations, or individual candidates could, in each electoral district, pool their surplus votes after the first distribution of seats.

44 D. N. Aidit, "For Broad Unity of All National Forces in Indonesia," *FALP,* Dec. 31, 1954, p. 4; *HR,* Oct. 15, 18, 20, 1954.

45 *TI*, Dec. 10, 1954.

46 *TI*, Oct. 29, 1954.

47 *HR*, Dec. 12, 1954.

48 *HR*, May 9, 11, 1955; *Buletin SOBSI* (May 15, 1955), pp. 3-5.

49 *HR*, June 22, 1955.

50 *HR*, June 30, 1955.

51 *HR*, July 12, 1955.

52 Aidit was belatedly brought to court at the end of 1954 and the beginning of 1955 for defaming Hatta in a statement on the Madiun rebellion. He was finally handed a three-month suspended jail sentence, and the Party was not prevented from publishing Aidit's defense which repeated and embellished the original defamation.

53 Sutan Sjahrir, "Problems the Country Faces," in "Perspective of Indonesia," *Atlantic Monthly,* Supplement (June, 1956), p. 24.

54 *HR*, July 27, 1955.

55 *HR*, Aug. 8, 1955.

56 D. N. Aidit, "The General Elections and the Tasks of the Indonesian Communist Party," *FALP,* Sept. 9, 1955, p. 3.

57 *HR*, Aug. 22, 1955.

58 *HR*, Aug. 23, 1955.

59 D. N. Aidit, *Pertahankan Republik Proklamasi 1945! [Defend the 1945 Proclamation Republic!]* (Djakarta, 1955), p. 31.

60 *HR*, Oct. 11, 1955.

61 *HR*, Nov. 16, 1955.

62 Sarmidi Mangunsarkoro, PNI general chairman, for example, on January 7, 1956, rejected the idea of PKI participation in the next cabinet, but said that PKI support was possible (*TI,* Jan. 9, 1956).

63 *HR*, Dec. 3, 1955.

64 The distribution of seats in the new, elected parliament was: PNI, 57; Masjumi, 57; NU, 45; PKI, 39; PSII, 8; Protestant Party, 8; Roman Catholic Party, 6; PSI, 5; IPKI, 4; Perti, 4; seventeen small parties, 23; and one individual.

65 *HR*, March 7, 1956.

66 *HR*, March 21, 1956.

67 *HR*, March 19, 1956.

68 Herbert Feith, "Indonesian Politics, 1949-1957: The Decline of Representative Government" (Ph.D. dissertation, Cornell University, 1961), p. 771.

69 *HR*, May 26, 1952.

70 "Bekerdja dikalangan Intelektuil" ["Working among the Intellectuals"], *BM* (Oct.-Nov. 1952), pp. 121-122.

71 Boyd R. Compton, *Indonesia, 1955*, Institute of Current World Affairs Report (New York, 1956), p. 11.

72 *HR*, Jan. 16, 1956. Sukarno presumably included in the figure of 16 million Communists the families of the 6 million who voted for PKI in the 1955 general elections.

73 PKI, "Bersatu dan Bantu Pemerintah untuk Mengatasi Peristiwa Sumatera Tengah dan Sumatera Utara" ["Unite and Assist the Government To Overcome the Central and North Sumatra Affairs"], *HR*, Dec. 24, 1956.

74 For the official Masjumi explantation of its withdrawal, see *Suara STII [Voice of STII]* (Jan. 1957), pp. 6-7.

75 *HR*, Jan. 11, 1957.

76 *HR*, Jan. 12, 1957.

77 *HR*, Feb. 8, 1957.

78 *TI*, Feb. 22, 1957.

79 *HR*, Feb. 18, 1957.

80 PKI, "Bung Karno's Concept Answers the Urgent Political Problems Faced by the Indonesian People Today," *RI*, Supplement (Feb., 1957), pp. 9-11.

81 *New Age* (weekly, New Delhi), April 21, 1957, p. 12.

82 *ITUN* (March, 1957), pp. 4-5.

83 *Ibid.*, p. 6. In response to this threat, the Djakarta military command announced that severe action would be taken against any political strike (*TI*, March 28, 1957).

84 *HR*, March 22, 1957.

85 Editorial, *HR*, April 5, 1957.

86 *RI* (April, 1957), pp. 8-9.

87 The "functional groups" represented in the National Council were workers, peasants, intellectuals, youth, national industrialists, artists, citizens of foreign descent, reporters, women, religious groups (Moslem, Protestant, Roman Catholic, and Bali-Hindu), the generation of 1945, the armed forces (including the police), the attorney-general, the cabinet, and the regions.

88 Quoted in *TI*, June 17, 1957.

89 *HR*, April 15, 1957.

90 In the September, 1955, parliamentary elections, PKI had been the second-largest party in Central and East Java, the third-largest in West Java, and the fourth-largest in Djakarta Raja.

91 *HR*, June 27, 1957.

92 *HR*, June 28, 1957.

93 *TI*, Nov. 1, 6, 1957; Feb. 5, 1958.

94 *TI*, Aug. 12, 1957.

95 *TI*, Nov. 1, 6, Dec. 28, 1957.

96 Editorial, *Suluh Indonesia*, Nov. 14, 1957.

97 For example, Abdulwahab, a member of the NU executive council, was reported as saying that PKI's advances were bringing Indonesia close to civil war, and as demanding that PKI and other Communist organizations be outlawed (Justus Maria van der Kroef, "Disunited Indonesia," *Far Eastern Survey*, XXVII (April, 1958), 57-58.

98 *HR*, Aug. 6, 1957.

99 *RI* (Oct.-Nov., 1957), pp. 19-20.

100 Nursuhud, *Menjingkap Tabir "Dewan-Banteng"* [*Lifting the Banteng Council's Curtain*] (Djakarta, 1958). The Banteng Council was the council established in Central Sumatra by Lieutenant Colonel Husein.

101 Reported in *TI*, Nov. 22, 28, 1957.

102 *RI* (Sept., 1957), pp. 28-29.

103 *Ibid.*, pp. 15-16.

104 Editorial, *HR*, Oct. 12, 1957.

105 *RI* (Dec., 1957), p. 25.

106 *HR*, Nov. 19, 1957.

107 *HR*, Oct. 21, 1957.

108 Sukarno told Louis Fischer that he had given the order for the take-over and that he had urged the confiscation of Dutch properties as early as 1950 when he had been opposed by the Natsir cabinet (Louis Fischer, *The Story of Indonesia* [London, 1959], p. 300).

109 Editorial, *HR*, Dec. 7, 1957.

110 PKI, "Memasuki Tahun 1958 dengan Fase Baru Perdjuangan Anti-Kolonialisme" ["Entering 1958 with a New Phase in the Anticolonial Struggle"], *BM* (Jan., 1958), p. 6.

111 *Ibid.*

112 *Ibid.*, p. 11.

113 *HR*, March 1, 1958.

114 *RI* (March, 1958), p. 7.

115 This claim was made to me by PKI and Pemuda Rakjat cadres. See also the reference to "people's guerrillas" fighting the PRRI-Permesta rebels, in PKI, *40 Tahun PKI* [*PKI 40 Years*] (Djakarta, 1960), p. 87.

116 The PKI leaders claimed that during the period from August, 1956, to August, 1959, Party membership was increased by 38 per cent in West Sumatra and by 40 per cent in North Sulawesi (Amir Anwar Sanusi, "Results of the First Three-Year Plan," mimeographed trans. [Djakarta, 1959], p. 3).

117 "Resolusi tentang Penurunan Harga Beras" ["Resolution on Lowering the Price of Rice"], *BM* (March-April, 1958), p. 178.

118 D. N. Aidit, "Pidato dihadapan Kongres ke-V Partai Persatuan Sosialis Djerman" ["Speech before the Fifth Congress of the German Socialist Unity Party"], *BM* (Aug., 1958), pp. 384-385.

119 *HR*, Nov. 1, 1958.

120 "Resolution on the General Report of the Central Bureau of SOBSI," *ITUN* (Jan., 1959), p. 3.

121 D. N. Aidit, "Bersatu Menempuh Djalan Demokrasi Terpimpin Menudju Pelaksanakaan Konsepsi Presiden Sukarno 100%" ["Unite along the Road of Guided Democracy toward the 100% Implementation of President Sukarno's Concept"], *HR*, Nov. 20, 1958.

122 My source for this report was a prominent politician, but one who must remain anonymous.

123 *HR*, Feb. 4, 1959.

124 D. N. Aidit, "Building the Organization Is Important, but Building Ideology Is Even More Important," *RI*, Supplement (June-July, 1959), pp. 4-5.

125 D. N. Aidit, "Mendukung Demokrasi Terpimpin Adalah Politik jang Paling Revolusioner" ["To Support Guided Democracy Is the Most Revolutionary Policy"], *HR*, Oct. 25, 1958.

126 *HR*, Dec. 31, 1958; Jan. 3, 1959.

127 *HR*, Jan. 12, 1959.

128 It should be noted again that under the 1945 constitution the president holds powers roughly equivalent to those of the president of the United States. The 1945 constitution was so brief and vague, however, that the president could take to himself powers far beyond those of his American counterpart.

129 Njoto, "Hold High the Spirit of 1945," *RI* (April-May, 1959), p. 17.

130 Sakirman, "Apa Arti Sokongan PKI kepada UUD 1945 dan Demokrasi Terpimpin" ["The Meaning of PKI's Support for the 1945 Constitution and Guided Democracy"], Part II, *BM* (July-Aug., 1960), pp. 320-328.

131 *RI* (June-July, 1959), pp. 16-17.

132 *Ibid.*, p. 11.

XXII. PKI AND GUIDED DEMOCRACY, JULY 1959–JULY, 1963

1 *TI*, April 22, 1960; also interviews with NU leaders.

2 *HR*, July 11, 1961.

3 SOBSI, *Tentang Aksi, Kader dan Demokrasi* [*Concerning Action, Cadres, and Democracy*] (Djakarta. 1961), pp. 25-26.

4 *Ibid.*, p. 37.

5 *HR*, July 6, 7, 8, 10, 1961; Oct. 15, Nov. 9, 1962.

6 *HR*, Feb. 14, 1963.

7 For the army's report on the current state of security in the various regions of Indonesia in April, 1963, see *HR*, April 11, 1963.

8 *HR*, Feb. 21, 1963.

9 For a commentary on the economic problems of the Sukarno cabinet see Justus Maria van der Kroef, "Indonesia's Economic Difficulties," *International Journal*, XVII (Autumn, 1962), 399-413.

10 Donald Hindley, "President Sukarno and the Communists: The Politics of Domestication," *American Political Science Review*, LVI (Dec., 1962), 915-926.

11 Stop-press supplement to *RI* (June-July, 1959), pp. 2-3.

12 See, for example, D. N. Aidit, *Berani, Berani, Sekali Lagi Berani!* [*Courageous, Courageous, and Again Courageous!*] (Djakarta, 1963), p. 39.

13 D. N. Aidit, *Perkuat Persatuan Nasional dan Persatuan Komunis!* [*Strengthen National Unity and Communist Unity!*] (Djakarta, 1961), pp. 17, 26.

14 D. N. Aidit, *Peladjaran dari Sedjarah PKI* [*Lessons from PKI's History*] (Djakarta, 1960), pp. 22-23.

15 *HR*, July 29, 1959; *RI* (Sept.-Oct., 1959), p. 8.

16 PKI, *Resolusi tentang Laporan Umum CC PKI kepada Kongres Nasional ke-VI* [*Resolution on the PKI Central Committee's General Report to the Sixth National Congress*] (Djakarta, 1959), pp. 33-34.

17 See, for example, Editorial, *HR*, Oct. 2, 1959.

18 The main speeches of the Communist representatives in the budget debates are given in abbreviated form in *RI* (Feb., 1960), pp. 10-15.

19 *RI* (April, 1960), p. 9.

20 *Ibid.*, p. 11.

21 When NU leaders protested at the low number of Moslems, Sukarno added an extra twenty-two members, mostly Islamic leaders.

22 *RI* (April, 1960), p. 12; *Suara Ibukota*, III (April, 1960), 1.

23 *HR*, May 24, 1962.

24 *HR*, June 27, 1960.

25 See, for example, *HR*, Dec. 3, 6, 19, 21, 23, 27, 1960.

26 In April, 1962, Aidit reported that about 50 per cent of the Communists had been removed from the provincial and local councils (D. N. Aidit, *Satu Fikiran—Satu Hati—Satu Tudjuan [One Thought—One Heart—One Goal]* [Djakarta, 1962], p. 57). It appears that Communist representation was most severely reduced outside Java, where Sukarno's personal supervision was weakest.

27 *HR*, May 23, 1961.

28 *HR*, Aug. 17, 1962.

29 *HR*, Sept. 12, 1962.

30 Aidit, *Berani*, pp. 7-8.

31 Editorial, *HR*, Feb. 14, 1963.

32 Aidit, *Perkuat Persatuan*, p. 13; *HR*, Jan. 5, 1962.

33 *HR*, Feb. 1, 1962.

34 *HR*, Dec. 21, 27, 1962.

35 *HR*, May 17, 22, 1963.

36 *HR*, Sept. 5, 1960.

37 *HR*, Feb. 9, 1962.

38 Aidit, *Berani*, pp. 34-35.

39 PKI, *Gerakan 1001 [The 1001 Movement]* (Semarang, 1962).

40 D. N. Aidit, "Back to the 1945 Constitution for a Change in Politics and Living Conditions," *RI*, Supplement (Sept.-Oct., 1959), pp. 3-11.

41 Editorial, "After the Proclamation of the Presidential Decree," *ITUN* (Sept., 1959), pp. 2-3.

42 *BB*, Jan. 15, 1960, p. 1; *HR*, Jan. 11, 1960.

43 See, for example, *HR*, Feb. 11, 1960; *RI* (April, 1960), pp. 4-5.

44 *Bintang Timur*, April 22, 1960.

45 PKI, "An Evaluation of the Kerdja Cabinet after One Year in Office," mimeographed (Djakarta, 1960). Kerdja [Work] Cabinet is the name given to Sukarno's cabinet. Of course the ministers criticized in this statement had been previously subject to criticism by PKI.

46 Aidit, *Berani*, pp. 5-41.

47 *HR*, Oct. 12, 1962.

48 *HR*, Dec. 27, 1962.

49 D. N. Aidit, *Untuk Demokrasi, Persatuan dan Mobilisasi [For Democracy, Unity, and Mobilization]* (Djakarta, 1962), p. 22.

50 *HR*, Jan. 8, 1963.

51 Sakirman, "Apa Arti," Part I, *BM* (May-June, 1960), pp. 194-219; Part II, *BM* (July-Aug., 1960), pp. 320-340, 348. See esp. pp. 194, 325, 328-329, 339, 340.

52 Aidit, *Perkuat Persatuan*, pp. 29-31.

53 *HR*, Jan. 13, 1962.

54 Aidit, *Untuk Demokrasi*, pp. 81-82.

55 Aidit, *Berani*, p. 58.

56 M. H. Lukman, *Tentang Front Persatuan Nasional [Concerning the National United Front]* (Djakarta, 1960), pp. 37-38.

57 M. H. Lukman, *Adjakan PKI Kepada kaum Pengusaha Nasional [PKI Support to the National Businessmen]* (Djakarta, 1963).

58 For a more recent discussion of the position of PKI in the deepening dispute

within the international Communist movement, see Donald Hindley, "The Indonesian Communist Party and the Conflict in the International Communist Movement," *The China Quarterly* (1964). Since early 1963, PKI has come down unequivocally on the side of the Chinese Communist Party and against the CPSU. Even so, there has been as yet no indication of any disagreement within PKI concerning its position in the dispute.

59 Aidit, *Berani*, p. 38.

60 The officer corps of the national army was drawn from some who had received military training from the Dutch, some who first received military training from the Japanese, and others who took up arms during the revolution as members of the national army, associated regular corps, and irregular guerrilla bands.

61 There were persistent rumors during 1962 that a Communist would be given charge of a ministry in the economic sphere. Even this need not be dangerous for any but PKI. The minister would be closely watched by his fellow ministers and by his non-Communist officials so that he could not abuse his position. Any success he might achieve would be claimed by the government as a whole, and would consolidate the position of the government as a whole; any failure in this very difficult sphere would be placed firmly on his and his party's shoulders.

Select Bibliography

Select Bibliography

The following bibliography is highly selective and focuses narrowly on the period since December 1949. Only the most important or illuminating secondary sources are cited. I have listed those Communist journals and newspapers that I managed to obtain; only their most important articles are cited separately. The list of Communist books, booklets, and pamphlets excludes only the most irrelevant.

Special mention ought to be made of the reports issued between 1952 and 1960 under the auspices of, first, the Institute of Current World Affairs and then the American Universities' Field Staff. The reports are too numerous to mention individually, but they were most useful, especially those by Boyd R. Compton in the period 1952 to 1955. It should be noted that I have not listed the following periodicals of which I was able to obtain only one or two scattered numbers: *Berita Gerwani* for 1959 and 1960, *Buletin Pemuda Rakjat* for 1955, and Gerwani's *Wanita Indonesia* for 1955 and 1956.

BOOKS, PAMPHLETS, MISCELLANEOUS DOCUMENTS

Aidit, D. N. *Aidit Menggugat Peristiwa Madiun.* Djakarta, 1955. 64 pp.
——. *Anti-Imperialisme dan Front Nasional.* Djakarta, 1962. 64 pp.
——. *Berani, Berani, Sekali Lagi Berani!* Djakarta, 1963. 72 pp.
——. *Bersatu untuk Menjelesaikan Tuntutan-Tuntutan Revolusi Agustus 1945 dan Bahan-Bahan Lain dari Sidang Pleno ke-IV CC PKI jang Perluas.* Djakarta, 1956. 100 pp.

——. *The Birth and Growth of the Communist Party of Indonesia.* Djakarta, 1958. 49 pp.
——. *Dari Sembilan Negeri Sosialis.* Djakarta, 1959. 164 pp.
——. *Djalan ke Demokrasi Rakjat bagi Indonesia.* Djakarta, 1955. 63 pp.
——. *Introduksi tentang Soal-Soal Pokok Revolusi Indonesia.* Djakarta, 1959. 16 pp.
——. *Konfrontasi Peristiwa Madiun 1948; Peristiwa Sumatera 1956.* Djakarta, 1957. 47 pp.
——. *Lenin dan Indonesia.* Djakarta, 1960. 32 pp.
——. *Madju Terus Menggempur Imperialisme dan Feodalisme!* Djakarta, 1961. 51 pp.
——. *Masjarakat Indonesia dan Revolusi Indonesia.* Djakarta, 1957. 72 pp.
——. *Menempuh Djalan Rakjat.* 4th ed. Djakarta, 1954. 38 pp.
——. *Menudju Indonesia Baru.* 2d ed. Djakarta, 1955. 48 pp.
——. *Peladjaran dari Sedjarah PKI.* Djakarta, 1960. 31 pp.
——. *Pengantar Etika dan Moral Komunis.* Djakarta, 1962. 32 pp.
——. *Perdjuangan dan Adjaran-Adjaran Karl Marx.* Djakarta, 1950. 64 pp.
——. *Perkuat Persatuan Nasional dan Persatuan Komunis!* Djakarta, 1961. 31 pp
——. *Pertahankan Republik Proklamasi 1945!* Djakarta, 1955. 36 pp.
——. *Pilihan Tulisan.* Djakarta, 1959, 1960. 2 vols.
——. *Satu Fikiran—Satu Hati—Satu Tudjuan.* Djakarta, 1962. 72 pp.
——. *Sedjarah Gerakan Buruh Indonesia.* Djakarta, 1952. 64 pp.
——. *Selamatkan dan Konsolidasi Kemenangan Front Persatuan.* Djakarta, 1955. 19 pp.
——. *Sendjata ditangan Rakjat.* Djakarta, 1958. 24 pp.
——. *Setudju Manipol Harus Setudju Nasakom!* Djakarta, 1962. 64 pp.
——. *Sosialisme Indonesia dan Sjarat-Sjarat Pelaksanaannja.* Djakarta, 1962. 310 pp.
——. *Tiga Interviu.* Djakarta, 1954. 16 pp.
——. *Untuk Demokrasi dan Kabinet Gotong Rojong.* Djakarta, 1959. 181 pp.
——. *Untuk Demokrasi, Persatuan dan Mobilisasi.* Djakarta, 1962. 103 pp.
——. *Untuk Kemenangan Front Nasional dalam Pemilihan Umum.* Djakarta, 1955. 28 pp.
——. *Untuk Konstitusi Republik Proklamasi 1945.* Djakarta, 1957. 32 pp.
——. *Untuk Persatuan jang Lebih Luas dari Semua Kekuatan Nasional di Indonesia.* Djakarta, 1955. 36 pp.
Aidit, D. N., et al. *Patriotisme dan Internasionalisme.* Djakarta, 1962. 92 pp.
——. *37 Tahun Partai Komunis Indonesia.* Djakarta, 1957. 28 pp.
——. *Untuk Bekerdja Lebih Baik dikalangan kaum Tani.* Djakarta, 1958. 40 pp.
Alimin. *Peladjaran Karl Marx.* Djakarta, 1958. 15 pp.
——. *Perdjuangan Klas Karl Marx.* Djakarta, 1959. 12 pp.
——. *Riwajat Hidupku.* Djakarta, 1954. 52 pp.
Anwar Sanusi, Amir. "The Results of the First Three-Year Plan." Mimeographed trans. Djakarta, 1959. 5 pp.
Barisan Tani Indonesia. *Konstitusi Barisan Tani Indonesia.* Djakarta, 1954. 67 pp.
——. *Konstitusi Barisan Tani Indonesia.* Djakarta, 1955. 104 pp.
——. *Konstitusi Barisan Tani Indonesia.* Djakarta, 1957. 71 pp.
——. *Tentang Agitasi dan Propaganda.* Djakarta, 1954. 13 pp.
Brackman, Arnold C. *Indonesian Communism: A History.* New York, 1963. 336 pp.
Burger, D. H. *Structural Changes in Javanese Society: The Supra-Village Sphere.* Ithaca, New York, 1956. 38 pp.

——. *Structural Changes in Javanese Society: The Village Sphere.* Ithaca, New York, 1957. 17 pp.

Central Bureau of Statistics. *Statistical Pocketbook of Indonesia, 1960.* Djakarta, 1960. 269 pp.

Comite Partai Komunis Indonesia Daerah Jogjakarta. *Manifes Pemilihan Umum Partai Komunis Indonesia untuk Dewan Perwakilan ˙Rakjat Daerah Daerah Istimewa Jogjakarta.* Jogjakarta, 1957. 31 pp.

Fadjar Harapan. *Constitution of Fadjar Harapan.* Djakarta, 1960. 4 pp.

Feith, Herbert. *The Decline of Constitutional Democracy in Indonesia.* Ithaca, New York, 1962. 618 pp.

——. *The Indonesian Elections of 1955.* Ithaca, New York, 1957. 91 pp.

——. *The Wilopo Cabinet, 1952-1953: A Turning Point in Post-Revolutionary Indonesia.* Ithaca, New York, 1958. 212 pp.

Fischer, Louis. *The Story of Indonesia.* London, 1959. 341 pp.

Geertz, Clifford. *The Development of the Javanese Economy: A Socio-Cultural Approach.* Cambridge, Mass., 1956. 130 pp.

——. *The Religion of Java.* Glencoe, Illinois, 1960. 396 pp.

——. *The Social Context of Economic Change: An Indonesian Case Study.* Cambridge, Mass., 1956. 179 pp.

Geertz, Hildred. *The Javanese Family.* Glencoe, Illinois, 1961. 176 pp.

Gerakan Tani Indonesia. *17 September 1953.* Bogor, 1953. 10 pp.

Gerakan Wanita Indonesia. *Lebih Giat Meluaskan Gerakan untuk Terlaksananja Piagam Hak-Hak Wanita Indonesia.* Djakarta, 1958. 144 pp.

——. *Meluaskan Aksi-Aksi untuk Memperkuat Tuntutan Hak-Hak Wanita-Anak-Anak dan Perdamaian.* Djakarta, 1956. 36 pp.

——. *Peraturan Dasar Gerwani.* Djakarta, 1954. 42 pp.

——. *Seminar Nasional Wanita Tani.* Djakarta, 1962. 92 pp.

Goldberg, Harry. *Gerakan Buruh di Indonesia.* Djakarta, 1952. 32 pp.

Hanna, Willard A. *Bung Karno's Indonesia.* New York, 1960. 232 pp.

Holland, William L., ed. *Asian Nationalism and the West.* New York, 1953. 449 pp.

Hutomo Supardan, et al. *Menudju Otonomi Daerah Seluas-Luasnja.* Djakarta, 1958. 3 vols.

Kahin, George McTurnan. *Nationalism and Revolution in Indonesia.* Ithaca, New York, 1952, 490 pp.

Kementerian Penerangan. *Kami Perkenalkan.* Djakarta, 1950. 108 pp.

——. *Kami Perkenalkan.* Djakarta, 1954. 158 pp.

——. *Kepartaian dan Parlementaria Indonesia.* Djakarta, 1954. 704 pp.

——. *Kepartaian di Indonesia.* Djakarta, 1951. 431 pp.

——. *Kepartaian di Indonesia.* Jogjakarta, 1950. 203 pp.

Kementerian Perburuhan. *Dokumentasi Pemogokan Sarbupri sampai 28-8-1950.* Jogjakarta, 1950. 24 pp.

——. *Laporan Kementerian Perburuhan, April 1957–April 1959.* Djakarta, 1959. 81 pp.

Kementerian Pertanian. *Himpunan Keputusan Kongres / Konperensi Organisasi-Organisasi Tani Massa.* Djakarta, 1951. 55 pp.

——. *Pemandangan tentang Organisasi Tani Massa.* Djakarta, 1952. 18 pp.

——. *Pergerakan Tani di Indonesia.* Djakarta, 1954. 266 pp.

——. *Supplement No. 1, Maret 1952, pada Himpunan Keputusan Kongres / Konperensi Organisasi-Organisasi Tani Massa.* Djakarta, 1953. 27 pp.

Kerdjasama Partai–Organisasi Djakarta Raja. *20 Mei.* Djakarta, 1954. 55 pp.

Komite Perdamaian Indonesia. *Musjawarah Nasional untuk Perdamaian.* Bandung, 1960. 39 pp.

Laqueur, Walter, and Leopold Labedz, eds. *Polycentrism: The New Factor in International Communism.* New York, 1962. 291 pp.

Legge, John D. *Problems of Regional Autonomy in Contemporary Indonesia.* Ithaca, New York, 1957. 71 pp.

Lembaga Kebudajaan Rakjat. *Keputusan-Keputusan Kongres Nasional ke-I Lekra.* N.p., 1959. 11 pp.

———. *Laporan Umum Pengurus Pusat LEKRA kepada Kongres Nasional ke-1 LEKRA.* N.p., 1959, 27 pp.

———. *Menjambut Kongres Kebudajaan.* N.p., 1951. 49 pp.

Lukman, M. H. *Adjakan PKI kepada kaum Pengusaha Nasional.* Djakarta, 1963. 32 pp.

———. *Mengamalkan Tjinta Tanahair.* Djakarta, 1957. 24 pp.

———. *Tentang Front Persatuan Nasional.* Djakarta, 1960. 61 pp.

———. *Tentang Konstitusi PKI.* Djakarta, 1959. 92 pp.

———. *Tentang Konstitusi PKI dan Penpres No. 7/1959.* Djakarta, 1962. 23 pp.

McVey, Ruth T. *The Soviet View of the Indonesian Revolution.* Ithaca, New York, 1957. 83 pp.

Metcalf, John E. *The Agricultural Economy of Indonesia.* Washington, 1952. 100 pp.

Munir, Moh. *Introduksi tentang Manifesto Politik Republik Indonesia.* Djakarta, 1960. 16 pp.

———. *Kader Tulangpunggung Organisasi.* Djakarta, 1961. 16 pp.

———. *Pedoman Penjelesaian Plan Organisasi 1958.* Djakarta, 1959. 34 pp.

Nasution, Abdul Haris. *Tjatatan-Tjatatan sekitar Politik Militer Indonesia.* Djakarta, 1955. 388 pp.

Njono. *Tegakkan Pandji-Pandji Persatuan.* Djakarta, 1956. 36 pp.

———. *Untuk Mempertahankan dan Memperluas Hak-Hak kaum Buruh.* Djakarta, 1959. 79 pp.

Njoto. *Marxisme, Ilmu dan Amalnja.* Djakarta, 1962. 100 pp.

———. *Perkenalan Pertama dengan Dunia Baru.* Djakarta, 1953. 31 pp.

———. *Pers dan Massa.* Djakarta, 1958. 136 pp.

———. *PKI dan Pantjasila.* Djakarta, 1958. 64 pp.

———. *Revolusi Sosialis Oktober dan Pengaruhnja atas Gerakan Kemerdekaan Indonesia.* Djakarta, 1954. 24 pp.

———. *Tentang Program PKI.* Djakarta, 1959. 63 pp.

Nursuhud. *Menjingkap Tabir "Dewan-Banteng."* Djakarta, 1958. 36 pp.

Parlaungan. *Hasil Rakjat Memilih Tokoh-Tokoh Parlemen.* Djakarta, 1956. 440 pp.

Partai Komunis Indonesia. *ABC Revolusi Indonesia.* Djakarta, 1958. 24 pp.

———. *AD-ART (Konstitusi) PKI.* Djakarta, 1962. 94 pp.

———. *Bahan-Bahan untuk Kongres Nasional ke-VI Partai Komunis Indonesia.* Djakarta, 1958. 115 pp.

———. *Buku Programa Memperingati Ulang Tahun ke-35 Partai Komunis Indonesia, 23-30 Mei 1955.* Djakarta, 1955. 48 pp.

———. *Buku Putih tentang Peristiwa Madiun.* Djakarta, 1953. 32 pp.

———. *Development of Work among Fishermen.* Djakarta, 1960. 5 pp.

———. *Djalan Baru untuk Republik Indonesia.* 7th ed. Djakarta, 1953. 34 pp.

———. *Documents of the Sixth Plenum of the Central Committee of the Communist Party of Indonesia.* Djakarta, 1958. 123 pp.

——. *Dokumen-Dokumen Kongres Nasional ke-VI Partai Komunis Indonesia.* Djakarta, 1960. 3 vols.

——. *An Evaluation of the Kerdja Cabinet, after One Year in Office.* Djakarta, 1960. 14 pp.

——. *40 Tahun PKI.* Djakarta, 1960. 99 pp.

——. *Gerakan 1001.* Semarang, 1962. 32 pp.

——. *Kepalsuan Masjumi.* Djakarta, 1955. 20 pp.

——. *Keputusan-Keputusan Sidang Pleno Ke-III CC PKI.* Djakarta, 1962. 61 pp.

——. *Kewadjiban Front Persatuan Buruh.* Djakarta, 1952. 24 pp.

——. *Konfernas Tani ke-II PKI.* Djakarta, 1962. 52 pp.

——. *Konstitusi Partai Komunis Indonesia.* Djakarta, 1951. 64 pp.

——. *Konstitusi Partai Komunis Indonesia.* 3d printing. Djakarta, 1956. 71 pp.

——. *Lahirnja Partai Komunis Indonesia dan Perkembangannja.* Djakarta, 1951. 29 pp.

——. *Manifes Pemilihan Umum PKI.* Djakarta, 1954. 20 pp.

——. *Menanggulangi Kesulitan-Kesulitan Ekonomi dengan Semangat Trikora.* Djakarta, 1962. 24 pp.

——. *Mengapa Front Nasional.* Djakarta, 1957. 12 pp.

——. *Pedoman Organisasi.* Djakarta, 1951. 30 pp.

——. *Pemilihan Umum untuk Pemerintah Koalisi Nasional.* Djakarta, 1955. 23 pp.

——. *Pengakuan Masjumi.* Djakarta, 1955. 52 pp.

——. *PKI dan Konstituante.* Djakarta, 1955. 16 pp.

——. *Program Partai Komunis Indonesia.* Djakarta, 1962. 31 pp.

——. *Program PKI.* Djakarta, 1954. 31 pp.

——. *Putusan-Putusan Sidang Pleno Central Comite Partai Komunis Indonesia.* Djakarta, 1953. 63 pp.

——. *Resolusi-Resolusi Kongres Nasional ke-VI PKI.* Djakarta, 1959. 103 pp.

——. *Resolusi-Resolusi Kongres Nasional ke-VII (Luarbiasa) Partai Komunis Indonesia.* Djakarta, 1962. 72 pp.

——. *Resolusi tentang Laporan Umum CC PKI kepada Kongres Nasional ke-VI.* Djakarta, 1959. 99 pp.

——. *Serba-Serbi Dokumen Partai 1961.* Djakarta, 1962. 151 pp.

——. *Tuntunan untuk Bekerdja dikalangan kaum Tani.* Djakarta, 1955. 48 pp.

——. *Tuntutan P.K.I. sekitar Kabinet Baru dan Program Pemerintah Ali ke-II.* Surabaja, 1956. 23 pp.

——. *Untuk Pendidikan Nasional, Kerakjatan dan Ilmiah!* Djakarta, 1962. 83 pp.

Partai Komunis Indonesia, *et al. Menempuh tahun 1959.* Djakarta, 1959. 31 pp.

Pemuda Rakjat. *Diktat.* Djakarta, n.d. 38 pp.

——. *Laporan Umum pada Sidang Dewan Nasional ke-III 17 July 1958.* Djakarta, 1958. 19 pp.

——. *Menudju Persatuan Pemuda Indonesia jang Luas.* Djakarta, 1956. 68 pp.

——. *Pemuda Pengawal Kemerdekaan Nasional Indonesia.* Djakarta, 1957. 36 pp.

——. *Peraturan Dasar Pemuda Rakjat.* 3d printing. Djakarta, 1954. 46 pp.

——. *Peraturan Dasar Pemuda Rakjat.* 5th printing. Djakarta, 1958. 51 pp.

——. *Program dan Peraturan Dasar Pemuda Rakjat.* Djakarta, 1962. 54 pp.

——. *Rol Pemuda dalam Perdjuangan untuk Kemerdekaan Nasional dan Perdamaian Dunia.* Djakarta, 1955. 73 pp.

——. *Setia Mengabdi Kepentingan-Kepentingan Vital Pemuda Indonesia dan Tjita-Tjita Revolusi Agustus 1945.* Djakarta, 1962. 71 pp.

——. *21 Februari, Hari Pemuda Melawan Kolonialisme.* Djakarta, 1955. 32 pp.

Persatuan Pamong Desa Indonesia. *Peraturan Dasar Persatuan Pamong Desa Indonesia.* Surakarta, 1957. 93 pp.

Runturambi, F. *Politik Pembangunan Sekarang.* Djakarta, 1957. 22 pp.

Sakirman. *Tentang Pemilihan Umum.* Djakarta, 1952. 128 pp.

Sandra Nitidihardjo. *Gerakan Buruh Indonesia.* Djakarta, 1957. 125 pp.

Sarekat Buruh Perkebunan Republik Indonesia. *Untuk Kebebasan Demokrasi dan Melawan Pemerasan jang Kedjam.* Djakarta, .1954. 32 pp.

Seksi Comite Partai Komunis Indonesia Kotabesar Jogjakarta. *Manifes Pemilihan Umum Partai Komunis Indonesia untuk Dewan Perwakilan Rakjat Daerah Kotapradja Jogjakarta.* Jogjakarta, 1957. 46 pp.

Seksi Comite Partai Komunis Indonesia Kota Pradja Surabaja. *Program untuk Pemilihan DPRD Kota Pradja Surabaja.* Surabaja, 1957. 19 pp.

Seksi Comite Partai Komunis Indonesia Sleman. *Program Untuk Pemilihan Umum DPRD Sleman.* Sleman, Jogjakarta, 1957. 6 pp.

Sentral Organisasi Buruh Seluruh Indonesia. *Dokumen-Dokumen Konferensi Nasional SOBSI (1957).* Djakarta, 1958. 129 pp.

——. *Dorong Madju Demokrasi dan Produksi serta Landjutkan Perdjuangan Pembebasan Irian Barat.* Djakarta, 1962. 34 pp.

——. *Forward for the Consistent Realization of the Political Manifesto.* Djakarta, 1960. 6 pp.

——. *Konstitusi SOBSI.* Djakarta, 1955. 60 pp.

——. *Koperasi dan Serikatburuh.* Djakarta, 1959. 24 pp.

——. *Masaalah Front Persatuan Buruh.* Djakarta, 1959. 42 pp.

——. *Masaalah-Masaalah Organisasi.* Djakarta, 1959. 57 pp.

——. *Mengatasi Keuangan dalam Serikat-Buruh.* Djakarta, 1956. 29 pp.

——. *Pendemokrasian Pembangunan Nasional.* Djakarta, 1961. 68 pp.

——. *Peranan Buruh Wanita Dalam Pembangunan.* Djakarta, 1961. 87 pp.

——. *Plan Organisasi 1958.* Djakarta, 1957. 15 pp.

——. *Program SOBSI Mengenai Perbaikan Ekonomi guna Perbaikan Upah dan Djaminan Sosial kaum Buruh.* Djakarta, 1955. 27 pp.

——. *Program Tuntutan SOBSI: Untuk Sandang Pangan dan Demokrasi.* Djakarta, 1960. 74 pp.

——. *Resolusi-Resolusi Kongres Nasional ke-III SOBSI.* Djakarta, 1960. 35 pp.

——. *Sedjarah Gerakan Buruh Indonesia.* Djakarta, 1958. 104 pp.

——. *Tentang Aksi, Kader dan Demokrasi.* Djakarta, 1961. 53 pp.

——. *Untuk Mempertinggi Produksi dan Melantjarkan Distribusi Pangan.* Djakarta, 1962. 32 pp.

——. *Untuk Sandang-Pangan dan Demokrasi.* Djakarta, 1961. 127 pp.

Sidik Kertapati. *Untuk Persatuan dan Memperluas Perdjuangan Tani.* Djakarta, 1955. 49 pp.

Skinner, G. William, ed. *Local, Ethnic, and National Loyalties in Village Indonesia: A Symposium.* New Haven, Conn., 1959. 68 pp.

Suharti, *et al. Undang-Undang Perkawinan.* Djakarta, 1960. 132 pp.

Susilo Prawiroatmodjo. *Tindjauan Singkat Organisasi Tani di Indonesia.* Djakarta, 1955. 74 pp.

Tauchid, Mochammad. *Mengapa Saja Tidak Menjetudjui Fusi BTI-RTI.* Bogor, 1953. 25 pp.

Tedjasukmana, Iskandar. *The Political Character of the Indonesian Trade Union Movement.* Ithaca, New York, 1958. 130 pp.

Ter Haar, B. *Adat Law in Indonesia.* New York, 1948. 255 pp.

Van der Kroef, Justus Maria. *Indonesia in the Modern World*. Bandung, 1954, 1956. 2 vols.

Widjojo Nitisastro and J. E. Ismael. *The Government, Economy and Taxes of a Central Javanese Village*. Ithaca, New York, 1959. 37 pp.

Willmott, Donald E. *The National Status of the Chinese in Indonesia*. Ithaca, New York, 1956. 88 pp.

PERIODICAL AND NEWSPAPER ARTICLES

Adina, A. M. "Menjambut Lahirnja Konstitusi Baru SOBSI," *Zaman Baru*, Oct. 15, 1952, pp. 2-3.

Adjitorop, Jusuf. "Kongres jang didukung Rakjat," *Bintang Merah* (Sept.-Oct., 1959), pp. 370-374.

——. "Rol Grup dalam Kehidupan Intern Partai," *Kehidupan Partai*, April 1, 1955, pp. 49-53.

Aidit, D. N. "Back to the 1945 Constitution for a Change in Policies and Living Conditions," *Review of Indonesia*, Supplement (Sept.-Oct., 1959), pp. 3-17.

——. "Building the Organization Is Important, but Building Ideology Is Even More Important," *Review of Indonesia*, Supplement (June-July, 1959). 8 pp.

——. "Communist Party Gets Ready for Elections," *New Age* (weekly, New Delhi), May 29, 1955, p. 5.

——. "Economic Difficulties and the Communist Party's Proposals," *World Marxist Review* (Sept., 1958), pp. 71-72.

——. "Fase Baru dan Penjesuaian Organisasi dengan Situasi," *Bintang Merah* (March-April, 1958), pp. 97-152.

——. "Fly High the Banners of 'Land to the Peasants' and Fight for One Victory after the Other," *Review of Indonesia*, Supplement (June-July, 1959), pp. 11-14.

——. "For National Unity," *World Marxist Review* (Feb., 1960), pp. 20-26.

——. "Front Persatuan Nasional dan Sedjarahnja," *Bintang Merah* (Aug., 1952), pp. 3-8.

——. "The General Elections and the Tasks of the Indonesian Communist Party," *For a Lasting Peace, For a People's Democracy!* Sept. 9, 1955, pp. 3-4.

——. "Haridepan Gerakan Tani Indonesia," *Bintang Merah* (July, 1953), pp. 332-340.

——. "Ideological Work in the Communist Party of Indonesia," *World Marxist Review* (July, 1959), pp. 24-27.

——. "Indonesian Situation," *New Age* (monthly, New Delhi) (April, 1959), pp. 15-28.

——. "Membolsewikkan PKI," *Bintang Merah* (March 1, 1951), pp. 129-134.

——. "Referat tentang Tan Ling Djie-isme," *Harian Rakjat*, March 19, 1954.

——. "Revolusi Oktober dan Rakjat-Rakjat Timur," *Bintang Merah* (Oct.-Nov., 1957), pp. 373-383.

——. "The Sixth National Congress of the Communist Party of Indonesia," *Review of Indonesia* (Nov.-Dec., 1959), pp. 40-48.

——. "Some Results of Vth National Congress of Indonesian Communist Party," *For a Lasting Peace, For a People's Democracy!* Oct. 15, 1954, p. 3.

——. "Ubah Imbangan Kekuatan untuk Melaksanakan Konsepsi Presiden Soekarno 100%," *Harian Rakjat*, July 5, 1957.

Alamputra, *pseud.* "Mengatasi Kelemahan-Kelemahan," *Bintang Merah* (Aug.-Sept., 1951), pp. 16-39.

Amar Hanafiah. "Pengalaman Tjara Menarik Simpati Kijai-Kijai," *Kehidupan Partai* (May-Aug., 1957), pp. 69-72.

Anwar Sanusi, Amir. "Sedikit tentang Penarikan Iuran dan Penjetorannja," *Kehidupan Partai* (Oct., 1956), pp. 8-12.

Asmu. "Beladjar dari Sidang-Pleno DPP-BTI ke-III untuk Mengatasi Kelemaham Pekerdjaan Partai dilapangan Perdjuangan Tani," *Bintang Merah* (Feb.-March, 1955), pp. 57-64.

——. "Masalah Landreform," *Bintang Merah* (Jan., 1960), pp. 14-28.

Banggas. "Memperbaiki Pekerdjaan Partai dikalangan Mahasiswa," *Bintang Merah* (Feb., 1958), pp. 57-65.

Barisan Tani Indonesia. "Laporan Umum dan Putusan-Putusan Sidang DPP Pleno II BTI," *Suara Tani*, Supplement (May-June, 1959). 60 pp.

——. "Memperluas dan Mengkonsolidasi Organisasi B.T.I.," *Suara Tani* (March, 1955), pp. 1, 6-7.

——. "Menjambut Kongres Nasional ke-VI BTI," *Suara Tani* (Aug.-Oct., 1962). 46 pp.

Budiardjo, Miriam S. "The Provisional Parliament of Indonesia," *Far Eastern Survey*, XXV (Feb., 1956), 17-23.

Feith, Herbert. "Towards Elections in Indonesia," *Pacific Affairs*, XXVII (Sept., 1954), 236-254.

Geertz, Clifford. "Religious Belief and Economic Behavior in a Central Javanese Town: Some Preliminary Considerations," *Economic Development and Cultural Change*, IV (Jan., 1956), 134-158.

——. "Ritual and Social Change: A Javanese Example," *American Anthropologist*, LIX (1957), 32-54.

Hartojo. "Luaskan Aksi-Aksi kaum Tani untuk Mengembangkan Kekuatan Progresif," *Suara Tani* (Oct., 1957), pp. 5-11.

Hatta, Mohammad. "Indonesia between the Power Blocs," *Foreign Affairs*, XXXVI (April, 1958), 480-490.

Hutapea, B. O. "Sikap SOBSI Terhadap 'Modal Nasional,'" *Zaman Baru*, Sept. 30, 1952, pp. 11-13, 16.

——. "Some Lessons from the First National Peasants Conference of the CPI," *Review of Indonesia* (Aug., 1959), pp. 30-34.

Imam Suprapto. "Bagaimana Menerobos Daerah Kosong," *Kehidupan Partai* (July, 1958), pp. 111-113.

Iman, *pseud.* "Razzia Agustus: Satu Bagian dari Rentjana Pengeluasan Perang Amerika," *Bintang Merah* (Aug.-Sept., 1951), pp. 5-9.

Isk. "Mendjadikan Soal Keuangan Masaalah Bagi Seluruh Partai," *Kehidupan Partai* (Nov., 1956), pp. 24-27.

Jay, Robert R. "Local Government in Rural Central Java," *Far Eastern Quarterly*, XV (Feb., 1956), 215-227.

Kahin, George McT. "Communist Leadership in Indonesia," *Far Eastern Survey*, XVIII (Aug. 10, 1949), 188-189.

Lubis, Mochtar. "Party Confusion in Indonesia," *Far Eastern Survey*, XXI (Oct. 29, 1952), 155-158.

Lukman, M. H. "Bagaimana Mentjiptakan Kader Wanita," *Kehidupan Partai* (Jan. 1, 1955), pp. 4-6.

——. "Menudju Front Persatuan," *Bintang Merah* (Feb. 1, 1951), pp. 57-59.

——. "Mewudjudkan Front Nasional," *Bintang Merah* (March 15–April 1, 1951), pp. 172-174.

——. "Partai dan Organisasi Massa," *Bintang Merah* (Feb. 15, 1951), pp. 104-105, 119.

——. "Tentang Agitasi dan Propaganda Partai," *Bintang Merah* (Sept., 1952), pp. 57-64.

Mirajadi, *pseud.* "Tiga Tahun Provokasi Madiun," *Bintang Merah* (Aug.-Sept., 1951), pp. 39-52.

Njono. "Beberapa Peladjaran dari Kongres Nasional ke-II SOBSI," *Bintang Merah* (Jan., 1955), pp. 7-10.

Njoto. "Masaalah Pendidikan didalam Partai," *Harian Rakjat*, Aug. 3, 1956.

——. "Pemalsuan Marxisme," *Bintang Merah* (Jan. 1-15, 1951), pp. 16-17.

——. "Soal Pendidikan dan kaum Inteligensia," *Harian Rakjat*, July 5, 1957.

Pardede, Peris. "Daerah Majoritet Mutlak Komunis Selama Setahun," *Bintang Merah* (Jan.-Feb., 1959), pp. 39-43.

Partai Komunis Indonesia. "Apa Sebab PKI Memberi Kesempatan Bekerdja pada Kabinet Wilopo," *Harian Rakjat*, July 14, 1952.

——. "Laporan Mengenai Pekerdjaan Partai dikalangan kaum Tani," *Bintang Merah* (April-May, 1959), pp. 128-146.

——. "Laporan Tambahan Mengenai Masaalah Mengembangkan Pekerdjaan Massa kaum Tani," *Harian Rakjat*, July 10, 1957.

——. "Masaalah Tani di Indonesia," *Bintang Merah* (June 15–July 1, 1951), pp. 303-306.

——. "PKI Berkampanje untuk Pemilihan Konstituante," *Harian Rakjat*, Nov. 18, 1955.

——. "Program Perubahan Tanah dan Tuntutan kaum Tani," *Bintang Merah* (Dec., 1951), pp. 1-36.

——. "Resolusi CC tentang Peluasan Keanggotaan Partai," *PKI-Buletin*, March 7, 1952, pp. 3-6.

Pauker, Guy J. "The Role of Political Organizations in Indonesia," *Far Eastern Survey*, XXVII (Sept., 1958), 129-142.

Rewang. "Apa jang Harus diperhatikan oleh Kader jang dimutasi," *Kehidupan Partai* (Jan.-March, 1958), pp. 3-5.

Sakirman. "Apa Arti Sokongan PKI kepada UUD 1945 dan Demokrasi Terpimpin," Part I, *Bintang Merah* (May-June, 1960), pp. 194-219; Part II, *ibid.* (July-Aug., 1960), pp. 320-340, 348.

Siswojo. "Seni untuk Menang dalam Pemilihan Umum," *Kehidupan Partai* (April 1, 1955), pp. 57-58.

Sjahrir, Sutan. "Problems the Country Faces," in "Perspective of Indonesia," Supplement to *Atlantic Monthly* (June, 1956), pp. 21-25.

Sobromalisi, *pseud.* "Tentang Perebutan Kekuasaan," *Bintang Merah* (Aug.-Sept., 1951), pp. 10-15.

Sudisman. "Untuk Perluas Pengaruh Partai dikalangan Massa Wanita," *Harian Rakjat*, July 5, 1957.

Suharti. "Menghidupkan Grup Wanita dan Meluaskan Keanggotaan Partai dikalangan Wanita," *Bintang Merah* (June, 1958), pp. 252-260.

Suroso. "The Indonesian Council for Asian-African People's Solidarity," *Dian Setia-kawan. Torch of Solidarity* (Dec., 1958), pp. 33-36.

"Trade Unions in Indonesia," *Indonesian Review* (Dec., 1950), pp. 6-10.

Van der Kroef, Justus Maria. "Agrarian Reform and the Indonesian Communist Party," *Far Eastern Survey*, XXIX (Jan. 1960), 5-13.

——. "Disunited Indonesia," *Far Eastern Survey*, XXVII (April, 1958), 49-63; (May, 1958), 73-80.

——. "Indonesian Communism under Aidit," *Problems of Communism*, VII (Nov.-Dec., 1958), 15-23.

——. "Indonesian Communist Policy and the Sixth Party Congress," *Pacific Affairs*, XXXIII (Sept., 1960), 227-249.

——. "Indonesia's First National Election: A Sociological Analysis," *American Journal of Economics and Sociology*, XVI (April, 1957), 237-249; (July, 1957), 407-420.

——. "Indonesia's Labour Movement: Its Development and Prospects," *United Asia*, V (Aug., 1953), 223-231.

Van Marle, A. "The First Indonesian Parliamentary Elections," *Indonesie*, IX (1956), 257-264.

Willner, Ann Ruth. "Social Change in Javanese Town-Village Life," *Economic Development and Cultural Change*, VI (April, 1958), 229-242.

THESES

Fagg, Donald R. "Authority and Social Structure: A Study in Javanese Bureaucracy." Ph.D. dissertation. Harvard University, 1958. 599 pp.

Feith, Herbert. "Indonesian Politics, 1949-1957: The Decline of Representative Government." Ph.D. dissertation. Cornell University, 1961. 928 pp.

Hartono. "The Indonesian Communist Movement, 1945-1948: Its Development and Relations with the Soviet Union." M.A. thesis. Columbia University, 1959. 116 pp.

Jay, Robert Ravenelle. "Santri and Abangan: Religious Schism in Rural Central Java." Ph.D. dissertation. Harvard University, 1957. 394 pp.

Meek, John Paul. "The Government and Economic Development in Indonesia, 1950-1954." Ph.D. dissertation. University of Virginia, 1956. 349 pp.

Munawir Sjadzali. "Indonesia's Muslim Parties and Their Political Concepts." M.A. thesis. Georgetown University, 1959. 145 pp.

Myers, Robert J. "The Development of the Indonesian Socialist Party." Ph.D. dissertation. University of Chicago, 1959. 256 pp.

Purwoto Gondosubroto. "Provisional Report on Research in Villages in Banjumas Residency." Unpublished manuscript. University of Indonesia, 1959. 79 pp.

Selosoemardjan. "Social Changes in Jogjakarta." Ph.D. dissertation. Cornell University, 1959. 529 pp.

Subandrio, Hurustiati. "Javanese Peasant Life: Villages in East Java." Academic Postgraduate Diploma in Anthropology dissertation. University of London, 1951. 198 pp.

NEWSPAPERS, PERIODICALS, PARLIAMENTARY DEBATES, ANNUAL REPORTS*

Api Kartini, June, 1959–Jan., 1963.
Bank Indonesia, *Annual Reports*, 1953–1959.

*Unless otherwise indicated, these papers were published in Djakarta.

Bendera Buruh, March, 1956–July, 1960.

Bintang Merah, Nov., 1950–Oct., 1960.

Bintang Timur, June, 1962–July, 1963.

Buletin Perdamaian, Sept. 22, 1958–Dec., 1959.

Buletin SOBSI, May, 1955–Feb., 1956.

Damai, Nov., 1952–Sept., 1953.

Ekonomi dan Keuangan Indonesia, 1953–1960.

Ekonomi dan Masjarakat, March, 1959–Oct., 1960.

For a Lasting Peace, For a People's Democracy! (Bucharest), Aug., 1948–April, 1956.

Harian Rakjat, July, 1951–July, 1963.

Ichtisar Gerakan Tani, Dec., 1950–Oct., 1953.

Indonesian Trade Union News, July, 1955–March, 1960.

Java Bank Annual Reports, 1941–1953.

Kehidupan Partai, Jan., 1955–Dec., 1958.

Madjalah PKI Surabaja (Surabaja), Jan., 1962–June, 1962.

New Age (weekly, New Delhi), 1955–1957.

PKI-Buletin, Feb., 1952–Oct., 1954.

PKI dan DPR (name changed to *PKI dan Perwakilan* in 1956), First Quarter, 1956–Third Quarter, 1960.

Review of Indonesia, Jan., 1957–Oct., 1960.

Risalah Dewan Perwakilan Rakjat Republik Indonesia Serikat, 1950.

Risalah Perundingan Dewan Perwakilan Rakjat Republik Indonesia, 1950–1951.

Sin Po, Nov., 1949–Dec., 1951.

Suara Pamong Desa (Surakarta), Nov., 1957–Jan., 1959.

Suara Tani, March, 1955–July, 1963.

Times of Indonesia, Jan., 1953–Oct., 1960.

Wanita Sedar, Oct., 1950–Aug., 1952.

World Trade Union Movement (London), 1952-1959.

Zaman Baru (Surabaja), May, 1952–Feb., 1955.

Index

Index